BOB DYLAN
IN AMERICA

Also by Sean Wilentz

The Age of Reagan: A History, 1974–2008

The Rise of American Democracy: Jefferson to Lincoln

Andrew Jackson

The Rose and the Briar:
Death, Love, and Liberty in the American Ballad (ed., with Greil Marcus)

The Kingdom of Matthias (with Paul E. Johnson)

The Key of Liberty:
The Life and Democratic Writings of William Manning, "A Laborer," 1747–1814
(with Michael Merrill)

Chants Democratic:
New York City and the Rise of the American Working Class, 1788–1850

→ 14 A

BOB DYLAN
IN AMERICA

SEAN WILENTZ

DOUBLEDAY

NEW YORK LONDON TORONTO

SYDNEY AUCKLAND

DOUBLEDAY

DOUBLEDAY and the DD colophon are registered trademarks of Random House, Inc.

Portions of this work previously appeared in slightly different form in the following: www.bobdylan.com; *The Bridge*; *The Daily Beast*; *The Oxford American*; *A New Literary History of America*, edited by Greil Marcus and Werner Sollors (Cambridge, Mass.: Belknap Press of Harvard University Press, 2009); *The Rose and the Briar: Death, Love, and Liberty in the American Ballad*, edited by Sean Wilentz and Greil Marcus (New York: W. W. Norton and Company, 2005); and as liner notes for *The Bootleg Series Volume 6: Bob Dylan Live 1964, Concert at Philharmonic Hall* and *Bob Dylan Live at the Gaslight 1962*.

Grateful acknowledgment is made to Ginsberg, LLC, for permission to excerpt from "Wichita Vortex Sutra" by Allen Ginsberg and to Special Rider Music for permission to reprint the following: [page 122]: excerpts from "Absolutely Sweet Marie" by Bob Dylan, copyright © 1966 and renewed 1994 by Dwarf Music; [page 200]: excerpt from "Blind Willie McTell" by Bob Dylan (as sung on version released on *Bootleg Series Vols. 1–3*), copyright © 1983 by Special Rider Music; [page 74]: excerpt from liner notes by Bob Dylan from *Bringing It All Back Home*, copyright © 1965 by Bob Dylan; [page 273]: excerpts from "Bye and Bye" by Bob Dylan, copyright © 2001 by Special Rider Music; [page 69]: excerpt from "Chimes of Freedom" by Bob Dylan (from unpublished poetry manuscripts, late 1963–early 1964), copyright © 1964 by Warner Bros. Inc. and renewed 1992 by Special Rider Music; [page 274]: excerpts from "Cry a While" by Bob Dylan, copyright © 2001 by Special Rider Music; [page 233]: excerpts from "Delia" by Bob Dylan (as sung on version released on *World Gone Wrong*), copyright © 1993 by Special Rider Music; [page 169]: excerpt from "Dusty Old Fairgrounds" by Bob Dylan, copyright © 1973 by Warner Bros. Inc.; [page 277]: excerpt from "For Dave Glover" by Bob Dylan; [page 280]: excerpt from "Highway 61 Revisited" by Bob Dylan, copyright © 1965 and renewed 1993 by Special Rider Music; [page 155]: excerpt from "Hurricane" by Bob Dylan and Jacques Levy, copyright © 1975 by Ram's Horn Music; [page 95]: excerpt from "I Shall Be Free No. 10" by Bob Dylan, copyright © 1964 and renewed 1992 by Special Rider Music; [page 165]: excerpt from "Just Like a Woman" by Bob Dylan, copyright © 1966 and renewed 1994 by Dwarf Music; [page 274]: excerpt from "Lonesome Day Blues" by Bob Dylan, copyright © 2001 by Special Rider Music; [page 272]: excerpt from "Moonlight" by Bob Dylan, copyright © 2001 by Special Rider Music; [page 315]: excerpts from "Nettie Moore" by Bob Dylan, copyright © 2006 by Special Rider Music; [page 125]: excerpt from "Visions of Johanna" by Bob Dylan, copyright © 1966 and renewed 1994 by Dwarf Music; [page 92]: excerpt from "Advice for Geraldine on Her Miscellaneous Birthday" from *Writings and Drawings* by Bob Dylan, copyright © 1964 by Bob Dylan (New York: Alfred A. Knopf, Inc., 1973). Reprinted by permission of Special Rider Music.

Book design by Michael Collica

Library of Congress Cataloging-in-Publication Data
Wilentz, Sean.
Bob Dylan in America / Sean Wilentz.—1st ed.
    p. cm.
Includes bibliographical references and index.
1. Dylan, Bob, 1941– 2. Singers—United States—Biography. I. Title.
ML420.D98W53 2010
782.42164092—dc22
    [B]   2009047636

ISBN 978-0-385-52988-4

PRINTED IN THE UNITED STATES OF AMERICA

1 3 5 7 9 10 8 6 4 2

First Edition

Frontispiece: Bob Dylan with, at rear, left to right, Robbie Robertson, Levon Helm, and Garth Hudson, at the Woody Guthrie Memorial Concert, Carnegie Hall, New York City, January 20, 1968.

"Only a few hints—a few diffused, faint clues and indirections . . ."

—Walt Whitman

CONTENTS

INTRODUCTION

For thirty years I have tried to write about American history, especially the history of American politics. It is extremely hard work, but gratifying over the long haul. Writing historical pieces about American music and about Bob Dylan wouldn't have been in the cards but for a fluke, the result of strange good fortune dating back to my childhood.

While I was growing up in Brooklyn Heights, my family ran the 8th Street Bookshop in Greenwich Village, a place that helped nurture the Beat poets of the 1950s and the folk revivalists of the early 1960s. My father, Elias Wilentz, edited *The Beat Scene*, one of the earliest anthologies of Beat poetry. Down from the shop, on MacDougal Street, was an epicenter of the folk-music explosion, the Folklore Center, run by my father's friend Israel Young, whom everyone called Izzy, an outsized enthusiast with an impish grin and a heavy Bronx-Jewish accent. Nothing in that setting was anything I had sought out, or had any idea was going to become important. As things turned out, I was just lucky.

On occasional pleasant Sundays, we'd take family strolls that almost always included a stop at the Folklore Center, which was crowded wall to wall with records and stringed instruments and had a little room in the back where musicians hung out. My first memories of Bob Dylan, or at least of hearing his name, are from there—Izzy and my dad would talk about what was happening on the street, and I (a son who wanted to look and act like his father) would eavesdrop. Only much later did I learn that Dylan first met Allen Ginsberg, late in 1963, in my uncle's apartment above the bookshop.

A few buildings north of Izzy's store, next to the Kettle of Fish bar, a staircase led down into a basement club, where Dylan acquired what it took to make himself a star. The Gaslight Cafe, at 116 MacDougal, was the focal point of a block-long spectacle of hangouts and showcases, including the Café Wha? (where Dylan played his first shows in the winter of 1961). Down adjoining tiny Minetta Lane, around the bend on Minetta Street, there was another coffeehouse, the Commons, later known as the Fat Black Pussycat. These places, along with the Bitter End and Mills Tavern on far more touristy Bleecker Street, and Gerde's Folk City on West Fourth Street, were Bob Dylan's Yale College and his Harvard.

The neighborhood had a distinguished bohemian pedigree. A century before, over on the corner of Bleecker and Broadway, Walt Whitman loafed in a beer cellar called Pfaff's, safe from the gibing mainstream critics, whom he called "hooters." A little earlier, a few blocks up MacDougal in a long-gone house on Waverly Place, Anne Charlotte Lynch ran a literary salon that hosted Herman Melville and Margaret Fuller, and where a neighbor, Edgar Allan Poe, first read to an audience his poem "The Raven." Eugene O'Neill, Edna St. Vincent Millay, e. e. cummings, Maxwell Bodenheim, and Joe Gould, among others, were twentieth-century habitués of MacDougal Street.

When Dylan arrived in the Village, the Gaslight was the premier MacDougal Street venue for folksingers and stand-up comics. Opened at the end of the 1950s as a Beat poets' café—for which it received a curious write-up in the New York *Daily News,* then the quintessential reactionary city tabloid—the Gaslight proclaimed itself, carnival-style, as "world famous for the best entertainment in the Village." Unlike many of the other clubs, it was not a so-called basket house, where walk-on performers of widely ranging competence earned only what they managed to collect in a basket they passed around the audience. The Gaslight was an elite spot where talent certified by Dave Van Ronk and other insiders, as many as six performers a night, received regular pay.

Not that the place was fancy in any way. Pine paneled (until its owners stripped it down to its brick walls) and faintly illuminated by fake Tiffany (or, as Van Ronk called them, "Tiffanoid") lamps, the Gaslight had leaky pipes that dripped on what passed for a stage, no liquor license (that's what brown paper bags and the Kettle of Fish were for), a tolerable sound system, and hardly any room. If one used a crowbar and a mallet, it might have been possible to jimmy a hundred people in there. The threat of a police raid—for noisiness, or overcrowding, or refusing to play along and pay off the Mob—was constant. But on MacDougal Street, playing the Gaslight was like playing Carnegie Hall.

Van Ronk was the king of the hill among the Gaslight's folksingers; the emcee was Noel Stookey (who became the Paul of Peter, Paul, and Mary); and the headliners included Tom Paxton, Len Chandler, Hugh Romney (better known as the late-1960s psychedelic prankster and communalist Wavy Gravy), and young comics like Bill Cosby and Woody Allen. When Dylan, with Van Ronk's imprimatur, cracked the Gaslight's prestigious performers' circle in 1961, he secured sixty dollars a week, which gave him enough to afford the rent on a Fourth Street apartment—and took a big step toward real fame and fortune. "It was a club I wanted to play, needed to," Dylan recalls in his memoir, *Chronicles: Volume One*.

A remarkable tape survives of what appears to have been a splicing together of two of Dylan's Gaslight performances, recorded in October 1962, in accord with what then qualified as professional recording standards. (Widely circulated for many years as a bootleg, the tape was eventually released in abbreviated form in 2005 as a limited-edition compact disc, *Live at the Gaslight 1962*.) The singer may have left his harmonica rack at home; in any case, this is one of the few early recordings where he performs for an audience without his harmonicas. But for all of its unpretentious, even impromptu qualities, the tape reveals how greatly and rapidly Dylan's creativity was growing.

A year earlier, Van Ronk's first wife, Terri Thal, had recorded Dylan, also at the Gaslight but with far inferior equipment, in an attempt to persuade club owners in nearby cities to hire the young singer. (Thal reports that someone stole the tape; it has long been available as a vinyl LP and on compact disc, known to collectors as "The First Gaslight Tape.") As a business scheme, the recording flopped, even though it included the best of Dylan's first songs, "Song to Woody." A year later, though, Dylan had jumped to the level of composing "A Hard Rain's A-Gonna Fall"—a song the world beyond the Village and the folk revival would not hear until its release more than six months later on Dylan's second album, *The Freewheelin' Bob Dylan*. It might be the ghostly singing along by the audience on "Hard Rain," or it could just be the benefits of hindsight, but this second Gaslight tape vibrates with a sensation that Bob Dylan was turning into something very different from what anyone had ever heard, an artist whose imagination stretched far beyond those of even the most accomplished folk-song writers of the day.

I first heard Dylan perform two years after that—at Philharmonic Hall, not the Gaslight. It was another bit of luck: my father got hold of a pair of free tickets. And even though I was only thirteen, I'd been made acutely aware of Dylan's work. A slightly older friend had presented *Freewheelin'* to a little knot of kids in my (liberal, Unitarian) church group as if it were a piece of just-revealed scripture. I didn't understand half of the album; mostly, I was fixed on its sleeve cover, with its now famous photograph of Dylan, shoulders hunched against the cold, arm in arm with a gorgeous girl, walking on Jones Street—a picture that, with its hip sexiness, was more arousing than anything I'd glimpsed in furtive schoolboy copies of *Playboy*.

Some of what I did understand in the songs was funny, some of it was uplifting, and a lot of it was frightening: the line "I saw a black branch with blood that kept drippin' " from "Hard Rain" stood out as particularly chilling. But I loved the music and Dylan's sound, the guitar, the harmonica, and a voice that I never thought especially raspy or grating, just plain. Getting the chance to see him in concert was a treat, about which I have more to say below. In time, it proved to be a source of even greater luck.

The next turn in the story, almost forty years later, is more mysterious to me. After a long and deep attachment through high school, college, and after, my interest in Dylan's work began to wane about the time *Infidels* appeared in 1983. Although his religious turn was perplexing, even off-putting, the early gospel recordings at the end of the 1970s and beginning of the 1980s had also, I thought, been gripping, taking an old American spiritual tradition, already updated by groups such as the Staple Singers, and recharging it with full-blast rock and roll. Dylan had seemed to be doing to "Precious Lord" what he once had done to "Pretty Polly" and "Penny's Farm." Now, though, except for a few cuts on *Infidels* and on *Oh Mercy* six years later, his music sounded to me tired and torn, as if mired in a set of convictions that, lacking deeper faith, were substituting for art.

I came back to Dylan's music in the early 1990s when he released a couple of solo acoustic albums of traditional ballads and folk tunes, sung in a now-aging, melancholy voice, yet with some of the same sonic sensations I remembered from the early records. The critic Greil Marcus (who, several years later, became my friend and collaborator) has written that with these recordings, Dylan began retrieving his own artistic core—but I had more personal reasons for admiring them with a special intensity. When my father fell mortally ill in 1994, hearing Dylan's hushed, breathy rendition on the second of the albums, *World Gone Wrong,* of the 1830s-vintage hymn "Lone Pilgrim" brought me tears and consolation I wouldn't have gone looking for in any church or synagogue.

By now I was writing about the arts as well as about history. On a lark, in 1998, I wrote an article for the political magazine *Dissent* about Marcus's Dylan book, *Invisible Republic,* and Dylan's latest release, *Time Out of Mind,* all prompted by a Dylan show I attended, goaded by a clairvoyant friend, the previous summer at Wolf Trap in Virginia. In 2001 a phone call came out of the blue from Dylan's office in New York asking if I would like to write something about a forthcoming album, called *"Love and Theft,"* for Dylan's official Web site, www.bobdylan.com. Once I'd established it wasn't somebody playing a practical joke, I agreed, provided that I liked the album, which in the end I very much did. I wrote more for the Web site over the following months and invented the somewhat facetious title of the site's "historian-in-residence," a job nobody else seemed to be angling for, at a home office suspended in cyberspace.

Sometime in 2003, plans took shape for an official release, as part of a retrospective series, of the tape made on that long-ago night when I first heard Bob Dylan in concert. When called upon to write the liner notes for what would become *The Bootleg Series, Vol. 6: Bob Dylan Live 1964, Concert at Philharmonic Hall,* I found the assignment intimidating. Dylan has always managed to land truly fine writers and experts, including Johnny Cash, Allen Ginsberg, Tony Glover, Pete Hamill, Nat Hentoff, Greil Marcus, and Tom Piazza, when he hasn't written the liner notes himself. I also worried about what it would be like trying to describe a scene from so long ago without sounding either coy or pedantic. How much would I even remember?

The memory part turned out to be easy. Listening to the recording brought back in a rush the feel of the occasion—the evening's warmth; the golden glow of the still-new Philharmonic Hall in the still-under-construction Lincoln Center for the Performing Arts; the sometimes giddy rapport that Dylan had with the audience (unimaginable in today's arena rock concerts). But as a historian, I also felt a responsibility to fill in the larger context: what the world was going through and what Dylan was up to in the autumn of 1964. The murders of three civil-rights workers in Mississippi, the first signs that America would escalate its involvement in Vietnam, the successful test of an atomic weapon by Communist China, had all marked the beginning of a scarier phase in national and world affairs. Dylan, meanwhile, had been moving away from the fixed moral position of his earlier work into a more personal and impressionistic vein, and would soon return, though in wholly new ways, to the electrified music that had been his first love as a teenager.

I tried to braid the background together with my memories, hoping to recapture the sense of what it was like to see things through thirteen-year-old eyes (and say it with a bit of a thirteen-year-old's voice) while sustaining what authority I had as a professional historian who by now was more than twice as old as Bob Dylan was that night. I tried to evoke the feeling of being a teenage cultural insider, self-consciously nestled as close to the center of hipness as possible, with an edge of callow smugness and little awareness of my own good fortune. Maybe half of us in the audience had worked an honest day in our lives, and few had come close to getting our skulls cracked defying Jim Crow. But we thought we were advanced and special, and for us the concert was partly an act of collective self-ratification. I wanted my notes to evoke the joy as well as the folly of that youthful New York moment.

The notes were eventually nominated for a Grammy Award, which was another kind of ratification, although the idea of middle-aged folly occurred to me as well. The attention that the nomination received surprised me. The recording industry's manufacture of spectacle had become so grand that even the low-priority Best Album Notes category got newspaper play. I tried not to kid myself too much about the hoopla: an Ivy League history professor getting picked to go to Los Angeles along with Usher and Green Day and Alicia Keys is an obvious "man bites dog" filler story. I did, though, take pride in how what I wrote interested people well outside my usual circles. As awards day closed in, I began to get that self-consciously hip feeling back again: going to the Grammys was pretty exciting. By the time I arrived in Los Angeles, I badly wanted to win.

I didn't. It hurt when the presenter read someone else's name, and I couldn't hide it. From the row in front of mine, an elegantly dressed woman, older than I, noticed my dejection and extended her hand.

"Don't you worry, honey, I didn't win myself, and ain't it great being here?" I kissed her hand, suddenly feeling better, grateful to be welcomed, if only for a weekend, into the ranks of hardworking musicians and artists.

I returned to writing my history books and teaching my history classes, but also continued to write an occasional essay and deliver an occasional lecture on aspects of American music, including Dylan's work. In 2004, with Greil Marcus, I co-edited *The Rose and the Briar,* an anthology of essays, short stories, poetry, and cartoons based on various American ballads, to which I contributed an essay on the old blues song "Delia," performed by Dylan on *World Gone Wrong.* Then, three years after losing the Grammy, with another history book done, I began thinking about attempting a more ambitious piece of music writing, a coherent commentary on Dylan's development as well as his achievements, and on his connections to enduring currents in American history and culture.

To be sure, my essays had skipped over a lot, ignoring almost completely the years from 1966 to 1992—a quarter century in which, according to the not entirely ironic announcement by Al Santos, Dylan's stage manager, that precedes every live show, Dylan "disappeared into a haze of substance abuse [and] emerged to find Jesus" before he "suddenly shifted gears, releasing some of the strongest music of his career beginning in the late nineties." All that made sense to me, and I thought that the years I had covered in my essays coincidentally had brought Dylan's most concentrated periods of powerful creativity, including the most powerful of all, between 1964 and 1966. Without quite realizing it, I had written about some of the high points of two of the major phases in Dylan's career—reason enough, I told myself, to see what they might look like assembled between two covers, revised as the chapters of a much longer book. I had also written about certain musical genres and figures to whom Dylan himself had alluded, if only tacitly, as personal influences, ranging from the shape-note choral music in the nineteenth-century Sacred Harp tradition to the leftist-influenced orchestral Americana of Aaron Copland. These pieces were no more comprehensive in their coverage than my essays on Dylan were. But they hinted at some connections I wanted to make between Dylan's work and American history and culture.

There is plenty of fascinating commentary on Dylan's songs, and there are several informative biographies. But even the best of these books do not contain all of what I have wanted to know about Dylan's music and the strains in American life that have provoked and informed it. I have never been interested in simply tracking down, listing, and analyzing the songs and recordings that influenced Dylan, important though this task is to understanding his work. I have instead been curious about when, how, and why Dylan picked up on certain forerunners, as well as certain of his own contemporaries; about the milieu in which those influences lived and labored and how they had evolved; and about how Dylan, ever evolving himself, finally combined and transformed their work. What do those tangled influences tell us about America? What do they tell us about Bob Dylan? What does *America* tell us about Bob Dylan—and what does Dylan's work tell us about America? These are the questions that finally pushed me to write this book.

While I was preparing to write about *"Love and Theft"* in late summer 2001, I thought I perceived (and it turned out to be a pretty obvious observation) that the album was a kind of minstrel show, in which Dylan had assembled bits and pieces of older American music and literature (and not just American music and literature) and recombined them in his own way. The musical reconstructions appeared to be rooted in what Pete Seeger has called "the folk process," and in Dylan's lifelong practice of transforming words and melodies for his own use. But they also now appeared to be more sophisticated, self-conscious, and elusive as well as allusive, drawing upon sources from well outside the folk mainstream (ranging from Virgil's *Aeneid* to mainstream pop tunes from the 1920s and 1930s), as well as from classic blues recordings by Charley Patton and the Mississippi Sheiks. I came to see it as an urbane if, to some, problematic twist in Dylan's art, the latest of his reshapings of old American musical traditions shared by the minstrels, songsters, and vaudevillians, as well as the folk and blues singers. I called his reshapings of those traditions modern minstrelsy.

I originally imagined writing a book that would build on my essay about *"Love and Theft"* and examine how older forms of adaptation prepared the way for Dylan the modern minstrel—but I quickly scrapped that idea. For one thing, as interesting as his later endeavors have been, I think that Dylan completed by far his strongest work, mixing tradition and utter originality, in the mid-1960s and mid-1970s, a judgment he himself appears to share.* A narrative that even appeared to climb ever upward toward Dylan's fully mature output would be nonsense. For another thing, Dylan's career has been an unsteady pilgrimage, passing through deep troughs as well as high points, including a prolonged period in the 1980s when, again by his own admission, his work seemed to be spinning in circles. Any account of Dylan's cultural importance must be built out of his ups and downs, zigs and zags, and relate how he has carried his art from one phase to another. Finally, although Dylan has long been a constant innovator—or, as the Irish troubadour Liam Clancy once called him, a "shape-changer"—his work has also exhibited strong continuities. Dylan has never stuck to one style for too long, but neither has he forgotten or forsaken or wasted anything he has ever learned. Anyone interested in appreciating Dylan's body of work must face the challenge of owning its paradoxical and unstable combination of tradition and defiance.

I decided instead to examine some of the more important early influences on Dylan and then focus on Dylan's work from the 1960s to the present at certain important junctures. The opening chapters might seem to have little to do with Dylan, especially in their early sections, as they trace the origins and cultural importance of influential people or currents, but they do in time bring Dylan into the story, and show how he connected with the forerunners, sometimes directly, sometimes not. A chapter about Dylan's song "Blind Willie McTell," as well as chapters about "Delia" and another song from *World Gone Wrong*, "Lone Pilgrim," also require extended passages explaining important background material. I ask for the reader's indulgence to hang on during all of these chapters, assured that the connections to Bob Dylan will be revealed soon enough. The remaining chapters deal more directly with Dylan from the start.

Accounts of Dylan's music normally begin with his immersion in the songs and style of Woody Guthrie, his first musical idol (and, he has said, his last), and with the folk revival that grew out of the left-wing hootenannies of the 1940s. This approach makes sense, but it has become overly familiar, and it slights the influence of the much larger cultural

---

* In a television interview with Ed Bradley, broadcast by CBS late in 2004, Dylan marveled at the lyrics of old songs such as "It's Alright, Ma (I'm Only Bleeding)" and mused: "I don't do that anymore. I don't know how I got to write those songs. Those early songs were almost magically written."

and political spirit, initially associated with the Communist Party and its so-called Popular Front efforts to broaden its political appeal in the mid-1930s, which pervaded American life during the 1940s—Bob Dylan's formative boyhood years.

In order to take a fuller and fresher look at this important part of Dylan's cultural background, I decided to focus on Popular Front music seemingly very different from Guthrie's ballads and talking blues—the orchestral compositions of Aaron Copland. The choice may seem extremely odd. Yet even though the connections are now largely forgotten, Copland belonged to leftist musical circles in New York in the mid-1930s that also included some of the major figures in what was becoming the world of folk-music collecting. Copland's beloved compositions of the late 1930s and the 1940s, including *Billy the Kid* and *Rodeo,* may sound today like pleasant, panoramic Americana, but they in fact contained some of the same leftist political impulses that drove the forerunners of the folk-music revival of the 1950s and '60s. Dylan, meanwhile, grew up in a 1940s America where Copland was becoming the living embodiment of serious American music. Copland's music and persona had no obvious or direct effect on the kinds of music Dylan performed and wrote as a young man, but the broader cultural mood that Copland represented certainly did. And insofar as Dylan's career has in part involved translating the materials of American popular song into a new kind of high popular art—challenging yet accessible to ordinary listeners—his artistic aspirations and achievements are not dissimilar to Copland's.

The second chapter concerns the Beat generation writers, in particular Allen Ginsberg. Not only did Dylan eagerly read the Beats before he arrived in Greenwich Village; he and Ginsberg befriended each other at what was, fortuitously, a critical moment in both of their careers. Once again, though, much as with the folk revival, understanding the Beats and their influence on Dylan requires moving back before the 1950s, to battles over literature and aesthetics fought out during World War II on and around the campus of Columbia University. The echoes of those battles—and the spirit of the so-called New Vision that the young Ginsberg and his odd friends promulgated—reappeared later in Dylan's music, most emphatically in the songs on his two great albums completed in 1965, *Bringing It All Back Home* and *Highway 61 Revisited.* Dylan's influence on Ginsberg, at several levels, in turn helped the poet write his great work of 1966, "Wichita Vortex Sutra." And Ginsberg and Dylan's personal and artistic connections, begun at the end of 1963, would last until Ginsberg's death in 1997.

The remainder of *Bob Dylan in America* takes up Dylan's career at selected and arbitrary but far from random moments: his concert at Philharmonic Hall at the end of October 1964, in which he tried out startling new songs such as "Gates of Eden" and "It's Alright, Ma" (and which I happened to attend); the making of Dylan's landmark album *Blonde on Blonde* in New York and Nashville in 1965–66; the Rolling Thunder Revue tour of 1975; and the birth of one of Dylan's greatest songs, "Blind Willie McTell," recorded (but not released) in 1983. The book then takes a long jump to 1992–93, when Dylan, his career out of joint for a decade, reached back for inspiration in traditional folk music and the early blues. The book covers this pivotal moment in Dylan's career by examining two very different songs that Dylan recorded in 1993: "Delia," one of the first blues songs ever written; and "Lone Pilgrim," an old Sacred Harp hymn. The final chapters consider Dylan's work from *"Love and Theft"* in 2001 through his album of Christmas music, *Christmas in the Heart,* released late in 2009. Although each chapter after Chapter Two takes a particular composition or event as its initial focus, none confines itself strictly to that subject. By roaming through other related material, sometimes leaping back and forth in time, I hope to discuss most of Dylan's greatest work, including albums such as *Blood on the Tracks,* without losing sight of the other great work, in and out of the recording studio, on which I concentrate. I also hope to present some reevaluations of material I heard very differently when first released.

Approaching my subject this way means that people, places, and things sometimes appear and vanish, only to reappear later under somewhat different circumstances. The folklorist John Lomax, for example, turns up in the very first chapter as the head of the Archive of American Folk Song, in connection with the invention of a folksy, Popular Front aesthetic; then he turns up again, five chapters later, in connection with the blues singer Blind Willie McTell. Or to take a smaller but still important example: in Chapter One, the writers in and around the influential periodical *Partisan Review* turn up as anti-Stalinist leftist critics of Aaron Copland; in Chapter Two, the *Partisan Review* intellectual, critic, and Columbia English professor Lionel Trilling appears, at roughly the same time, the mid-1940s, as the ambivalent antagonist of Allen Ginsberg and the incipient Beat generation. Where absolutely necessary to keeping the story line clear, I have alluded to earlier appearances by various figures or groups. But to pause and point out all of these recurrences, and the cultural circuits they represent, would interrupt the flow of the narrative and turn the book into an overlong encyclopedia of music and literary history. Readers should thus be prepared to encounter characters or institutions already discussed earlier in the book, but in very different contexts—and, much as when these kinds of things happen in the rest of life, make the necessary adjustments of perception and understanding.

Although it traces the jagged arc of a mercurial artist, through thrilling highs and (more cursorily) crushing lows, *Bob Dylan in America* is chiefly concerned with placing Dylan's work in its wider historical and artistic contexts. This has required recognizing Dylan as an artist who is deeply attuned to American history as well as American culture, and to the connections between the past and the present. Reflecting on *"Love and Theft"* before its release, I was impressed all over again by Dylan's immersion in literature and popular music, especially American literature and music— something he would discuss at length a few years later in the first volume of *Chronicles.* But I was also impressed by his ability to crisscross through time and space. It could be 1927 or 1840 or biblical time in a Bob Dylan song, and it is always right now too. Dylan's genius rests not simply on his knowledge of all of these eras and their sounds and images but also on his ability to write and sing in more than one era at once. Partly, this skill bespeaks the magpie quality that is the essence of Dylan's modern minstrelsy—what many friends and critics early in his career called his sponge-like thirst for material that he might appropriate and make his own. Partly, it stems from some very specific innovations that Dylan undertook in the mid-1970s. But every artist is, to some extent, a thief; the trick is to get away with it by making of it something new. Dylan at his best has the singular ability not only to do this superbly but also to make the present and the past feel like each other.

Dylan has never limited himself to loving and stealing things from other Americans. But his historical as well as melodic themes have constantly recurred to the American past and the American present, and are built mainly out of American tropes and chords. There are many ways to understand him and his work; the efforts presented here describe him not simply as someone who comes out of the United States, or whose art does, but also as someone who has dug inside America as deeply as any artist ever has. He belongs to an American entertainment tradition that runs back at least as far as Daniel Decatur Emmett (the Ohio-born, anti-slavery minstrel who wrote "Dixie") and that Dylan helped reinvent in the subterranean Gaslight Cafe in the 1960s. But he belongs to another tradition as well, that of Whitman, Melville, and Poe, which sees the everyday in American symbols and the symbolic in the everyday, and then tells stories about it. Some of those stories can be taken to be, literally, about America, but they are all constructed in America, out of all of its bafflements and mysticism, hopes and hurts.

One of the trickier difficulties in appreciating Dylan's art involves distinguishing it, as far as is possible, from his carefully crafted, continually changing public image. To be sure, his image and his art are closely related, and each affects the other. The same could be said for any performing artist and for any number of literary figures, not just in our own time, but going back at least as far as that of Jenny Lind and Walt Whitman. But Dylan has been particularly skilled at manufacturing and handling his persona and then hiding behind it, and this can mislead any writer. In good times, as in recent years—when he has presented himself as the living embodiment of all the previous Bob Dylans wrapped into one, as well as of almost every variety of traditional and commercial American popular music—the image is powerful enough to transfix his admirers and deflect criticism of his music. (It can also invite contrarian debunking.) In bad times, as in much of the 1980s, Dylan's unfocused image can prompt either unduly harsh criticism of everything he produces or loyalist efforts to praise it all, or at least some of it, beyond its worth.

Although I have backed away from focusing too much on Dylan's image in American culture, an interesting topic in itself, I have tried to check my own evolving enthusiasms for and disappointments in Dylan as a public figure in considering his art—or at least, as in the chapter on the Philharmonic Hall concert in 1964, I have tried to acknowledge those feelings and incorporate them into my analysis. More an exercise in the historical appreciation of an artist's work than a piece of conventional cultural criticism, the book dwells on some of the more interesting phases of Dylan's career, and spends far less time on the less interesting ones. In order not simply to rehash familiar material, I have also devoted less space than I might have to the years from 1962 to 1966, which have attracted the most attention until now, while devoting more to Dylan's work in recent years, on which historical writing has just begun to appear. Throughout, though, the book takes account of where and when I think

Dylan has succeeded and where and when he has stumbled, even in his most fruitful periods.

Here, then, are a series of takes on Dylan in America. Read them as hints and provocations, written in the spirit that holds hints, diffused clues, and indirections as the most we can look forward to before returning to the work itself—to Dylan's work and to each of our own.

The stairway down to the Gaslight Cafe, New York.

PART I: BEFORE

1

MUSIC FOR THE COMMON MAN:

The Popular Front and Aaron Copland's America

Early in October 2001, Bob Dylan began a two-month concert tour of the northern United States. In his first performances since the terrorist attacks of September 11, Dylan debuted many of the songs on his new album, *"Love and Theft,"* including the prescient song of disaster, "High Water (for Charley Patton)." Columbia Records, eerily, had released *"Love and Theft"* on the same day that the terrorists struck. How, if at all, would Dylan now respond to the nation's trauma? Would he, for once, speak to the audience? What would he play?

The new tour had no opening act, but as a concert prelude the audience heard (as had become commonplace at Dylan's shows) a prerecorded selection of orchestral music. And on this tour, Dylan began playing what may have seemed a curious choice: a recording of the "Hoe-Down" section of Aaron Copland's *Rodeo.* Then Dylan and his band took the stage and, with acoustic instruments, further acknowledged the awfulness of the moment, while also marking Dylan's changes and continuities over the years, by playing the country songwriter Fred Rose's "Wait for the Light to Shine":

When the road is rocky and you got a heavy load
  Wait for the light to shine

For the rest of the month, through fifteen shows, Dylan opened with "Wait for the Light to Shine," often after hitting the stage to "Hoe-Down." He would continue to play snatches of *Rodeo* at his concerts for several tours to come, and now and then he would throw in the opening blasts of Copland's *Fanfare for the Common Man* or bits of *Appalachian Spring*. Copland's music from the 1940s served as Dylan's call to order, his American invocation. Sixty years on, whether he knew it or not, Dylan had closed a mysterious circle, one that arced back through the folk-music revival where he got his start to the left-wing New York musical milieu of the Great Depression and World War II.

Anyone familiar with Dylan's music knows about its connections to the 1930s and 1940s through the influences of Woody Guthrie and, to a lesser extent, Pete Seeger. But there are other connections as well, to a broader world of experimentation with American music and radical politics during the Depression years and after. These larger connections are at times quite startling, especially during the mid-1930s, when shared leftist politics brought together in New York a wide range of composers and musicians not usually associated with one another. Thereafter, many of the connections are elliptical and very difficult to pin down. They sometimes involve not direct influence but shared affinities and artistic similarities recognized only in retrospect. Yet they all speak to Dylan's career, and illuminate his artistic achievement, in ways that Guthrie's and Seeger's work alone do not. The most important of these connections leads back to Aaron Copland and his circle of politically radical composers in the mid-1930s.

On March 16, 1934, Copland participated in a concert of his own compositions, sponsored by the Composers' Collective of the Communist Party–affiliated Workers Music League and held at the party's Pierre Degeyter Club on Nineteenth Street in New York. Copland was still known, at age thirty-three, a decade after first making his mark, as a young, iconoclastic, modernist composer. The collective, with which Copland was closely associated, had been founded in 1932 to nurture the development of proletarian music, and it consisted of about thirty members. The Degeyter Club took its name from the composer of the melody of "The Internationale."

The review of the concert in the Communist newspaper *Daily Worker* praised Copland for his "progress from [the] ivory tower" and hailed his difficult *Piano Variations,* written in 1930, as a major, "undeniably revolutionary" work, even though Copland "was not 'conscious' of this at the time." A few months later, Copland, increasingly drawn to the leftist composers and musicians, won a songwriting contest, cosponsored by the collective and the pro-Communist periodical *New Masses,* for composing a quasi-modernist accompaniment to the militant poem "Into the Streets May First," written by the poet Alfred Hayes, who is best-known today for his lyrics to the song "Joe Hill." In the 1950s, Copland would publicly disown the piece as "the silliest thing I did." At the time, though, he was proud enough of what he called "my communist song" to bring it to the attention of his friend the Mexican composer Carlos Chávez, and to note that it had been republished in

Aaron Copland, circa 1930.

the Soviet Union. The *Daily Worker*'s music reviewer later recalled that the contest judges agreed that Copland's song was "a splendid thing."

That reviewer, who was one of the founders of the Composers' Collective and wrote under the pseudonym Carl Sands, was the Harvard-trained composer, professor, and eminent musicologist Charles Seeger. At this point, Seeger, a musical modernist, had little use for traditional folk music as a model for revolutionary culture. "Many folksongs are complacent, melancholy, defeatist," he wrote, "intended to make the slaves endure their lot—pretty, but not the stuff for a militant proletariat to feed on." A year later, though, the Communist Party, on instructions from the Comintern, abandoned its hyper-militant politics and avant-garde artistic leanings in favor of the broad political and cultural populism of the so-called Popular Front. The Composers' Collective duly folded in 1936, but Seeger took the shift in stride. In 1935, he moved his family to Washington, D.C., to work as an adviser to the Music Unit of the Special Skills Division of the Resettlement Administration, the forerunner of the New Deal's Farm Security Administration; and he and his second wife, the avant-garde composer Ruth Crawford Seeger, were able to collaborate with their friend John Lomax and his son Alan in helping to build the Archive of American Folk Song at the Library of Congress. In addition to collecting and transcribing traditional songs that were in danger of disappearing, the archive and its friends would encourage

Members of the Seeger family, circa 1937. Left to right: Ruth Crawford Seeger, Mike Seeger, Charles Seeger, Peggy Seeger. Not shown are Charles's children from his first marriage, including son Pete, then eighteen.

the development of folk music as a tool for radical politics—efforts that eventually helped inspire Bob Dylan and the folk revival of the 1950s and 1960s.

Charles's son Peter, then a teenager, had accompanied his father and stepmother to hear Copland discourse at the Degeyter Club, and during the summer of 1935 he traveled with his father to a square dance and music festival in Asheville, North Carolina, run by the legendary folklorist and mountain musician Bascom Lamar Lunsford. The youngster was already a crack ukulele player, but in Asheville he heard traditional folk music for the first time, played by Lunsford on a cross between a mandolin and a five-string banjo—and it changed his life forever.

A few years later, after dropping out of Harvard and working under Alan Lomax at the Library of Congress, Pete Seeger teamed up with a revolving commune of folk artists, including a young songwriter discovered and recorded by Lomax, Woody Guthrie, to form the leftist Almanac Singers, who promoted union organizing, racial justice, and other causes with their topical songs. (The supervisor for one of the Almanacs' recording sessions in 1942, Earl Robinson, had written the tunes for "Joe Hill" and the Popular Front classic "Ballad for Americans"—and in 1935 he had studied piano with Copland at the Workers Music League's school.) In the late 1940s, the Almanac Singers evolved into the Weavers.

The Weavers' recordings would later prove essential in introducing a

The Almanac Singers, 1942. Left to right: Agnes "Sis" Cunningham, Cisco Houston, Woody Guthrie, Pete Seeger, Bess Lomax Hawes. Hawes was John Lomax's daughter.

younger generation, including Bob Dylan, to the music of Woody Guthrie and in sparking the broader folk-music revival. But the Weavers were not the only influential musical descendants of the Composers' Collective—and not the only ones drawn to American folk music.

Like the Seegers, Aaron Copland continued his musical career with his politics intact. After winning his Communist song award in 1934, Copland spent the summer with his teenage lover, the photographer and aspiring violinist Victor Kraft, at a cabin his cousin owned in Lavinia, Minnesota, alongside Lake Bemidji and just to the west of the Mesabi Iron Range. Copland worked hard on his abstract and purposefully radical formal work, *Statements for Orchestra,* but also relaxed and took in what he called the "amusing town" of Bemidji, nearby. As he told a radical friend in New York, the amusements included some political escapades:

> It began when Victor spied a little wizened woman selling a Daily Worker on the street corners . . . From that, we learned to know the farmers who were Reds around these parts, attended an all-day election campaign meeting of the C.P. unit, partook of their picnic supper and [I] made my first political speech! . . . I was being drawn, you see, into the political struggle with the peasantry! I wish you could have seen them—the true Third Estate, the very material that makes revolution . . . When S. K. Davis, Communist candidate for Gov. in Minn. came to town and spoke in the public park, the farmers asked me to talk to the crowd. It's one thing to think revolution, or talk about it to one's friends, but to preach it from the streets—OUT LOUD—Well, I made my speech (Victor says it was a good one) and I'll probably never be the same!

The "good one" for the Communist candidate in Bemidji was, as far as we know, the last political stump speech Copland ever delivered, and his slightly bemused, slightly awkward, and maybe self-ironic description— "the peasantry"? "the true Third Estate"? in northern Minnesota?—makes it sound out of character. But Copland and Kraft did seek out the "Reds around these parts" and joined in their political activity. "The summer of 1934," Copland's most thorough biographer writes, "found him no mere fellow traveler, but rather an active, vocal 'red.' " Thereafter, and until

1949, Copland, if not a member of the Communist Party, was aligned with the party, its campaigns, and its satellite organizations, connections he would later try to minimize and evade under hateful and intense political pressure—and under oath.

Soon after he returned to New York, via Chicago, for the winter, Copland had his own reckoning with the Popular Front. But the first great musical sensation to come out of the Composers' Collective group and Copland's circle of friends after 1935 involved another young composer, Marc Blitzstein—who, many years later, would have a direct and profound impact on Bob Dylan, independent of the Popular Front folksingers. Born to an affluent Philadelphia family in 1905, Blitzstein had been a prodigy and made his professional debut at age twenty-one with the Philadelphia Orchestra, playing Liszt's E-flat piano concerto. Like Copland, Blitzstein had studied piano and composition in Paris in the 1920s with the formidable Nadia Boulanger, but after the onset of the Depression, living in New York, he found himself attracted to the radical theater more than to the concert hall. He felt a special kinship with the founders of the left-wing, socially conscious Group Theatre, including Harold Clurman (who had shared an apartment with Copland in Paris), Clifford Odets, and Elia Kazan.

In 1932, Blitzstein wrote a one-act musical drama, *The Condemned*, based on the Sacco and Vanzetti case, a leftist cause célèbre, that was never produced. Through the mid-1930s, as a member of the Composers' Collective, he wrote film scores and workers' songs, including a submission to the songwriting contest that Copland won. All along, Blitzstein had begun turning to concepts of populist, modernist, left-wing musical theater, blending Marxist politics with jazz, Igor Stravinsky, cabaret, and folk songs. Bertolt Brecht and his musical collaborators Hanns Eisler and Kurt Weill had conceived and advanced these ideas in Germany before the Nazi takeover in 1933, and Eisler and Weill had brought them to New York as political émigrés. Earlier, Blitzstein had condemned Weill's music as vulgar pandering, but now he had completely changed his mind. In the late summer of 1936, working at what he called a white heat, he completed a new proletarian musical play, *The Cradle Will Rock*.

A hard-bitten allegory of capitalist greed and corruption, capped by an uprising of organized steelworkers, *The Cradle Will Rock* was the first important American adaptation of the Brecht-Eisler-Weill style—and it caused a firestorm. As the show took shape, Blitzstein's sponsor, the New Deal's government-funded Federal Theatre Project, already suffering reprisals from conservatives in Congress, became panicky. Practically on the eve of the first scheduled preview performance, the project, citing impending budget cuts, shut down the production and ordered the theater padlocked. Thinking fast, Blitzstein's collaborators—the young director Orson Welles and the producer John Houseman—vowed to defy the order, rented another theater, redirected ticket holders for the first preview to the new venue, and mounted an astounding sold-out debut. (The audience swelled into a standing-room-only crowd when the company invited passersby in for free.) The Actors' Equity union had forbidden the cast to perform the piece, just as the musicians' union had refused to allow its members to play in what had formally become a commercial production for less

Poster for the original production of *The Cradle Will Rock*, 1937.

than union scale, and so, with Blitzstein himself playing the score from a piano onstage, the actors spoke and sang their parts from the house. The hastily planned, seemingly spur-of-the-moment debut was a political as well as an artistic sensation. After a brief run, *Cradle* reopened some months later, by popular demand, under the auspices of Welles and Houseman's new Mercury Theatre company, and ran for an additional 108 performances.

Aaron Copland was among those present for the impromptu premiere, and it thrilled him. ("The opening night of *The Cradle* made history," he wrote thirty years later, "none of us who were there will ever forget it.") Defending the show against charges that it was nothing but leftist propaganda, Copland allowed that "a certain sectarianism" limited its appeal, but he praised its innovative combination of "social drama, musical revue, and opera," and its clipped prosody and score.* Copland, meanwhile, had moved away from the dis-

---

* Copland also had an interesting indirect connection to the show. Welles—all of twenty-two years old and already a celebrated prodigy when *Cradle* debuted—was not a political

sonant modernism of his earlier work, and he would soon venture beyond orchestral music to write film scores and ballets. But Copland's own new direction had more in common with the all-American folk-song collecting of Charles Seeger and the Lomaxes that would later strongly affect Bob Dylan than it did with Blitzstein's Brechtian musical theater (which would also affect Dylan's work). Theirs were two very distinct artistic responses to the times, made by two ambitious, left-wing American Jewish composers and friends, one who was destined for international fame, the other for relative obscurity. Yet their sensibilities were closely related, at least in the mind of Aaron Copland.

Copland's new, more open and melodious composing style, which he adopted around 1935 and called "imposed simplicity," emerged in full in 1938, when he completed, for the impresario and writer Lincoln Kirstein, the music for a ballet, *Billy the Kid*, a stylized depiction of the outlaw's life and death. At Kirstein's suggestion, Copland consulted various cowboy song collections edited by John Lomax, looking for possible themes. Copland wound up choosing six cowboy songs and adapting them to his score. All of them appeared, at one point or another, in collections published by Lomax. Three—"Whoopie Ti Yi Yo," "The Old Chisholm Trail," and "Old Paint"—would in turn be recorded by Woody Guthrie in a famous series of sessions in 1944 and 1945 for the record producer Moe Asch, the founder of Folkways Records.

Copland's simplified and more self-consciously popular music distressed some of his admirers, including the young composer David Diamond, who feared that Copland was selling out "to the mongrel commercialized interests." And Copland himself, the vanguard innovator, seems to have been initially uneasy about quoting directly from American folk music, or at least the music of the Old West. He had, to be sure, borrowed from Mexican folk songs for *El Salón México*, a one-movement tone poem that he wrote between 1932 and 1936. That effort helped him shed the received artistic wisdom that folk music was intrinsically a

radical, yet he was drawn to Blitzstein and his score, and was fascinated by the possibility of directing a musical play. His fascination deepened when, in April 1937, he briefly staged, for the Henry Street Settlement, a new children's opera, *The Second Hurricane,* composed by Aaron Copland.

static form that lacked vitality. He had also experimented with jazz elements in the 1920s, believing that they helped diminish what he called the "too European" sound of his music. And there certainly were precedents for incorporating American folk music into serious composition. The pioneering American modernist composer Charles Ives, whose work Copland had begun to champion in the early 1930s, had been including American folk songs, band music, and bugle calls in his songs, chamber pieces, and orchestral music for decades.

But Ives, who was something of a hermit, wrote music that was difficult for musicians to play and for audiences to understand, and he had been largely ignored. The Mexican tunes of *El Salón* had the advantage of at least sounding exotic. Jazz contained the rhythmic and modal magic of African-American music, which impressed even the Europeans. American cowboy music was different. Copland later said that he was "rather wary of tackling a cowboy subject," since he had been born in Brooklyn, but there were artistic concerns as well. "I have never been particularly impressed with the musical beauties of the cowboy songs as such," Copland wrote in a note published to accompany *Billy the Kid*'s premiere.

Kirstein pushed Copland and persuaded him that having worked with Mexican folk songs, he should see what he could do with homegrown ones. Only after he sailed to Paris, however, where he composed the ballet while living on the Rue de Rennes, did Copland become "hopelessly involved" in rearranging Old West tunes. "Perhaps there is something different about the cowboy song in Paris," he mused, not for a minute relinquishing his urbane cosmopolitanism. In his hands, what he called "the poverty stricken tunes Billy himself must have heard" became modern art.

Still, the songs were indubitably present in *Billy the Kid;* anybody could recognize them; indeed, Copland's whole endeavor involved making sure that they were easily recognized. And if their presence helped make Copland's music more popular and commercially viable, it also underscored Copland's newfound attachment to his own variation of Popular Front aesthetics. By these lights, popular folk music, stories, and legends contained raw materials for new forms of art—and for a better world to come. The revolutionary artist's task was to help entwine the party with the fabric of national life by seizing upon these popular cultural forms—from detective thrillers to high, lonesome ballads—and infusing them with revolutionary élan. Copland started out this program by mining and reinventing the cowboy tunes.

The compositional task he set himself was by no means simple, even though the results sounded that way. "It's a rather delicate operation," he wrote, "to put fresh and unconventional harmonies to well-known melodies without spoiling their naturalness. Moreover, for an orchestral score, one must expand, contract, rearrange and superimpose the bare tunes themselves, giving them if possible something of one's own touch. That, at any rate, is what I tried to do."

Copland succeeded, and in doing so created something special, a music unlike any that had ever been written, even by George Gershwin with his jazz-inflected rhapsodies and tone poems—an amalgamation of traditional American folk songs and avant-garde harmonics that retained, unspoiled, the songs' "naturalness," a synthesis that employed the unconventional modal and chromatic shifts characteristic of "difficult" music, yet that did not require a practiced ear to understand and enjoy.

After opening in Chicago in October 1938, *Billy the Kid,* and particularly its score, won both popular and critical acclaim. Over the next three years, Copland devoted himself chiefly to writing film scores, teaching, publishing two books, making a concert and lecture tour of Latin America, and serving as president of the American Composers Alliance, an enterprise he had helped to establish in 1937 to promote serious contemporary American music. As it happened, his pause from concert-hall composing coincided with a confusing period for the American Left. The signing of the Nazi-Soviet nonaggression pact in 1939 signaled a complete reversal of the Communist Party line, from endorsing antifascism to endorsing peace, and it formally brought an end to the Popular Front. But after Hitler invaded the Soviet Union in June 1941 (one month after Robert Zimmerman was born in Duluth), the party line changed again—and the renewal of antifascism caused a revival of the basic tenets of Popular Front politics and culture.

Copland, who unlike some artists in the Communists' orbit remained loyal to the party during the Nazi-Soviet alliance, was happy to embrace and advance that revived sensibility—and so was the American public, as never before. After Japan's attack on Pearl Harbor and the United States' entry into World War II allied with the Soviets, the Popular Front style began spreading out far beyond the political and cultural margins. Enlisted against the Axis powers, what had once been a sectarian leftist impulse now looked and sounded patriotic, unifying, and mainstream. The war became popularized as the fight of the common man—the ordinary, dog-faced GI foot soldier—to vindicate democracy, alongside the common men of the other Allies. In politics, idealizations of the People, and of the international struggle against class and racial oppression, began turning up in the rhetoric of the warmer, deeply liberal elements of the New Deal. And in virtually every realm of American culture, high and low, Popular Front motifs and mannerisms helped to define the 1940s.

Copland did his part for the war effort by returning to his composing. In 1942 alone, he completed three of what would become his most beloved works—*Lincoln Portrait, Fanfare for the Common Man,* and, for the young choreographer Agnes de Mille, the ballet *Rodeo.* (Copland also received a commission initiated by his friend Martha Graham to write another ballet, which would appear in 1944 as *Appalachian Spring.*) All three pieces extended the "imposed simplicity" of *Billy the Kid.* Two of them celebrated the nation's popular culture and democratic politics; the third was a lucid, modernist orchestral tribute, solemn but vibrant, to the unshackled egalitarian masses.

American folk music remained, for Copland, a major resource, in the Popular Front vein. *Lincoln Portrait* incorporated Stephen Foster's "Camptown Races" and the old New England folk song "Springfield Mountain," in a cowboy rendition that John Lomax had included (one critic called it a "stammering version") in his first published song collection, and that Woody Guthrie later recorded for Moe Asch. These tunes helped Copland evoke what he perceived as Lincoln's plebeian simplicity as well as the 1850s and 1860s, as part of a Popular Front paean to the Great Emancipator as a revolutionary democratic leader—a radical ideal that was also patriotic and blended easily enough with more anodyne celebrations of Honest Abe, typified by the sentimental early installments of Carl Sandburg's widely read multivolume biography of Lincoln.

Rodeo included the cowboy song "Old Paint," which Copland had used in *Billy the Kid*—but Copland also utilized American folk music that was country but not western. In 1937, Alan Lomax and his wife, Elizabeth, had trudged a Presto disc-recording machine across rutted roads in the hills of eastern Kentucky. In the town of Salyersville, they found the fiddler William Hamilton Stepp. The recording they made of Stepp performing a juiced-up version of the old fiddler's march "Bonaparte's Retreat" was so powerful that a transcription of it appeared in a song collection that John and Alan Lomax published in 1941, *Our Sing-*

ing Country. Copland may have heard the Lomaxes' recording, but the scrupulous transcription (made by Pete Seeger's stepmother, Ruth) would have been sufficient to provide him with what he turned into the opening melody of *Rodeo*'s "Hoe-Down" section, which would be loved by generations to come—including Bob Dylan.*

Befitting the occasion of its composition, *Fanfare for the Common Man* sounds, in contrast to *Rodeo*, abstract and declamatory as well as majestic. Written on commission for the Cincinnati Symphony as a concert prelude to honor the Allies—one of seventeen commissioned by the orchestra's conductor, Eugene Goossens—*Fanfare* can be understood as a coda to *Lincoln Portrait*, which Copland completed only a few months earlier. The title contains an obvious paradox. Fanfares, rooted in the music of the court, are supposed to herald the arrival of a great man, a noble. Copland's *Fanfare*, however, heralded the noble groundlings, grunts, and ordinary men—not just their service and sacrifice in the war, but their very existence and their arrival in history. The title had more specific political connotations as well—for Copland borrowed it, as

William Hamilton Stepp, circa 1937.

he later informed Goossens, from a widely publicized speech, "The Century of the Common Man," delivered earlier in 1942 by the New Dealer most closely identified with pro-Soviet and Popular Front politics, Vice President Henry Wallace.

Copland reinvented the fanfare musically as well as thematically. Virtually all of the pieces that Goossens received—including one by an old comrade of Copland's from the Composers' Collective, Henry Cowell—

---

* In some program notes, Copland wrote simply that the version of what he called "a square dance tune called 'Bonyparte' " which he used for "Hoe-Down" could be found in the Lomaxes' anthology. See Copland to Louis Kaufman, Nov. 1, 1945, Aaron Copland Collection, Library of Congress.

conformed to the same basic model: brief and snappy; heavy on trumpets and on rolling, military snare drums; filled with triplets and other traditional flourishes; and either starting out at full blast or quickly building to it. Copland's *Fanfare*, though, is stately and deliberate, perhaps the most austere fanfare ever written. Beginning with its opening crash and rumble, it builds slowly in sonority and complexity, moving by stages from dark, obscure tones to an almost metallic brilliance, soaring and then concluding with a bang, in a different key from where it began. In its dignified simplicity, it is also complex—a subtly esoteric piece of music written for the democratic masses as well as to honor them.

Copland's works from 1942 vastly increased his popularity, and they remain, to this day, admired standards in the orchestral repertoire. Yet Copland's broadening appeal also got him into trouble with some high-toned critics—a foreshadowing of greater trouble to come. The detractors included the composer and scholar Arthur Berger, who, though a leftist sympathizer and for a long time Copland's friend, criticized Copland in the influential *Partisan Review* for his switch from writing what Berger called "severe" music to writing "simple" music. When Copland, unfazed, inserted *Fanfare* as the opening to the fourth movement of his Third Symphony in 1946, even his erstwhile kindred spirit the composer Virgil Thomson derided the symphony as evocative of "the speeches of Henry Wallace, striking in phraseology but all too reminiscent of Moscow."

These criticisms were of a piece with a more general repudiation of Popular Front culture—both in its explicitly left-wing political form and in the broader "little guy" impulses of the 1940s—that had been brewing for several years inside the anti-Stalinist Left. An up-and-coming critical avant-garde was refashioning the idea of modernism along the lines articulated by several of the critics in and around *Partisan Review*, above all Clement Greenberg—a view hostile to accessibility and that regarded any hint of the programmatic in the arts as redolent of realist philistinism, suspiciously Stalinist as well as aesthetically vapid. *Fanfare*, along with the rest of Copland's work from the late 1930s on, fit in perfectly with what Greenberg had been denouncing since 1939 as "kitsch" and what Dwight Macdonald eventually defined as "mid-cult"—a style, Macdonald wrote, that "pretends to respect the standards of High Culture while in fact it waters them down and vulgarizes them."

The detractors had an important point when they attacked the purposeful subordination of art to politics. But they did not adequately appreciate Copland's art when they failed to comprehend efforts to cut through the distinctions between sophistication and simplicity as anything other than pursuit of the party line. Simplifying music, Copland believed, need not mean cheapening it; it could, in fact, help form the basis of an American artistic style that would fuse "high," "middle," and "low," elevating creatively interesting forms of popular culture while also popularizing more serious culture. That effort had aesthetic intentions and merits above and beyond politics. "The conventional concert public continued apathetic or indifferent to anything but the established classics," he recalled, whereas "an entirely new public for music had grown up around the radio and phonograph. It made no sense to ignore them and to continue writing as if they did not exist. I felt that it was worth the effort to see if I couldn't say what I had to say in the simplest possible terms."

It is always important to remember that the idea of using popular culture as a takeoff point for a larger artistic quest was not limited to the music of the Popular Front; neither was it limited to the Left nor to musicians alone nor to the ferment of the 1930s and 1940s. Numerous giants in modern American culture, from across a wide political spectrum, tried to build something new and larger out of popular forms, among them Louis Armstrong, Willa Cather, John Ford, William Carlos Williams, Duke Ellington, Walker Evans, Edward Hopper, and Frank Lloyd Wright. Copland understood and felt a kinship with their efforts, with no narrow political agenda.

Still, for Copland, the principles of "imposed simplicity" were inevitably bound up with his Popular Front political loyalties of the 1930s

People's Songs magazine, June 1947.

and 1940s, even as a diluted form of those loyalties entered the cultural mainstream. And although Copland was chiefly identified with the symphony concert hall, he did not completely lose touch with the more populist adaptations of American folk music being undertaken by his friend

Charles Seeger's boy Pete and by Pete's leftist folksinger friends—adaptations that Copland found musically and politically sympathetic. At the very end of 1945, the younger Seeger, recently discharged from the army, was instrumental in founding a new organization, People's Songs, which over the next five years promoted the use of radical-minded folk music in order to encourage left-wing union organizing and related causes. Joining Seeger on the group's founding committee were members of the Almanac Singers and other notables on the New York leftist folk-music scene, including Woody Guthrie, Lee Hays, Agnes "Sis" Cunningham, Alan Lomax, and Josh White. A few years later, the Board of Sponsors of the expanded People's Songs Inc. included Aaron Copland as well as Paul Robeson and Leonard Bernstein.

During the same summer of 1934 that Copland roused the "peasantry" of northern Minnesota, the newlyweds Abraham Zimmerman and Beatrice Stone Zimmerman, by complete coincidence, settled in Abraham's hometown, Duluth—the port city of the Mesabi Iron Range, about 150 miles from Copland's vacation cabin on Lake Bemidji. Zimmerman had a good job working as a senior manager for the Standard Oil Company, and he ran the company union. Seven years later, on May 24, 1941, Beatrice, known to all as Beatty, gave birth to the first of the couple's two sons, Robert.

Bob Dylan's proximity and debt to the World War II era and its aftermath always need emphasis. It is said that he owns the 1960s—but he is, of course, largely a product of the 1940s and 1950s. At the very end of the 1950s, he heard for the first time John and Alan Lomax's greatest discovery in the field, the Louisiana ex-convict and folksinger Huddie "Leadbelly" Ledbetter. Then he heard an album of Odetta's, picked up on the folk revival, and traded in his electric guitar for a double-O Martin acoustic; a year later, he immersed himself in the romance of Woody Guthrie's *Bound for Glory* and was well on the way to becoming Bob Dylan. Before that, when he was still Bob Zimmerman, a mixture of country and western, rhythm and blues, and early rock and roll dominated his listening and his first expeditions as a performer, while his reading, at Hibbing High School, embraced Shakespeare and the classics, Mark Twain, and Popular Front stalwarts like his particular favorite, the novelist John Steinbeck. Throughout the 1940s and 1950s, he was immersed in the singers and musicians whom everyone heard: Frank Sinatra, the Andrews Sisters, Bing Crosby, Frankie Laine, and the original cast recording of *Oklahoma!* (choreographed by Copland's sometime collaborator de Mille); Whoopee John Wilfahrt, Frankie Yankovic, and a host of other Midwest polka band leaders. And, at the movies, there were

Whoopee John Wilfahrt, bottom of stairway, and his band in a playful pose at the Wold-Chamberlain Minneapolis and St. Paul Airport, 1947.

Woman of the North Country, On the Waterfront, The Law vs. Billy the Kid, and (above all for Zimmerman and his friends) Marlon Brando in *The Wild One* and James Dean in *Rebel Without a Cause* and *Giant.* Finally, although far less popular, on stacks of twelve-inch records (and then the flood of long-playing records released after 1948), as well as on the radio and on early television as well as in school, there was classical music, old and new—including the music of Aaron Copland.

Copland was virtually inescapable in the 1940s and 1950s, even for the less musically inclined. The leading music-appreciation textbooks of the day, by Martin Bernstein and Joseph Machlis, hailed him as "one of America's greatest composers," his music "straightforward without being banal, and thoroughly American in spirit," including compositions in which local and regional music "is dissolved in personal lyricism, thereby assuming a value that extends beyond the particular time or place." Copland wrote works intended especially for young performers and listeners; his *Young Pioneers* and *Suite No. 1 for Young Pianists,* performed by Marga Richter, appeared on an MGM Records album, *Piano Music for Children by Modern American Composers* in 1954. Early in its premier season in 1952, the pioneering "highbrow" television show *Omnibus* broadcast *Rodeo,* and a year later it aired *Billy the Kid.* A portion of *Billy the Kid* also served as the opening theme for the first and only "live" television Western series, *Action in the Afternoon,* starring Jack Valentine as a singing, guitar-playing cowboy, broadcast by CBS in 1953, two years before it began running a televised version of the radio series *Gunsmoke,* starring James Arness as Marshal Matt Dillon. (As Abe Zimmerman was in the appliance business, his family became the first in town to own a television, in 1952.) Copland also scored music for several movies, including those based on Steinbeck's novels *Of Mice and Men* (1939) and *The Red Pony* (1949), and in 1950 his music for a William Wyler film, *The Heiress,* won the Academy Award for Best Original Musical Score.

Dylan has never disclosed when he first heard Copland's music, and as it was so ubiquitous on the American scene, he may not even recall. Dylan did not take any music-appreciation course after the eighth grade, so he likely did not hear Copland at school. Still, in light of where and when he grew up, it would have been extraordinary if Dylan, as a boy or a teenager, had not heard, somewhere, something composed by Copland. And whether he first heard Copland's music then or later, it has clearly impressed itself on him—as has, just maybe, Copland's example. Although born forty years apart, both Copland and Dylan descended from Jewish immigrant forebears from Lithuania. Both were drawn to the legends of underdogs and outlaws like Billy the Kid, as well as to the youthful, leftist New York musical precincts of their respective times. Both soaked up the popular music of the American past (taking special interest in the balladry and mythos of the Southwest) and transformed it into their art, reconfiguring old songs and raising them to creative and iconic levels that the purist folklorists could never have reached.

Those are interpolations and interesting parallels. Without question, though, Copland contributed to the blend of music and downtown left-wing politics that in time produced the folk-music revival which in turn helped produce Bob Dylan. Long before Dylan had picked up *Bound for Glory*, Copland's reinventions of folk songs and paeans to the common man had been part of the soundscape of 1940s and early 1950s America. The most familiar way of understanding Dylan's musical origins goes back to Woody Guthrie. But another, strangely related way goes back to Aaron Copland, whose orchestral work raises some of the same conundrums that Dylan's songs do—about art and politics, simplicity and difficulty, compromise and genius, love and theft.

Those connections might have been clearer long before Dylan played "Hoe-Down" in 2001 had Copland acknowledged, more than he did, that he and some of his closest associates had been downtown left-wing composers and performers. Yet because of the course of Copland's career in the late 1940s and after—when he broke from the pro-Communist Left, touched up his political past, and became a widely beloved elder statesman—that link was almost invisible, especially to Dylan and the rising generation.

Copland's music moved in both familiar and startlingly fresh directions after World War II. He worked on new experiments with jazz and choral music as well as further compositions in the "imposed simplicity" style. But he also turned to writing with the twelve-tone system of Arnold Schoenberg that he had long abjured—and that young composers after the war had embraced while regarding Copland as outmoded—resulting in his *Piano Quartet* of 1950.*

His political loyalties, meanwhile, became troubled—and in time, to

---

* When Leonard Bernstein asked Copland why he, of all people, had turned to the twelve-tone system, Copland replied, "Because I need more chords. I've run out of chords." Bernstein was later put in mind of Paul Simon's telling him that when he met Bob Dylan for the first time in the early 1960s, Dylan's first sentence had been "Hey, you got any new chords? *I've run out of chords.*" Another coincidence.

Copland, troublesome. Through the opening years of the Cold War, he remained attached to the pro-Soviet Left. At the notorious Cultural and Scientific Conference for World Peace, held at the Waldorf-Astoria hotel in New York in 1949, he gave an address in which he described himself as "a democratic American artist, with no political affiliations of any kind," and criticized the Soviets' condemnations of Western music and modern art—but also expressed concern that the Truman administration's foreign policies were leading to a third world war, blamed the United States for provoking the Kremlin's repressive arts' policies, and generally relieved the Soviets of any blame for initiating the Cold War.

Yet as the decade ended, Copland was beginning to have new and serious doubts about his leftist connections. Stalin's manipulation and mistreatment of the Soviet composer Dmitri Shostakovich disturbed him, as did his growing feeling that the American Communists were manipulating him in order to batten on his fame. (He was particularly perturbed by the *Daily Worker*'s brief report on his speech to the Waldorf conference, which completely omitted its criticisms of the Soviets' attack on modern art and exaggerated his misgivings about Truman's foreign policies.) In 1950, Copland began cutting his ties with the Stalinist Left. In 1951–52, in a set of lectures delivered at Harvard, he made a point of criticizing "each fiat of Soviet musical policy." By 1954, when he resigned from the Workers' Music Association, one of the last such groups to which he still belonged, Copland's old romance with pro-Communist politics was dead.

Copland's break, however, came too late to ward off the agents of the 1950s Red Scare. Amid the controversy in 1949 over the Waldorf conference, *Life* magazine had run Copland's photograph (and misspelled his name "Copeland") as one of a group of fifty of the better-known participants, to illustrate an article entitled "Red Visitors Cause Rumpus." (The others included Leonard Bernstein, Albert Einstein, Arthur Miller, and F. O. Matthiessen, described by *Life* as "a representative selection ranging from hard-working fellow travelers to soft-headed do-gooders.") The following year, a right-wing newsletter, *Counterattack,* published *Red Channels,* a compilation of the names of 151 actors, singers, composers, and other entertainers who supposedly had strong Communist links or sympathies and who immediately became targets for blacklisting; Copland was named, along with Marc Blitzstein, Alan Lomax, Earl Robinson, and Pete Seeger. In 1953, an Illinois Republican congressman, prepped in part by *Red Channels,* fingered Copland as a Communist, which forced

Protestors picket the Cultural and Scientific Conference for World Peace, Waldorf-Astoria hotel, New York City, March 26, 1949. Aaron Copland at the Waldorf Peace Conference.

the cancellation of a performance of *Lincoln Portrait* as part of the inauguration festivities for Dwight D. Eisenhower. Later that year, Copland appeared as a putatively friendly but highly unforthcoming witness in closed session before Senator Joseph McCarthy's Senate Permanent Subcommittee on Investigations.

Some suspected Reds hauled before congressional committees, such as Marc Blitzstein, confessed their personal involvement but refused to name names. (Blitzstein had broken from the party in 1949 and cited the Communists' hostility to his homosexuality as the chief reason.) Others invoked their Fifth Amendment rights against self-incrimination. Still others (including Pete Seeger) stood on the First Amendment and refused to answer any questions about their political associations. (Seeger was cited for contempt of Congress, and later convicted, but finally won his case on appeal.) Copland, though, preferred to present himself to McCarthy's committee as an apolitical artist who had innocently stumbled into certain political connections out of humanitarian motives—a composer consumed by his music who cared little about politics and knew even less.

Copland admitted he had been a member of the National Council of

American-Soviet Friendship, had helped sponsor a concert in support of Hanns Eisler to protest Eisler's deportation in 1948, and had participated in the Waldorf conference. But he testified not only that he had never been a member of the Communist Party but, parsing his words carefully, that he "had never thought of myself as a Communist sympathizer," had "never sympathized with Communists as such," and had "never attended any specific Communist function of any kind," which was not so. When backed into a corner about one affiliation or another, Copland claimed that his memory failed him, although he also pointed out, reasonably, that he had only just received his subpoena, which had given him little time to prepare. When confronted with undeniable facts, he answered cleverly as well as evasively. Pressed about the Waldorf conference, for example, he testified that he was happy he had attended "because it gave me firsthand knowledge in what ways the Communists were able to use such movements for their own ends," but he said nothing about his remarks to the conference, and he claimed that he was completely unaware of the widely publicized Communist domination of the conference and had attended simply to encourage Russian-American cultural and diplomatic relations.

The exasperated senators finally decided that there was no point in pursuing the questioning and excused Copland from giving any further testimony. McCarthy's critics called the episode an egregious attempt to humiliate a great American artist, which it was. Copland, for his own part, could take relief at how, having broken with the Communist commissars, he had parried the right-wing persecutors. While he would always remain something of a social utopian, he became thereafter a staunch political liberal—a firm supporter of the civil-rights movement in the 1960s and an opponent of the Vietnam War. But he would wear his public mask of political innocence for the rest of his life, while he shrouded his radical past in vagueness, circumspection, and platitudes.

In 1955, Copland completed his only full-scale opera, *The Tender Land,* written in his popular style. Then his composing output sharply declined, "exactly as if," he said, "someone had simply turned off a faucet." He devoted the last thirty-five years of his life mainly to conducting, recording, teaching, writing, and traveling around the world as an unofficial ambassador for American music. By 1960, when RCA Victor released a celebrated recording of Copland conducting the Boston Symphony Orchestra in the orchestral suites to *Appalachian Spring* and *The Tender Land,* his best years as a composer were behind him. By the time he finished his last significant work, the *Duo for Flute and Piano,* in 1971, he had become an owlish, benign elder statesman, the dean of serious American music.

Something profound had also happened to the place of Copland's music in American life—another strange turn of the screw. The left-wing Popular Front politics that had helped animate his most popular work had crumbled; yet despite *Red Channels* and Senator McCarthy, Copland's reputation, after a brief period of blacklisting, had survived the Red Scare virtually unscathed, thanks in part to his own evasiveness and in part to his rejection of the Communist Left. Thereafter, his stature among the general public as well as concertgoers continued to grow.

In the 1940s, Copland's mingling of folk music and orchestral form, informed by his leftist political sensibilities, became more generally accepted as an embodiment of American democratic culture embattled in Europe and the Pacific. Thereafter, that Popular Front aesthetic, stripped of its left-wing or even New Deal connotations, helped turn Copland's most prominent works into landmark, all-embracing, modern statements of the American musical imagination. The former pro-Communist revolutionary became, in effect, America's composer, his music a celebration of the nation itself—the essence of what listeners around the country and around the world regarded as American art music. Musically, this land was his

land. Twenty-eight years after *Lincoln Portrait* was banned from Eisenhower's inauguration ceremonies, *Fanfare for the Common Man* was featured at Ronald Reagan's inauguration, and in 1986, Reagan—a man of the 1930s and 1940s Left who, unlike Copland, had become a man of the Right—bestowed upon him the National Medal of Arts, to go along with the Congressional Gold Medal presented by the House of Representatives.

Copland's was not the sort of music—and Copland was not the sort of figure—that attracted Bob Dylan to New York in 1961, even though, unknown to Dylan, Copland and his music shared common

Aaron Copland on the Brooklyn Bridge, 1969.

political origins and sensibilities with the folk revival, and even though Copland, while still on the left in the 1940s, had done as much as any American to celebrate and elevate American folk song. Dylan came looking for the authentic hobo troubadour Woody Guthrie and for a different piece of the legacy of the radical 1930s and 1940s. Yet that journey, inevitably, brought Dylan into contact with what remained of a New York musical world once inhabited by Aaron Copland as well as the Seegers—including one shard that would affect him deeply.

In 1950, just before the blacklisting began—and just after the People's Songs movement, beleaguered by the Cold War political backlash, fell apart—the Weavers enjoyed a national number one hit with their recording of "Goodnight, Irene," a slightly bowdlerized rendition of the version that John Lomax and Alan Lomax had picked up in 1933 from Leadbelly.* (Later that same year, "Goodnight, Irene" became a hit record for, among others, Frank Sinatra, Jo Stafford, and the Nashville duo of Ernest Tubb and Red Foley—but the Weavers' success dwarfed the others'.) The flip side of the Weavers' record, the exuberant Israeli hora "Tzena, Tzena, Tzena," was also a smash hit, reaching number two on the Billboard chart. Suddenly Pete Seeger and the rest of the quartet found themselves booked in proper supper clubs and hotels—which elicited swift denunciations of them from doctrinaire leftists for allegedly abandoning their political mission and selling out to big-money show business. For a moment, it seemed as if the quintessential folk-song leftists of the 1940s might make a successful commercial transition into the postwar era. But it all came crashing down when *Red Channels* named Pete Seeger as a subversive, the group was blacklisted, and Seeger defied the Un-American Activities Committee by standing on the First Amendment.

It is possible that nine-year-old Bob Zimmerman first heard Seeger and the Weavers on the radio or on a jukebox or at summer camp during their

---

* People's Songs was in effect succeeded by the more overtly doctrinaire leftist People's Artists group. In 1951, the new group undertook the publication of *Sing Out!* magazine, co-founded and edited by the former executive director of People's Songs, Irwin Silber, whose criticisms of Dylan's work in 1964 played a part in the singer's break with the radical political folk-song establishment. See below, pp. 89–90.

fleeting early success. He certainly heard Seeger and the Weavers—along with the Almanac Singers, Woody Guthrie, and a cavalcade of other folk performers—after he moved to Minneapolis in 1959 and gravitated to Jon Pankake, Tony Glover, and other local folk and blues sophisticates—and began to emerge as Bob Dylan. One biographer states that Dylan first saw Seeger in the flesh at one of Seeger's college concerts at the University of Wisconsin at Madison at the very end of 1960 or beginning of 1961. (Still blacklisted, Seeger had been keeping body and soul together for years by playing on the less-than-lucrative but open-minded campus circuit.) That story, unfortunately, is apocryphal. But Seeger's reputation, and his music, were very much in the air, and may have helped fire up Dylan's ambition to travel to New York and meet Guthrie, his newly acquired hero and musical model.

Dylan got his wish at the end of January 1961, about five days after he arrived in Manhattan, at a Sunday gathering at the home of Guthrie's friends Bob and Sidsel "Sid" Gleason in East Orange, New Jersey. Guthrie, ravaged by Huntington's chorea, was under permanent care at Greystone Park Hospital in Morris Plains, but the hospital released him to the Gleasons' care on weekends, when old friends and young admirers from New York would hop a bus to East Orange, pay their respects, eat, hang out, and play music. The elders included Pete Seeger and, now and then, Alan Lomax, as well as other spirits and comrades from the *Sing Out!* crowd and the old People's Songs movement. In his successful search for Guthrie, Dylan had stumbled upon the surviving remnants of the original folk revival that, along with Aaron Copland, had emerged out of the Composers' Collective and the rest of the left-wing music world in New York City at the depths of the Great Depression. He would remain closely identified with these circles, including Seeger, through the mid-1960s, and thereafter he would occasionally reappear to pay homage to Woody Guthrie, including, late in 2009, a televised appearance on a History Channel special presentation on which he sang Guthrie's Dust Bowl ballad "Do Re Mi."

By chance, Dylan also bumped into the work of another, very different, and far less renowned survivor from that same 1930s New York Communist and pro-Communist Left, who, though he had left the Communist Party, never renounced his leftist politics or his musical preoccupations of the 1930s. The effects on Dylan were profound. In the fall and winter of 1961–62, the Theatre de Lys on Christopher Street presented *Brecht*

Bob Dylan and Pete Seeger in Greenwood, Mississippi, July 6, 1963.

on Brecht, a new revue consisting of excerpts from Bertolt Brecht's varied works, starring Kurt Weill's widow, Lotte Lenya. A landmark production of Brecht and Weill's masterpiece, *The Threepenny Opera*—inspired by a concert performance sponsored by Copland's greatest protégé, Leonard Bernstein, at a Brandeis University music festival in 1952—was just ending a six-year run at the same theater. In *Brecht on Brecht,* Lenya, who had starred in the *Threepenny* production for its first two years, would return to perform once again her spine-chilling, showstopping song, "Pirate Jenny."

A year and several months later, Dylan's young girlfriend Suze Rotolo, the daughter of Communists, who had begun introducing him to the Village's bohemian drama world, was helping out backstage with a bare-bones production of *Brecht on Brecht* at the Sheridan Square Playhouse. One day, Dylan showed up at the theater, and while waiting for her, he caught the show and heard the black actress Micki Grant sing "Pirate Jenny." It bowled him over.

The young folksinger and aspiring songwriter—his second album, *The Freewheelin' Bob Dylan,* appeared in May—returned to his dumpy apartment, stunned. He would listen, over and over, to the original Off-Broadway cast album of *The Threepenny Opera,* with Lotte Lenya as

Pirate Jenny. "The raw intensity of the songs," he recalls in *Chronicles,* immediately aroused him:

> "Morning Anthem," "Wedding Song," "The World Is Mean," "Polly's Song," "Tango Ballad," "Ballad of the Easy Life." Songs with tough language. They were erratic, unrhythmical and herky-jerky—weird visions . . . They were like folk songs in nature, but unlike folk songs, too, because they were sophisticated.

Lotte Lenya in 1962, photograph by famed writer and artist Carl Van Vechten.

He pored over the lyrics of "Pirate Jenny"—a "nasty song, sung by an evil fiend," he now calls it, even though in Weill and Brecht's score Jenny was singing of sublime proletarian justice—with its repeated menacing image of "a ship, the black freighter." The free verse association, the strange melodic lines—everything about "Pirate Jenny" was, to Dylan, a revelation, although, he now recalls, he stayed "far away from its ideological heart." Inspired anew, he was headed in directions that would one day lead him to write the strong but imitative song of prophecy "When the Ship Comes In" (which suggested that, however much he disdained ideology, he at least partly absorbed Weill and Brecht's Marxist apocalypse as anything but nasty or evil). Those same impulses would later help lead him into the imagined twilight world of "Visions of Johanna" and the rest of *Blonde on Blonde.*

The words that laid Dylan flat on his back, and forever changed his thinking about songs and songwriting, came from an inventive, powerful new American translation of Brecht's German lyrics, written by Marc Blitzstein.

Blitzstein had been struggling for years to complete an expanded version of his 1932 song play about Sacco and Vanzetti, and the work would remain unfinished at his death early in 1964. It was disheartening, Aaron Copland wrote in an appreciative memorial note for his friend, that the present generation of musicians knew little or nothing about Blitzstein or about "the moral fervor that fired his work during the depression-haunted thirties." Although Blitzstein had quit the Communist Party in 1949, he had never lost that 1930s fervor—and, like Pete Seeger, he had been blacklisted by the television and movie industries. Copland, who unlike Blitzstein and Seeger had renounced his Communist sympathies out of artistic and political principle and then dodged the Red-baiters, enjoyed a very different career and entered a comfortable musical world very different from the Village bohemia that lured the young Bob Dylan.

On January 26, 1961—a day or two after Dylan first arrived in New York and played at the Café Wha?—Copland narrated a performance of *The Second Hurricane,* the children's opera he had composed and Orson Welles had staged in 1937, at a Composers' Showcase held at the Museum of Modern Art. It was the beginning of what would be another good year. Copland received various honors in 1961, including the prestigious Edward MacDowell Medal for contributions to American arts and letters from the MacDowell Colony. The American Ballet Theatre mounted a well-received production of *Billy the Kid*; a new Copland chamber piece, *Nonet,* had its first performance at the Dumbarton Oaks Research Library in Washington; and President Kennedy hosted a youth concert on the White House lawn that featured a performance of "Hoe-Down." There was also an official announcement that the New York Philharmonic, conducted by Leonard Bernstein, would offer the debut of a newly commissioned Copland work on the opening night of the new Philharmonic Hall at Lincoln Center for the Performing Arts in the fall of 1962. In addition, a few days after the opening, the Philharmonic would perform *Lincoln Portrait,* with the U.S. ambassador to the United Nations, Adlai Stevenson, onstage as the narrator.

By then, almost certainly, Dylan had heard Copland's music. Like Copland, he would go on to slough off charges of sell-out commercialism and reshuffle the very terms on which American music could be composed and comprehended, mingling Petrarch, Donizetti, and Herman Melville with Hambone Willie Newbern, appealing to a mass audience without sacrificing his own vision. And forty years later in 2001, after an American catastrophe, Dylan would turn to Copland's "Hoe-Down" to set his own concerts in motion.

Dylan's art, though built from the songs of others, would be all his own. After starting out in Hibbing by banging out Little Richard songs on the piano, he began his musical writing in Guthrie-esque style and then entered into every other folk-music style he could lay his hands on. Copland, by contrast, was first inspired to become a composer by the Polish composer, pianist, and national patriot Ignacy Paderewski and went on to study in Paris with Nadia Boulanger. Still, Copland's musical world in 1930s New York led, directly and indirectly, to Dylan's in 1960s New York. And Copland's amalgamating art, in time built partly out of old cowboy ballads and mountain fiddle tunes, anticipated Dylan's in ways that help make sense of both men's achievements.

By the time that Dylan, the high-school rock and roller turned songwriter-bard, began to make his mark, Copland had become the amiable patriarch of the American classical music establishment and had moved away from the Left, and so the connections were missed. But the aging master could still write with feeling about "the moral fervor" of "the depression-haunted thirties" that Dylan heard in Woody Guthrie. And the young Aaron Copland had been more like the young Bob Dylan than his older persona suggested.

Aaron Copland in Paris, circa 1920s. Bob Dylan during sound check prior to his concert at Philadelphia's Town Hall, September 1964.

In the late summer of 1924, Copland, still in his initial dissonant, modernist phase, finished his very first symphony. The premiere performance, given the following January at Aeolian Hall in Manhattan by the

New York Symphony Orchestra, was conducted by Walter Damrosch—who, at the concert's conclusion, turned to the shaken audience and announced that "when the gifted young American who wrote this symphony can compose, at the age of 23, a work like this one, it seems evident that in five years more he will be ready to commit murder." Dylan's earliest Greenwich Village admirers were similarly stunned when his own songs began pouring out of him after he settled in New York. And in less than four years, at the age of twenty-three, Dylan would be ready to play Philharmonic Hall.

2

PENETRATING AETHER:

The Beat Generation and Allen Ginsberg's America

Aaron Copland's first important musical project after *Billy the Kid* was to write the score, in 1939, for a film by the innovative director Lewis Milestone, made from John Steinbeck's novella about hard-luck migrant workers in California, *Of Mice and Men.* Copland had been trying to break into film work since 1937 but was still known in Hollywood as a composer of modernist art music and hence was considered too difficult for American moviegoers. Thanks in part to his good friend Harold Clurman of the Group Theatre, who had relocated to Hollywood, and inspired in part by Virgil Thomson's film work, Copland finally got his foot in the door, received the Steinbeck assignment, and produced a score in his new style of "imposed simplicity" (although without the obvious

Original poster for Lewis Milestone's film version of John Steinbeck's *Of Mice and Men*, 1939.

borrowing from folk music or cowboy songs). The film won immediate critical praise, as did Copland's accessible adaptation of modernist techniques—including, daringly for the time, dissonance—to his score's wide-open, pastoral evocations. The following year, Copland's music for *Of Mice and Men* earned him two Academy Award nominations and the National Board of Review Award.

Late one night in 1940, Jack Kerouac, not yet out of high school, saw Milestone's film—possibly in his hometown of Lowell, Massachusetts, but most likely in Manhattan's Times Square—and left the theater envisaging phantoms flitting out of sight beneath the streetlamps. The movie, as well as the ghostly aftermath, stuck with him, particularly its rackety opening scene, carried along by Copland's dramatic music. Fifteen years later, Kerouac described it in the "54th Chorus" of his large clutch of poems *Mexico City Blues:*

> *Once I went to a movie*
> *At midnight, 1940, Mice*
> *And Men, the name of it,*
> *The Red Block Boxcars*
> *Rolling by (on the Screen)*
> > *Yessir*
> > > *life*
> > > > *finally*
> > > > > *gets*
> > > > > > *tired*
> > > > > > > *of*
> > > > > > > > *living—*

Twenty years after Kerouac wrote those lines, on a crisp scarlet-ocher November afternoon at Edson Cemetery in Lowell, Bob Dylan and Allen Ginsberg visited Kerouac's grave, trailed by a reporter, a photographer, a film crew, and various others (including the young playwright Sam Shepard). Dylan had performed the night before at the University of Lowell, on a tour of New England with a thrown-together troupe of new friends and old, including Ginsberg, which called itself the Rolling Thunder Revue. Ginsberg, who became excited when the tour buses reached the city, met up with some of Kerouac's relatives and drinking buddies and tried to immerse Dylan's entourage in Kerouacian lore. Shepard, who had joined the troupe ostensibly to write the screenplay for a movie Dylan

Sam Shepard, Bob Dylan, and Allen Ginsberg at Jack Kerouac's grave, Edson Cemetery, Lowell, Massachusetts, November 3, 1975.

planned to make of the tour, duly recorded in his travel log the names of real-life Lowell sites described in the Duluoz Legend—Kerouac's collective, Faulknerian name for the autobiographical novels, revolving around his fictional alter ego Jack Duluoz, that constituted the main body of his work. But at Edson Cemetery, Ginsberg recited not from Kerouac's prose but from poetry out of *Mexico City Blues,* including "54th Chorus"— invoking specters, fatigue, mortality, Mexico, and John Steinbeck's boxcar America, while he and Dylan contemplated Kerouac's headstone. And when Dylan included footage of the event in the film he made in and about the Rolling Thunder tour, yet another complicated cultural circuit closed, linking Kerouac listening to Copland and watching Steinbeck's *Of Mice and Men* in 1940 with the scene at Kerouac's grave in *Renaldo and Clara* in 1977.

Dylan knew the poems, Ginsberg later claimed. "Someone handed me *Mexico City Blues* in St. Paul in 1959," Dylan told him. "It blew my mind." It was the first poetry he'd read that spoke his own American language, Dylan said—or so Ginsberg said he said. Maybe, maybe not. Without question, though, Dylan read *Mexico City Blues* and was deeply interested in Beat writing before he left Minneapolis for New York. (Like other Beats and hipsters, his friend Tony Glover ordered a paperback copy of William Burroughs's *Naked Lunch* from France, where it had been published by Olympia Press in Paris in 1959 as *The Naked Lunch*—uncertain whether the book, deemed obscene by American authorities, would clear customs. The book indeed arrived, and Glover lent it to Dylan, who returned it after a couple of weeks.) And Dylan's involvement with the writings of Kerouac, Ginsberg, Burroughs, and the rest of the Beat generation is nearly as essential to Dylan's biography as his immersion in rock and roll, rhythm and blues, and then Woody Guthrie. "I came out of the wilderness and just naturally fell in with the Beat scene, the bohemian, Be Bop crowd, it was all pretty much connected," Dylan said in 1985. "It was Jack Kerouac, Ginsberg, Corso, Ferlinghetti . . . I got in at the tail end of that and it was magic . . . it had just as big an impact on me as Elvis Presley."

Dylan's connection to Kerouac was mainly artistic. After he arrived in New York, he now says, he quickly outgrew the raw, aimless, "hungry for kicks" hipsterism personified by Neal Cassady's character, Dean Moriarty, in *On the Road*. Aimlessness would never suit Dylan. And by the time Dylan had begun making a name for himself, Kerouac had begun his descent into the alcoholism and paranoia that would kill him in 1969, at the age of forty-seven. Dylan never met him. But he still loved what he called Kerouac's "breathless, dynamic bop phrases," and always would. He could relate to Kerouac as a young man from a small declining industrial town who had come to New York as a cultural outsider more than twenty years earlier—an unknown bursting with ideas and whom the insiders proceeded either to lionize or to condemn, and, in any case, badly misconstrue. Now and then, over the years to come, recognizable lines and images of Kerouac's would surface in Dylan's lyrics, most conspicuously in the song "Desolation Row."

Dylan's continuing link to the Beat generation, though, came chiefly through his friend and sometime mentor Allen Ginsberg. Dylan's link with Ginsberg dated back to the end of 1963, a pivotal moment in the lives and careers of both men. Thereafter, in the mid-1960s, the two would complete important artistic transitions, each touched and supported by the other. On and off, their rapport lasted for decades. And in 1997, in New Brunswick, Canada, Dylan would dedicate a concert performance of "Desolation Row" to Ginsberg, his longtime comrade, telling the audience it was Allen's favorite of his songs, on the evening after Ginsberg died.

As with Dylan's connection to New York's Popular Front folk-music world, his connection with the Beats had a complicated backstory. The origins of the Beat impulse, like those of the folk revival, dated back much further than the 1950s, let alone the 1960s, to the days of Dylan's childhood in Duluth and Hibbing. For all the obvious differences between the Beats and the folk-music crowd—the Beats' affinities were with the arts of Arthur Rimbaud, William Blake, and Charlie Parker, and not Anglo-American backwoods balladry—the Beat writers found themselves, early, locked in conflict with some of the same liberal critical circles around *Partisan Review* that decried, for different reasons, the folksy leftism of the Popular Front, including its high- or middlebrow version in Aaron Copland's music. Out of that conflict emerged Beat artistic ideas that Dylan admired, remembered, and later seized upon when he moved beyond the folk revival. Even though Dylan invented himself within one current of musical populism that came out of the 1930s and 1940s, he escaped that current in the 1960s—without ever completely rejecting it—by embracing anew some of the spirit and imagery of the Beat generation's entirely different rebellious disaffiliation and poetic transcendence. Dylan in turn would make an enormous difference to the surviving, transformed Beats, especially Ginsberg, each influencing the other while their admirers forged the counterculture that profoundly affected American life at the end of the twentieth century.

Although they were distinct and in many ways antagonistic, the folk revival and the Beat scene shared certain ancestral connections in the Depression-era Left, and this may help explain why the liberal critics thought the Beats were so contemptible. Jack Kerouac's feel for some of the texture of lower-class life and for what he called "the warp of wood of old America"—his appreciation of "the switching moves of boxcars" in Steinbeck, Milestone, and Copland's *Of Mice and Men*—provided one set of similarities. Along with several others in the Beat orbit, including Ginsberg, Kerouac joined the left-wing National Maritime Union in order to ship out with the merchant marine. (Working at the NMU's headquarters on Sixteenth Street was Ginsberg's troubled mother, Naomi.) On the West Coast, Gary Snyder brought some of the traditions of Pacific northwoods radicalism into his Zen poesy. But the most powerful link was through Ginsberg, who would always be the most political of the Beat writers. In his poem "America," which he wrote in 1956, soon after the

McCarthy Red Scare, Ginsberg confessed that he had sentimental feelings for the Wobblies, described being brought as a boy to Communist-cell meetings, and chanted in praise of the anarchist martyrs of the 1920s Sacco and Vanzetti. The allusions were not merely historical.

Ginsberg's readers know about his mother, Naomi, the loyal Communist who took him to those cell meetings, as immortalized in his poem "Kaddish." But Naomi's was not the only left-wing political influence inside the Ginsberg household. Ginsberg's father, Louis, taught high school in Paterson, New Jersey, and was an accomplished mainstream lyric poet whose verses appeared in the *New York Times* and other respectable places. In his youth, though, the elder Ginsberg, then a Eugene V. Debs socialist, published poetry in Max Eastman's *Masses* and its successor, the *Liberator.* He then gravitated, in the late 1920s, to a loosely organized association called the Rebel Poets, co-founded by the "proletarian" novelist Jack Conroy (who wrote *The Disinherited* and was an influence on, among others, John Steinbeck and Richard Wright). Louis did not join his wife in the Communist Party, which added to his air of moderation. Yet, like his fellow New Jersey poet William Carlos Williams and other non-Communists, he published work in the Communist-leaning monthly *New Masses.* And he shared in the widespread outrage that led him to contribute a poem, "To Sacco and Vanzetti," to a commemorative volume published in 1928, shortly after the two convicted anarchists were executed.

Hints of the Beats' left-wing genealogy lasted through the 1960s and beyond—thanks, again, chiefly to Allen Ginsberg—and it made some difference to Dylan, who, whatever his thoughts about politics and political organizations, never lost his attraction to rebels and outlaws. The day after the Rolling Thunder Revue left Lowell, Ginsberg wrote a letter to his father:

> Beautiful day with Dylan, beginning early afternoon visiting
> Kerouac's grave plot & reading the stone . . . —We stood in the
> November sun brown leaves flying in wind & read poems from
> *Mexico City Blues* . . . Dylan wants to do some scene related to
> Sacco & Vanzetti when we get to Boston.

Boston's symbolic significance needed no explication between son and father: Sacco and Vanzetti had been executed there in 1927, for the murder they allegedly committed in nearby South Braintree seven years earlier. It is plausible that Dylan kindled to the idea of performing "some scene" about them—a reprise, perhaps, of one of Woody Guthrie's song tributes on his album *Ballads of Sacco and Vanzetti,* composed and recorded in 1946–47 at the prompting of Moe Asch, though not issued until 1960. But nothing came of the idea. By the time the Rolling Thunder Revue reached Boston, Joan Baez, one of the troupe's stars, had even ceased singing the Alfred Hayes–Earl Robinson anthem, "Joe Hill," about the Wobbly organizer and songwriter executed in 1915—a song she had featured at earlier stops during her allotted solo portion of the show.* Baez and Dylan did share the vocal on "I Dreamed I Saw St. Augustine," Dylan's rewrite of "Joe Hill." Traces of the old radical America persisted, long after Dylan had moved beyond writing topical songs. But Dylan had transformed those traces completely, as he transformed everything.

Dylan had hardly come to the Beats in search of a new political cause; rather, he was taken (as he had been before he left Minnesota) with their play of language as well as their spiritual estrangement that transcended conventional politics of any kind. In this sense, Ginsberg, Kerouac, and the others served Dylan a bit as rock and roll did—as something he had picked up in Minnesota, returned to, and absorbed anew after he had passed through the confining left-wing earnestness and orthodoxy of the folk revival. Ginsberg sensed Dylan's disquiet about politics when the two men first met, and it was one reason why he found Dylan so compelling.[†] "He had declared his independence of politics," Ginsberg later recalled, "because he didn't want to be a political puppet or feel obligated to take a stand all the time. He was above and beyond politics in an interesting way." Although he could not help himself, at first, from regarding Dylan, as he later put it, as "just a folksinger," Ginsberg had heard some of Dylan's songs and understood them as something much grander than imitative folk art or political storytelling, "an answering call or response to the kind of American prophecy that Kerouac had continued from Walt Whitman."

---

* Baez, too, would have sympathized with the idea of a Sacco and Vanzetti tribute, and would even have had songs of her own to contribute—a three-part composition, "The Ballad of Sacco and Vanzetti," and "Here's to You," all composed for the Giuliano Montaldo film *Sacco e Vanzetti,* which had been released in 1971.

[†] Ginsberg later misremembered meeting Dylan on the same night that Dylan gave his controversial speech accepting the Tom Paine Award from the left-wing Emergency Civil Liberties Committee. In fact, they met nearly two weeks later—but the controversy was still fresh in Dylan's mind. See below, pp. 67–69.

Dylan, for his part, could not yet have known—few if any of the Beats' young admirers did—how the original core members of the Beat generation had been hard at work for years before they established their reputations in the late 1950s. The Beat generation and its aesthetic had their own long foreground; the major Beat writers began to forge their friendships and find their literary voices in the same 1940s America that produced the Almanac Singers and *Appalachian Spring*. And the conflicts of the 1950s and early 1960s between the Beats and the liberal intellectuals— the most poignant, ambivalent, fateful, and intellectually interesting of the conflicts—began in the spring of 1944, nearly a decade before anyone had even heard the phrase "Beat generation," when the Columbia College freshman Allen Ginsberg signed up to take a Great Books course with the eminent literary critic and *Partisan Review* intellectual Lionel Trilling.

Ginsberg arrived at Columbia in 1943, having taken a solemn vow that he would dedicate his life to serving the working class, but he would soon change course. He fell in with another student, Lucien Carr, who introduced him to his older friend (and fellow St. Louis native) William S. Burroughs and to a Columbia dropout, Jack Kerouac, who was living on Morningside Heights with his girlfriend, having been honorably discharged from the U.S. Navy on psychological grounds. In conversation with Ginsberg, Carr formulated the aesthetics of what he called, borrowing from William Butler Yeats, Ralph Waldo Emerson, and, above all, Arthur Rimbaud, the "New Vision"—a Left Bank bohemian transcendentalism, at once Edenic and decadent, based on shameless self-expression, an unhinging of the senses, and renunciation of conventional morality.

Carr would, before long, become caught up in a bizarre honor murder that landed him in prison for two years, and he would never become a full-fledged author. But out of the New Vision, his friends built ideas about spontaneous renderings of direct experience that became the foundations of Beat writing. And through Ginsberg (whose run-ins with Columbia authorities over relatively minor incidents would lead to a year's suspension and delay his graduation until 1948), those ideas came into direct contact and conflict with Trilling's more measured conceptions of literature.

"In the early years, I tried to be open with him," Ginsberg later told his friend the journalist Al Aronowitz about Trilling, "and laid on him my understanding of Burroughs and Jack—stories about them, hoping he would be interested or see some freshness or light, but all he or the others at Columbia could see was me searching for a father or pushing myself or bucking for an instructorship, or whatever they had been conditioned to think in terms of."

In fact, Ginsberg and Trilling actually shared some important ground, over and against important currents in American culture, which had the effect of making their disagreements all the more rancorous. Both were estranged from the cult of scientific reason and the consumerist materialism that seemed to be swamping the country during the years just after World War II. Both had rejected the submission of art to any strict ideology or party line; despite Ginsberg's sentimental gestures (and an abiding sense of himself as a radical, no longer Marxist, but Blakean) neither teacher nor student had any use for Communist/Popular Front left doctrine.* Both recoiled from the regnant academicism of the so-called New Critics, including John Crowe Ransom, Allen Tate, and Cleanth Brooks, who called for the formalist "close reading" of literature, to the exclusion of history, morality, biography, or any other contextual considerations—thereby turning literary analysis, according to Trilling, into "a kind of intellectual calisthenic ritual."

Allen Ginsberg, 1945. This picture was taken in a photo booth in Brooklyn's Sheepshead Bay, in August 1945, while Ginsberg was in training for the merchant marine, which he joined during what proved to be a temporary expulsion from Columbia.

Yet if Ginsberg and Trilling both saw in literature an escape route from tyranny and torpor, they differed sharply over literature's spiritual dimen-

---

* Trilling had passed through a brief intense attraction to the Communist Party as a young man in the early 1930s, going so far as to sign a public statement endorsing the party's presidential ticket in 1932. But he never actually joined the CP, and by 1934 he openly opposed the party, though he would remain sympathetic to leftist ideas for some years thereafter.

sions and possibilities. In his repudiation of literary as well as political fellow traveling, the anti-Stalinist Trilling looked to poetry and fiction to affirm a skeptical liberalism, founded on what he called "the value of individual existence in all its variousness, complexity and difficulty."

He was especially drawn to probing the ironies and ambiguities in the works of Jane Austen, Charles Dickens, Henry James, E. M. Forster, George Orwell, F. Scott Fitzgerald, and other practitioners of what he called "moral realism"—defined not as merely "the awareness of morality itself but of the contradictions, paradoxes and dangers of living the moral life." Trilling's work took readers outside the traditional insight of literary criticism into essentially philosophical considerations of good and evil, nature and civilization, commitment and evasion.

Lionel Trilling, in an undated photograph.

These difficult proving grounds of the liberal imagination afforded little room for the kind of transcendent "freshness" and "light" that the young Ginsberg and his bohemian friends were proclaiming. In 1945, Ginsberg touted Rimbaud to Trilling as a prophet, "unaffected by moral compunction, by allegiance to the confused standards of a declining age." Trilling duly read up on Rimbaud and reported that he found in the poet's rejection of conventional social values "an absolutism which is foreign to my nature, and which I combat." The idea that artistic genius arose out of derangement of the senses was, to Trilling, a dismal legacy of what he called the Romantic movement's solipsistic, hedonist conceit that mental disturbance and aberration were sources of spiritual health and illumination "if only because they controvert the ways of respectable society."

Trilling's idea of transcending mundane reality through what he called great literature's sense of "largeness and cogency" and of the "infinite complication" of modern life struck Ginsberg as, finally, a dodge, a retreat into conformism masked by intellectual ambiguity—a "cheap trick," he told a friend years later, that Trilling performed to hide his own "inside irrational Life & Poetry & reduce everything to the intellectual standard of a Time magazine report on the present happiness and proper role of the American Egghead who's getting paid now & has a nice job & fits in with the whole silly system." In direct contrast, Ginsberg and the Beats developed an aesthetic that renounced intellectual abstractions and poeticized individual lived experience—what Ginsberg described in 1948, in a letter to Trilling, as "the shadowy and heterogeneous experience of life through the conscious mind."

By the time the teenage Bob Dylan first encountered Beat writing a decade later, these literary skirmishes on Morningside Heights had turned into battles between archetypes that helped lead, in turn, to the culture wars of the 1960s and after. Beat and liberal intellectual became locked in an antagonism that established each as the opposite of the other in their own minds. Dylan, in Dinkytown, had no trouble deciding which side he was on, and in Dinkytown, far from the political trench wars of Manhattan, there was an easy overlapping between Beat bohemianism and the scruffy authenticity of the folk clubs. But when he arrived in New York, his head full of Woody Guthrie, he would discover that although the two worlds intersected, Manhattan's cultural alignments were more convoluted.

In 1958, a resourceful entrepreneur, master carpenter, bohemian, and lover of poetry, John Mitchell, opened a coffee shop at 116 MacDougal Street, near Bleecker, in what was once a coal cellar and which more recently had sheltered a subterranean gay hangout, the MacDougal Street Bar. According to Al Aronowitz, Mitchell, a native of Brooklyn, had settled in Greenwich Village in the early 1950s, where he befriended and, for a time, roomed with the celebrated crumbling old Village bohemian *poète maudit* Maxwell Bodenheim, shortly before Bodenheim's shocking murder in 1954. Emerging as something of a neighborhood celebrity himself, Mitchell opened a Parisian-style coffeehouse, Le Figaro, on the corner of MacDougal and Bleecker, saw it become an instant hit with the locals as well as curious tourists, then sold it at a handsome profit.

Mitchell soon had his eye on the space at 116 MacDougal, which was dank and cramped but perfectly located for another coffee shop. Unable to raise the ceiling, he lowered the floor and opened for business, featuring sweet drinks and dessert items as well as coffee. (Having a boozeless menu reduced costs and avoided the hassles with the police and the Mob that went with securing a liquor license—and it catered well to those bohemians whose drug of choice was marijuana, not alcohol. In any case, drinking customers could sneak in bottles stuffed in brown paper bags, or repair to the Kettle of Fish.) Mitchell invited the growing legion of Village poets who broadly identified with the Beat movement to recite their material and entertain his customers, in exchange for the proceeds

Beat poets standing on MacDougal Street near the Gaslight Cafe, with the Kettle of Fish bar in the background. Left to right: Peter Orlovsky, Alan Ansen, Allen Ginsberg, unidentified man behind Orlovsky, 1959.

collected in a basket handed around the audience. He called his new coffee shop the Village Gaslight, and among the poets who would read there was Allen Ginsberg.

Ginsberg's breakthrough had come in San Francisco in October 1955, when a poetry reading in a converted old auto repair shop on Fillmore Street featured his first stunning recital of "Howl." The poem's publication, in *Howl and Other Poems,* by the local bookseller and poet Lawrence Ferlinghetti in 1956, followed by Ferlinghetti's failed prosecution on obscenity charges, brought Ginsberg wide public attention and acclaim. The Beats and their West Coast friends and kindred spirits—

who included the young poets Michael McClure, Gary Snyder, Philip Whalen, and Philip Lamantia, as well as the older, surrealist-influenced Kenneth Patchen—launched an enthusiasm for Beat and Beat-style poetry that sympathetic critics labeled the San Francisco Renaissance.

Ginsberg, who had spent 1957 in Morocco and, later, Paris, returned in June 1958 to the United States, where Manhattan would remain his main base of operations for most of the rest of his life. The New York Beat scene of bars and coffeehouses flourished in the 1950s along the main thoroughfares of Greenwich Village west of University Place. (Neighborhood rents climbed so high as a result that artists and poets, Ginsberg included, took up residence across town, east of Cooper Square.) A New York circle was closed, uptown, in February 1959, when Ginsberg returned to Columbia for a highly publicized public reading with Gregory Corso and Peter Orlovsky and recited "The Lion for Real," in honor, he said ironically, of Lionel Trilling.* "It's my old school I was kicked out of," Ginsberg wrote to Ferlinghetti a week later, "so I suppose I'm hung up on making it there and breaking its reactionary back."

All the while, a few blocks up MacDougal Street from where John Mitchell opened his Village Gaslight, the folksingers had been gathering in Washington Square. At some point either just before or just after the end of World War II, the story goes, a man named George Margolin began turning up on Sunday afternoons with his guitar in the square, to play union ballads and familiar folk songs (including "Old Paint," one of the songs Aaron Copland had borrowed). By the early 1950s, Sundays in Washington Square had become the focus for folk-music enthusiasts from around the city. Pete Seeger and his wife, Toshi, obtained the necessary police permit for playing music in public, and in time flocks of folk instrumentalists and singers of every variety crowded the dry fountain at the center of the square. Alongside Woody Guthrie's first great acolyte, Ramblin' Jack Elliott, there jostled the young Dave Van Ronk, and alongside him, the even younger Mary Travers, alongside whom were numerous others who, in the early 1960s, would lead the folk revival. Despite the blacklisting of Seeger and the Weavers, a New York folk scene had persisted with roots in the Popular Front cultural radicalism of the 1930s and 1940s—although it was also to prove more eclectic than its forerunner.

---

* Ginsberg and the others had hoped that Jack Kerouac would also read from his work, but Kerouac spent the evening in his refuge in Northport, Long Island, where he had bought a house with the proceeds from *On the Road* and lived with his mother, Gabrielle.

Ramblin' Jack Elliott playing in Washington Square Park, 1953.

The continuing presence of Earl Robinson, Alan Lomax, and Seeger, among others, guaranteed folk music's enduring connection to the 1940s Popular Front Communist worldview. (The Weavers proved resilient enough to enjoy a reunion concert at Carnegie Hall, under the professional hand of their former manager, Harold Leventhal, late in 1955.) A few key institutions—above all *Sing Out!* magazine, cofounded in 1950 and edited by the politically orthodox Irwin Silber—carried on the Popular Front outlook. And the New York folk-song scene would always have a strong leftist bent, which deepened when the southern civil-rights movement began making headway in the late 1950s. But at almost every level, a growing portion of the folk-song community had no strict or formal political connections and demanded none of its artists and performers.

Moe Asch, the founder of Folkways Records, was the son of the important Yiddish writer Sholem Asch and came to the United States when he was still a boy. A leftist radical who was involved with the People's Songs folk revivalists, Asch also kept his distance from Communist ideology—he once called himself a "goddamn anarchist"—and was happy to record strong music regardless of the performers' politics or the contents of the songs. (It was Asch who, in 1952, released the influential six-LP collection *Anthology of American Folk Music,* compiled by the eccentric filmmaker and occultist Harry Smith from previously recorded material.) Although best known for his folk recordings, Asch also worked closely with jazz musicians, including the pioneer of the stride-piano style James P. Johnson.

Then there was Israel "Izzy" Young. An aspiring bookseller and square-dance enthusiast from the Bronx, born in 1928, Young had developed a passion for folk music and had struck up friendships with some of the more talented and creative Washington Square regulars. (Among them were John Cohen and Tom Paley, who, with Pete Seeger's half brother, Mike, became the New Lost City Ramblers, and who recorded four albums of old-timey folk music, songs from the Great Depression, and children's songs by the end of the 1950s.) In time, Young decided to rent a storefront on MacDougal Street for selling folk-music records and books. (In order to cover the lease, he cashed in a thousand-dollar insurance policy.) He called the place the Folklore Center and opened for business in March 1957.

Fiercely independent in his leftish politics, Young prized music over ideology. His store—located a few doors down from the cellar where John

Izzy Young and Albert Grossman at the Folklore Center, circa 1964.

Mitchell would soon be showcasing the Beat poets—became a clearing-house for musicians, record company men, scholars, and enthusiasts. Young was also something of a concert promoter. One of the founders of the Friends of Old Time Music, he helped arrange, in 1959, a regular concert series at Gerde's bar on Fourth Street west of Broadway, which he called "The Fifth Peg at Gerde's." The bar's owner, Mike Porco, undertook the venture as a lark, but when the music began attracting steady crowds, Young got squeezed out of the operation. Gerde's Folk City was born.

Soon after, John Mitchell, having also noticed the trend, switched from using folksingers for turning the house between recitations by Beat poets to hiring folksingers regularly. By the time Bob Dylan arrived in January 1961, the Gaslight was the premier showcase for folksingers on MacDougal Street, and Dylan considered himself fortunate to break into the Gaslight lineup. In April, he secured his first important extended New York engagement, as an opening act for the blues great John Lee Hooker, at Gerde's. But it was still a long way from the Village clubs to musical stardom. A little more than six months after Dylan premiered at Gerde's, Young would lose money when he sponsored Dylan's first theatrical concert, at Carnegie Chapter Hall, and only fifty-three ticket buyers showed up. Dylan's big break only came months later, in September, when the *New York Times*

Bob Dylan performing at Gerde's Folk City in New York, September 26, 1961. Based on this performance, Robert Shelton wrote the *New York Times* review that first gave Dylan wide exposure.

critic Robert Shelton reviewed a show at Gerde's, dealt quickly with the headline act, the Greenbriar Boys, and devoted his own headline and the bulk of his story to celebrating Dylan as the prodigious new talent on the folk scene. After playing backup harmonica on a recording session for the folksinger Carolyn Hester the day after Shelton's article appeared, Dylan signed a five-year recording contract with Columbia Records, where the legendary John Hammond, who had worked with Benny Goodman, Billie Holiday, and Big Joe Turner, would be his producer.

Relations between the folkies and the Beats in New York were not necessarily close or even harmonious. The Beats' preferred music was, and always had been, jazz, from bebop to the free jazz experiments being undertaken by Ornette Coleman and others at the Five Spot on Cooper Square. On the West Coast, Kenneth Patchen had pioneered in reading what he called his "picture poems" to the accompaniment of the Charles Mingus combo. Kerouac appeared with a jazz group at the Village Vanguard on Seventh Avenue in 1958 and recorded readings of his prose and poetry with the saxophonists Al Cohn and Zoot Sims; he also collaborated with David Amram on the jazzy soundtrack, part spoken, part musical, for Robert Frank's Beat movie *Pull My Daisy.* The folksingers shared the Beats' disdain for consumerist materialism and conventional 1950s dress and mores, as symbolized by clean-cut, collegiate folk groups like the Kingston Trio, who had built on the earlier success of the Weavers. But the Beats had their own hip style that clashed with what the Afrosurrealist Beat Ted Joans (who for a time had shared a cold-water West Village flat with Charlie Parker) called, in 1959, the "silly milly" folksingers, "the squarest of squares," with "their boney banjo-shaped asses."

Still, as Moe Asch's recordings showed, the Beat jazz scene and the folk revival sometimes overlapped. Folkies and Beats could not help interacting as poetry cafés and music clubs proliferated cheek by jowl on and around MacDougal Street—the Café Bizarre (located in what had been Aaron Burr's livery stable), the Commons (which would later become the Fat Black Pussycat), the Bitter End, and many others. Dylan writes in his memoirs of seeing Thelonious Monk in one club, off-hours, sitting alone at the piano, and when Dylan informed him he was playing folk music up the street, Monk replied, "We all play folk music." Among the jazz musicians who played at the Fat Black Pussycat were the pianist Sonny Clark and the tenor saxophonist Lin Halliday.

The folkies were hardly uninterested in the jazz they heard all around them, on records as well as in the clubs. Van Ronk started in New York as a self-described "jazz snob," more interested in the jazz pioneers of the 1920s still to be found in the Village than in the earnest folk types. Dylan reports in *Chronicles* of listening at friends' houses to all sorts of jazz and bebop records, by artists ranging from Benny Goodman and Dizzy Gillespie to Gil Evans, who, he notes, recorded a version of Leadbelly's song "Ella Speed." ("I tried to discern melodies and structures," he recalls. "There were a lot of similarities between some kinds of jazz and folk music.") And at least some of the Beats listened to black rhythm and blues as well as jazz, just as the younger folkies like Dylan did. (Allen Ginsberg began his great poem about his mother, "Kaddish," describing a midwinter Manhattan scene in 1959, in which, after a sleepless night, he reads the Kaddish aloud "listening to Ray Charles blues shout blind on the phonograph.") All were influenced, in their sense of stagecraft and spontaneity, by the burgeoning Village Off-Broadway and experimental theater, ranging from Julian Beck and Judith Malina's Living Theatre and the avant-garde productions at the venerable Cherry Lane Theatre on tiny Commerce Street, to the first of the impromptu "happenings" in private apartments and lofts.

By 1961, the Beats and folkies also shared MacDougal and Bleecker streets with herds of tourists who would come to town to see the weirdos perform and get a whiff of bohemian danger. As recorded by the *Village Voice* photographer Fred McDarrah in his collection of pictures and articles *Kerouac and Friends,* a more serious Beat scene persisted, in readings at the Living Theatre, in nighttime conviviality at the Jazz Club, the Cedar Street Tavern, and Riker's Diner, and in book signings and parties at the 8th Street Bookshop, co-owned by my father and uncle, Eli and Ted Wilentz. But the Beats did not entirely disappear from MacDougal, even as the tourist trade burgeoned. (At the Folklore Center, Israel Young, an utterly indifferent businessman, would bolt the door when MacDougal got too crowded, to permit the folksingers to chat and to perform their songs for each other in peace.) Some of the poets turned into showmen, giving the customers all of the espresso and all the black-bereted soulful and titillating verse they could want. Some of the MacDougal and Bleecker cafés turned into vaudeville-like tourist traps, where cracked raconteurs and musical jabberwocks would appear on a rapidly changing bill with genuinely talented performers.

It was in one of those hole-in-the-wall MacDougal Street cabarets, the Café Wha?, that Bob Dylan performed on the same day he hit New York City in January 1961. The writings of Jack Kerouac and Allen Ginsberg were already in his brain, though his search for Woody Guthrie was fore-

The 8th Street Bookshop, New York, circa 1963.

most on his mind. And, although it might have seemed different in some of the other clubs, there were signs that, just as the folksingers were getting popular, the Beat phenomenon was running out of steam.

On January 26, 1961—the same day, just after Dylan's arrival in Manhattan, that Aaron Copland was narrating *The Second Hurricane* in midtown—a group of writers gathered at the apartment of the Belgian theater director Robert Cordier, on Christopher Street, to discuss (and, for some, to celebrate) the death of the Beat generation. Cordier's friend James Baldwin—who especially disliked Kerouac's work, considering it patronizing and ignorant in its projections about American blacks—was there. So were Norman Mailer, Susan Sontag, William Styron, and the Beats Ted Joans, Tuli Kupferberg (later of the rock band the Fugs), and the *Village Voice* journalist Seymour Krim. A few of the non-Beats, particularly Mailer, found the Beats very interesting. But most of the writers had gathered to bury what was left of a movement that they believed had been thoroughly co-opted by the commercial mainstream. What had begun as an iconoclastic literary style (whether one approved of it or not) had become, the detractors said, just another fad, a subject fit for television comedies. (*The*

Many Loves of Dobie Gillis, a popular TV sitcom that featured a comedic "beatnik" character, Maynard G. Krebs, had debuted in September 1959.)

The major Beat writers, meanwhile, were going their own ways. Two months after the meeting at Cordier's, Ginsberg and Peter Orlovsky set sail for Paris, in part to locate William Burroughs and in part to escape the malign publicity directed at them and their friends from critics high and low. Over the next two years, Ginsberg and Orlovsky would circumnavigate the globe, visiting Tangier (where they would finally find Burroughs), Greece, Israel, and East Africa, before reaching India, where they spent fifteen months in holy seeking before they ended their travels in Japan and headed home. The somewhat younger poet Gregory Corso, who had joined the Beats' inner circle in 1950 and whose City Lights volume of poems *Gasoline,* published in 1958, had greatly impressed Dylan in Minneapolis, had been sidelined by an addiction to heroin and alcohol. With Kerouac devoting most of his time during these years to drinking, writing, and living with his mother in Northport, Long Island, and Orlando, Florida, the Beat generation would never be the same.

Bob Dylan, who has said he "got in at the tail end," had read the Beats in Minneapolis, but apart from preparing him for the open road that he found in Woody Guthrie's *Bound for Glory,* the literary effects on his early lyrics are difficult to discern. The Beats' performance style was something else again, or so Dylan has recalled. "There used to be a folk music scene and jazz clubs just about every place," he remembered a quarter century later. "The two scenes were very much connected, where the poets would read to a small combo, so I was close up to that for a while. My songs were influenced not so much by poetry on the page but by poetry being recited by the poets who recited poems with jazz bands." The poetry on the page that mattered, he has said, were "the French guys, Rimbaud and François Villon," to whom he turned after reading Ginsberg and the others.

As the Beat presence in the Village faded, MacDougal Street became, more than ever, a showcase for the folk revival. Not that Dylan forgot the Beats, or failed to connect with the Beat writers and artists who remained in town. He still adored Allen Ginsberg's work and had a special kinship with the oft-incarcerated jazz poet Ray Bremser (whose "jail songs" he cited, along with Ginsberg's love poems, in the last of the "11 Outlined Epitaphs," free verse he substituted for liner notes on his third album). What he later called the "street ideologies" of Ginsberg, Kerouac, Corso, and the others still signaled to him the possibility of a new form of human existence. At some point in 1963, he met Lawrence Ferlinghetti, and the two discussed possibly publishing a book of Dylan's writing, alongside Ginsberg's and Corso's volumes, in the City Lights Pocket Poets Series. Still, Dylan's literary breakthroughs, taking him outside the idiom of traditional Anglo-American balladry, would come from other sources and experiences, not least from hearing Micki Grant sing Marc Blitzstein's translation of "Pirate Jenny." The Beat influence would rekindle only after Dylan had established himself as a rising star—the greatest young folk songwriter in the Village and, for that matter, in the country—when he met up with Allen Ginsberg.

In December 1963, Ginsberg and Orlovsky, having at last returned to New York from their travels, took up temporary residence in Ted Wilentz's family apartment above the 8th Street Bookshop, while they looked for an apartment of their own. It was, coincidentally, a moment of national trauma. The inauguration of President John F. Kennedy (less than a week before Dylan's arrival in New York and the writers' gathering in the Village to bury the Beat generation) had elevated new hopes for a great cultural as well as political change. It seemed as if the nation had suddenly decided, as Norman Mailer put it, "to enlist the romantic dream of itself" and to "vote for the image in the mirror of its unconscious." But now Ginsberg and Orlovsky came back to the Village less than a month after President Kennedy's assassination.

Although he would later deny it, Kennedy's murder hit Dylan as hard as it did everyone else, and maybe more than most. Three weeks later, receiving an award from the established left-wing Emergency Civil Liberties Committee, Dylan expressed his deep discomfort with the well-dressed, older audience—well-intentioned people, he perceived, who were on the sidelines and who wanted to change the world but at a safe distance. He identified more, he said, with James Forman and the young activists of the Student Nonviolent Coordinating Committee, who were putting their bodies as well as their goodwill on the line in the southern freedom struggle. Anyway, he declared, switching course, he did not see things in terms of black and white, left and right anymore—"there's only up and down," he said. Then he shocked everybody by confessing that, speaking as a young man, he could imagine seeing something of himself in the president's young assassin. Gasps, then boos and hisses followed, and Dylan stepped down. Unable to articulate his feelings any better than that—some reports say he had drunk a good deal of wine to fortify himself before the speech—Dylan seemed to be at loose ends.

While Dylan brooded and stumbled, Ginsberg and Orlovsky tried to pay Kerouac a visit in Northport—but Kerouac's formidable French-Canadian mother, Gabrielle, who despised Kerouac's Beat friends for what she thought they had done to her Ti Jean, turned them away. A transfiguration of the Beat generation would, though, commence at month's end, without Kerouac. Al Aronowitz, who had written extensively about the Beats for the *New York Post,* was now writing about Dylan—more or less, he admitted, in order to become part of his inner circle. Aronowitz got word of a welcome-home party for Ginsberg and Orlovsky, to be held at Ted Wilentz's Eighth Street apartment on Boxing Day, the day after Christmas, when the bookshop's distracting holiday season was done. Aronowitz thought it would be interesting to bring Dylan along to meet the author of "Howl." (As it happened, Dylan preferred "Kaddish," which Ferlinghetti had published as part of his Pocket Poets Series soon after Ginsberg and Orlovsky had left for Paris, in 1961.)

Weeks earlier, at a party in Bolinas, California, Ginsberg, on his way back to New York from India, had heard Dylan on *The Freewheelin' Bob*

Unidentified reporter, Allen Ginsberg, Al Aronowitz, and Bob Dylan backstage at McCarter Theater, Princeton, New Jersey, September 1964, about nine months after Aronowitz introduced Dylan and Ginsberg to each other.

Dylan singing "A Hard Rain's A-Gonna Fall"—and, he later said, wept with illuminated joy at what he sensed was a passing of the bohemian tradition to a younger generation. At Wilentz's apartment, Ginsberg and Dylan discussed poetry, and, according to Aronowitz, Ginsberg came on sexually to Dylan. ("Allen was really a flaming queer," Aronowitz later said.) Dylan, unfazed, invited Ginsberg to join him on a flight to Chicago, where he was scheduled to play at the august Orchestra Hall the following night. Ginsberg declined, worrying, he recalled, that "I might become his slave or something, his mascot."

Dylan had already been experimenting with writing free verse, without intending that it would serve him as lyrics. Not long before he met Ginsberg, he poured out a poem about the day of Kennedy's murder, which concluded:

> the colors of friday were dull
> as cathedral bells were gently burnin
> strikin for the gentle
> strikin for the kind
> strikin for the crippled ones
> an strikin for the blind.

Pulled together, the lines would form part of what Dylan called the "chain of flashing images" that soon went into "Chimes of Freedom"—marking both Dylan's reconnection to Beat aesthetics and the transformation of those aesthetics into song. And in 1964 and 1965, Ginsberg and Dylan influenced each other as both of them recast their public images and their art.

D. A. Pennebaker's cinema verité film about Dylan's concert tour of England in 1965, *Dont Look Back*, includes several scenes of Dylan and his entourage in his suite at London's Savoy Hotel. In one of them, Dylan squats on the floor amid a gaggle of English folkies and hangers-on, and slurring his words, he converses with Ramblin' Jack Elliott's old recording mate Derroll Adams, who had relocated to England and who suggests that they get together "and I'll turn you on to some things."

"Okay. Are there any poets like Allen Ginsberg around, man?" Dylan asks.

"No, no, nothing like that," Adams replies. He pauses for a split second. "Dominic Behan."

"Hey, yeah, yeah, you know, you know," Dylan says, then the name sinks in and he sounds repulsed. "No, I don't wanna hear nobody like Dominic Behan, man."

Dylan mutters the name again, contemptuously, "Dominic *Be*-un." A sodden English voice, off camera, spits out: "Dominic Behan is a friend of mine . . ."

"Hey, that's fine, man," Dylan says, evenly enough, "I just don't wanta hear anybody like that though."

It's no wonder that Dylan was annoyed. A couple of years earlier, he had lifted the melody of Behan's song "The Patriot Game" for his own "With God on Our Side," and the word was going around that Dylan had plagiarized him—even though Behan himself had based his song on a traditional Irish tune, "The Merry Month of May." But Behan, the brother of the playwright and novelist Brendan Behan, was also part of the Irish working-class equivalent of the folk revival in the United States. Dylan, having gone as far as he was going to go with the folkies, had been turning elsewhere, to his own variations on rock and roll (as the musical world would soon discover) and to American bop prosody as it was sliding into late-1960s hippie ecstasy. (Later in the scene, he would badly outmatch the latest British folk sensation, Donovan, laying down "It's All Over Now, Baby Blue" as a kind of response to Donovan's impromptu performance of his ditty "To Sing for You.") Intensely restless in the spring of 1965—still performing his old material, solo, on acoustic guitar and rack harmonica, but with his mind roaming—Dylan was on the cusp of something new, and he wanted to hear Ginsberg's poesy.

As it happened, unknown to Dylan (and as *Dont Look Back* does not reveal), Allen Ginsberg had just flown to London from Prague, suddenly ejected by Czech authorities as a corrupter of youth—he was now a year shy of forty—a week after a massing of a hundred thousand students, with rock bands blaring, had proclaimed him the King of May, as part of the revival of an annual festival that the Communists had suppressed for twenty years.

In the movie's next scene (shot, according to the transcript of the film, the following day), all is calm in the hotel room—and there, out of the blue, though only fleetingly on camera, is Ginsberg, seated and chatting softly with Dylan. The sequence is utterly fortuitous, spooky in its timing given what has just happened on-screen: Dylan asked for Ginsberg, and all of a sudden there he was, seemingly conjured up out of the vapors but in fact thanks to the apoplectic commissars of Prague. (Pennebaker confirms that nobody had any idea that Ginsberg was coming the night that Dylan brought up his name with Derroll Adams.) An important moment in Beat lore merged with an iconic moment in Dylan's career—although explaining all of that in the film would have taken the focus off Dylan and, in any case, would have taken too long. Instead, the camera records the hip-

Allen Ginsberg as the King of May (*Kral Majales*) in Prague, May 1, 1965.

pest of 1960s friendships—and makes possible a clever piece of image making, joining the singer as poet in the same documentary frame with the poet as cultural hero.

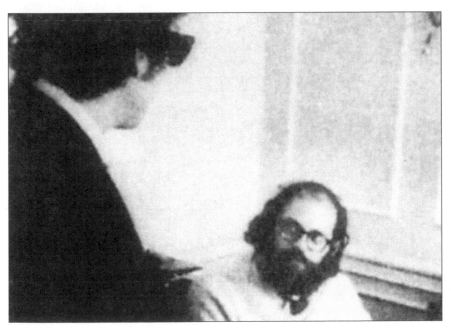

Bob Dylan and Allen Ginsberg at the Savoy Hotel in London, May 8, 1965. A still from D. A. Pennebaker's film *Dont Look Back,* 1967.

Over the two years since Dylan and Ginsberg had met, their connection had become a public fact as well as an artistic and personal alliance. It started off quietly enough. During part of the summer of 1964, Dylan stayed at the country retreat of his manager, Albert Grossman, on Striebel Road in Bearsville, New York, just west of Woodstock. Ginsberg, breaking away from various engagements in New York (including a cam-

Bob Dylan at Albert Grossman's house in Bearsville, New York, August 27, 1964. The next day, Dylan would meet the Beatles for the first time at the Delmonico Hotel in New York City.

paign to legalize marijuana), spent some time with Orlovsky at Grossman's, where Dylan taught him how to play a harmonium that Orlovsky had lugged back from India. In September, Ginsberg, Orlovsky, and one of Ginsberg's rare girlfriends, the young filmmaker Barbara Rubin, were part of Dylan's entourage at a concert in Princeton, New Jersey.

The following February, Dylan appeared on Les Crane's nationally broadcast, late-night TV talk show, dressed not in his customary suede and denim but in a modish suit and performing with an accompanist, Bruce Langhorne, who played an acoustic guitar with an electronic pickup. Between songs, Dylan bantered with Crane about a collaboration he had undertaken with Ginsberg—"sort of a horror cowboy movie," Dylan deadpanned, that Ginsberg was writing and he was rewriting, and

Allen Ginsberg, Peter Orlovsky, Barbara Rubin, Bob Dylan, and Daniel Kramer backstage at McCarter Theater in Princeton, New Jersey, September 1964.

that would take place on the New York State Thruway. "Yeah?" asked Crane, who seemed to get the put-on but was willing to play it straight. "Are you gonna star in it?"

Dylan: Yeah, yeah, I'm a hero.
Crane: You're the hero? You play the horrible cowboy?
Dylan: I play my mother (audience laughter).
Crane: You play your mother? In the movie?
Dylan: In the movie. You gotta see the movie (audience laughter).

Three months later, Ginsberg appeared in the movie that Pennebaker was making about Dylan. By then, Columbia had released *Bringing It All Back Home,* its back cover illustrated with photographs taken by Daniel Kramer in Princeton, including one of Ginsberg wearing Dylan's trademark top hat and another of Rubin massaging a weary Dylan's scalp. To top it off, and seal the symbolism, a small photo showed Dylan smiling impishly, wearing the same top hat Ginsberg was wearing in the first picture. The two shared an odd 1960s bohemian crown, with intimations of Lewis Carroll's Mad Hatter in *Alice's Adventures in Wonderland.* And just in case the message wasn't clear enough, Dylan wrote in the album's liner notes:

*i have
given up at making any attempt at perfection
the fact that the white house is filled with
leaders that've never been t' the apollo
theater amazes me. why allen ginsberg was
not chosen t' read poetry at the inauguration
boggles my mind / if someone thinks norman
mailer is more important than hank williams
that's fine.*

In early December, in San Francisco, Dylan stopped by Lawrence Fer-linghetti's bookstore, City Lights, where Ferlinghetti was staging what came to be called the Last Gathering of Beat poets and artists (five years after the "funeral" at Robert Cordier's apartment). A dozen or so Beat writers turned up, including Ginsberg, Orlovsky, and Michael McClure. Dylan, who had by now released "Subterranean Homesick Blues" and "Like a Rolling Stone," and was touring with his backup musicians, would play that evening at the Masonic Auditorium, having performed the previous two nights at the Berkeley Community Theater. He had had fun the day before at a press conference where Ginsberg asked a hipster question: "Do you think there will ever be a time when you'll be hung as a thief?" (Dylan, taken aback momentarily, smiled and replied, "You weren't supposed to say that.") Now he would mingle with Ginsberg and Ginsberg's friends at one of the Beat scene's literary headquarters, accom-panied by his band's lead guitarist, Robbie Robertson. The two musicians headed straight for the store's basement in order to avoid the crush of fans and not to intrude on what Dylan thought ought to be entirely the Beats' occasion. When the hubbub subsided, Dylan posed for some pictures in the alley that adjoined the store, alongside McClure, Ginsberg, Ferlin-ghetti, Robertson, and Orlovsky's brother, Julius.

Dylan had thought that some photographs of him with the poets might look good on the cover of the album he had just begun recording, which would become *Blonde on Blonde.* Even though the pictures, some of them made by the young photographer Larry Keenan, did not appear on the album, they would be widely reproduced in books as well as future Dylan record releases, affirming Dylan's place among the poets and theirs with him.

The Beats' gathering over, and the concert done, Dylan headed south with Ginsberg, Orlovsky, and McClure, riding in Ginsberg's Volkswagen

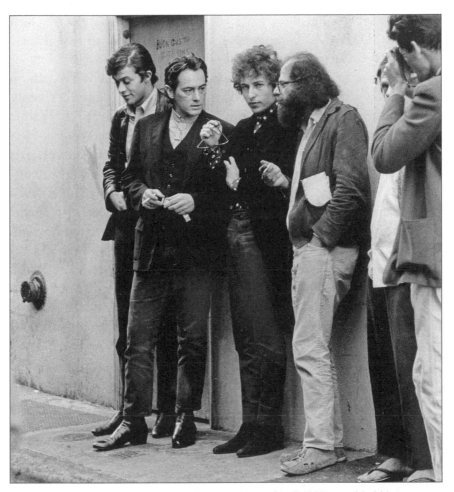

Outside City Lights Books in San Francisco, December 5, 1965, stand Robbie Robertson, Michael McClure, Bob Dylan, Allen Ginsberg, Julius Orlovsky (partially hidden), and unidentified photographer.

van (bought with the proceeds from a Guggenheim Fellowship) to San Jose, to meet up with the band for another concert before finishing off the tour with concerts in Pasadena and Santa Monica. Dylan had given Ginsberg a gift of six hundred dollars, enough to purchase a state-of-the-art, portable Uher tape recorder. (Ginsberg, in gratitude, taped one of Dylan's concerts in Berkeley, as well as approving members of the audience, to show Dylan that the hostility his new electric music had received from reviewers was undeserved. Rebutting charges that Dylan had sold out his fans, Ginsberg later remarked: "Dylan has sold out to God. That is to say, his command was to spread his beauty as widely as possible. It was an artistic challenge to see if great art can be done on a jukebox.") Dylan also presented McClure with an Autoharp, on which the poet would soon be composing in what was, for him, an entirely new kind of sung verse.

Then Dylan flew back to New York to resume work on his new album and prepare for a grueling tour of the continental United States, Hawaii, Australia, Europe, and Britain, which would culminate in his historic concerts at the Free Trade Hall in Manchester and at the Royal Albert Hall in London. Ginsberg, after a brief trip to Big Sur, returned to Los Angeles (where he met the Byrds and the record producer Phil Spector), then took off in the van headed east. Orlovsky drove; Ginsberg dictated poetry into the Uher recorder, which he had called, musician-style, his "new ax for composition." As the Volkswagen gyrated between Lincoln, Nebraska, and Wichita, Kansas, Ginsberg compressed radio announcements, highway advertising signs, pop lyrics of the Beatles, the Kinks, and Dylan, always Dylan, and the bleak farming landscape into verse, and composed, as taped spoken stanzas, the lengthy "Wichita Vortex Sutra"— one of his greatest poems and, along with Norman Mailer's *Armies of the Night,* the most powerful literary response to America's mounting military intrusion in Vietnam.

Dylan and Ginsberg's friendship was close and respectful but also complicated, as the New York poet Anne Waldman has explained. Fifteen years Dylan's senior, Ginsberg was hardly old enough to be a father figure, but Dylan sometimes cast him that way, as the patriarch of the entire hip cultural family. (In the film he made from the Rolling Thunder Revue in 1975, Dylan actually had Ginsberg play a role named Father.) Yet Dylan garnered by far a larger audience with his music than Ginsberg did with his poems, and Ginsberg became such a devotee of Dylan's that, during the Rolling Thunder tour, Waldman recalls, members of the troupe "joked that Ginsberg was Dylan's most dedicated groupie." Ginsberg's homosexuality and obvious desire for Dylan added an additional layer of tension and even curiosity. Certainly, by the 1970s, Dylan had eclipsed Ginsberg as a cultural, and countercultural, star; at times, especially during the Rolling Thunder Revue, Ginsberg seemed practically to be nipping at Dylan's heels, wanting but never quite reaching the aura of rock-and-roll adulation and glory. At these moments, Dylan, and not Ginsberg, seemed to be the more powerful man in the friendship, the older brother if not the father. On Dylan's part, Waldman writes, there was "a bit of taunt and tease in the relationship whose intimacy I notice[d] Ginsberg deeply enjoy[ed]." And, one might add, there was a bit of pathos on Ginsberg's part.

Still, in their odd tandem, Dylan and Ginsberg helped each other complete transitions into new phases of their careers after 1963. Part of the transitions had to do with image. Masters of self-protection and media presentation, Dylan and Ginsberg entered into, if only tacitly, a mutual-reinforcement pact. By the time they met, Dylan was already on the move artistically, yet that move had its risks. Trading in the soulful, Steinbeckian leftishness depicted in his portrait by Barry Feinstein on the cover of *The Times They Are A-Changin'* was bound to confuse and even offend a portion of Dylan's young pro-civil-rights, ban-the-bomb folkie base, as well as the folk-revival old leftists. The falloff became obvious when Dylan's second album of 1964, *Another Side of Bob Dylan*—which included the completed "Chimes of Freedom"—did not crack the Top 40 on the sales charts. (By contrast, *The Times They Are A-Changin'* had broken in at number twenty on the charts.)

Having Ginsberg as his visible ally helped Dylan negotiate the shift, as well as his return to rock and roll on the three albums that followed *Another Side* in 1965 and 1966. To be sure, Ginsberg and the Beats, with their mysticism, sexual frankness, and individualism, were politically unreliable as far as the Popular Front veterans were concerned. And some of the Beats (though not Ginsberg) shared a resentful view that the folk musicians, Dylan included, had shoved them aside at the very beginning of the 1960s.* But Ginsberg was enough of a leftist to satisfy the younger folkies. (Joan Baez—Dylan's lover through part of this period, and disconcerted at Dylan's growing detachment from politics—asked Ginsberg and McClure late in 1965 to act as Dylan's conscience.) As a cultural revolutionary, antibourgeois seer, and antagonist of the academy,

---

* Ginsberg did, though, always insist on the close links between Dylan and what he called an older generation of "bohemian or Beat illumination." Waldman writes: "In many of my own conversations with Ginsberg he forged, even *pressed* (being the legend builder he was) the ongoing link of Dylan to the Beats. As he was dying, he regretted there was no opportunity to do an 'Unplugged Ginsberg' session with Dylan, as he had hoped." (In fact, MTV had actually planned an "Unplugged Ginsberg" program.) In one sense, Ginsberg was anointing Dylan; in another, he was making sure nobody forgot how Dylan was really an extension of himself, Kerouac, and the other Beats. Once a salesman, always a salesman.

Ginsberg commanded respect on the left. Above all, Ginsberg stood for literary seriousness, on a level far above what even the most talented folkie lyricist, let alone rock and roller, could hope to attain.

Dylan, meanwhile, helped Ginsberg make his transition from Beat generation prophet to a kind of older avatar of the late-1960s counterculture—for the poet, a new kind of fame. If Dylan did not open the doors to the widest pop markets, he beckoned to audiences that no poet of the traditional sort could hope to reach—baby boomers, fully twenty years younger than the Beats, who listened to Top 40 radio and crammed into places like Orchestra Hall in Chicago and Carnegie Hall in New York to hear their hero Dylan perform. Apart from Andy Warhol, no artist on the New York scene in 1964 and 1965 was as shrewd a molder of his pop public image as Dylan—and for Ginsberg, himself a great self-publicist and promoter of his poet friends, the association with Dylan was one of the catalysts that transformed him into a celebrity emblem, young America's wild-haired poet.

None of this means that the connection between the two men was merely or even mainly about cultural marketing. Ginsberg wrote only a few brief verses in 1964 (complaining, in one of them, about the distracting telephone, "ringing at dawn ringing all afternoon ringing up midnight," and callers hoping to cash in on his celebrity), but in his poem of Prague in 1965, "Kral Majales," written during the unexpected flight to London where he immediately linked up with Dylan, he sprang to life as one of the Just Men who denounced lying Communists and lying capitalists, and who was chosen King of May "which is the power of sexual youth." Later, Ginsberg talked seriously with Dylan about future joint projects, possibly including a record album of Ginsberg's mantras.

In one of the culminations of "Wichita Vortex Sutra," Ginsberg, having already declared the Vietnam War over but still hearing the blab of the airwaves about death tolls and new military operations, wrote of how, at last, the radio bade new promise:

> *Angelic Dylan singing across the nation*
> *   "When all your children start to resent you*
> *   Won't you come see me Queen Jane?"*
> *His youthful voice making glad*
> *   the brown endless meadows*
> *His tenderness penetrating aether,*
> * soft prayer on the airwaves.*

Typescript of an early draft of Allen Ginsberg's "Wichita Vortex Sutra," 1966.

Five years later, Ginsberg would finally record with Dylan, performing mantras, William Blake songs that he had put to music, and at least one song that Dylan and Ginsberg wrote together. Ginsberg would, for the rest of his life, see Dylan's work (and not the Beat generation jazz experiments he linked to Patchen and Kenneth Rexroth) as aligned with his own practice of vocalizing poetry, in a vernacular, idiomatic, self-expressive form.

Dylan, for his part, was determined to make his own artistic break from the topical, folkie Left when he recorded *Another Side* in a single afternoon and evening on June 9, 1964, telling the journalist Nat

Hentoff, "There aren't any finger pointing songs in here . . . From now on, I want to write from inside me . . . for it to come out the way I walk or talk." Combined with a renewed attachment to Rimbaud, which he had affirmed to his friends months earlier, Dylan's dedication to writing from within—to capturing what Ginsberg had called, nearly twenty years earlier, "the shadowy and heterogeneous experience of life through the conscious mind"—placed him within the orbit of the Beats' spontaneous bop prosody even before he returned to playing with a band on electric guitar.

Dylan's transition, although rapid, was not flawless. *Another Side*— written amid a coast-to-coast concert tour, riding with friends and exploring the country in a station wagon; followed by his final breakup with Suze Rotolo; followed then by his first concert tour of Britain and a trip through Europe that ended in a village outside Athens—contains the occasional poetic clinker. (From "Ballad in Plain D": "With unseen consciousness, I possessed in my grip / A magnificent mantelpiece, though its heart being chipped.") The album is not uniformly successful in its experiments with what Ginsberg described as "join[ing] images as they are joined in the mind"—efforts influenced by sources as diverse as Japanese haiku and what T. S. Eliot called the "telescoping of images." "Howl" had evoked "horrors of Third Avenue iron dreams"* and "the crack of doom on the hydrogen jukebox"; Dylan's "My Back Pages"—a strong, expressionist song about looking back and moving on—offers apprentice images of "corpse evangelists" and "confusion boats."

Still, *Another Side* was, by any measure, an artistic breakthrough. Typing and scribbling on notepad paper from London's Mayfair hotel, Dylan composed lyrics in bursts of wordplay, including little narratives and collage-like experiments. Writing on the other side of what would eventually become the lyrics for "To Ramona," he tried out little riffs, some of which would turn up in "I Shall Be Free No. 10," and some of which would be discarded. (The latter included a pair of couplets set off in alternating lines, one on the left about getting his monkey to do the dog atop a lumberjack log, the other on the right, about joining Ingmar Bergman in singing "Blowing in the Wind," written out as if each couplet was coming in from a different side of a set of earphones.) In their

---

* The reference here was to the Third Avenue Elevated Railway, a part of Manhattan's subway system, which was demolished in May 1955.

finished form, the album's simpler songs of love and anti-love—sung to the cracked-lipped Ramona, to the gypsy fortune-teller of Spanish Harlem, and about the unnamed watery-mouthed lover who turns him into a one-night stand—show an inventiveness in language, narration, and characters far more sophisticated than anything on *Freewheelin'*. Whatever its slips, "My Back Pages" contains interesting turns about "half-wracked prejudice" and ideas as maps, along with its unforgettable chorus about being younger than before.

Above all, there is "Chimes of Freedom"—an expansion of the free verse lines that Dylan had written about the day President Kennedy died, but reworked into a pealing of thunder and lightning for all the world's confused and abused, one dazzling image following another: "majestic bells of bolts" supplanting clinging church bells in "the wild cathedral evening," flashing, tolling, striking, tolling, as "the sky cracked its poems in naked wonder." Making music out of nature's sights and sounds had attracted Dylan before, in his mystical song "Lay Down Your Weary Tune" (just as Jack Kerouac tried to render the ocean's roar as poetry in his book *Big Sur*, published in 1962). But in "Chimes of Freedom," strong metaphors replace similes; sight and sound uncannily merge in the flashing chimes; and a simple story of a couple crouching in a doorway turns into a hail-ripped carillon—and a song of tender empathy as well, far outside the old politics of left and right, black and white.

A year later, Dylan divulged his indebtedness to the Beats. In March 1965, the same month that Columbia Records released *Bringing It All Back Home*, with its encomiums to Ginsberg, Kerouac published *Desolation Angels*, his last great novel of his experiences inside the Beat generation circle. Part of the Duluoz cycle, the book covered events and developments in 1956 and 1957: Ginsberg's unveiling of "Howl," the San Francisco Renaissance, Kerouac's growing disillusionment with his Beat friends, his bringing his mother out to California from Lowell and then his plunge into the weirdness and mystery of impoverished Mexico, only to have his Beat friends, the Desolation Angels, catch up with him. In early August, Dylan recorded "Desolation Row" for his sixth album, *Highway 61 Revisited*, and the correspondences with Kerouac, beginning with the title, were too exact to be coincidental.

Various readers have plucked out lines in the novel—Kerouac's descriptions of the poet David D'Angeli (Philip Lamantia) as "the perfect image of a priest" or of all the authorities who condemn hot-blooded embracers of life as sinners, when, in fact, "they sin by lifelessness!"—that turn up verbatim or nearly so in Dylan's song.* The ambience of "Desolation Row" is reminiscent of Kerouac's Mexico, a mixture of cheap food and fun (and ladies for hire) but with "a certain drear, even sad darkness." After the recording of the song was done, Dylan suddenly decided to add a swirling, Tex-Mex acoustic guitar run, played by the visiting Nashville sideman Charlie McCoy, which dominates the track's sound. Later, asked at a press conference to name Desolation Row's location, Dylan replied, "Oh, that's someplace in Mexico." Decades after that, when he returned to play the Newport Folk Festival in 2002, Dylan and his band performed "Desolation Row" in the style of a Mexican border song.

"Desolation Row" presents a kind of carnival (the critic Christopher Ricks calls it a "masque") of fragments, shards of a civilization that has gone to pieces, in a modernist tradition that runs from Eliot's *Waste Land* to Ginsberg's "Howl." Curious listeners have had a field day claiming particular references in every line, beginning with the very first, "They're selling postcards of the hanging." Clearly, some would have it, this alludes to the Hanged Man tarot card that turns up in the opening section of *The Waste Land;* not at all, others retort, it's about a notorious lynching that occurred in Dylan's birthplace, Duluth, in 1920, when his father was just a boy, and when, indeed, postcards of the two hanged blacks were made and sold as souvenirs. Who knows? With its repeated images of drowning and the sea—in references to the *Titanic,* Shakespeare's Ophelia, Nero's Neptune, Noah's ark and the great rainbow—the song almost certainly echoes *The Waste Land*'s repeated invocations of death by water. But no matter. Here on "Desolation Row" (conceivably a Beat-influenced updating of Steinbeck's *Cannery Row*) it is enough to see the characters from the Bible, Shakespeare, folktales, the circus, and Victor Hugo, most of them doomed, as well as Albert Einstein disguised as a noble outlaw, sniffing drainpipes and reciting the alphabet—strange sights and sounds,

---

* Readers have also noted that *Desolation Angels* speaks of "Housing Project hill," a line that turns up in another song on *Highway 61 Revisited,* "Just Like Tom Thumb's Blues," which begins with an evocation of being lost during a rainy Easter time in the Mexican border town of Juárez. The music critic Bill Flanagan reports having a conversation around 2001 with the novelist Robert Stone in which Stone (who was part of the crowd surrounding Ken Kesey and the Beat legend Neal Cassady) reminisced about Cassady's exile in Mexico and claimed that there was no better account of that time and that place than "Just Like Tom Thumb's Blues."

but all too real, everything a symbol of itself, viewed by the singer and his Lady looking out on it all, detached, from inside Desolation Row.

In all of its strangeness, the song mocks orthodoxies and confining loyalties of every kind—loyalties to religion, sex, science, romance, politics, medicine, money—which the singer has rejected. The least mysterious verse (although it is mysterious enough) comes next to last. Crammed aboard the damned *Titanic,* the people are oblivious to what is happening; instead, they shout an old reliable left-wing folkie tune (made popular by the Weavers), "Which Side Are You On?" T. S. Eliot and Ezra Pound, respectively the author and the editor of *The Waste Land,* struggle for command of the ship; but it is all a laugh to the calypso singers; and down beneath the dreamlike sea where lovely mermaids flow, and where (simple) fishermen hold (simple) flowers, thoughts of Desolation Row are unnecessary. Neither strait-minded politics nor modernist high art will save the ship from crashing and going down.

In 1985, a review of mine for the *Village Voice* of *Kerouac and Friends,* Fred McDarrah's collection of photographs and articles related to the Beats, mentioned how writers and critics have differed over when and why the Beat generation disappeared. Soon after the piece was published, Al Aronowitz, whom I'd never met and never would, phoned to inform me that the Beat generation died the minute that he introduced Ginsberg to Dylan in my uncle's apartment. Self-dramatizing though he was, Aronowitz had a point—for by the time Dylan recorded "Desolation Row," he had found his way out of the limitations of the folk revival, having reawakened to Beat literary practice and sensibilities and absorbed them into his electrified music. He had thereby completed (according to Ginsberg himself) a merger of poetry and song that Ezra Pound had foreseen as modernism's future. Thereafter, it would be Ginsberg who sought artistic enlightenment from Dylan, turning his long-line verse into musical lyrics, and at times even becoming—as he did during the Rolling Thunder Revue tour of 1975—the willing mascot he had initially feared he might become. At the beginning of the 1970s, Ginsberg persuaded Dylan to collaborate on some studio recordings, the best of which, "September on Jessore Road," would not be released until 1994, a few years before Ginsberg's death. Finally, Ginsberg would partially fulfill what one punk rock musician from the 1980s called his firm desire "to be a rock star," by working with, among others, Joe Strummer of the Clash and Paul McCartney.*

The changing of the guard, though, had occurred between when Aronowitz said it did in late December 1963 and the recording of "Desolation Row" a little more than eighteen months later. On the day he made *Another Side* in June 1964, Dylan recorded a version of a new song, "Mr. Tambourine Man," but he wisely decided it was too important to include on an album completed in a one-off session. He played the song twice at the Newport Folk Festival in late July, to rapturous applause and cheers. And by the middle of autumn, he had written two more compositions that sang of bread-crumb sins and of walking upside down inside handcuffs, which completed the transition. He tried out the new songs on the road in Philadelphia, Princeton, Detroit, and Boston. Then, on Halloween night in New York City at Philharmonic Hall, he sprang them on an audience that included Allen Ginsberg (who had brought along with him Gregory Corso)—and, coincidentally, this author.

---

* At a reading at Princeton University on February 12, 1996, Ginsberg called to the stage the film director Gus Van Sant, who happened to be in town and happened to play the guitar; Van Sant duly accompanied Ginsberg's reading/performance of "The Ballad of the Skeletons," which Ginsberg had recently recorded with McCartney.

PART II: EARLY

3

DARKNESS AT THE
BREAK OF NOON:

The Concert at Philharmonic Hall,
New York City, October 31, 1964

On Halloween night 1964, a twenty-three-year-old Bob Dylan spellbound an adoring audience at Philharmonic Hall in New York. Relaxed and high-spirited, he sang seventeen songs, three of them with his guest Joan Baez, plus one encore. Many of the songs, although less than two years old, were so familiar that the crowd knew every word. Others were brand-new and baffling. Dylan played his heart out on these new compositions, as he did on the older ones, but only after a turn as the mischievous tease.

"This is called 'A Sacrilegious Lullaby in, in D minor,' " he announced, before beginning one of the first public performances ever of "Gates of Eden."

He was the cynosure of hip, when hipness still wore pressed slacks and light brown suede boots (as I remember he did that night). Yet hipness was transforming right onstage. Dylan had already moved on, well beyond the knowing New Yorkers in the hall, and he was singing about what he was finding. The show was in part a summation of past work and in part a summons to an explosion for which none of us, not even he, was fully prepared.

Bob Dylan at Philharmonic Hall, New York City, on October 31, 1964.

The times seemed increasingly out of joint during the weeks before the concert. The trauma of John F. Kennedy's assassination less than a year earlier had barely abated. Over the summer, the disappearance in Mississippi of the young civil-rights workers James Chaney, Andrew Goodman, and Michael Schwerner, and the recovery of their beaten and murdered bodies, had created traumas anew. President Lyndon Johnson managed to push a civil-rights bill through Congress in July 1964; by early autumn, it seemed as if he would trounce the archconservative Barry Goldwater in the coming election and usher in an updated New Deal. But in August, Johnson received a congressional blank check to escalate American involvement in the Vietnam conflict. On a single day in mid-October, the Soviet leader, Nikita Khrushchev, was overthrown and Communist China exploded its first atomic bomb. A hopeful phase of the decade was quickly winding down, and a scarier phase loomed.

Dylan's style and his art were changing too, with an accelerating and bewildering swiftness befitting the times. As early as the summer of 1963, he had put the folk establishment on notice in "For Dave Glover," a prose poem he was asked to write for the Newport Folk Festival program, asserting that, although he had great respect for the older folk songs and their traditions, he would write new songs as he liked, for himself and his friends. In January 1964, he complained in a letter to *Broadside* magazine about the pressures and guilt that had come with his growing fame. Out of the blue, a letter then appeared in *Broadside* from Johnny Cash, praising Dylan as "a Poet Troubadour" and bidding the world to "SHUT UP! . . . AND LET HIM SING." But the din around Dylan had barely begun. In late July, his performances at the Newport Folk Festival of new material, including "Chimes of Freedom," followed, two weeks later, by the release of *Another Side of Bob Dylan,* badly shook the older folk-music establishment. In *Sing Out!* magazine, Irwin Silber published "An Open Letter to Bob Dylan," complaining that Dylan's "new songs seem to be all inner-directed now, inner probing, self-conscious—maybe even a little maudlin or a little cruel on occasion." Noting, with a familiar left-wing combination of vagueness and menace, that he was not alone in his disquiet, Silber warned Dylan not to turn into "a different Bob Dylan than the one we knew." (Dylan responded by instructing his manager, Albert Grossman, to inform *Sing Out!* that he would no longer send the magazine his songs for publication.)

Little did Silber know that Dylan was not simply becoming different; he had also been listening to the Beatles. But neither did Dylan's approving fans, for whom Dylan remained the great folk-music star, no matter what he sang. At Newport, Dylan stuck almost entirely to playing his new songs, including one he introduced to an afternoon workshop session as "Hey, Mr. Tambourine Man, Play a Song for Me"—and the response was enthusiastic. Amid what the Top 40 disc jockeys hyped as the English rock invasion, led by the Beatles, Dylan still stood onstage alone, singing and playing with nothing more than his acoustic guitar and rack-clamped harmonica. When he wasn't alone, he performed, at Newport and elsewhere, with Joan Baez, whose presence and endorsement of Dylan's new songs banished any doubts about their legitimacy. Dylan's politics actually hadn't disappeared, as Silber charged, but only become less preachy and much funnier, as in the joke-saga "Motorpsycho Nitemare" on *Another Side*. Dylan had always sung intensely personal songs. His most powerful political material often involved human-sized stories, like "The Lonesome Death of Hattie Carroll." And amid the disorientation of late 1963 and 1964, who was to say that a turn to introspection was out of place?

The Beatles, with their odd chords and joyful harmonies, were exciting, but what was "She Loves You" compared to the long-stemmed word imagery in "Chimes of Freedom"? Who else but Dylan would be brainy enough and with-it enough to toss off allusions in his songs to a Fellini film and Cassius Clay? To his fans—among whom, as a self-centered precocious thirteen-year-old, I counted myself one—he may have been evolving, but so were we. The Bob Dylan we now heard and saw seemed basically the same as the Bob Dylan we knew, only better.

That Dylan's management booked Philharmonic Hall for its star's biggest show of the year, on Halloween night, was testimony to his allure and growing stature. Opened only two years earlier as the first showcase of the neighborhood killer Robert Moses's new Lincoln Center for the Performing Arts, Philharmonic Hall (now Avery Fisher Hall) was, with its imperial grandeur and bad acoustics, the most prestigious auditorium in Manhattan—and for that matter in the entire country. Within two years of the release of his first album, Dylan's New York venues had shot upward in cachet (and farther uptown), from Town Hall to Carnegie Hall and now to the sparkling new home of Leonard Bernstein and the New York Philharmonic. When the expectant audience streamed out of the old mosaic-tiled IRT subway stop at Sixty-sixth Street, and then crammed into the cavernous gilded theater, it must have looked to the uptowners (and the ushers) like a bizarre invasion of the beatnik, civil-rights, ban-the-bomb young.

Philharmonic Hall.

As if to make sure that we knew our place, a man appeared onstage at showtime to warn us that there would be no picture taking or smoking permitted in the house. Then, like Bernstein striding to his podium, Dylan walked out of the wings, no announcement necessary, a fanfare of applause proclaiming who he was. He started the concert, as he normally did, with "The Times They Are A-Changin'." Here we all were, the self-consciously sensitive and discerning, settling in—at a Dylan show like any other, whatever the plush surroundings.

Two hours later, we would leave the premises and head back underground to the IRT, exhilarated, entertained, and ratified in our self-assured enlightenment, but also confused about the snatches of lines we'd gleaned from the strange new songs. What was that weird lullaby in D minor? What in God's name is a perfumed gull (or did he sing "curfewed gal")? Had Dylan really written a ballad based on Arthur Koestler's *Darkness at Noon*? The melodies were strong, and the playing on the "darkness" song had been ominous and overpowering, but it had all moved so fast that comprehension was impossible. It had turned into a Dylan show unlike any we'd ever heard or heard about. And in our programs, there was Dylan's latest prose poem, "Advice for Geraldine on Her Miscellaneous Birthday," which warned that if one crossed the line, people will "feel / something's going on up there that / they don't know about. revenge / will set in." The piece concluded with a string of injunctions, some serious, some comic, some Dada-esque: "beware of bathroom walls that've not / been written on. when told t' look at / yourself . . . never look. when asked / t' give your real name . . . never give it." Way ahead of his listeners, Dylan was already mulling over sentiments, thoughts, and even lines that would one day wind up in "Ballad of a Thin Man" and "Subterranean Homesick Blues."

Thanks to an excellent tape, finally released in its entirety to the public as a compact disc forty years later, it is possible to appreciate what happened that night—not just in what Dylan sang, but in what he said, and in the amazing audible rapport he had with his audience.

The show was divided in two, with a fifteen-minute intermission. The first half was for innovation as well as for some glances at where Dylan had already been. Two of the most pointedly political older songs, interestingly, had never been issued on record, but the audience knew them anyway, or at least knew about them, and responded enthusiastically.

Back in May 1963, Dylan had been booked on *The Ed Sullivan Show,* the premier Sunday night television variety program, where Elvis Presley had made three breakthrough appearances seven years earlier and had agreed, on the final show, to be shown performing only from the waist up. The downtown Irish traditional folk group the Clancy Brothers and Tommy Makem had appeared on *Sullivan* twice, vastly enlarging their following. (They played Philharmonic Hall a year before Dylan did.) The Limeliters, the Lettermen, the Belafonte Folk Singers, and other mainstream folk acts had also performed on Sullivan's program; in March 1963, Sullivan hosted the popular Chad Mitchell Trio. For Dylan, an edgy topical singer, playing *The Ed Sullivan Show* would mean huge exposure. He chose as his number the satirical "Talkin' John Birch Society Blues."

(For readers too young to remember: the John Birch Society, which still exists, was notorious as a hard-right political group that saw Communist

Bob Dylan in rehearsal for *The Ed Sullivan Show* prior to his walkout on
May 12, 1963.

conspiracies everywhere. The Chad Mitchell Trio had enjoyed a minor
hit with its own mocking song, "The John Birch Society," in 1962.)

Upon hearing Dylan's selection at the rehearsal, just before airtime, a
CBS executive got cold feet and, over Sullivan's objections, ordered him
to sing something less controversial. Unlike Presley, Dylan would not
be censored, and he refused to appear. Word of his principled walkout
burnished Dylan's reputation among his established fans, old and young.
Little did we know that the song had also been dropped, along with three
others, from the original version of Dylan's second album, *The Freewheelin' Bob Dylan.*

Dylan included the banned number on his 1964 Halloween program.
It required no introduction, as its notorious identity is revealed early in the
song's first verse, but Dylan wanted to make a point, and so he introduced
it, with a mixture of defiance and good humor, as "Talkin' John Birch
Paranoid Blues"—a title that now to us seemed to cover the craven main-

stream media as well as the right-wing extremists who were thumping their tubs for their favorite, Senator Goldwater. It was a thrilling moment for the audience, getting to hear what CBS had forbidden the nation to hear while also exulting in our own political righteousness. It also sustained Dylan's connection—and our vicarious one—to the left-wing moral dramaturgy surrounding the right-wing 1950s blacklist, which had carried on for some key figures long after Senator Joseph McCarthy had fallen in disgrace. "Got a shock from my feet that hit my brain / Them Reds did it, the ones on *Hootenanny,*" Dylan sang—a jokey slap at the ABC-TV officials who had banned Pete Seeger from appearing on their weekly show that had capitalized on folksinging's new popularity (and had recently gone off the air), and a note of support for Joan Baez, Ramblin' Jack Elliott, and others who had boycotted the show in protest.

Davey Moore following his bout with Sugar Ramos at the Dodger Stadium in Los Angeles, March 21, 1963. Although he recovered consciousness, Moore slipped into a coma in his dressing room and died four days later.

"Who Killed Davey Moore?" the other older political song, was about the death of a young featherweight boxer who, after losing a title bout to Sugar Ramos in Los Angeles in 1963, fell into a coma and died. The incident sparked public debate about whether boxing should be banned in the United States. It also inspired the political songwriter (and Dylan's rival) Phil Ochs to compose a narrative song, describing in detail the flying fists and pouring sweat inside the ring and the "money-chasing vultures" and blood-lusting fans outside it. Dylan's musical take on the episode was at once simpler—a reworking of the ancient "Who Killed Cock Robin?" theme—and more complex, pointing out the many people who bore responsibility for Moore's death and reciting their lame excuses.

On the concert tape, the audience's instant adulatory reaction stands out most of all. As soon as Dylan sings "Who killed . . . ," the cheering starts. Although Dylan had not released a recording of the song, he had been performing it in concert as early as his Town Hall show in April

1963, less than three weeks after Davey Moore died. It was a time when a folksinger, at least this one, could have a song achieve familiarity without even putting it on a record, let alone getting it played on the radio.

Another response to "Davey Moore" also stands out on the tape, when Dylan comes to the song's line about boxing no longer being permitted in Fidel Castro's Cuba and elicits scattered but determined applause. Maybe some of the *Sing Out!* old guard were in the audience—momentarily, if just momentarily, relieved and encouraged.* Certainly there were younger people there, the Red-diaper babies and other political types, who still wanted to hold on to Dylan as the troubadour of the revolution.

Dylan, however, would not be typecast as anything, and even his rendering of "Davey Moore" pulled in other directions. "This is a song about a boxer," he said before he sang it. "It's got nothing to do with boxing; it's just a song about a boxer really. And, uh, it's not even having to do with a boxer, really. It's got nothing to do with nothing. But I fit all these words together, that's all." The irreverent introduction undercut solemnity, even though some people wanted and expected and even demanded solemnity. (Others in the audience did not, and made that clear in their impromptu badinage with the singer.) Dylan's laughter in the middle of his introduction even sounded intoxicated. Was he drunk on Beaujolais—we all knew from one magazine story or another that Dylan drank Beaujolais—or maybe, even cooler (this was 1964, and some of us were very young), had Dylan been smoking pot? (It would only come out much later that he had already moved from Burgundy on to much harder stuff than marijuana, including his first LSD trip back in April.) Perhaps he was intoxicated in a different way, giddy from the hall and the affectionate crowd and the joy of playing Lincoln Center. No matter: his mellow, at times merry mood was infectious, and it had nothing to do with sermonizing.

It did, however, have something to do with sex. Nobody in the audience had yet heard "If You Gotta Go, Go Now," and its rollicking monologue of a sly, self-aware, take-it-or-leave-it seduction sent everybody into stitches. Coming after "Gates of Eden," it was a bit of comic relief, but

---

* The relief would have been all the greater given they had heard "I Shall Be Free No. 10," one of the songs on *Another Side* that Dylan did not perform at the concert, which included the following lyrics: "Now, I'm liberal, but to a degree / I want ev'rybody to be free / But if you think that I'll let Barry Goldwater / Move in next door and marry my daughter / You must think I'm crazy! / I wouldn't let him do it for all the farms in Cuba."

hip comic relief. In the song, the singer knows very well that the object of his affections is no virgin. Casual sex is no longer taboo; the repression surrounding this part of life has lifted. But what Presley had done with his body and his voice, Dylan was doing with his words—coy, conversational, and comical, feeding the youth conspiracy of candid pleasure (and pleasant candor) but with jesting, gentle persuasion.

Sometimes, the audience knew Dylan's words better than he did. Nearing the end of the show's first half, Dylan strummed his guitar but completely forgot the next song's opening line. As if he were still performing at the Gaslight down in Greenwich Village, or at a Newport festival workshop, and not in serious Philharmonic Hall, Dylan asked the audience to help him out, and it did. On the tape, two voices, unmistakably New York voices, carry above all the others, one rapidly following the other with the cue: "I can't understand . . ." The song, "I Don't Believe You (She Acts Like We Never Have Met)," had appeared on *Another Side* less than three months earlier, but his fans knew it so well that it might have been "Pretty Peggy-O." (It may even have been more familiar to most of the audience than "Pretty Peggy-O.") Dylan, a master of timing, did not miss a beat, picked up the line, and then sang the song flawlessly.

Dylan interspersed these funny moments with his new masterpieces, "Gates of Eden" and "It's Alright, Ma (I'm Only Bleeding)," calling the latter "It's Alright, Ma, It's Life and Life Only," and he performed "Mr. Tambourine Man" for the first time in New York. These songs have become such iconic pieces over the intervening decades, their twisting images so much a part of a generation's subconscious, that it is difficult to recall what they sounded like when heard for the first time, and in concert. Dylan knew that they were special, and that they would fly over his listeners' heads the first time around. He even joked about that onstage. (On the tape, some laughter greets Dylan's announcement of "It's Alright, Ma," as if the song title were a put-on, and he pipes up, "Yes, it's a very funny song.") During these performances, the audience was utterly silent, trying at first to catch all the words, but finally bowled over by the intensity of both the lyrics and Dylan's playing, even when he muffed a line. We would not get the chance to figure the songs out for another five months, when they appeared on *Bringing It All Back Home*—and even then it would take repeated listening for any of it to make sense. At the time, it just sounded like demanding poetry, at times epic narrative, proving once again that Bob Dylan was leading us into new places, the exact destination unknown but still deeply tempting.

Dylan did not waste any words of introduction to "Mr. Tambourine Man" even though he'd yet to release it on record. (The truncated rock version by the Byrds, which became a number one hit on the *Billboard* singles charts, did not appear until the following April, two weeks after Dylan finally released his own version on *Bringing It All Back Home.*) But enough of the audience had heard the song, at Newport or perhaps at one of the shows leading up to this one, so that its opening words brought an outburst of applause. The rest of us, uninitiated, sat back to wonder how lyrics about weariness and stripped senses could fit such a delightful, dancing melody.

It turned out to be a song of Dylan singing again to his muse. He had done so in one of his earliest compositions—"Hey, hey, Woody Guthrie, I wrote you a song"—but now he called out to an abstract figure—"Hey! Mr. Tambourine Man"—and wanted a song played to him. Dylan would later point to an oversized Turkish tambourine, played by Bruce Lang-horne, as an inspiration, but neither Langhorne nor anybody else any longer served Dylan as Guthrie had done. He was weary, unable to keep a grip, but also unsleepy, and with no particular place to go, he would follow the musical figure to his "magic swirling ship," out to the inspired windy beach beyond crazy sorrow.

Like all of Dylan's compositions, "Mr. Tambourine Man" contained bits and pieces gathered from hither and yon. Dylan himself had alluded in an interview to Federico Fellini's film *La strada* (The Road), in which an innocent, sprightly young woman falls into the clutches of a brutish he-man performer; much later, the brute, alone, learns that the woman has died, and the film ends with him sobbing uncontrollably on a beach.* Dylan aficionados have located some specific references, including the words "jingle jangle," which appear on a recording by the hip British comic monologist Lord Buckley, whom Dylan is known to have enjoyed. Finally, though, the song is not a direct translation of anything else; it is about precisely what it says it is about—an artist, at his wit's end, looking for respite from his distress if only for a night, and turning to a shadowy musical spirit to play him a song that he will follow.

The other two new songs showed where his muse had taken him, and

---

* Alternatively, the allusion could be to the famous final, freeze-frame scene on a beach in François Truffaut's *Les quatre cents coups* (*The 400 Blows*).

Bob Dylan playing "Mr. Tambourine Man" in its first public performance, at the Newport Folk Festival on July 24, 1964.

they were more obscure—as they remain. The title of "It's Alright, Ma" evoked Arthur "Big Boy" Crudup's "That's All Right, Mama," one of the first songs that Elvis Presley recorded in Memphis—but the reference certainly didn't occur to me at the time, and probably didn't to more than a few others. Instead, the title got a laugh, then Dylan joked about it being a funny song, and then he began hammering dropped-D tuning runs in a minor key which announced that something dark and sinister was about to come. The opening line swipes the title of Koestler's novel about Communism's stupid cruelties, but changes it so that darkness arrives not simply at noon but at the break of noon. The break of noon? Dawn cracks and breaks, and in Ginsberg's "Howl" doom cracks on the hydrogen jukebox. But noon doesn't break—except that now it did, making the darkness at noon sound all the scarier.

The song didn't seem to have anything to do with Koestler's book, and its opening verses about "the handmade blade" and "the fool's gold mouthpiece" made it difficult to understand what the song actually did have to do with. But some startling images and proclamations, restating Dylan's escape from folk-revival pieties, carried listeners along: "He not busy being born / Is busy dying"; "While others say don't hate nothing at all / Except hatred." One line leaped out, about how even the president of the United States must sometimes stand naked. After Vietnam, Watergate, and the long age of Reagan that followed, the line has brought predictable, beery anti-authoritarian cheers from concertgoers. But nobody cheered in 1964—nobody knew it was coming—and the line was actually perplexing, given our assumption that the incumbent was the good guy in the upcoming presidential election. The rest of the song charted dishonesties, blasphemies, and hypocrisy in American life in a manner more like Allen Ginsberg's "Howl" than like any folk song ever written. The hypnosis that is modern advertising, the fake morals that limit sex but bow down to money, the rat-race society that twists people into meanness and conformity: Dylan had written a song of Ginsberg's Moloch, exposing the human corruption and self-delusion that had driven the best minds mad. What hopeful sound there is comes from a solitary individual, directed at another individual—but the words are trembling, distant, unclear, seeking a human and humane connection, and they are directed at someone who is asleep. The subversive singer is tolerated only because he keeps his truly dangerous thought-dreams under wraps. Otherwise, he'd probably get his head cut off.

"The Gates of Eden," as he called it that night, took us furthest out into the realm of the imagination, to a point beyond logic and reason. Like "It's Alright, Ma," the song mentions a book title in its first line, but the song is more reminiscent of the poems of William Blake (and, perhaps, of Blake's disciple Ginsberg) than it is of Tolstoy's *War and Peace,* vaunting the truth that lies in surreal imagery.

After an almost impenetrable first verse, the song approaches themes that were becoming familiar to Dylan's listeners. In Genesis, Eden is the paradise where Adam and Eve had direct communication with God. According to "Gates of Eden," it is where truth resides, without bewitching illusions. And the song is basically a list, verse after verse, of the corrosive illusions that Dylan would sing about constantly from the mid-1960s on: illusions about obedience to authority; about false religions and idols (the "utopian hermit monks" riding on the golden calf); about possessions and desire; about sexual repression and conformity (embodied by "the gray flannel dwarf"); about high-toned intellectualism. None of these count for much or even exist inside the gates of Eden.

The kicker comes in the final verse, where the singer talks of his lover telling him of her dreams without any attempt at interpretation—and that at times, the singer thinks that the only truth is that there is no truth outside the gates of Eden. It's a familiar conundrum: If there is no truth, isn't saying as much really an illusion, too, unless we are all in Eden? ("All Cretans are liars," says the Cretan.) What makes that one truth so special? But the point, as the lover knows, is that outside of paradise, interpretation is futile. Don't try to figure out what the song, or what any work of art, "really" means; the meaning is in the imagery itself; attempting to define it is to succumb to the illusion that truth can be reached through human logic. So Dylan's song told us, as he took the measure in his lyrics of what had begun as the "New Vision," two and a half miles up Broadway from Lincoln Center at Columbia, in the mid-1940s. Apart from Dylan, Allen Ginsberg and Gregory Corso may have been the only people in Philharmonic Hall who got it.

I can't recall much about the intermission, except that a goodly number of people were smokers and there was a rush to the entry hall for a fifteen-minute nicotine break. (Too young to smoke, and seated in the top tier, I didn't stray downstairs.) The evening's second half brought us back to familiar ground: songs from *Freewheelin'* and *The Times They Are*

Joan Baez and Bob Dylan at Philharmonic Hall, New York City, October 31, 1964.

A-Changin', including what has proven to be one of Dylan's most enduring ballads, "The Lonesome Death of Hattie Carroll," a song of contained outrage so expertly written that it has outlived almost all of the
era's other finger-pointing songs. Then came three duets with Joan Baez,
she sporting at least part of the time a plaid Glengarry cap. (Baez also sang
"Silver Dagger," accompanied by Dylan on the harmonica.) Dylan and
Baez—the king and queen of the folk movement, known to be lovers—
had been performing together off and on for well over a year. Baez had
brought Dylan to the stage during several of her concerts, including one
at Forest Hills in August, and now Dylan was returning the compliment.
They sang of desire, rejected and requited, and American history, their
harmonizing ragged in places, but with an ease between them that further
mellowed the mood even as it upped the star wattage onstage.

Plenty has been made since about Dylan and Baez's relationship in
these years, some of it unflattering to one or the other or both of them.
Much as the Kennedys' Camelot would have its debunkers, so the magi-
cal kingdom we conjured up around Bob Dylan and Joan Baez would
come crashing down. Nearly forgotten, however—but captured on the
Philharmonic tape, even in that night's laid-back, knockabout performances—have been the rich fruits of their singing collaborations. Joan
always seemed, onstage, the earnest, worshipful one, overly so, in the
presence of the Boy Genius, and Bob would sometimes lightly mock that
earnestness, as he did between songs at the Philharmonic. But when singing together, they were quite a pair, their harmony lines adding depth to
the melodies, their sheer pleasure in each other's company showing in
their voices.

When I listen to the Philharmonic tape, my favorite duet is of the then-
unreleased song "Mama, You Been on My Mind." Baez sings "Daddy"
instead of "Mama." Then, during one of the brief instrumental inter-
ludes, she interjects a "shooka-shooka-shooka, shooka-shooka"—nothing
one would expect from the folk queen, something more like pop or rock
and roll or even rhythm and blues than folk music. Was our Joan listening
to the Beatles, too? I don't recall hearing it this way at the time, but now
it sounds like another little portent of things to come.

Dylan closed, solo, with his encore. Shouted requests filled the air,
for "Chimes of Freedom," for anything, even for "Mary Had a Little
Lamb." "God, did I record that?" Dylan joked back, basking in the rev-
elry. "Is that a protest song?" He chose "All I Really Want to Do," another
crowd-pleaser from *Another Side.* He seemed to start out with an attitude,

his voice rising, half snapping near the end of the opening line—"I ain't looking to com-PETE with you"—but he settled into a kind of emphatic exuberance. Was this a cryptic envoi to Joan Baez? (If it was, she didn't get it, and maybe Dylan didn't either, not fully.) Was it an envoi to us, or the part of us that wanted to make of Dylan, in our own way, something more than he could possibly be? Or was he just itching to plug in to an amp and play rock and roll?

During the first half of the concert, after singing "Gates of Eden," Dylan got into a little riff about how the song shouldn't scare anybody, that it was only Halloween, and that he had his Bob Dylan mask on. "I'm masquerading!" he joked, elongating the second word into a smoke-ringed laugh. The joke was serious. Bob Dylan, né Zimmerman, brilliantly cultivated his celebrity, but he was really an artist and singer, a man behind a mask, a great entertainer, maybe, but basically just that—someone who threw words together, astounding as they were. The burden of being something else—a guru, a political theorist, "the voice of a generation," as he facetiously put it in an interview some years ago—was too much to ask of anyone. Indeed, it missed the whole point as he was laying it out in his songs, which was that the songs themselves were what mattered, their words and images alone. We in the audience were asking him to be a leader and more, but Dylan was slipping the yoke. He certainly enjoyed the fame and fortune that had headed his way. But beyond a certain level of acceptance, all he really wanted to do was to be a friend, if possible, and an artist writing and singing his songs. He was telling us so, but we didn't want to believe it, and wouldn't let him leave it at that. We wanted more.

Less than three months after the Philharmonic Hall concert, Bob Dylan showed up at Columbia Records' Studio A in Manhattan for the second session of recording *Bringing It All Back Home*—and he brought with him three guitarists, two bassists, a drummer, and a piano player. One of the first songs they recorded was "Subterranean Homesick Blues," a Chuck Berry–ish rock number, less sung than recited, about lures, snares, chaos, not following leaders, cooking up illegal drugs, and keeping an eye out for the cops. That spring, Dylan would tour England and return to his acoustic playlist, but the film made of that tour, *Dont Look Back,* shows him a conscientious trouper who is obviously bored with the material and

the audiences' predictable responses. The new half-electric album appeared in March; by midsummer, "Like a Rolling Stone," recorded in June in the opening sessions for what would become *Highway 61 Revisited,* was all over the radio; and in late July came the famous all-electric set at Newport that sparked a civil war among Dylan's fans.

He was no longer standing alone with his guitar and harmonica. The once pleasant joker now wore menacing black leather boots and a shiny matching jacket. No more Joan Baez. A bit of the old rapport reappeared when Dylan was coaxed back onstage to play some of his acoustic material. "Does anybody have an E harmonica, an E harmonica, anybody?" he asked—and E harmonicas came raining out from the crowd and thumped onstage. But now the envoi was unmistakable as Dylan serenaded the folkies with "It's All Over Now, Baby Blue," as well as "Mr. Tambourine Man." A year after that—with the Vietnam War tearing the country apart, urban ghettos beset by arson and riots, and a conservative backlash coming on strong—Dylan would suffer his famous motorcycle crack-up, concluding the wild period when he pushed his innovations to the limit with *Blonde on Blonde* and with his astonishing concerts with the Hawks (with Bobby Gregg, then Sandy Konikoff, and finally Mickey Jones playing drums), not least the "Judas" show at the Free Trade Hall in Manchester, England.

In retrospect, the concert at Philharmonic Hall was Dylan's springboard into that turmoil, turmoil that he somehow survived. His trial would reach a spiritual, musical, and literary apex sixteen months later in Nashville, Tennessee.

Bob Dylan at the sessions for *Highway 61 Revisited,*
Columbia Records' Studio A, New York City, June 1965.

4

THE SOUND OF 3:00 A.M.:

The Making of *Blonde on Blonde,* New York City and Nashville, October 5, 1965–March 10 (?), 1966

A memory from the summer of 1966: Across the Top 40 airwaves, an insistent drumbeat led off a strange, new hit song. Some listeners thought the song too explicit, its subject of madness and persecution too coarse, even cruel. Several radio-station directors banned it. Yet despite the controversy, or more likely because of it, the record shot to number three on the *Billboard* pop-singles chart. The singer-songwriter likened the song, which really was more of a rap, to a sick joke. His name was Jerry Samuels, but he billed himself as Napoleon XIV, performing "They're Coming to Take Me Away, Ha-Haaa!"

That spring, an equally controversial single, with an eerily similar opening, had quickly hit number two, and by summer "Rainy Day Women #12 & 35" had reappeared as the opening track on the mysterious double album *Blonde on Blonde* by Bob Dylan, who said the song was about "a minority of, you know, cripples and orientals and, uh, you know, and the world in which they live." Over Coppertone-slicked bodies on Santa Monica Beach and out of secluded make-out spots and shopping-center parking lots and everywhere else American teenagers gathered that summer, it seemed that the ba-de-de-bum-de-bum announcing Dylan's hit about getting stoned was blaring from car radios and transistor radios, inevitably followed by the ba-de-de-bum-de-bum announcing Jerry Samuels's hit about insanity. It would be Samuels's only big recording, and in July, Dylan suddenly left the scene and retreated into seclusion in Woodstock.

Such were the cultural antinomies of the time as Bob Dylan crossed over to pop stardom. *Blonde on Blonde* might well have included a character named Napoleon XIV, and the album sometimes seemed a little crazy, but it was no joke (not even the frivolous "Rainy Day Women"), and it was hardly the work of a madman, pretended or otherwise. At age twenty-four, Dylan, spinning on the edge, had a well-ordered mind and an intense, at times biting rapport with reality. The songs are rich meditations on desire, frailty, promises, boredom, hurt, envy, connections, missed connections, paranoia, and transcendent beauty—in short, the lures and snares of love, stock themes of rock and pop music, but written with a powerful literary imagination and played out in a pop netherworld.

Blonde on Blonde borrows from several musical styles, including 1940s Memphis and Chicago blues, turn-of-the-century vintage New Orleans processionals, contemporary pop, and blast-furnace rock and roll. With every appropriation, Dylan moved closer to a sound of his own. Years later, he famously commended some of the album's tracks for "that thin, that wild mercury sound," which he had begun to capture on his previous albums *Bringing It All Back Home* and *Highway 61 Revisited*—a sound achieved from whorls of harmonica, organ, and guitar. Dylan's organist

Al Kooper and Bob Dylan in 1966.

Publicity photograph of the Hawks, circa 1964. Left to right: Jerry Penfound, Rick Danko, Levon Helm, Richard Manuel, Garth Hudson, Robbie Robertson.

and musical go-between Al Kooper has said that "nobody has ever cap-tured the sound of 3 a.m. better than that album. Nobody, not even Sina-tra, gets it as good." These descriptions are accurate, but neither of them applies to all the songs, nor to all of the sounds in most of the songs. Nor do they offer clues about the album's origins and evolution—including how its being recorded mostly in the wee, small hours may have contrib-uted to its 3:00 a.m. aura.

Reminiscences and scraps of official information have added up to a general story line. During the autumn and winter of 1965–66, after his electric show at the Newport Folk Festival in July and amid a crowded concert schedule, Dylan tried to cut his third album inside of a year at Columbia Records' Studio A in New York with his newly hired touring band, Levon and the Hawks, which until 1964 had been the backup band for the rhythm-and-blues and rockabilly star Ronnie Hawkins.*

---

* After leaving Hawkins, the band appeared first as the Levon Helm Sextet (led by the drummer, Levon Helm, and including a saxophone player, Jerry Penfound), then (without Penfound) as Levon and the Hawks. In 1965, they released a single on the

The results were unsatisfactory. *Blonde on Blonde* arose from Dylan's decision to quit New York and record in Nashville with a collection of seasoned country-music session men joined by Al Kooper and the Hawks' guitarist, Robbie Robertson. But that story line is incomplete.

From the time he began recording regularly with electric instruments, Dylan, his palette enlarged, fixated on reproducing the sounds inside his mind with minimal editing artifice. The making of *Blonde on Blonde* combined perfectionism with spontaneous improvisation to capture what Dylan heard but could not completely articulate in words. "He never did anything twice," the album's producer, Bob Johnston, recalls of Dylan's mercurial manner in the studio, "and if he did it twice, you probably didn't get it." Making the record also involved happenstance, necessity, uncertainty, wrongheaded excess, virtuosity, and retrieval. One of the album's finest musical performances, maybe its finest, unfolded in New York, not Nashville, perfected by a combo that included three musicians—Rick Danko, Bobby Gregg, and Paul Griffin—who have never received proper credit for working on the album. Some of the other standout songs were compact compositions that took shape quickly during the final Nashville sessions. And what has come to be remembered as the musical big bang in Nashville actually grew out of a singular evolution that turned one grand Dylan experiment into something grander.

"THAT'S NOT THE SOUND"

The first recording date at all connected to *Blonde on Blonde* took place with the Hawks in New York on October 5, 1965, barely a month after the release of *Highway 61 Revisited*. Dylan had just performed his half-electric show at Carnegie Hall and in Newark (only his fifth and sixth concerts ever with any of the Hawks) and received a warmer response than expected. "Like a Rolling Stone" had hit number two on *Billboard*

---

small Ware Records label under the name the Canadian Squires—all of the members except the Arkansan Helm hailed from Canada—but then reverted to Levon and the Hawks and recorded another single for Atco Records that same year. The group had been playing a regular engagement at Tony Mart's, a club at Somers Point on the New Jersey shore, when Dylan hired them in the late summer of 1965, based on strong recommendations from the young blues singer and son of Dylan's first producer, John Hammond (who had recorded with Helm, the keyboard player Garth Hudson, and the guitarist Robbie Robertson earlier in the year), and from Albert Grossman's secretary, Mary Martin.

At the discotheque Ondine in Manhattan on the evening of the first recording session for *Blonde on Blonde,* October 5, 1965. Left to right: Rick Danko, Bob Dylan, Bob Neuwirth, David Blue, and unidentified [Venetia Cunningham?].

over the summer; now, following successful concerts at the Hollywood Bowl, and in Austin and Dallas, the booing furies of Newport and Forest Hills seemed to have receded, at least temporarily. Dylan's new sound initially went over much better with audiences down south, where rock and roll was born, than in most other places, and so the applause at Carnegie Hall was unexpected. Dylan was also still learning about how to play onstage with a band, and the Hawks were still getting used to playing with him; the kinks would surface inside Studio A.

The producer Bob Johnston, a Texas-born protégé of John Hammond's, had overseen the last four of the six *Highway 61* sessions (replacing Tom Wilson, Dylan's record producer since *The Times They Are A-Changin'*), and Johnston was back for *Blonde on Blonde.* Not surprisingly, Dylan had not written any new material that approached "Like a Rolling Stone" or "Desolation Row." This first day's efforts included two takes of "Medicine Sunday," an early version of what would evolve into "Temporary Like Achilles," and two takes (separated by a good deal of sketchy instrumental riffs) of another song that became two songs with very different lyrics: the first, a downtown hipster joke given the title "Jet Pilot"; the second, a quasi-parody of the Beatles' "I Wanna Be Your Man." The parody

Left to right: Dylan, Johnny Cash, unidentified, and Bob Johnston, Nashville, Tennessee, 1969.

morphed, later in the session, into six takes of what Dylan, on the session tape, calls "I Don't Wanna Be Your Partner, I Wanna Be Your Man," and was later labeled "I Wanna Be Your Lover." The parody improved during the session and had some intriguing lines—fragments from the entire day's work would later reappear on *Blonde on Blonde*—but the results, maybe intentionally, amounted to musical warm-ups. The session ended with an untitled instrumental, later called "Number One," also unreleased on *Blonde on Blonde* but later bootlegged. The date's bright spot was recording new takes of "Can You Please Crawl Out Your Window?" a single left over from the *Highway 61* sessions.

Over the next two months, Dylan and the Hawks resumed touring—from Toronto, Canada, to Washington, D.C.—and the booing resumed, though not in Memphis. On November 22, Dylan married Sara Lownds, née Shirley Noznisky, a recently divorced former actress and fashion model whom he had met privately in New York through Albert Grossman's wife, Sally. Eight days after the wedding, two days after the Washington concert, and one day before flying off for a West Coast tour, he was back in the studio with the Hawks, minus the leader, Levon Helm, who had wearied of playing in a backup band and quit; Bobby Gregg played drums in his stead. The newlywed now carried with him a masterpiece he had to record right away. "This is called 'Freeze Out,'" Dylan

Bob Dylan and the Hawks at the War Memorial, Syracuse, New York, November 21, 1965.

announced with a note of triumph as the tape started rolling for the first session take.

"Freeze Out" was "Visions of Johanna," virtually intact, but Dylan was even less certain about how he wanted it played than he was about the title. On the session tape, he and the Hawks change the key and slow the tempo at the start of the second take, if only to hear more closely. "That's not right," Dylan interrupts. He speeds things up again—"like that"— and bids Gregg to go to his cowbell, but some more scorching tests are no good either. "Stop . . . That's not the sound, that's not it," he breaks in early on. "I can't . . . 'at's not . . . *bauoom* . . . it's, it's more of a *bauoom, bauoom* . . . It'snota, it'snota, it's not hard rock. The only thing in it, man, that's *hard* is Robbie." A broken attempt features a harpsichord, possibly played by Garth Hudson. "Naah," Dylan decides, though he keeps the harpsichord in the background. Out of nowhere comes the idea for a new introduction, starting off with Dylan on harmonica, preceding a slower, hair-raising, bar-band rock version. But Dylan doesn't hear "Freeze Out" that way either, so he quiets things down, inching closer to what will eventually appear on *Blonde on Blonde*—and it is still not right. Dylan had written an extraordinary song—he would boast of it at a San Francisco press conference a few days later—but had not rendered its sound. Over the coming months, starting in Berkeley, he would perform the song constantly in concert, but in the solo acoustic half of the show. (The first "Visions of Johanna" date did yield, in an evening session, a forceful final take of "Crawl Out Your Window"—but the single's ill-timed release, just after Christmas, generated mediocre American sales.)

Dylan became frustrated and angry at the next *Blonde on Blonde* date, held three weeks into the new year during a break from touring. In nine hours of recording, through nineteen listed takes, only one song was attempted, for which Dylan supplied the instantly improvised title "Just a Little Glass of Water." Eventually renamed "She's Your Lover Now," it is a lengthy, cinematic vignette of a hurt, confused man lashing out at his ex-girlfriend and her new lover. Nobody expected it would be recorded easily. (Dylan's manager, Albert Grossman, interjects on the tape, just before the recording starts, that there is a supply of "raw meat coming up for everybody in the band.") The first take rolls at a stately pace, but Dylan is restless and the day has just begun.

On successive takes, the tempo speeds, then slows a bit, then speeds up again. Dylan tries singing a line in each verse accompanied only by Garth Hudson's organ, shifting the song's dynamics, but the idea survives for only two takes. After some false starts, Dylan says, "It's not right . . . it's not right," as if something just keeps eluding him, and soon he despairs: "No, fuck it, I'm losing the whole fucking song." He again changes tempos and fiddles with some chords and periodically scolds himself as well as the band: "I don't give a fuck if it's good or not, just play it together . . . just, just, make it all together, you don't have to play anything fancy or nothing, just . . . just together." A strong, nearly complete version ensues, but Dylan flubs the last verse. "I can't hear the song anymore," he finally confesses. He wants the song back, so he plays it alone, slowly, on the tack piano he has been playing for the entire session, and nails every verse.* He reacts to his own performance with a little "huh" that could have been registering puzzlement or rediscovery. But Dylan would end up discarding "She's Your Lover Now," just as he would abandon a later, interesting take of an older song, originally written for the blond European chanteuse Nico, "I'll Keep It with Mine."

For better or worse, Dylan had become used to honing his songs and

---

* A tack piano, which produces a sound reminiscent of saloons in movie and television Westerns, is an ordinary piano with tacks or nails attached to the hammers in order to produce a tinny, percussive timbre. Dylan first recorded with one two years earlier on the song "Black Crow Blues," on *Another Side of Bob Dylan.*

then working quickly in the studio, even when he played with sidemen. He had finished *Bringing It All Back Home* in just three studio dates involving fewer than sixteen hours of studio time. It took five dates, one overdub session, and twenty-eight hours for *Highway 61 Revisited* (along with the single "Positively 4th Street"). After three dates and more than eighteen hours in the studio on this new endeavor, Dylan had one unrealized tour de force, one potentially big song, and one marginally popular single, but little in the way of an album. One way to move forward was to bring in veterans of earlier Dylan sessions. Four days after failing on "She's Your Lover Now," Dylan recorded with Paul Griffin on piano, William E. Lee on bass, and, fortuitously, Al Kooper (who stopped by to see his friend Griffin but wound up sitting in on organ). Bobby Gregg returned once again to substitute for Levon Helm on the drums and was joined this time by the Hawks' guitarist, Robbie Robertson, and bassist, Rick Danko. Dylan also brought two new songs: the funny, jealous put-down blues "Leopard-Skin Pill-Box Hat" (based in part on Memphis Minnie's "Me and My Chauffeur Blues," and in part on Lightnin' Hopkins's "Automobile Blues," but laid aside temporarily after two strong takes) and "One of Us Must Know (Sooner or Later)," recorded simply as "Song Unknown" after Dylan pondered in the studio but could not come up with a title. The results on "Song Unknown" were stunning.*

The lyrics are straightforward, even ordinary, tracking a burned-out love affair's misunderstandings. Dylan shifted tempos and pieced together the lyrics section by section inside the studio, working off the line, later

---

* One writer's listing for all of this day's sessions credits Michael Bloomfield on guitar and William E. Lee on bass; another listing omits Paul Griffin. The playing and talk on the session tape, though, show conclusively that Rick Danko was the bassist on "One of Us Must Know," that Robbie Robertson played guitar, and that Griffin was, indeed, the pianist. After all these years, Bobby Gregg, Paul Griffin, and Rick Danko, whose names have never appeared in the album's liner notes either on LP or on CD, deserve their share of credit for playing on *Blonde on Blonde*. My thanks to Diane Lapson for helping to sort out the identities of the various musicians on the recordings, as well as to Jeff Rosen and Robert Bowers for guiding me to and through the recordings themselves.

The first take of "Leopard-Skin Pill-Box Hat" was also strong and ended up being released forty years later on the CD collection that accompanied Martin Scorsese's documentary *No Direction Home*. Curiously, this version sounded more like the one actually included on *Blonde on Blonde* (and recorded in Nashville at the very last studio session) than many of the numerous intervening takes. For once, Dylan ended up, musically, more or less where he began.

abandoned, "Now you're glad it's through"; the title chorus only began to emerge on the fifth take. But the sound texture that makes "One of Us Must Know" so remarkable was built steadily, late into the night and into the next morning. After take seventeen, Dylan heeds the producer Johnston's advice to start with a harmonica swoop. Crescendos off of an extended fifth chord, led by Paul Griffin's astonishing piano swells ("half Gershwin, half gospel, all heart," an astute critic later wrote), climax in choruses dominated by piano, organ, and Bobby Gregg's drumrolls; Robbie Robertson's guitar hits its full strength at the finale. Intimations of the thin, wild mercury sound underpin rock-and-roll symphonics. Johnston delivers a pep talk before one last take—"it's gotta be that soul feel"— there is a false start, then Gregg snaps a quick click opener, and less than five minutes later the keeper is in the can.

"AFTER THAT, IT WENT REAL EASY"

"We knew we had cut a good 'un when it was over," Al Kooper remembers. But despite the successful experiment, the next day's recording was canceled, as were two other New York dates; during the one completed session, on January 27, Dylan played around with words and driving melodies and tried to nail down some songs, but the work produced nothing of lasting consequence for the new album.* A change in venue had been in the works, and despite the results on "One of Us Must Know" it would go forward. During the *Highway 61* sessions, Bob Johnston had suggested that Dylan try recording in Nashville, but according to Johnston, Grossman and Columbia objected and insisted everything was going fine in New York. Dylan, though, finally went along with Johnston. He had been listening to Nashville-recorded music since he was a boy and knew firsthand how Johnston's Nashville friends might sound on his songs. At Johnston's invitation, the multi-instrumentalist Charlie McCoy had sat in on a *Highway 61* session and overdubbed the borderland acoustic guitar

---

* According to one dating of the Columbia reels, this session occurred on January 22, the day after the failure to capture "She's Your Lover Now"—but all other accounts of Dylan's recording sessions state that the date was January 27, and Columbia recording numbers given each song affirm the later date. The musicians included Robbie Robertson, Rick Danko, Al Kooper, and Bobby Gregg as well as Dylan. The session was mainly devoted to recording revised versions of "Leopard-Skin Pill-Box Hat" and a pair of incomplete, preliminary run-throughs of "I'll Keep It with Mine." Every take was discarded for *Blonde on Blonde.*

runs that grace the released version of "Desolation Row," strongly reminiscent of the great session guitarist Grady Martin's work on Marty Robbins's "El Paso." It was an impressive calling card. "After that," McCoy remembers, "it went real easy."

Nashville had been ascending as a major recording center since the 1940s. By 1963, it boasted eleven hundred musicians and fifteen recording studios. After Steve Sholes's and Chet Atkins's pioneering work in the 1950s with Elvis Presley, Nashville also proved it could produce superb rock and roll as well as country and western, rhythm and blues, and Brenda Lee pop. That held especially true for the session crew Johnston assembled for Dylan's Nashville dates. Trying to plug songs for Presley's movies, Johnston had hooked up for demo recordings with younger players, many of whom, like McCoy, had moved to Nashville from other parts

Charlie McCoy and the Escorts, Cadence Records publicity photograph, 1960s. McCoy is in the center playing harmonica; standing are (left) the drummer Kenny Buttrey holding a guitar and (right) the guitarist Wayne Moss.

of the South. Charlie McCoy and the Escorts, in fact, were reputed to be Nashville's tightest and busiest weekend rock band in the mid-1960s; the members included the guitarist Wayne Moss and the drummer Kenneth Buttrey, who, along with McCoy, would be vital to *Blonde on Blonde*.

Johnston's choices (also including the guitarist Jerry Kennedy, the pianist Hargus "Pig" Robbins, the bass player Henry Strzelecki, and the great Joseph Souter Jr.—a.k.a. Joe South—the guitarist and singer who would hit it big nationally in three years with a single, "Games People Play") were certainly among Nashville's top session men. Some of them had worked with stars ranging from Patsy Cline, Elvis Presley, and Roy Orbison to Ann-Margret. But apart from the A-list regular McCoy (whose harmonica skills were in special demand), they were still up-and-coming members of the Nashville elite, roughly Dylan's age. (Robbins, at twenty-eight, was a relative old-timer; McCoy, at twenty-four, was only two months older than Dylan; Buttrey was just turning twenty-one.) Although they were too professional to be starstruck, McCoy says, "everybody knew what a brilliant songwriter [Dylan] was" from songs such as "Blowin' in

Joe "South" Souter, Hargus "Pig" Robbins in Nashville, Tennessee, circa 1975. Jerry Kennedy at the Mercury Records studio in Nashville, Tennessee, circa 1975.

the Wind," but as a performer, and especially as a rock performer, Dylan's reputation did not precede him. Still, the session men were much more in touch with what Dylan was up to on *Blonde on Blonde* than is allowed by the stereotype of long-haired New York hipsters colliding with well-scrubbed Nashville good ol' boys. One of Dylan's biographers reports that Robbie Robertson found the Nashville musicians "standoffish." But the outgoing Al Kooper, who had more recording experience, recalls the scene differently: "Those guys welcomed us in, respected us, and played better than any other studio guys I had ever played with previously."

(What aloofness there was seems mainly to have come from Dylan's end. Kris Kristofferson, then an aspiring songwriter working as a janitor at the studio, recalls that police had been stationed around the building to keep out unwanted intruders. Asked if he got to meet the star, he told an interviewer, emphatically, he did not: "I wouldn't have *dared* talk to him. I'd have been fired.")

Johnston, apparently at Dylan's request, helped bring everybody together by emptying the studio of baffles—tall partitions that separate musicians to reduce sonic reflections and prevent the sounds from one player bleeding into the microphone of another. The producer wanted to create an ambience fit for an ensemble, and he succeeded—so much so that Kenny Buttrey later credited the album's distinctive sound to that alteration alone. "It made all the difference in our playing together," he later told an interviewer, "as if we were on a tight stage, as opposed to playing in a big hall where you're ninety miles apart. From that night on, our entire outlook was changed. We started having a good time."

Of course, Nashville, for all of its musical sophistication, was not Manhattan. Kooper tells of going to the country-music star Ernest Tubb's famous record store downtown and getting chased in broad daylight by some tough guys who disliked his looks. There were differences inside the studio, too. The Nashville musicians were accustomed to cutting three- to four-minute sides, several a day, where, McCoy says, "the artist and the song was always the number-one item." Dylan, though, had undertaken some remarkably long songs, and apart from "Visions of Johanna" none of them was finished. Departing from his reputation for recording rapidly, Dylan kept sketching and revising in his hotel room and even in the studio—sometimes laboriously, sometimes spontaneously, seizing on inspiration so quickly it seemed like free association (and sometimes *was* free association). The first day of Nashville sessions passed briskly enough, but none of the remaining marathon dates ended before midnight, and they usually lasted until after daybreak. Late-night work was not uncommon in Nashville, especially when Elvis Presley was recording, but McCoy relates that it "was just unheard of at that time" to devote so much studio time and money to recording any single song.

Dylan came to Nashville after playing a show in Norfolk, having resumed his touring with the Hawks (now joined by their old backup drummer, Sandy Konikoff). He was determined to finish "Visions of Johanna," the masterpiece that had initiated the entire enterprise. It emerged in its final recorded form at the first date and inside just four takes (only one of them complete). Dylan now knew what he wanted, and the sidemen quickly caught on: Kooper swirled his ghostly organ riffs around Dylan's subtle, bottom-heavy acoustic strumming and Joe South's funk hillbilly bass; Robbie Robertson's feral lead electric guitar sneaked in at the "key chain" line in the second verse; Kenny Buttrey mixed steady snare drum with tolling cymbal taps that came to the fore during Dylan's lonesome-whistle harmonica breaks. The thin, wild mercury sound hinted at in New York was now a fact, spun out of what had been the underlying triad of Kooper's organ, Dylan's harmonica, and the guitars—Dylan's acoustic and Robertson's electric. Yet Dylan was still experimenting. The date had begun with a song in 3/4 time, "4th Time Around," which critics call Dylan's reply to the Beatles' "Norwegian Wood." Like "Visions of Johanna," "4th Time Around" evolved little in the studio, and even with Charlie McCoy buttressing the band on his bass harmonica, it was a much slighter song, like Bob Dylan impersonating John Lennon impersonating Bob Dylan. In still another vein, numerous takes that reworked "Leopard-Skin Pill-Box Hat" into a sort of knock-knock joke complete with a ringing doorbell, shouts of "Who's there?" and car honks fell completely flat.

The strangest Nashville recording dates were the second and third. The second began at six in the evening and did not end until five thirty the next morning, but Dylan played only for the final ninety minutes, and on only one song: "Sad-Eyed Lady of the Lowlands." He would later call it a piece of religious carnival music, which makes sense given its faint melodic echoes of Johann Sebastian Bach, especially the chorale "Jesu, Joy of Man's Desiring." Unlike "Visions of Johanna," though, this epic needed work, and Dylan toiled over the lyrics for hours. The level of efficiency was military: hurry up and wait.

Kristofferson has described the scene: "I saw Dylan sitting out in the studio at the piano, writing all night long by himself. Dark glasses on." Bob Johnston recalled to the journalist Louis Black that Dylan did not even get up to go to the bathroom despite consuming so many Cokes, chocolate bars, and other sweets that Johnston began to think the artist was a junkie: "But he wasn't; he wasn't hooked on anything but time and space." The tired, strung-along musicians shot the breeze and played Ping-Pong while racking up their pay. (They may even have laid down ten takes of their own instrumental number, which appears on the session tape, though Charlie McCoy doesn't recollect doing this, and the recording may come from a different date.) Finally, at 4:00 a.m., Dylan was ready. "I don't think we'll take a break," he told the musicians. "Let's just make it, see what it sounds like."

"It's two verses and a chorus—five times," one of the Nashville musicians says, half-inquisitively, on the tape, just to make sure he understood right. But none of the accompanists knew what they were in for. "After you've tried to stay awake 'til four o'clock in the morning, to play something so slow and long was really, really tough," McCoy recalls. After he finished an abbreviated run-through, Dylan counted off, and the musicians fell in. Kenny Buttrey recalled that they were prepared for a two- or three-minute song and started out accordingly: "If you notice that record, that thing after like the second chorus starts building and building like crazy, and everybody's just peaking it up 'cause we thought, Man, this is it . . . After about ten minutes of this thing we're cracking up at each other, at what we were doing. I mean, we peaked five minutes ago. Where do we go from here?"

Yet if the session men were baffled, it didn't show once the tape started rolling. They were among the best artists in the business, and once they actually began playing, the song came to life about as swiftly as any of Dylan's ever had—an astonishing feat for a track that, on the album, clocked in at eleven minutes and twenty-three seconds. After a single, beautiful, complete preliminary take—with the lyrics finished and the musical arrangement, amazingly, set—that final version was done.

"NEXT!"

At the third session, the recording of another epic, "Stuck Inside of Mobile with the Memphis Blues Again," began at 4:00 a.m. after another long wait. The lyrics cohere gradually on a surviving part-typed, part-handwritten manuscript page, which begins with a standard line about honey, it being too hard (which had survived from "Medicine Sunday" at the very first New York session with the Hawks). Then the words meander through random combinations and disconnected fragments and images about people getting uglier, and musical instrument eyes, and toting a .22 caliber rifle that is really just a single shot, before suddenly, in Dylan's own hand, amid many crossings-out, there appears the first rough version of Mama being in Mobile, Alabama, with the Memphis blues again. Inside the studio, several musical revisions and false starts followed, and frustration began setting in, when suddenly, on take fourteen, everything fell into place.

There is some disagreement about what happened next. According to most accounts, based on the logs and files kept by Columbia Records, Dylan departed Nashville, then returned with Kooper and Robertson less than three weeks later to finish recording. Supposedly, Dylan, in the interim, adapted and came up with the rudiments of eight more songs, most of them in the three-and-a-half- to four-minute range, closer to the traditional pop-song form. Al Kooper, however, insists that the entire album was recorded in a single visit to Nashville, most likely in February, meaning that Dylan had all of the songs sketched out from the get-go; Charlie McCoy, too, says he remembers only one set of dates, although he also concedes he just might be mistaken. The official documented version jibes better with Dylan's known touring schedule. It also jibes with the fact that five of the eight songs first recorded after "Memphis Blues Again," but none of those recorded earlier, include a Tin Pan Alley middle-eight or bridge section—Dylan's first extensive foray as a writer into that conventional song structure.* Nevertheless, the testimony of two key participants carries weight, especially when set against an easily misconstrued paper trail.

But whether the Nashville sessions occurred in two clusters or just one, New York hip and Nashville virtuosity converged; indeed, musically, the two seem never to have been much apart. It produced enough solid material to demand an oddly configured double album, the first of its kind in contemporary popular music.

The songs recorded after "Memphis Blues Again" fell into three categories: straight-ahead eight- and twelve-bar electric blues; blistering rock and roll; and a miscellany of hip pop songs. A few of the tracks retrieved sounds from the early New York sessions with the Hawks, but in tighter and richer forms. The others ventured into entirely new territory.

The recording at the fourth Nashville date began well after midnight, with a pair of run-through takes by what sounds like an ensemble of piano, two guitars (one played by Robbie Robertson), bass, organ, and drums. Dylan, rich voiced, practically croons at times. The lyrics to what

---

* The outstanding early use of a bridge in Dylan's work appears in the verse beginning, "You have many contacts," in "Ballad of a Thin Man."

Bob Dylan, 1965.

was then called "Where Are You Tonight, Sweet Marie?" are not quite done, and Dylan sings some dummy lines ("And the eagle's teeth / Down above the train line"). The band even changes key between takes, but the song seems basically set—though, on these preliminary takes, Kenny Buttrey shifts his snare beat half a minute or so into the song and then steadily increases the layered patterns of his drumming. On the last take, the one we know from the album, Buttrey builds the complexities to the point where he is defying gravity or maybe Newton's third law of motion. By the time Dylan sings of the six white horses and of the Persian drunkard, Buttrey and the song are soaring—and then Dylan launches a harmonica break. The band stays in overdrive, but Dylan and Buttrey, pushing each other forward, nearly pop the clutch. For just under a minute, the song becomes an overpowering rock-and-roll concerto for harmonica and drums. "Absolutely Sweet Marie" is esteemed chiefly for lines like "But to live outside the law, you must be honest" and "Well, anybody can be just like me, obviously / But then, now again, not too many can be like you, fortunately"—the second phrase one of many that Dylan has freely mutated in concert over the last forty years. But with the sound of "Sweet Marie," *Blonde on Blonde* entered fully and sublimely into what is now considered classic rock and roll.

Less than twelve hours later, everybody was back in the studio to start in on what Dylan called "Like a Woman." The lyrics, once again, needed work; on several early takes, Dylan sang disconnected lines and semi-gibberish. He was unsure about what the person described in the song does that is just like a woman, rejecting "shakes," "wakes," and "makes mistakes." The improvisational spirit inspired a weird, double-time fourth take, somewhere between Bo Diddley and Jamaican ska, that on the tape finally disintegrates into a voice in the background admitting, "We lost, man." That escapade prompted a time-out. Robbie Robertson and the pianist Pig Robbins then joined the band, and laying aside "Just Like a Woman," they helped change Dylan's boogie-woogie piano number "What You Can Do with My Wigwam" into "Pledging My Time," driven by Robertson's screaming guitar. Only then, after several false starts and near misses, the final proud, pained version of "Just Like a Woman" surfaced. The concluding date produced six songs in thirteen hours of booked studio time, no time at all compared with the earlier sessions—and serendipity had not departed. They were rolling. "Most Likely You Go Your Way and I'll Go Mine" was originally a straightforward rock song, dominated by Robertson's guitar—until Charlie McCoy picked up a trumpet between takes and asked to repeat a little lick along-side Dylan on the harmonica. The song's sound changed utterly, and for the better. The boys then made quick work of "Temporary Like Achilles," ending with a performance steered by Robbins's dusky barrelhouse piano—doubtless the only stroll like it ever to carry the name of a character from the *Iliad*.

Round midnight, the mood on the session tape gets giddy. As later related by Johnston to Louis Black, Dylan had roughed out the next song on the piano.

"That sounds like the damn Salvation Army Band," Johnston said.

"Can you get one?" Dylan replied, either perplexed, inspired, joking, or a little of all three.

After a couple of quick phone calls, the trombonist Wayne "Doc" Butler showed up, the only extra musician (with McCoy playing trumpet) whom Johnston thought was needed. But at this point in the story recollections clash once again. Legend has it—and more than one of the session musicians have affirmed in great detail—that at someone's insistence, possibly Dylan's, potent marijuana got passed around, along with a batch of demonic drink ordered in from a local bar. But not everybody was interested. And Charlie McCoy, who by all accounts did not partake, denies categorically that anybody was intoxicated. "It just didn't happen," he insists, either at this session or (with isolated exceptions) at any of the many thousands of others on which he has performed in Nashville. Al Kooper, who had given up alcohol years earlier, agrees that the *Blonde on Blonde* sessions were sober and says that the hyper-professionals Dylan and Albert Grossman would never have permitted pot or drink inside the studio.

The chatter on the tape and the studio tape version of the song are, if not necessarily seriously whacked, certainly jacked up and high-spirited—much as Johnston recalled to Black, with "all of us walking around, yelling, playing, and singing. That was it!" The excited musicians chip in with their own musical ideas. When Johnston asks for the song's title, Dylan's off-the-cuff answer, "A Long-Haired Mule and a Porcupine Here" (later changed to "Rainy Day Women #12 & 35"), is perfectly in character. "It's the only one time that I ever heard Dylan really laugh, really belly-laugh, on and on, going around that studio, marching in that thing," Johnston said. In only one take, the recording is done. And, it is important to note, three more tracks would be recorded that night, all of which would appear on the album.

It is now long past the midnight hour, and songs are getting churned out at a rapid clip. After each final take, Johnston announces, "Next!" sounding, Texas drawl and all, like a New York deli counterman hustling things along. When the playing of "Black Dog Blues" (later "Obviously 5 Believers") breaks down, Dylan complains, "This is very easy, man" and "I don't wanna spend no time with this song, man." Charlie McCoy seizes a harmonica signature line; Kooper lays down a fuzzy bass run on a Lowrey organ; a percussion shaker effaces Buttrey; and Robertson blazes. In four takes, the song is done.

"Next!"

Johnston gets Dylan to start one last retake of "Leopard-Skin Pill-Box Hat" with a clangy lead guitar—"Okay," Dylan says, sounding almost boyish, before asking the other musicians to play along with him—but Robertson's searing performance abducts the song. "Robbie, the whole world'll marry you on that one," Charlie McCoy raves.

"Next!"

"I Want You" had been Kooper's favorite song all along, and he has said Dylan saved it for last just to bug him. More like "Memphis Blues Again" than like the other songs cut at this final session, "I Want You" starts off in manuscript with lyrical experiments that fail, about deputies asking him his name and being unable to explain what he wants from you. Sometimes, Dylan stopped to work on a phrase over and over, fiddling around with lines about all his fathers going down hugging one another and about their daughters putting him down because he isn't their brother, until he strikes on what more or less becomes the final version. Once Dylan has finished writing, though, little changes through five takes except the tempo. Johnston expresses surprise that Dylan can sing all the words so swiftly; Wayne Moss's rapid-fire sixteenth notes on the guitar are nearly as impressive. And then the recording of *Blonde on Blonde* ends.

GHOST, HOWLS, BONES, AND FACES

After the record was mixed in Los Angeles in April, it was obvious that the riches of the Nashville sessions could not fit on a single LP.

During the recording, dating back to October in New York, and through all of the changes in personnel, there had been some constants. Al Kooper played on every track of the final album, his contributions essential not just as a musician and impromptu arranger but also as a conduit between Dylan and the changing lineup of session men. Kooper's

Nashville roommate, Robbie Robertson, had been involved from the start and refined his playing from unsubtle rock lead to restrained, even delicate performances, along with blues keenings that won praise from some of the most discerning ears on the planet. Kooper and Robertson, familiar with Dylan's spur-of-the-moment ways, also helped as translators for the Nashville musicians, working mainly through Charlie McCoy. "They couldn't have any charts or anything, so they were following where he was putting his hand," Johnston told Black. "It was so spontaneous. Al Kooper used to call it the road map to hell!"

And, of course, dominating everything was Bob Dylan's voice, figuratively as the author and literally as one of the album's main musical instruments. Dylan did not completely relinquish his own version of what Jack Kerouac had called "spontaneous bop prosody," but crucially, in violation of Kerouac's alleged miraculous practice, Dylan constantly and carefully revised, as he always had and still does, even to the point of abandoning entire songs. Three years earlier, Dylan's deft change of a single word of "A Hard Rain's A-Gonna Fall," from "my" to "young," strengthened the song's narrative, while it brought the lyric closer to the traditional Scots song on which it was based, "Lord Randall." With the songs on *Blonde on Blonde*, the alterations were sometimes extensive and always unerring. Changing the line "I gave you those pearls" to "with her fog, her amphetamine, and her pearls" was one example out of dozens of how Dylan, in the studio and in his Nashville hotel room, improved the timbre of the songs' lyrics as well as their imagery. And Dylan's voice, as ever an evolving invention, was one of the album's touchstones, a smooth, even sweet surprise to listeners who had gotten used to him sounding harsh and raspy. By turns sibilant, sibylline, injured, cocky, sardonic, and wry, Dylan's voice on *Blonde on Blonde* more than made up in tone and phrasing what it gave away in range. It was even more challenging to sing out than it was to write out "But like Louise always says / 'Ya can't look at much, can ya, man?' / As she, herself, prepares for him," in "Visions of Johanna," but Dylan pulled it off.

Blonde on Blonde was, and remains, a gigantic peak in Dylan's career. From more than a dozen angles, it describes basic, not always flattering, human desire and the inner movements of an individual being in the world. The lyric manuscripts from the Nashville sessions show Dylan working in a 1960s mode of what T. S. Eliot had called, regretfully, the dissociation of sensibility—cutting off discursive thought or wit from poetic value, substituting emotion for coherence. Dylan had begun experimenting with that mode at least as early as 1964 in composing the songs that turned up on *Another Side,* with their obvious debts to the Beats. The less-finished lyrics-in-formation for *Blonde on Blonde* that survive in manuscript—like the archipelago of flashing images that led, finally, to intimations of "Memphis Blues Again"—became much tighter but would never completely lose their delirious quality. Along with its ruptures between image and meaning, its Rimbaud-like symbolism and Beat generation cut-up images, *Blonde on Blonde* evokes William Blake's song cycle of innocence and experience, when it depicts how they can mingle, as in "Just Like a Woman," but also when it depicts the gulf that lies between them. Many of the album's songs, for all of their self-involved temptations and frustrations, express a kind of solidarity in the struggle to live inside that gulf. Although the songs are sometimes mordant, even accusatory, they are not at all hard or cynical. *Blonde on Blonde* never degrades or mocks primary experience. Its doomed, hurtful love affairs do not negate love, or abandon efforts to remake love, to liberate it: quite the opposite, as is shown in the litanies of its concluding psalm to the mysteriously wise Sad-Eyed Lady. *Blonde on Blonde,* as finally assembled, is a disillusioned but seriously hopeful work of art.

The album is Blakean in other ways as well. As the young critic Jonny Thakkar has pointed out, there are allusions to Blake's writing in the third verse of "Visions of Johanna," where the song's perspective temporarily shifts to that of the delicate but prosaic Louise, and which mocks Louise's distracted lover, the singer, as "little boy lost." The phrase repeats the title of one selection in *Songs of Innocence* and one in *Songs of Experience,* contrapuntal poems in which Blake's little boy first is disappointed when he pursues a holy vision—"The night was dark, no father was there, / The child was wet with dew; / The mire was deep, and the child did weep, / And away the vapour flew"—and later is cruelly punished. On his earlier recordings, Dylan asked questions and supplied answers, adhering to the standard folk-ballad form if only to say that the answer was blowin' in the wind. But some of his songs on *Blonde on Blonde,* like some of Blake's poems in *Songs of Experience,* pose questions without providing any answers at all. Blake's "Tyger" consists entirely of unanswered questions—"What immortal hand or eye / Could frame thy fearful symmetry?"—and so does "Sad-Eyed Lady of the Lowlands."

The album changed how listeners and ambitious writers and performers thought about Bob Dylan and about the possibilities of rock and roll. It also affected its makers. A year later, after the breakup of the group he was

William Blake manuscript of "The Tyger," one of the poems in his collection *Songs of Experience,* published in 1794. See lower right.

in, the Blues Project, Al Kooper headed a new band that fused jazz with rock and roll and pop but took its name from an album of Johnny Cash's released in 1963, *Blood, Sweat, and Tears* (as well as from the phrase's original coiner, Winston Churchill). Soon after they finished *Blonde on Blonde,* several of the Nashville musicians reassembled as the Mystic Knights Band and Street Singers. Under the producer Bob Johnston (renamed, for the occasion, Colonel Jubilation B. Johnston), they recorded and released on Columbia one of the most obscure rock albums of the 1960s, *Moldy Goldies*—"as goofy as we could be," Charlie McCoy remembers—sending up hits from the Young Rascals' "Good Lovin' " to Sonny and Cher's "Bang Bang." They also spoofed a hit of their own, namely "Rainy Day

Women #12 & 35," except with one "Luscious Norma Jean Owen" singing instead of Bob Dylan, her southern voice hovering between coyness and confusion.

Dylan helped oversee the mixing of *Blonde on Blonde* in Los Angeles, then departed on his famous, furious world tour with the Hawks (Mickey Jones now sitting in for Levon Helm). Despite the heckling in England and France, the instant commercial success of "Rainy Day Women" back home matched the

Album sleeve of *Moldy Goldies*, Columbia Records, 1966.

earlier success of "Like a Rolling Stone," and it seemed as if Dylan's new sound had blasted away the booers for good, at least in America. Artistically complicated though it was, *Blonde on Blonde* affirmed Dylan's enormous new popularity, reaching number nine on *Billboard.* In July, though, Dylan cracked up his motorcycle on a back road outside Woodstock, and in his new seclusion he recorded near Saugerties what became known as *The Basement Tapes* with all of the Hawks, soon renamed the Band. He would not return to a Columbia recording studio until a year and a half after he'd completed *Blonde on Blonde*—back in Nashville with Charlie McCoy and Kenny Buttrey by his side, and with Bob Johnston producing, to complete *John Wesley Harding,* which was released just after Christmas. Innocence and experience remained on Dylan's mind, but the stripped-down song that took shape quickly during the first session, "Drifter's Escape," sounded completely unlike what had come before. "Everything was different," McCoy remembers, referring to the efficiency of the sessions (which required fewer than ten hours of studio time) but also to the singer's voice: "To me, he sounded almost like he was singing different." Bob Dylan refused to be locked up or pinned down, even to the rapturous sounds of *Blonde on Blonde*. He drifted, as he still drifts, toward new peaks and valleys and peaks.

PART III: LATER

5

CHILDREN OF PARADISE:

The Rolling Thunder Revue, New Haven, Connecticut, November 13, 1975

The New Haven Veterans Memorial Coliseum was an uninspiring place to see and hear the Rolling Thunder Revue. Built just three years earlier, and stretched out behind the Knights of Columbus's national headquarters tower, the building would have epitomized the drab futurism of mainstream American public architecture from the mid-1960s through the 1970s—if only it had been a little more charming and better designed. The geology of the Connecticut shoreline prevented

The Knights of Columbus tower and the New Haven Veterans Memorial Coliseum, undated photograph.

construction of an underground garage, so the architects planted a parking lot on the roof—an ill-planned as well as off-putting innovation that caused the building to crumble, until it was finally demolished in 2007. Dylan's revue was a tribute of sorts to the old-time carnivals and medicine shows, and it often performed, especially during its early weeks, in historic old theaters. Turning the New Haven Coliseum into something carnivalesque, let alone something historic, would require a great deal of stagecraft and make-believe.

Even so, there was a buzz inside, up near the front of the hall. New Haven was the closest to New York City that the revue would get until its very final date, so VIPs came up to hear one or both of the shows. Being one of the supremely unconnected—in my second year of graduate school at Yale and attending only my third Dylan concert ever, the Village long gone, my brain too full of history books and academic anxiety to have even thought too much about music for a while—I simply could not have known just how big the buzz was. Joni Mitchell had decided to join the tour in New Haven, flown into town, and slipped in through the stage door (though, alas, she only appeared in the evening performance, and I had a ticket for the matinee). The latest "new Dylan," Bruce Springsteen (whom my Yale apartment mate had seen in college and always raved about), was prowling around, and would meet with the star in Dylan's dressing room. Bill Graham, Patti Smith, and John Prine also showed up.

I was aware enough to recognize Albert Grossman standing in the aisle, no longer the scary, suited manager from *Dont Look Back,* but a white-maned, jolly-looking fellow wearing what, from a distance, looked like a campesino's white smock. Everyone else in the first ten rows or so, especially the women, was far better heeled and more glamorous than the people I'd remembered seeing at Dylan's Philharmonic Hall concert in 1964, let alone the unruly crowd I'd seen at a Dylan concert at Forest Hills one year later. Whatever this "revue" was to bring, the A-list Dylan fans had certainly become elegant, more outwardly taken with high style than a decade earlier. I forget how my roommate and I managed to score such good seats, behind the important people but downstairs and with a good full view of the stage. Most likely, we'd lucked out.

As the buzz built before the houselights dimmed, there was also an odd onstage curtain to consider. Whether it was pure circus sideshow or just mockery of one was hard to tell: a yellow contrivance depicting a faux proscenium arch (emblazoned with the revue's name) and with

Top: The opening credits of *Les enfants du paradis,* 1945. Bottom: Rolling Thunder Revue curtain, 1975.

a trompe l'oeil curtain beneath it, covered with cartoony pictures of a
he-man lifting barbells, a trained seal, and other carny acts. A man and a
woman, painted in 1890s-style gymnasts' suits and flying-trapeze boots,
stared coyly from the middle of the curtain, standing on a globe colored
in cobalt blue.

I would not make the connection until many years later, but it resembled an Americanized repeat of the opening credits to Marcel Carné's
great film of 1945, *Les enfants du paradis* (Children of Paradise)—which,
as it turns out, was very much on Dylan's mind at the time. Who knew—
and who knows? What seemed certain, though, was that we were about to
watch and listen to something very different from a rock concert, something more like a pageant or a fete.

Suddenly, unannounced, Dylan hit the stage with his band, to sing
about wasting time inside the true Coliseum, in his first number, "When
I Paint My Masterpiece." More confusion. One of the two singers up
front *sounded* like Dylan, but his face was covered by a weird, shiny semi-
transparency that turned out to be a clear plastic mask. Three minutes
into the show, Dylan had his audience thoroughly mystified, and—oddly,
happily—it didn't matter anymore that we were sitting in the New Haven
Veterans Memorial Coliseum.

Dylan's motorcycle crack-up shortly after the release of *Blonde on Blonde*
had caused him to reassess his life and his music, and prompted a prolonged withdrawal from concert touring. Yet contrary to one widespread
view, the accident did not cause a caesura, and it did not stem Dylan's
creativity. During the ensuing year, folded into the protective Woodstock
comforts of his new family and his bandmates, he completed his work
on the film *Eat the Document*, and he laid down the hours of informal
playing that became, much truncated, *The Basement Tapes* double album
in 1975. The original tapes—since analyzed imaginatively by Greil
Marcus—included a good deal of folk music and other writers' songs, but
also enough original and cowritten material, quite apart from cover versions of older songs, to fill at least two albums, and some of that material
was stunning, including "Tears of Rage," "I Shall Be Released," and "Too
Much of Nothing." In retrospect, the tapes show that when Dylan had
returned to the rock and roll of his youth in 1965 and 1966, he hardly
had severed his roots in all sorts of popular American songs, including

Bob Dylan, Woody Guthrie Memorial Concert, Carnegie Hall, New York City, January 20, 1968.

country and western, rhythm and blues, and the wide repertoire of the folk revival.

In October 1967, Dylan returned to Nashville to record the sparse, poetic *John Wesley Harding* with Bob Johnston, Charlie McCoy, and Kenny Buttrey. The album appeared in December, and over the next eight years Dylan released seven albums of original material and covers (beginning with *Nashville Skyline* and culminating in *Planet Waves* and *Blood on the Tracks,* as well as *The Basement Tapes*), an album of greatest hits, an outlaw-political-song single ("George Jackson"), the soundtrack album for *Pat Garrett and Billy the Kid,* and a double album of performances of his comeback tour with the Band in 1974. He also played with the Hawks at a Woody Guthrie memorial concert at Carnegie Hall in 1968, published a book of his lyrics and prose poems accompanied with some of his line sketches, entitled *Writings and Drawings,* and played a minor role in the Pat Garrett and Billy the Kid film, directed by Sam Peckinpah. Compared with his astonishing peak from 1962 until 1966, these have seemed like fallow artistic years for Dylan—but for any other musical artist, the results of his retrenchment would qualify as a strong achievement.

Dylan's biographers have written in detail of his personal turmoil during this period, spent largely offstage and out of the public eye: the beginnings of the fitful disintegration of his marriage to Sara Dylan, which left them basically separated by 1975; the business battles that caused him to break with his original recording label, Columbia (which in turn prompted Columbia, holding him to his contract, to release what has been called a revenge album of inferior outtakes and entitle it *Dylan*), before he returned to the label in 1974; the fierce strains with his manager, Grossman; and Dylan's ill-starred decision, in 1969, to move his growing family back to the heart of Greenwich Village, followed by a later relocation to Malibu.

Dylan also spoke of a kind of artistic crisis, as if, despite his productivity, he had lost touch with his basic gifts and aspirations. "It's like I had amnesia all of a sudden . . . I couldn't learn what I had been able to do naturally—like *Highway 61 Revisited.* I mean, you can't sit down and write that consciously because it has to do with the break-up of time." The "amnesia" became so bad that by 1974, Dylan felt as if, while chasing his muse, he was only going "down, down, down . . . I was convinced I wasn't going to do anything else." Yet Dylan remained open to fresh ideas—as much now, perhaps, as at any time since his career began.

One of Dylan's more interesting experiments—from the vantage point of his cultural genealogy, one of the richest; from that of his aesthetic, one of the most profound—had to do not with songwriting and performing but with painting. Dylan's lyrics had always contained especially strong visual as well as narrative elements. In "Visions of Johanna," he even wittily described the paintings in the museums where infinity goes up on trial, including Mona Lisa with the highway blues. During the Australia leg of the 1966 tour, he sometimes introduced one song as the tale of a painter with the name of an old P. T. Barnum circus performer who lived near Juárez, Mexico, and who had had an especially productive "blue period": hence (ha, ha!), "Just Like Tom Thumb's Blues." In 1968, one of his own paintings, of various musicians and an onlooking circus elephant, served as album art for the debut album of the reborn Hawks, the Band's *Music from Big Pink,* and in the early 1970s, when Dylan sang of one day painting his masterpiece, he also made a painted self-portrait as the cover art for his double album *Self Portrait,* and featured some of his drawings in the new book of song lyrics and writings.

Dylan's early absorption in Woody Guthrie's work included Guthrie's whimsical pencil drawings, which obviously influenced Dylan's own sketches, as published in *Writings and Drawings.* His surviving song manuscripts dating back to the early 1960s contain several elaborate sketches and doodles. Suze Rotolo, a fine professional artist, had encouraged him to take his interests deeper, helping him to appreciate the work of, among others, her favorite, Red Grooms, whose madcap creations seem also to have influenced Dylan's drawings. Dylan also delved into New York's museums and saw many things for the first time, including an exhibition of Gauguin paintings at the Metropolitan Museum of Art. "I found I could stand in front of any one of them for as long as I'd sit in the movies," he later recounted, "yet not get tired on my feet. I'd lose all sense of time."

In the spring of 1974, after his tour with the Band, Dylan turned up at the studio of the painter and instructor Norman Raeben on the eleventh floor of Carnegie Hall—and immediately, whether he knew it or not, encountered a rich set of historical links, as well as a formidable, charismatic new teacher. Born in Russia in 1901, Raeben was the youngest child of the great émigré Yiddish writer Sholem Aleichem (born Sholem Naumovich Rabinovich), whose vast output of novels and stories on shtetl life earned him a reputation as "the Jewish Mark Twain." (Sholem Aleichem became best known, nearly half a century after his death in

1916, for his stories about Tevye the milkman, which became the source for the musical *Fiddler on the Roof*.) From his father, Raeben learned to regard the sacred texts of Judaism not simply as religious and philosophical but as deeply metaphorical evocations of suffering and endurance, open to the realm of imagination—and fit for appropriation, alternatively comic and dark, as he sprinkled holy verse, sometimes in mangled form, in the speeches of his most ordinary characters, from Tevye to the *schlimazel* Menakhem-Mendl.

Having moved with his family to New York in 1914, young Norman studied painting with some of the leading lights of the so-called Ashcan school, including Robert Henri, John Sloan, and George Luks. Six years before Sholem Aleichem arrived with his family, Henri, Sloan, Luks, and five other painters had caused a sensation with a group exhibition at the Macbeth Gallery of their realist pictures, many of which showed rough, poverty-stricken sides of Manhattan life. The work of the painters known loosely as the Eight, and especially Henri, would influence the work of their associate George Bellows, Edward Hopper, and, in time, the younger Norman Raeben.

At some point before 1920, Raeben returned to Europe to connect with the more dynamic taproots of artistic innovation—which meant traveling to Paris. There, by his own account, he fell in with the bohemian circles that included Pablo Picasso, Marc Chagall, Amedeo Modigliani, and (most important) the expressionist Chaim Soutine, with whom, he said, he shared lodgings. (Raeben's widow, Victoria, later denied his more high-flown claims, although he may at least have been Soutine's neighbor.) Soutine's love of old masters, whom he studied in the Louvre, translated into heavy, bursting brushwork that could convey tenderness as easily as it did turbulence. The combination of inner expression, traditional influence, and Jewish metaphor, as transformed by Raeben—like him, Soutine, Chagall, and much

Norman Raeben, circa 1974.

of his circle were Jews—would have a profound effect on Bob Dylan's songwriting. But by the 1970s, Raeben had given himself over mainly to teaching about both art and Judaism—in a studio fittingly located in defiant independence directly across Fifty-seventh Street from the Art Students League, where Luks, Bellows, Sloan, and Henri had taught.

Norman Raeben's *Times Square*, circa 1959–63, 24" x 16", oil on linen.

Dylan, who had heard of Raeben from Sara's friend Robin Fertik, sought Raeben out with the intention of learning more about Jewish philosophy, but he ended up spending two months working at Raeben's studio, five days a week, from eight thirty until four. Dylan later described his fellow pupils as a thrown-together assortment: "rich old ladies from Florida—standing next to an off-duty policeman, standing next to a bus driver, a lawyer. Just all kinds." Dylan does not appear to have been anyone special, at least to Raeben, who, though he knew of Dylan's fame, regularly berated him as an idiot (much as he did the other students). It is unclear how much the sessions actually improved Dylan's sketching and painting; at neither would he ever become especially skilled. But Dylan credited Raeben with nothing less than teaching him "how to see," by putting "my mind and my hand and my eye together, in a way that allowed me to do consciously what I unconsciously felt."

Dylan has from time to time spoken of mentors whose principles or systems pulled him out of an artistic and spiritual trough. In the first volume of *Chronicles,* he relates how recalling a particular "mathematical" tone structure that he had learned years earlier from the old blues star Lonnie Johnson helped revitalize his playing in the mid-1980s. With Raeben, he learned to eschew conceptualization (the bane, in Raeben's view, of the contemporary art scene), and to see things plain, as they really are, always aware of perspective, both straight on and from above, simultaneously. He also learned how to abandon the sense of linear time

to which he had clung automatically, and to understand the artistic possibilities of pulling together the past, present, and future, as if they were
of a piece, permitting a clearer, more concentrated focus on the objects
or object at hand.

That summer of 1974, working mainly in a house around back on a
farm he had purchased in Minnesota alongside the Crow River (with his
brother David's house in front, closer to the road), Dylan pored over a
small red notebook, writing lyrics for a new album that would capture the
wounds, scars, and sorrowed wisdom of love. His writing included, early
on, what would become "Tangled Up in Blue," a song he would later
describe as directly beholden to Raeben:

> I was just trying to make it like a painting where you can see the
> different parts but then you also see the whole of it. With that
> particular song, that's what I was trying to do . . . with the concept
> of time, and the way the characters change from the first person to
> the third person, and you're never quite sure if the third person is
> talking or the first person is talking. But as you look at the whole
> thing, it really doesn't matter.

Nor did it matter who the "she" was in the song, or how many shes
there really were, or when anything happened; the song hangs together
as one that took ten years for Dylan to live and two years for him to
write.

Indeed, it appears that Raeben affected Dylan and "Tangled Up in
Blue" in several ways. Manic, brusque, and unsparing, Raeben would
dress down his pupils as a means to help instruct them, sometimes revising students' work right on the canvas in his loose rapid style, to show
them how it was done. According to the artist John Amato, another student of Raeben's at the time, Dylan was one day painting a still life of
a vase—the quintessential artistic effort to stop time—and was working heavily in blue, a favorite pigment of novice students, when Raeben
looked at the canvas dismissively, telling Dylan that he was all tangled
up in blue. A few days later, Amato recalls, Dylan astonished his fellow
students by bringing in lyrics of a now unknown song with that title. He
would do the same, as far as his fellow students could tell, when he used
as a title one of Raeben's favorite terms of abuse, "Idiot Wind"—although
the phrase more likely came from the poem "June 1940" by the proto-

Beat writer and composer, legendary in older underground literary and artistic circles, Weldon Kees.*

The new album, *Blood on the Tracks,* was full of blues, although only one song, "Meet Me in the Morning," was written in standard twelve-bar form. It included songs of longing, gratitude, and fury, and an elliptical narrative about the Jack of Hearts that sounded like brave, possibly self-inflating allegory (even if it wasn't). It ended with a grace note of hope, "Buckets of Rain."

Some of the stanzas in some of the songs were painterly. Part of "Simple Twist of Fate" (alternatively titled "Fourth Street Affair") took place inside "a strange hotel with a neon burnin' bright":

He woke up, the room was bare
He didn't see her anywhere
He told himself he didn't care, pushed the window open wide
Felt an emptiness inside to which he just could not relate
Brought on by a simple twist of fate.

Dylan's lyrics of aloneness conjured up the spirit and even the composition of a Hopper canvas.

Curiously, *Blood on the Tracks,* now widely considered one of Dylan's greatest albums, met with some harsh reviews upon its release in January 1975, as critics complained chiefly about what one called the "indifferent" musicianship of Dylan's accompanists. Perhaps the sustained mood of

---

* Published in the September/October 1940 issue of *Partisan Review,* "June 1940" concluded: "It is summer again, the evening is warm and silent. / The windows are dark and the mountains are miles away. / And the men who were haters of war are mounting the platforms. / An idiot wind is blowing; the conscience dies." Although in keeping with what was the Communist Party line at the time of the Nazi-Soviet pact, the poem in fact reflected a broader antiwar view, common among intellectuals who had come of age in the disillusioned decades after World War I, and who did not want to see the United States again involved in an imperial European war. Kees, a Nebraskan who visited New York in 1940 and moved there in 1943, frequented left-wing anti-Stalinist literary circles that included Lionel Trilling and Dwight Macdonald, among other *Partisan Review* writers, but he later turned to painting, and became a notable figure among the early abstract expressionists of the so-called New York school. Kees's involvement in music composition and criticism deepened after he relocated to the San Francisco Bay area in 1950, where he mysteriously disappeared five years later. Thanks to Nina Goss for the reference.

resigned melancholy, occasionally broken by songs such as "Idiot Wind" and "Lily, Rosemary, and the Jack of Hearts," blocked listeners from hearing the first mature musical reflections to come out of the 1960s and early 1970s by a popular artist who had survived them. But no matter; Dylan flew the coop and spent several weeks during the late spring of 1975 in France with the artist David Oppenheim, staying in touch by phone with Sara but spending much of his time in aimless, amiable dissolution, at one point meeting the king of the Gypsies in southern France.* Then, at the end of June, he turned up again in Greenwich Village.

At some point that spring, according to Roger McGuinn, erstwhile mainstay of the Byrds, he and Dylan were tossing basketballs around at McGuinn's home in Malibu. Dylan suddenly paused, grabbed a ball, stared out at the ocean, and said that he wanted to do "something different."

Knowing that "different" could mean just about anything to Dylan, McGuinn asked what he had in mind.

"I don't know . . . something like a circus."

At the Rolling Thunder concert in New Haven, "When I Paint My Masterpiece" opened the show, booming and stately, with Dylan and Bob Neuwirth singing a duo that was a little ragged but forceful. With full orchestration, including a running mandolin line that sounded more Eye-tie than Okie, it was wholly different from the acoustic version of the song that had found its way onto a greatest-hits compilation a few years earlier. Above all, Dylan seemed to have a pent-up vehemence in his voice, at once elongating and spitting out the line about wishing he were back in the land of Coca-Cola—"Co-HO-LA," he sang it, as if he wanted to make sure we knew exactly what that last word was. Musicians strayed all over the stage, none of them recognizable to me. At the song's end, Dylan lifted what looked like a flower-bedecked sombrero to take

---

* Dylan has also claimed that Raeben's influence had by then added new strains to Dylan's marriage to Sara. "Needless to say, it changed me," he told Pete Oppel. "I went home after that and my wife never did understand me ever since that day. That's when our marriage started breaking up. She never knew what I was talking about, what I was thinking about, and I couldn't possibly explain it." Dylan quoted in Andy Gill and Kevin Odegard, *A Simple Twist of Fate: Bob Dylan and the Making of "Blood on the Tracks"* (New York, 2004), 39.

off his mask, and sure enough it was certainly he, the now-unmasked marvel—except that Dylan's face, which at first just looked pale, turned out to be covered by a thin coating of white makeup, or this is how I have remembered it. Because I have seen so much film from the tour of Dylan in thicker streaks of whiteface, my memory could be faulty (though photographers still seem to bear me out), just as I may be wrong about his wearing a plastic mask in New Haven.

Dedicated by Dylan, quickly, to Leonardo da Vinci, the performance of "It Ain't Me, Babe" turned the old favorite into another new song, performed with a syncopated, semi-reggae beat, highlighted musically by a concluding trading-off between rippling pedal steel guitar and Dylan's first brief but blistering solo on his mouth harp (which brought great cheers from the audience). When Dylan and the band next played "The Lonesome Death of Hattie Carroll," one of the finest songs he would ever write, with a deliberate thumping beat, it became even more obvious that Dylan's vehemence was a matter of diction and enunciation—that rather than slurring in a folkie drawl he was making certain that no syllable of the ballad could be mistaken.

Then the proceedings began getting truly weird. Dylan introduced a tall, raven-haired female fiddler as Scarlet Rivera, knowing full well that she was a stranger to us all, but he spoke as if she should be a friend. "We're gonna dedicate this to Sam Peckinpah," he continued. Everyone recognized who *he* was—*Pat Garrett and Billy the Kid* had been released nearly two years earlier—but it seemed odd to call the name of a filmmaker, until the band moved into "Romance in Durango" from the as-yet-unreleased *Desire,* which began with a line about hot chili peppers and sounded appropriately south of the border.

Everything went haywire during the next number. Dylan laid down his guitar, said something about "a true story," and proceeded to act out another new song that started out being about diamonds and the world's biggest necklace—a song I mistook to be about someone or something or some things called "Ices." Punctuated by a blasting harmonica riff with the band in full swell, this was plainly rock music, but it also sounded incantatory, as if Dylan were half-reciting, half-shouting a bizarre short story while stretching out his arms and waving his fingers. The lyrics were completely unfamiliar and, thus, hard to follow, no matter how cleanly Dylan punched them out. Only when the band quieted for the lines beginning, "She said, 'Where you been?' " did I begin to catch that this was a song about yet another romantic pas de deux. But "Ices" was soon done, Dylan announced an intermission, and the houselights rose. Everybody cheered and applauded, and some people whistled, but what had just happened deeply perplexed me, and I could not have been alone.

The curtain was prominently in place onstage after the break; from behind it came guitar-strumming sounds, and the curtain slowly rose to reveal Dylan and Joan Baez singing "The Times They Are A-Changin'." Dylan was wearing his first-half sombrero gear, including a vest and flowing scarf; Baez, dressed in what looked like gigantically flared blue bell bottoms, had her trademark long hair cropped to her shoulders; and so the duo weren't the same as in 1964, and yet they were, at least aurally— a numinous throwback to an earlier, more earnest time. "Thank you," Dylan replied to the applause; then he called out, "Bob Dylan and Joan Baez"—announcing himself in the third person, as if we had just seen the return of a beloved but bygone act, as if the Bob Dylan doing the talking were not the same person who had just performed. He was playing around with his persona again, and hers, and he was mixing up the past with the present.

Dylan and Baez—or was it "Dylan and Baez"?—sang four more numbers, none of them familiar from their old repertoire together: Merle Travis's mining song from the mid-1940s "Dark as a Dungeon"; a new, bouncy arrangement of "I Dreamed I Saw St. Augustine" from *John Wesley Harding* (which Dylan dedicated to the people of Lowell, Massachusetts); Johnny Ace's 1950s rhythm-and-blues ballad hit "Never Let Me Go"; and "I Shall Be Released," dedicated to Richard Manuel, and accompanied by the backup band. The little duet concert within the revue had wafted back and forth from country music from before the folk revival to reworked Dylan compositions from his not-so-quiet years of retreat in Woodstock, leavened by a scoop of early soul. In its own way, the dreamlike set encapsulated—musically, visually, and spiritually—how Dylan had pulled together the circus that he had forecast, vaguely, to Roger McGuinn.

"Roger!" Dylan shouted, spilling drinks all over the table as he sprang up to embrace his friend. "Where you been, man, we been waiting for you all night."

It was after 2:00 a.m., sometime in late October 1975. McGuinn had been in Gerde's Folk City before he went down to Chinatown for

Joan Baez and Bob Dylan in the Rolling Thunder Revue, performing in New Haven, Connecticut, on November 13, 1975.

a meal with his band's guitarist, his road manager, and the writer Larry Sloman, from whose book about the Rolling Thunder Revue this story comes. When they had finished eating, Sloman persuaded McGuinn not to return to his hotel but to stop for a nightcap at the old Bitter End on Bleecker Street (which had been closed and reopened as the Other End), where McGuinn had played years earlier as an accompanist for the clean-cut Chad Mitchell Trio. "C'mon Roger," Sloman importuned, "I hear Dylan just got into town and even if he's not there I'm sure Levy'll be there," meaning Jacques Levy, the Off-Broadway director who had co-written McGuinn's best-known post-Byrds number, "Chestnut Mare." The night finally ended at four in the morning, in the Kettle of Fish bar, with Dylan, animated, very much the center of action and attention, talking about his new cause, which was to win freedom for the imprisoned prizefighter Rubin "Hurricane" Carter. He mused about old friends and rivals like Phil Ochs and talked about his impending and practically impromptu tour. He offhandedly invited McGuinn and Sloman to join the troupe as, respectively, performer and scribe.

The largely—though not completely—haphazard recruitment for the tour matched Dylan's improvisational instincts, but it was also the product of Dylan's return to a familiar staging ground, safe and surrounded by new friends and old. As the summer began, the Village was fairly desolate: New York's fiscal woes had become critical, and the old downtown coffeehouse scene had long since succumbed to an influx of head shops, fast-food joints, and schlocky "hippie" clothing stores. Things began happening, quietly, once Dylan started popping up late in June. Just before the Fourth of July weekend, he joined Ramblin' Jack Elliott onstage at the Other End and played several numbers, including the debut of a new song, "Abandoned Love"; later in the summer, he recorded a backing harmonica track for a studio album by David Blue. Word got around that Dylan was back in town when he wasn't holed up out on Long Island with Jacques Levy, working on a new batch of songs; then, in late July, Dylan recorded the songs at the Columbia studio in midtown with an ever-changing pickup band (which included, at one session, both Eric Clapton and Emmylou Harris). Old-timers as well as denizens of the rising punk rock scene along the Bowery—including the new sensation, Patti Smith—played at and frequented the remaining folkie outposts, Gerde's, the Other End, and the Kettle of Fish.

The culmination came on October 22, when Dylan and friends gathered for an appearance by David Blue at the Other End, followed the night after by an invitation-only surprise birthday party for Gerde's owner, Mike Porco, which Sloman's book describes well. The very next day, Dylan finished up work on the new album, *Desire,* and on October 30, after only a couple of days' worth of spur-of-the-moment rehearsing, the Rolling Thunder Revue opened in Plymouth, Massachusetts. Maybe, it occurred to me much later, that mask of Dylan's had something to do with Halloween.

Although the roster was not exactly a "come one, come all" affair, it amply reflected Dylan's past. From the old Village scene, Ramblin' Jack Elliott (Woody Guthrie's living alter ego) and Bob Neuwirth (Dylan's sharp-tongued sidekick from the mid 1960s who had reestablished himself, in New York, as one of Dylan's alter egos) made the cut; bloated, hollow-eyed Phil Ochs (who would commit suicide five months later) and a disappointed Eric Andersen did not. Dylan deepened the tour's 1960s connection by inviting Joan Baez, who, after citing her own schedule, signed on. Roger McGuinn was another link, as was the lesser-known David Blue (who would not actually perform onstage), as were Allen Ginsberg and Peter Orlovsky (who were supposed to be, respectively, the tour's bard and the chief baggage handler), as was the Beat-circle poet Anne Waldman. Going back a bit further was the rock and roller Ronnie Hawkins, whose former accompanists the Hawks, later the Band, had been Dylan's steady backup musicians until now.

Yet Dylan had no intention of touring in an oldies show. Patti Smith amiably turned him down, but one of her old boyfriends, the up-and-coming playwright Sam Shepard, signed on, ostensibly to help write the screenplay for a movie Dylan hoped to make out of the show. Totally out of the blue, Dylan also hired Mick Ronson, lately the lead guitarist in David Bowie's glitter band, the Spiders from Mars. From the *Desire* sessions band, he recruited the bassist and bandleader Rob Stoner (lately a member of the band Jake and the Family Jewels, performing as Raquin Rob Rothstein), the drummer Howie Wyeth (a nephew of the painter Andrew Wyeth), and the violinist Scarlet Rivera, whom Dylan had spied walking down Second Avenue, brought in for an audition, and hired on the spot. When Emmylou Harris dropped off the scene, Dylan signed up Ronee Blakley, a singer best known for her role in Robert Altman's recently released film, *Nashville,* for which she would win an Oscar nomination, and whom Dylan met at the David Blue show at the Other End barely a week before the tour began. The Fort Worth–raised guitarist T Bone Burnett, the multi-instrumentalist David Mansfield (not yet twenty and most recently a member of a band called Quacky Duck and His Barnyard Friends), and the percussionist Luther Rix (who had played congas on "Hurricane" and earlier recorded as a sideman with, among others, Bette Midler) filled out the band, although space on the bill was set aside for other performers to join once the tour had picked up steam.

There was never any question who the star was, but Baez (singing solo as well as in duets with Dylan), Elliott, McGuinn, Blakley, Neuwirth, and (during her brief stints on the tour) Joni Mitchell all got their individual turns. Ginsberg was supposed to recite poetry, but almost all of these appearances were cut; Ginsberg did appear onstage, though, for what became the revue's nightly closing number, "This Land Is Your Land." The rest of the musically motley congregation took the band name Guam, which, depending on which source you believe, signified either a place that none of the band members had ever visited or the island from which U.S. bombers had taken off on their first set of runs over Vietnam in 1965, under the official military name Operation Rolling Thunder.

Another odd refraction—and updating—of old times was Dylan's championing of the ex-middleweight Rubin "Hurricane" Carter. After never quite living up to his enormous promise in the ring, Carter had been convicted of first-degree murder in connection with a robbery-related shoot-out that killed three people at a bar and grill in Paterson, New Jersey, in 1966.* Carter insisted that he had been framed, singled out because of what he called his staunch advocacy of civil rights and criticism of police brutality; the police and prosecution contended that he had been part of a revenge killing following the murder by a white man of a black tavern owner in his own Paterson establishment a few hours earlier. In 1974 Carter published his side of the story as a book, *The 16th Round,* and sent a copy to Dylan. The singer took the book with him to France, found the story compelling, visited Carter in Rahway State Prison after he returned to the States, and rallied to the former boxer's defense.

---

* Dylan and Jacques Levy's song "Hurricane" states that, at the time of the murders, Carter was "Number one contender for the middleweight crown." In fact, Carter did fight the reigning middleweight champion, Joey Giardello, for the title, but at the end of 1964, and he lost in a unanimous decision. Never ranked higher than number three by *Ring* magazine, Carter suffered a rapid fall-off after the Giardello fight, losing four out of five matches against top contenders in 1965, and losing three of his six fights in 1966, including his final bout, less than two months after the murders, against Juan "Rocky" Rivero. Carter, well past his prime, had by then slipped to number nine in the *Ring* ratings.

Two years before the slaying in Paterson, Dylan was singing in concert about professional boxing as cruel, exploitative, and immoral, in one of his early songs of protest, "Who Killed Davey Moore?":

"Not me," says the man whose fists
    Laid him low in a cloud of mist,
Who came here from Cuba's door
    Where boxing ain't allowed no more.
"I hit him, yes, it's true,
    But that's what I am paid to do.
Don't say 'murder,' don't say 'kill.'
    It was destiny, it was God's will."

Now Dylan was sticking up for a fighter who, he would later write, "could take a man out with just one punch," but who truly fought just to make money and then be on his way, "up to some paradise"—a soulful man who, Dylan believed, had been railroaded because he was black and had a reputation as a militant, a "revolutionary bum" to white people, a "crazy nigger" to blacks.

This was not exactly the story of Medgar Evers or Hattie Carroll—but it was a story, Dylan was convinced, of gross official manipulation and racial injustice, regular themes in his earlier writing. Dylan had stepped away from political movements long ago, but now he had found a single cause he could help lead. By writing and recording a song, he told his friends and associates, he would help set Hurricane Carter free.

As the Rolling Thunder tour got under way, Dylan was leaning on Columbia to release his song about Carter as a single and to do so as quickly as possible, in order to achieve maximum political effect; "Hurricane, Parts 1 and 2" duly appeared in November. It was the sole song from *Desire* that would be available in stores while the revue was touring, which was more than strange. This was still an age when artists and their record labels scheduled tours in order to promote newly released recordings (whereas today, thanks to downloading and the Internet, recordings often do more to help promote the concert tours). Dylan had never completely heeded the convention; the three newly written songs he performed at the Halloween concert in 1964, for example, did not appear on record for nearly five months. Still, according to the merchandising wisdom of the day, a Dylan tour in the fall of 1975 made little sense. (The album would not finally appear until just after New Year's.) But Dylan was on fire, eager to perform his newest work, and not just "Hurricane," along with revised versions of older material.

All of this—the collapsing of old and new, the impulsiveness, the additional elements of poetry and politics—meant that the Rolling Thunder enterprise would be utterly different from Dylan's tour with the Band in 1974. And at the very heart of the show, the music was bound to be something new, as Dylan and his bandmates experimented with rock and folk-music sounds, in combinations as yet unheard. It would further complicate any comprehension of what the Rolling Thunder Revue was supposed to be, and what it actually was.

When the "Bob Dylan and Joan Baez" duets ended, Baez departed the stage, and Dylan performed "Tangled Up in Blue," solo, on acoustic guitar and harmonica. It was one of only two performances during the entire concert of a song, already released, that sounded reasonably close to the recording, and Dylan sang and played it beautifully. Yet even now, he did not ignore the injunction to make it new.

As a crude audience bootleg tape of the concert affirms, Dylan changed the pronouns in the second verse, removing any sense that the singer was the man described in the song. He changed a pronoun and more in the next verse. "He"—not "I"—"had a job in Santa Fe, working in an old hotel," Dylan sang:

> But he knew he didn't like it all that much,
> And one day it just went to hell,
> So he drifted down to New Orleans,
> Lucky not to be destroyed,
> Lived for a while on a fishing boat,
> Docked outside of Delacroix.

This darkened the song considerably. Dylan also cut my favorite verse in the song (which I missed at the time), about reading poetry by an Italian poet from the thirteenth century. In the final verse, he vowed to get back to "them," not "her." The former friends who originally had become "carpenters' wives" had now become "truck drivin' wives."

Dylan's onstage lyric improvisations over the succeeding decades, notably with "Tangled Up in Blue," have become one of his concert trademarks, and they can sometimes sound like mere exercises in verbal dexterity.* But changing the pronouns in "Tangled Up in Blue"—the pronouns being, as Dylan himself has said, one of the keys to the song—matters a great deal, in this instance distancing the singer from the stories in his song while diminishing the song's romance. Above all, maybe, Dylan showed that he had written a song whose meanings could change as much and as often as he desired, by flipping just a word or two.†

After the applause died, Dylan returned to the microphone. "I want to dedicate this to Brigham Young," he said—a funny if slightly screwy introduction to a song that began, "Oh, sister," the song's eventual title on *Desire*. Playing slowly, Dylan's guitar and harmonica interwove with Rivera's violin to form a new variation on the thin, wild mercury sound. (Curiously, after the years of playing with Paul Griffin, Al Kooper, and Garth Hudson, Dylan did not include a keyboard on the Rolling Thunder Revue apart from some occasional piano playing by Howie Wyeth; he worked out a different timbre with Rivera and David Mansfield's fiddles and Mansfield's pedal steel guitar.) Yet as the song proceeded—Dylan's words were easy to understand here—it turned into a demand for sex as a woman's religious duty, and the Brigham Young dedication didn't seem odd at all, and *that* was deeply odd. This song's holy seduction lines were very different from the jokey, hip "If You Gotta Go, Go Now" of 1964. The new song's lyric "We died and were reborn / And then mysteriously saved" sounded more evangelical Christian than Mormon, but certainly sacred. The last verse—saying, basically, sleep with me tonight, for tomorrow I may be gone—was more in the old Dylan vein, even the traditional ballad vein, but did not efface the song's sanctified injunctions. Since when had Dylan become so *religious*?

---

* On the other hand, Dylan almost completely changed the lyrics of "If You See Her, Say Hello" during the opening show in Florida of the second leg of the Rolling Thunder Revue, in 1976. What had once been a wistful song of separation and loss became an embittered diatribe, the singer hoping he will have the strength to spurn his ex-lover when she (inevitably) returns, and including such nastiness as: "If you're makin' love to her / Watch it from the rear / You never know when I'll be back / Or liable to appear."

† If Dylan did improvise the changes in New Haven, he liked them enough to stick with them, more or less, during his handful of subsequent performances of "Tangled Up in Blue" on the tour. Listen, for example, to the version recorded just over a week later in Boston, on the official Sony/Legacy Recordings release *Live 1975: The Rolling Thunder Revue*.

Then the revue took another sharp turn. " 'Hurricane,' " Dylan said. The audience clapped hard, having already heard Dylan's new political cause song as a 45 rpm single, and there were yelps as soon as Scarlet Rivera's fiddle started keening.

Although known early on as a protest singer, Dylan had never been consistently good at writing narrative songs out of the newspaper head-lines.* Some of Dylan's early compositions about civil rights and vari-ous injustices—"The Death of Emmett Till" and "Ballad of Donald White"—sounded forced and formulaic, and they concluded with plati-tudes. "Oxford Town" was better, its anger leavened by a sense of unhe-roic, even comical idiosyncrasy, in its lines about how "me and my gal, my gal's son / we got met with a tear gas bomb" and turned tail for home.

"Only a Pawn in Their Game" was a major advance, bidding listen-ers to understand the inner and outer worlds of the white racist who had murdered the civil-rights leader Medgar Evers. With fierce inter-nal rhymes—"From the poverty shacks, he looks from the cracks to the tracks / And the hoofbeats pound in his brain"—Dylan shifted the onus of moral condemnation from white supremacy alone to murkier areas of politics and class. The dramaturgy of racial conflict turned out not to be as simple as Dylan had depicted it in "Emmett Till." "Only a Pawn"—which Dylan sang to the crowd at the March on Washington in August 1963—forced its listeners of goodwill to think again, and think much harder, about a struggle they thought they fully understood.

Then, in "The Lonesome Death of Hattie Carroll," Dylan created a surpassing work of art—a song of indignation about an incident that, unlike the others he had written about, might easily have gone unnoticed. The song is perfectly economical and at times almost hushed; its lyrics, like its outrage, are completely under control. Recall the verse about Hat-tie Carroll and her children, never sitting once at the head of the table, not even speaking to those at the table, just cleaning up all the food from the table—the table, the table, the table, Dylan's rendering of that element of oppression which is deadening monotony. The song's conclu-

---

* Interestingly, Dylan's true-life "protest" ballads did not include his best-known antiwar songs. Although it is often linked to the Cuban missile crisis, he first performed "A Hard Rain's A-Gonna Fall" in September 1962, a few weeks before the crisis, and Dylan took pains to deny that it had anything to do with nuclear fallout. "Masters of War" was an imprecation, and not, strictly speaking, a "topical" song; "John Brown," a ballad reminiscent of Dalton Trumbo's antiwar novel of 1939, *Johnny Got His Gun,* was wholly fictional.

sion required changing only a few words in the four-line chorus—turning "Take" into a fearsome "Bury," "away from" into "deep in," and "ain't" into another elision, "now's"—to deliver Dylan's devastating point: that what's truly so terrible isn't the kitchen maid Hattie Carroll's lonesome death as much as the law's injustice.

Compared with "Hattie Carroll," Dylan's single "George Jackson," appearing eight years later, marked a huge decline. Dylan apparently dashed off the song and recorded it instantly in November 1971, after reading an account of the jailed black Marxist militant's death in a prison shoot-out three months earlier. Whatever information he had about what happened, Dylan, plainly, was sincerely moved, less by the story's politics than by its broader human dimensions. Yet the song is a trifle, and may even be worse than a trifle. Musically, the bright, upbeat melody sounds almost ghoulish when it carries insincere lines like "They killed a man I really loved / Shot him through the head." Although Dylan took literary license with the story of Hattie Carroll (including melodramatic touches that enraged the song's protagonist, William Zantzinger, for the rest of his life), the changes did not mar the song's artistry. By contrast, the ellipses and sentimentalism in "George Jackson" are the stuff of agitprop, and so is the song's concluding grand cliché about the world being divided between prisoners and guards.* "George Jackson" did mark the first time Dylan recorded an offending four-letter word—"He wouldn't take shit from no one"—which may have been calculated partly to instigate radio stations into censorship. If so, it worked, as station directors beeped out the offensive word on the air—but no great uproar ensued and the First Amendment survived.

Dylan himself seems to have had second thoughts about "George

---

* The song tells of Jackson's imprisonment, at age eighteen, for a seventy-dollar armed robbery of a gas station, but says nothing about his previous run-ins with the law, nor about his alleged participation in the killing of a prison guard in 1970, nor about the foiled violent effort, shortly thereafter, to free three San Quentin inmates, a spectacular incident led by Jackson's younger brother, Jonathan, that ended in the slaying, by police, of a judge taken hostage, two of the prisoners, and young Jackson. Nor was Dylan bothered about the contested facts surrounding George Jackson's death. Instead, the song takes for granted and then romanticizes the version of events propagated by left-wing publicists and intellectuals at home and abroad, including Michel Foucault and Jean Genet, who called Jackson's death a "political assassination." Although Dylan, working from his gut, crafted his response in human and not political terms—and although, as ever, he was an artist, not a political spokesman—the song amounted to a strangled piece of political advocacy.

Jackson," and he has never performed it in public. "Hurricane" did not fare much better, in the long run. Just prior to the Rolling Thunder tour, Dylan said he hoped Carter would be freed in ninety days: "That's our slogan, ninety days or we fight." The tour would end its first leg six weeks later in a gigantic benefit performance for Carter, dubbed "The Night of the Hurricane," at Madison Square Garden, and at the start of the new year the revue recapped the benefit in Houston. Carter, meanwhile, won an appeal for a new trial in 1976—later than the ninety days Dylan had vowed, but a victory. A second jury, though, convicted him for a second time and again sentenced him to life in prison. The New Jersey Supreme Court upheld the conviction in 1982. Three years later, a federal judge overturned the conviction; New Jersey authorities decided it was unfeasible to mount a third trial; and more than twenty years after the murders, Carter, finally free, relocated to Toronto, Canada, where he still resides. By the time Carter left prison, though, Dylan had long since abandoned any public interest in the case; indeed, as of the end of 2009, he had not performed "Hurricane" in concert for well over thirty years, since the Houston benefit at the start of 1976.

Coming five years after Nixon's invasion of Cambodia and the trial in New Haven of the Black Panther Bobby Seale, and more than a year after Nixon's resignation over Watergate, "Hurricane" sounded stale as a political provocation. Yet, just as with "George Jackson," Dylan's simple sincerity was hard to question. He easily (perhaps all too easily) construed Carter much as he had Jackson—as a tough, politically aware black man who, deep down, was a literate, beautiful soul and who had been locked up by a rigged and racist legal system. And there was an additional angle—for even though Dylan defended Carter's innocence, the aura of robbery, violence, and prison also struck the old ballad chord of the charming romantic outlaw, from Robin Hood to Pretty Boy Floyd. It was the same romance that led Dylan to write another song for *Desire* that glorified the brief life and violent death of the Brooklyn mobster Joey Gallo, a convicted racketeer and gang boss who read Victor Hugo and Albert Camus and who built close ties to black gangsters.

"Hurricane" is vastly inferior to "Hattie Carroll" and "Only a Pawn," but aesthetically an improvement over "George Jackson." With considerable poetic license, the song describes the murders and Carter's trial (based on assertions that remain hotly disputed to this day); it alleges that the local police conspired to pin the crime on Carter (based on similarly disputed evidence); and it vows to clear Carter's name and get the authorities, somehow, to give him back the time he has served in prison. Dylan's lyrics feature street slang—"stir" for "prison," "heat" for "police"—and "shit" reappears, along with "sonofabitch." The song divides the ghetto into a world of white cops and black victims. There is some interesting wordplay, as in the lines "We want to put his ass in stir / We want to pin this triple murder on him / He ain't no Gentleman Jim," with "murder" broken down into "mur-der" in order to preserve the meter and with the close of the line syncopated and elided—sung as "deron him"—to emphasize the rhymes. But "Hurricane" is notable mainly for its visual imagery, which, when combined with sound effects, lyrical and instrumental, gives the song the feel of a crime-thriller film treatment.

"Pistol shots ring out in the barroom night / Enter Patty Valentine from the upper hall": these are stage directions, or lines from a movie script, written in the present tense, and not the usual start of a crime ballad or any other kind of song. With "Hurricane," the influence of the song's co-author, the theater director Jacques Levy, becomes perfectly obvious. At one level, "Hurricane" is a legal brief, recounting one event after another from the viewpoint of Carter's defense, capped with a lawyerly summation: "Rubin Carter was falsely tried." At another level, it is Dylan's testament to Carter's essential goodness. But throughout, it is a graphic drama, describing a dead man lying in a pool of blood, Patty Valentine's shriek of "My God, they killed 'em all," police cars screeching, their "red lights flashin' / In the hot New Jersey night," a film noir scene of the cops putting the screws to a petty thief to get him to testify falsely. Whereas "George Jackson" (like "Emmett Till" before it) ended in a trite abstraction, "Hurricane" ends with a movie shot—"Now all the criminals in their coats and their ties / Are free to drink martinis and watch the sun rise."

Dylan and his troupe were taking risks with his audience. Having acted out whatever "Ices" was (it turned out to be "Isis"), having brought to the stage "Bob Dylan and Joan Baez," having offered rewrites of some of his greatest songs, Dylan was now reinventing what used to be called topical song, adding a musical movie to the revue's playbill. And although the audience could not know it, he was making a real movie as well, on the stage and off.

Dylan's fascination with the films he had seen at his family's Lybba Theater in Hibbing did not end with his self-invention as a folksinger. On one of the early surviving tapes of him playing in Minneapolis, Dylan brags about some photographs of him in a turtleneck shirt (taken by the mother of his pal Dave Whitaker's wife, Greta), saying that they make him look "just like Marlon Brando, uh, James Dean!" In the Village, he and Suze Rotolo saw classic as well as new-wave European films at the Art Theater on Eighth Street. (Rotolo remembers that they both loved François Truffaut's *Shoot the Piano Player,* but couldn't make heads or tails out of Alain Resnais's *Last Year at Marienbad.*) The songs that first made him famous included numerous playful references to Anita Ekberg, Elizabeth Taylor (and Richard Burton), Sophia Loren, and Brigitte Bardot (about whom he once said he wrote his very first song in Hibbing). Early in 1965, Dylan joked with the TV talk-show host Les Crane about the film he was supposedly writing with Allen Ginsberg, the cowboy horror flick in which he would play his own mother. And that spring, in England, the rising filmmaker D. A. Pennebaker shot the footage for a full-length documentary about Dylan.

Pennebaker had worked with Richard Leacock and others in the shop of Robert Drew, a *Life* magazine journalist turned filmmaker, where the aesthetic and technical essentials emerged for the fly-on-the-wall technique that became known as cinema verité. In 1963, the Drew Associates shot their finest film, *Crisis: Behind a Presidential Commitment,* covering from very different angles the momentous desegregation of the University of Alabama. Assigned to the film crew working in Tuscaloosa, Pennebaker captured on film, behind the scenes, the tense events that led to Governor George C. Wallace's famous effort to thwart the courts and the Kennedy administration with his "stand in the schoolhouse door," followed that same day by Wallace's capitulation.

Approached by Dylan's manager, Albert Grossman, Pennebaker (who knew just a little about Dylan) agreed, on a hunch, to film the singer during a string of concert appearances in England, and he began work on what became *Dont Look Back.* The movie would bear all of the distinguishing features of cinema verité—unrehearsed, candid footage, filmed with small, unobtrusive cameras—as well as some innovations. (These included the now famous, highly staged opening scene, suggested by Dylan himself, of the soundtrack playing "Subterranean Homesick Blues" while the performer held up and tossed away, more or less in sync, cue cards of words and phrases from the song's lyrics.) Shot in black and white during an eleven-day, six-city tour in April and May, *Dont Look Back* captures several aspects of life on the road, from frenzied post-concert stage-door departures to Dylan jousting with journalists. Above all, though, as its title suggests, the film is about Dylan on the edgy cusp of change.

Although he was hearing rock and roll in his head, Dylan was still playing an all-acoustic show, much as he had at Philharmonic Hall the previous October—now bored with his material but, ever the professional, giving it his best. In the film, he inhabits the same world as Joan Baez, Donovan, and the Irish balladeer Dominic Behan (whose name gets mentioned by Jack Elliott's old sidekick Derroll Adams), but he also dismisses them. Dylan is on the move, far beyond where some of his fans wished he would stay, and although he has not yet arrived at his next destination, it will be closer to the world of Allen Ginsberg. The "Subterranean Homesick Blues" opening—where Ginsberg stands in the background, gripping a long staff, looking like a Blakean Jewish prophet, and with Dylan's sharp-witted hipster friend Bob Neuwirth acting as Ginsberg's interlocutor (or perhaps disciple)—is one tip-off. Another is a brief scene of Dylan, in his Ray-Ban shades and black leather jacket, marveling at a London shopwindow filled with electric guitars, followed by a quick cut to Dylan backstage, banging out on a piano the chords of what sounds like an early version of "Like a Rolling Stone."

After he expressed some initial horrified concerns at a prerelease screening of *Dont Look Back,* Dylan saw the film again the following evening and pronounced it perfect. Yet he was also turning serious about his own ideas on cinema. Pennebaker and his camera crew accompanied Dylan to Britain to film his "electric" tour the following year, and Pennebaker sensed, joyously, that everything, indeed, was different. ("He was having such a fantastic time," Pennebaker recalls. "He was jumping around like a cricket out there. The whole scene had changed instantly. It was a different kind of music.") But now Dylan rejected Pennebaker's rough cut of a film contracted to ABC Television, gathered up Pennebaker's original reels, and went his own way, joined by Pennebaker's fellow cameraman and filmmaker, Howard Alk.

Alk had been a founding member of Chicago's Second City comedy troupe and an impresario, with Albert Grossman, of a folk club, the Bear (where he first met Dylan in 1962)—and he was now becoming an important experimental filmmaker in his own right. Working broadly in the verité style, Alk would in time tackle subjects that ranged from the tumultuous Democratic National Convention in 1968 to the peregrinations of the wandering, visionary minstrels in West Bengal known as the

Bauls.* More drawn to radical politics than was Pennebaker, Alk also had his own ideas about filmmaking. Pennebaker always had dramatic intentions—"Really, I'm trying to be Ibsen," he once told an interviewer—but he aimed to dramatize what he thought of as real things happening to real people, without enacting or writing them out beforehand. Alk was more open to intervention and less strictly tied to real things, and he saw film as a place where truth met fiction—and where he could blend improvised staginess with cinema verité.

Over the winter of 1966–67, Dylan and Alk recut Pennebaker's footage of the 1966 tour into what became the first half of *Eat the Document,* a stylized reimagining of the drug-fueled concertizing and its attendant frolics, with intercuttings that became little commentaries on dogs and women, prophets and policemen—all punctuated by footage of Dylan playing with the Hawks. (Although rarely credited, Robbie Robertson edited the film's more conventionally organized second half.) *Eat the Document* lacks a clear narrative line. Staged or at least semi-staged scenes appear like mini-happenings (including an encounter in a room and on a patio at the Hotel George V in Paris between a jaded, fake-mustachioed Dylan and a pixieish young French woman who speaks not a word of English). It is a chaotic film that appears to be about chaos, in the spirit of Rimbaud's derangement of the senses. Here, as Dylan saw it, was a filmic version of where he had arrived out of the crisis that Pennebaker had depicted in *Dont Look Back.*

By the time he dreamed up the Rolling Thunder Revue nearly a decade later, Dylan had also tried his hand as a film actor, with shaky results. As early as 1962, he agreed to play the starring role in a BBC teleplay, *Madhouse on Castle Street,* but he was so awkward in rehearsals that his part got cut, and he simply played a few songs. Dylan's experience with *Pat Garrett and Billy the Kid* ten years later was similarly frustrating. Having been commissioned to write music for the film, Dylan showed up on the set in Durango, Mexico, forced by MGM studios on the director Sam Peckinpah, by now

---

* The greatest of the Baul singers, Purna Das, turned up with one of his fellow Bauls, Lakshman Das, as well as with Dylan and a local Woodstock stonemason, Charlie Joy, in the photograph on the cover of *John Wesley Harding* in 1968. Alk's film *Luxman Baul's Movie,* completed three years later, was financed with funds raised by Albert Grossman (who first brought the Bauls to Woodstock) and featured a voice-over by Grossman's wife, Sally.

legendary for his violent films of the mythic Old West, and was given the role of Alias, a close pal of Billy, who was played by Kris Kristofferson, who had come a long way since his studio janitor days. (Interestingly, Dylan's role came from the same novel that Aaron Copland had used for his ballet: Walter Noble Burns's *Saga of Billy the Kid*, published in 1926.) Dylan received no assistance from Peckinpah, and amid unforeseen difficulties between the director and the studio, Dylan's part dwindled down to a few lines and some amusing Chaplinesque turns. Some of the music that Dylan provided, especially "Knockin' on Heaven's Door," survived, but not his acting. Still, Dylan yearned to act in films as well as to make them.

From the start of the Rolling Thunder experiment, Dylan had a movie in mind, and he brought along a camera crew headed by Howard Alk. On the surface, it would be a third "tour" film, following those of 1965 and 1966, which included plenty of concert performances along with offstage material. But now the action behind the scenes (as well as in the concerts) would be scripted, a drama instead of a documentary—and instead of reinforcing the persona of Bob Dylan, as *Dont Look Back* had done, this film would attempt to undermine and finally shatter Dylan's public image. The celebrated artist would die and be reborn, as in one of Dylan's new songs. The three-ring-circus conceits of the concerts, especially the masking and the whiteface, would work in sync with the movie. (Indeed, some of the conceits were invented, and others later improvised, with the movie in mind.) Whereas Pennebaker had filmed Bob Dylan and his entourage waiting for drama to break out, there now would be a very different story with very different, fictional characters who only looked like Bob Dylan and his entourage. It would all emerge, three years later, as *Renaldo and Clara.*

When Sam Shepard signed on to the tour as writer, he believed that he would be composing a conventional dramatic script, and Dylan has said this is what he originally had planned. But any sense of formal boundaries or genres quickly broke down once the shooting began. Dylan later remarked that about one-third of *Renaldo and Clara* "is improvised, about a third is determined, and about a third is blind luck." There are elements in the film of cinema verité, of John Cassavetes–like situational spontaneous drama, and of the mini-happening experimentation of *Eat the Document.* There are also elements of the avant-garde European filmmaking of the 1930s and after that had first made a strong impression on Dylan in the early 1960s.

Renaldo and Clara, despite Dylan and Alk's densely plotted symbolism, is incoherent. It seems, at times, to be a film about a troubled couple—Robert and Sara?—being tracked by one of Renaldo's former lovers, the Woman in White, played by Joan Baez. But *Renaldo and Clara* unfolds in odd fits and starts, like a dream. (Dylan had, of course, already written several comic, surreal dream songs, and he has said that *Renaldo and Clara* actually *is* a dream, not his own, but Renaldo's.) Logical progressions advance and then take wing. Faces and names get reshuffled. (A figure who looks like Ronnie Hawkins appears as Bob Dylan, and Ronee Blakley plays Mrs. Dylan—except when she appears in one caustic scene as another man's wife.) Then, suddenly, there are scenes that bear some resemblance to the world as we think we know it. (The most direct of these pick up where *Dont Look Back* left off, showing Baez confronting Dylan about their old romance. The most amusing are recurring shots of David Blue smoking a cigarette and playing a visceral game of pinball, while he reminisces about Dylan and the folkie days in the Village.)

With its long sequences of pre-concert technical preparations, and with its improvised domestic quarrels, man-on-the-street interviews about Hurricane Carter, and protracted takes of attempted pickups, *Renaldo and Clara* seems to go on forever, even though, at just under four hours, it is about only half the length of a good night's sleep. Still, Dylan insists that the film has a thematic core: "naked alienation of the inner self against the outer self . . . integrity . . . knowing yourself." And it certainly has a theatrical core that is deeply connected to the theatrics of the Rolling Thunder Revue.

When Dylan first encountered Sam Shepard just before the touring began, he asked the playwright if he had ever seen the films *Children of Paradise* and *Shoot the Piano Player.* (Shepard confessed he had, although it had been a while.) Both are films about performers under stress, but *Children of Paradise* in particular would remain one of the templates for *Renaldo and Clara* long after Shepard's job description had changed from writer to bit-part actor. And *Children of Paradise*'s impact on Dylan had everything to do with timing. Dylan had closely watched Truffaut's films since the early 1960s. *Children of Paradise,* though, was one of Norman Raeben's favorites, and it was Raeben who introduced the film to Dylan, at some point after they met in 1974. The lessons on experimenting with time, perspective, and texture that had helped produce "Tangled Up in Blue" influenced Dylan's thinking about film as well.

Directed by Marcel Carné, written by the sometime surrealist poet Jacques Prévert, and starring Jean-Louis Barrault, *Children of Paradise* is a long film about the world of the popular theater in Paris during the 1820s and 1830s, when revolution was very much in the air. (Made furtively during the Nazi occupation and completed in 1944, the film held its own claims as a statement of resistance through art.) Garance, a beautiful, lusty courtesan played by the great French actress Arletty, is pursued by four men: a womanizing actor, a thief, an aristocrat, and Barrault's character, the mime Baptiste Debureau. Baptiste is the key. Wearing the whiteface of the stock pantomime character Pierrot, Baptiste performs at the Théâtre des Funambules (or "tight-rope walkers"), one of many theatrical venues on the crowded, working-class Boulevard du Temple. In an early scene, Baptiste appears before the milling spectators outside the Funambules—dressed and painted in white from head to toe, a thin scarf tied loosely around his neck, and wearing a broad-brimmed white hat decorated with white flowers.

At different points in the film, the irresistible Garance becomes briefly involved with all four of her suitors, but she also insists on her independence—and when they try to impose love on their own terms, she leaves them. Her most tragic liaison, though, is with Baptiste. After overcoming a rocky relationship with his father, the mime becomes an enormous star, particularly popular with the fun-loving, rambunctious denizens perched in the second balcony, way up with the "gods" (and thus known as the children of paradise). Unlike his rivals, Baptiste loves Garance purely and wholly, and one night she all but directly invites him into bed—but he runs away. The film then proceeds through a long series of ricocheting intrigues. Baptiste, his stardom ever rising, marries another woman and starts a family. But years later, Garance (now the aristocrat's kept woman) reappears in Baptiste's life, and the two finally spend the night together. Discovered the next morning by Baptiste's wife, Nathalie, Garance flees by carriage along the boulevard, now crowded with carnival celebrators in full costume. Baptiste becomes engulfed by the revelers. The film suddenly ends as a mock theater curtain descends over the screen.

Was the story of Baptiste and Garance—the shy, forlorn star and the woman whom he desired, then from whom he ran away—lodged in Dylan's mind when he blocked out *Renaldo and Clara*? It's possible, although the convergence cannot be taken too literally. Jacques Levy later recalled that Dylan wanted to make "a kind of *Children of Paradise*" and was interested mainly in "the atmosphere—and having a love story go through it." When Shepard asked him if he wanted to make a film like Carné's or Truffaut's, Dylan replied simply, "Something like that."

Still, as various critics have pointed out, the two films are intimately connected. A leitmotif of a lover's flower in Carné's film also turns up in Dylan's (where, Dylan has said, it symbolizes the vagina). Baptiste/Barrault's whiteface is an obvious link, as are his scarf and flowered hat, as, indeed, is the bevy of masks that appears throughout *Children of Paradise*. The second part of Carné's film is entitled "The Man in White" (although Dylan might well have borrowed his Woman in White from the spooky novel of the same name by Wilkie Collins). The star performer Renaldo/Dylan physically resembles the thin but wiry star performer Baptiste/Barrault, in his face as well as his body, just as the characters played by Baez and Sara Dylan vaguely resemble Garance and Nathalie. (As the Woman in White, Baez even affects a French accent from time to time.) In a climactic, confrontational scene, Baptiste/Barrault's wife, who has found him snuggling with his long-ago love, Garance, bids him to be honest

Left: Jean-Louis Barrault as Baptiste in *Les enfants du paradis,* 1945. Right: Bob Dylan in whiteface during the Rolling Thunder Revue, 1975.

with her; in a corresponding scene near the very end, the Woman in White (the long-ago love) confronts Renaldo/Dylan (who has been snuggling with his wife, Clara), and both women in the triangle tell him to decide, and to say, directly, which of the two of them he loves. The configurations, as well as the outcomes, are different, but the scene in *Renaldo and Clara* strongly echoes the one in *Children of Paradise.*

Above all, the two films share a distinctive theatricality. Barrault's Baptiste performs several brilliant pantomimes that are closely knit thematically with the rest of *Children of Paradise.* Likewise, the concert sequences of Dylan performing in whiteface are intrinsic to the dreamscape of *Renaldo and Clara.* One layered sequence out of many, late in the movie, begins with Renaldo staring at an actual newspaper photograph of Bob Dylan and Joan Baez, appearing together in the Rolling Thunder Revue. The film then abruptly cuts to Dylan and Baez onstage, singing "Never Let Me Go." Next we see and hear Clara talking about the newspaper photograph as a picture not of Dylan and Baez but of Renaldo and the Woman in White; then Renaldo starts daubing himself with his white makeup before the next performance. All along, deep in the background, we can hear "Sad-Eyed Lady of the Lowlands" from *Blonde on Blonde,* as recorded during the Rolling Thunder rehearsals—a love song, *Desire* had since disclosed, that Bob Dylan wrote for Sara Dylan.

The concert footage in *Renaldo and Clara* should not be interpreted as standing distinct from the film (although, much like his earlier movie appearances, Dylan's best acting in *Renaldo and Clara,* by far, is in his musical performances). Yet that footage also stands up extremely well on its own, as powerful, at times stunning recordings of Bob Dylan singing, playing, and even miming his heart out in the Rolling Thunder Revue, much as I remember him at the Veterans Memorial Coliseum. And here, the film's tone and texture, as informed by the plebeian theater in *Children of Paradise,* help to further explain the Rolling Thunder Revue. At one point during the tour, Dylan referred, in an interview, to sixteenth-century Italian commedia dell'arte as one of the conceptual models for the revue, and he could easily have mentioned many other models, including the Bauls of West Bengal. But backstage in New Haven, when Bruce Springsteen's girlfriend inquired about why he was wearing whiteface, Dylan muttered about having seen something once in a movie.

"Hurricane" ended as an instrumental footrace between Rivera's violin and Dylan's harmonica, pushed along by Howie Wyeth's pounding drums and cymbals and Rob Stoner's bass. Suddenly everyone reached the finish line in a tie, the music slowed for a split second, and the final chord changed the key from minor to major, which always sounds hopeful. Musically, the show had hit a peak. "One More Cup of Coffee," the next song, was a comedown, a slow melody bearing words I could hardly make out, mainly because Dylan's artfully wavering vocal, early on—singing that sounded distinctly Hebraic, like a cantor's High Holy day cantillation of sacred text—threw me off. Later, I would read the song's lyrics and realize I was mistaken, but at the time I wondered if Dylan had actually composed a song about the Middle East.

"Sara" was much softer—Dylan singing with his guitar, along with Rivera on her violin, and with Wyeth and Stoner providing a tactful rhythm line. It was also a much sadder tune, shifting the key from E minor to C major for the chorus but then reverting. Knowing nothing about the state of the Dylans' marriage, I didn't at first comprehend that the song was a plea for Sara's unending love as well as an avowal of his own. By any standard, it was a gripping, graphic sorrow song, and for Dylan it was startlingly autobiographical, full of vivid, loving family memories and adoring images of his wife.

Yet the song's reconciliation plea rang hollow. Even as he rhapsodized about Sara's charms, wisdom, and devotion, Dylan seemed self-absorbed and all too willing to place responsibility chiefly on her for the marriage's souring. Apart from some superficial self-abasement—"You must forgive me my unworthiness"—the lyrics lacked contrition, and at one point even affected cluelessness about why things had gone wrong. "Whatever made you want to change your mind?" Dylan sang, as if he didn't know. When the song told of how Dylan spent several sleepless nights in the Hotel Chelsea writing "Sad-Eyed Lady of the Lowlands" for Sara, it sounded as if he thought he was handing her some sort of trophy, by telling the whole world that she and she alone was the muse behind his masterpiece.

There is more emotional humility (and economy) in Dave Van Ronk's version of "Come Back, Baby," which at least asks the woman in question to talk things over "one more time." Still, the fans in New Haven seemed deeply affected by "Sara," and judging by their whistling, cheering response, they were entirely in Dylan's corner. The references to the Chelsea and "Sad-Eyed Lady" elicited scattered appreciative yips of hip recognition from some of the rowdier male patrons, in an audience that, as I recall, was mainly composed of men. Then came some shouted requests. The show was drawing to a close.

The New Haven Rolling Thunder afternoon show has not been described by Dylan's chroniclers as one of the musical highlights of the tour, in part because it included none of the solos by Baez, McGuinn, Elliott, and Mitchell that brightened other shows, and in part because it was not professionally recorded. Aside from the four duets with Baez, the New Haven matinee was all Dylan, all the time. Yet that yielded some treats, including the first public performance ever of "Tangled Up in Blue." And by the time the troupe reached Connecticut, it was following a strong regular set list toward the end of the concert, which led from Dylan's current anguish in "Sara" to his song of despair from *Blonde on Blonde,* "Just Like a Woman."

If "Sara" has been too easily accepted as simply a loving, autobiographical tribute, "Just Like a Woman" has come in for a good deal of unfair scorn. Some lyrics in the chorus—above all, those that say the woman in the song "breaks just like a little girl"—have caused critics and ordinary listeners to hear the entire song as one of Dylan's acidic put-downs, and they have even prompted some to denounce him as a misogynist. In fact, the song is more like a flashback to a howl, recounted after the protagonist has numbed the pain.

The song is the mirror image of "Sara," describing a man trying to break off a relationship gone haywire. The singer describes how he fell in love with a passionate woman who was wreathed in fog, amphetamine, and pearls, but then came to realize that she was fragile, afflicted, and deceptive, playing the little girl, and that the affair was a train wreck in the making. The song shows him struggling to express his feelings honestly and find the proper parting words, although he is never quite definite. In all of Dylan's songs, there are few lyrics more distraught (as well as technically sharp) than the bridge section in "Just Like a Woman" and the lyrics immediately after:

> *It was raining from the first*
> *And I was dying there of thirst*
> *So I came in here*
> *And your long-time curse hurts*
> *But what's worse*
> *Is this pain in here*
> *I can't stay in here*
> *Ain't it clear that—*
>
> > *I just can't fit*
> > *Yes, I believe it's time for us to quit.*

The lyrics that follow are calculating as well as sad: the couple will certainly meet again, and he asks her not to shame him, but to be discreet about their past, when he was down and the world was hers. The lines actually intensify the song's pathos.

The performance of "Just Like a Woman" on *Blonde on Blonde* emphasizes the bridge: Dylan's singing builds in volume and passion, then falls into hushed resignation at "just can't fit." In New Haven, Dylan and Guam produced the same effect, only now Dylan actually did howl and wail—"suh-oh I came in heeeeee-ah-uh-ah-uh-ah-uh," "long time CURSE HURTS but what's WORSE," "AIN'T IT CLEEEEEEEEEEah"—before dropping.

The chord changes for "Just Like a Woman" moved effortlessly, beneath the crashing applause, into "Knockin' on Heaven's Door," already a reliable crowd-pleaser. Roger McGuinn sang the solo on the second verse, the entire ensemble gathered for the chorus, then dramatically halted, waiting out a pause, slowly took up a sweet instrumental interlude, and finally sang one more chorus.

The Rolling Thunder Revue finale, 1975.

The troupe then fell into unconcerted milling onstage. A fast fiddle line floated up. The stars gathered in front of the band for a disheveled grand-finale singing of what had become the counterculture's national anthem, Woody Guthrie's "This Land Is Your Land." The relief among the smiling performers was obvious: another closing, another show. Joan Baez took a verse of the song, McGuinn took another, then Jack Elliott, and then Bob Neuwirth. Baez teased the audience that the performers knew no more songs, and won some loud cheers with a couple of her high-soprano flourishes. There the show ended, in a tribute to Guthrie, concluding where Dylan's proper artistic career had begun—a beginning more than fifteen years earlier, by which time much of the romance evoked by the Rolling Thunder Revue had already entered Dylan's soul.

Moving from commedia dell'arte to Marcel Carné to Woody Guthrie cut a huge swirl through time and space, far bigger than assembling the Greenwich Village folk revival with newer musical currents and then making a movie out of it. Meant to make history, or at least make a statement about the past and the present, the Rolling Thunder Revue had plenty of historical elements embedded in its spirit. Allen Ginsberg acted as a kind of historical consultant as well as poet to the troupe—Ginsberg was especially taken with the never-executed idea of pairing Hurricane Carter's travails with the Sacco and Vanzetti case, in some form of musical-poetic homage—and he worked out some of what he thought of as the tour's strange patriotic bicentennial implications. The revue began and ended, after all, during the autumn following the two hundredth anniversary of the battles of Lexington and Concord, outside Boston. New England was already gripped by what Sam Shepard would call "Bicentennial madness, as though desperately trying to resurrect the past to reassure ourselves that we sprang from somewhere." During the summer after the tour—when, as it happened, the revue would regroup for a second, southern swing—the entire country would undertake a gigantic celebration of 1776 (or an attempt at celebration, in the sour public mood that lingered after the Watergate affair). Now Bob Dylan, who had picked up the American bardic cudgel from Ginsberg, who had earlier picked it up from Walt Whitman, would kick off the patriotic commemoration by making music, theater, film, and poetry with his friends on a tour that wound its way past village and farm in the very cradle of the American Revolution. Dylan would steal a march on the culture. Ginsberg told his father that Dylan was making "a Bicentennial picture."

Dylan had long had his own strong, if surreal, historical sense of early America, as he had written it out in "Bob Dylan's 115th Dream" on

Bringing It All Back Home—a cut-up story inspired as much by Herman Melville and Chuck Berry's "Too Much Monkey Business" and Ray Stevens's "Ahab the Arab" as by any book of history. The song begins with the singer describing how he had hit the American shore after riding on the *Mayflower* with Captain Ahab/Arab and his crew. And sure enough, as the Rolling Thunder tour began, there was Dylan aboard the modern replica of the *Mayflower,* parked in Plymouth harbor, gazing out over the waves with a crew that now consisted of Roger McGuinn and Ramblin' Jack Elliott, among others. In a semi-scripted encounter, which would become a long passage in *Renaldo and Clara,* the revue also visited a gathering of Tuscarora Indian families in a run-down meeting hall (and with a chief, Rolling Thunder, who added another dimension to the tour's name). In the movie, the musicians also gather for what looks like a sundown ceremony by the sea, mixing American Indian drums and Buddhist chants with improvised doo-wop. It could all have been a Dada Thanksgiving, with Dylan (or Renaldo in the movie) acting kindly to the awestruck Indians but also striding about as the true star: Miles Standish as celebrity troubadour.

There was another, even richer historical layer to the tour, more out of the American 1920s, 1930s, and 1940s, at the outer edge of Dylan's own experience and just beyond it, sheltered in some of the old redbrick New England towns and cities where the revue played, like Lowell, Massachusetts, and Waterbury, Connecticut. Here was an America that had all but disappeared, flattened by structures such as the New Haven Veterans Memorial Coliseum, hollowed out by time and tide, much as Dylan's hometown had been. A few Rolling Thunder shows took place in grand big-city arenas, including Madison Square Garden, to help recoup costs and build up Rubin Carter's defense fund, but for the most part the tour's setting and atmosphere—the little theaters, not unlike the old Lybba in Hibbing; the very fact that the performers and the entourage traveled by bus and car—turned this into an adventure out of another time.

At the center of the tour's historical romance, though, was what Dylan had first mentioned to McGuinn, the American circus or carnival—and a particular romance of popular entertainment. This circus would have nothing to do with the star-studded, one-off *Rock and Roll Circus* that the Rolling Stones had staged for television in London a few years earlier. Rolling Thunder would be more like the real McCoy; among other things, it actually would roll from town to town. *Children of Paradise* added a thematic and cinematic gloss to the theatrical romance, but the

Rolling Thunder Revue had most in common with an American caravan lodged deep in Dylan's imagination.

In the tall-tale versions of his show-business past that he bandied about during his early days in New York, Dylan claimed that he had been rousting with the circus for a long time. (He actually knew a lot about the details and mentioned one troupe in particular, the Roy B. Thomas Show.) In a radio interview early in 1962, he told Cynthia Gooding that he had spent six years, "off and on," in the carnival, working all sorts of odd jobs, learning about reading playing cards (which he didn't trust) and reading palms (which he did, "for a bunch of personal things, I don't . . . personal experiences"). A year later, at Town Hall, he debuted "Dusty Old Fairgrounds," a song mostly about work and travel—he told the audience it was "a route song"—but also about camaraderie and magic and fate:

> *It's a-many a friend that follows the bend,*
> *The jugglers, the hustlers, the gamblers.*
> *Well, I've spent my time with the fortune-telling kind*
> *Following them fairgrounds a-calling.*

Dylan has returned to the circus images repeatedly over the years, vividly in "Ballad of a Thin Man" and most recently in the various sideshow scenes in his film *Masked and Anonymous,* in his interviews included in the Martin Scorsese documentary *No Direction Home,* and in an interview posted on Dylan's official Web site in conjunction with the release of *Together Through Life* in 2009. In the latter, Dylan talks of a boyhood, still outside the reach of mass media, when he was drawn to "the traveling performers passing through":

> The side show performers—bluegrass singers, the black cowboy with chaps and a lariat doing rope tricks. Miss Europe, Quasimodo, the Bearded Lady, the half-man half-woman, the deformed and the bent, Atlas the Dwarf, the fire-eaters, the teachers and preachers, the blues singers. I remember it like it was yesterday. I got close to some of these people. I learned about dignity from them. Freedom too. Civil rights, human rights. How to stay within yourself.

By 2009, Dylan, knowingly or not, was mixing other allusions with his carnival reveries—Atlas the Dwarf and Miss Europe probably come out of Juvenal's *Satires*—but then again, the late Roman Empire was a circus, too.

Always, it has been the midway freaks, mystics, novelty acts, and conjurers that most captivated Dylan—the sword swallowers, the fortune-tellers, the geeks. These are circus people who may be bent and misshapen, maybe, but who are also talented and very smart, who can get up onstage and, as he told Gooding, "wanna make you have two thoughts," getting you to believe that they don't feel bad about themselves but also getting you to feel sorry for them. It is magic and these are illusions, but they are also dead real, playing around with identities, perception, self-perception: which is to say, they are psychological insight made into entertainment, and vice versa.

The Rolling Thunder Revue was, finally, that kind of a many-layered entertainment, featuring intense performances by Bob Dylan unlike any he had ever given before or would ever give again. The theater of the mind in his old songs became flesh and then got fleshed out even more, partly in the assembly of acts, but above all in Dylan's own singing and dancing and miming—insistent, driven, attentive to stagecraft in ways that Dylan never had been, renewing the old and, at his best, making the new sound old. And then, in a flash, like the circus—or like the meaning one thought was taking shape in a Dylan song, the meaning that for an instant seemed so concise and so clear—the revue was gone, vanished, never to be exactly the same way again, heading for another joint, or for a dusty old theater that looked a lot like the Lybba, the past permuting and combining with the present.

And the future? Dylan led the revue on a second leg that traveled through the South in 1976, featuring the same basic band and many of the same costars (including Joan Baez, but not Ramblin' Jack Elliott, who was brusquely replaced with Kinky Friedman). Yet with the Dylans' marriage entering its nasty, terminal phases, and with the novelty of the gypsy caravan worn thin, the frivolity and magic of the New England tour faded away. The mélange still produced some fine music—some of which turns up on the album *Hard Rain,* including a searing reworking of "Maggie's Farm"—but without the multilayered theatrics and overpowering performances of the previous year. Even though Dylan told Baez, at the second tour's conclusion, that he planned to keep the revue going forever, the future would be a very different proposition.

As the decade wound down, Dylan's art jumped into an entirely new phase, another seemingly utter break from his past that shocked and infuriated many of his devotees. And this time, Dylan would finally under-mine his persona, as neither the Rolling Thunder Revue nor *Renaldo and Clara* ever managed to do. Yet the all-American carny would never be too far from Dylan's imagination. And in time, he would circle back to a shrewd, blind Georgia artist from the 1930s and 1940s—a novelty act of a kind, a bit of a freak—who as a boy had lit out with the circus (or who later claimed that he had) and who grew up to sing the blues like nobody else.

6

MANY MARTYRS FELL:

"Blind Willie McTell," New York City, May 5, 1983

wonder," John Lomax asked Blind Willie McTell, "I wonder if, if you know any songs about colored people havin' hard times here in the South."

It was a bright morning in Atlanta, in early November 1940, still warm enough to keep the windows open. Lomax and his second wife, Ruby, had come to town the day before on one of their field recording trips for the Archive of American Folk Song of the Library of Congress, coordinated by the archive's assistant in charge, John's son Alan Lomax. As they drove around the city at dinnertime, Ruby spotted a guitarist singing and playing outside a whites-only drive-in barbecue restaurant, the Pig 'n' Whistle. They were unfamiliar with McTell and his recordings, but a friend had tipped them off that while in Atlanta, they should try to find him. And they had. For a payment of one dollar plus cab fare, the singer agreed to meet the Lomaxes at nine the next morning in their room at the Robert Fulton Hotel and perform into their acetate disc recorder.

McTell showed up right on time, and over the next two hours he played more than two dozen songs—one of the most remarkable field recording sessions in the history of American music. The early going, though, was difficult. McTell began by announcing a medley of spirituals. "I will demonstrate how the mothers and fathers used to wander about their work," he said, "when they used to sing those old-fashioned hymns"—

his tone oddly formal, like a folklore instructor, befitting a recording session for the Library of Congress. When the medley was done, John Lomax announced the singer's name, the place, and the date, in a cultivated accent still marked by his Texas upbringing, but then he presumed to call the tune, requesting the songs about colored people and hard times.

Blind Willie McTell recording for John and Ruby Lomax in Atlanta, Georgia, on November 5, 1940.

"Well," McTell replied, "that's all songs that have a reference to our old people here. They hasn't very much stuff of the people nowadays, because they're . . ."

Lomax, impatient, broke in.

"Any complainin' songs, complainin' about the hard times and sometimes mistreatment of the whites? Have you got any songs that talk about that?"

No, McTell said at once, he had no such songs, "not at the present

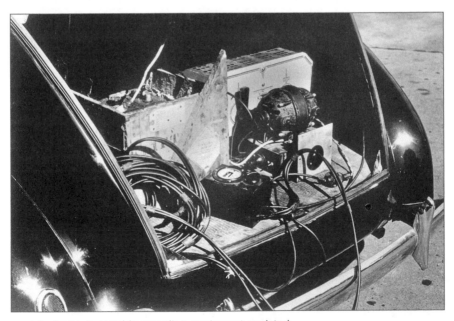

John Lomax's portable recording equipment, undated.

time." Those were songs of another era, but now "the white peoples is mighty good to the southern people, as far as I *know.*" The qualifying last five words came out emphatically, after a tiny pause.

Lomax would not be deterred.

" 'Ain't It Hard to Be a Nigger, Nigger,' do you know that one?"

"That's not . . . in our time," McTell said. He did have a spiritual, "It's a Mean World to Live In," but it still made no reference to the hard times.

Lomax, unfazed, asked McTell why it's a mean world to live in; McTell replied that it's not altogether, and that the song "has reference to *everybody.*"

"It's—it's as mean for the whites as it 'tis for the blacks, is that it?"

"That's the idea."

Lomax thought he caught the singer squirming.

"You keep movin' around like you're uncomfortable, what's the matter, Willie?"

McTell immediately said that he'd been injured in an automobile accident the night before, nothing serious, no one got hurt, just got a little shook up is all, still sore—an unlikely story. Then, after a break, the next sounds on Lomax's acetate are of McTell playing his twelve-string guitar and singing "Boll Weevil" in his sweet, lilting tenor—a song that at least bordered on a hard-times blues.

Read one way, Lomax's conversation with McTell is a tense social transcript from the Jim Crow South. Lomax, the overbearing if well-intentioned white visitor, wants musical documents of poverty and racial oppression. The request may connote obliviousness on his part, as well as a condescending sympathy for blacks, but it is nevertheless rude and insulting, demanding that the singer violate basic, unspoken southern norms that should have been familiar to anyone reared in Texas. McTell knows much better than to say anything against white people, let alone sing it, to a white man with even the hint of a southern accent and his wife, especially if the man is some sort of government official and a recorder is running. Although McTell makes it clear that he knows the kinds of songs that Lomax wants to hear, he would never play them under these circumstances, even under duress—but to say as much and explain why would also violate the Jim Crow norms by making them explicit. Lomax's insistence unsettles and embarrasses McTell, but the singer hangs in there and dissembles, while he slyly slips in phrases—"as far as I *know*"—that covertly disclose the truth. God, after all, is his witness.

But there is another, very different way to understand the conversation.

John Lomax, the archivist and collector, certainly wants what he wants, but Blind Willie McTell simply doesn't have it. The music that McTell knows best and prefers to perform carries no overt or even hidden social or political meaning. There are no old-fashioned sorrow songs about the black man's plight in his regular repertoire (and certainly not on his records, even though they are intended for the black "race record" market). His songs are up-to-date, and they are about sadness in love and gladness in love, drinking too much, benign nonsense, God, gambling, violence (much of it involving blacks attacking or killing other blacks), honoring life and death. For the Library of Congress, he will perform a little of each.

To be sure, McTell does play music from earlier times for the Lomaxes, including a remorseful blues from sometime between 1908 and 1914—"back in the days when the blues started being original," he says—but mainly the older material is sacred music that is timeless and relevant to all of God's children, even though traditionally sung by rural blacks. McTell may well be heeding the submissive Jim Crow etiquette code, especially when Lomax pushes. But then again, McTell is not a sharecropper or big-city laborer; he is a professional performer in a growing southern city. He lives within the iron structures of segregation, yet even though he was blind, he must have known his skin was brown and that he thus had white ancestors. As a youth, he had benefited from the generosity of a kindly white man in his country hometown, and now he is making a very decent living playing music for whites as well as blacks and getting recorded commercially. For a black Atlantan in 1940, this amounted to a comparatively easy experience with white people—while taking their money—which may help to explain McTell's bemusement at Lomax's fixation on the "complainin' songs."

In any event, McTell is an artist as well as a performer, and his songs are about meanness and joy on both sides of the color line—with "reference to *every*body"—and not just in hard times. Lomax doesn't quite get it.

Whichever reading of the conversation is correct—and elements of both probably are—the initial tension dissipated after McTell sang "Boll Weevil," and the rest of the recording session went smoothly. McTell performed spirituals and murder ballads, songs about falling in and out of love, folk songs, ragtime, and a long, rollicking number about the deathbed wishes of a hard-hearted crapshooter. Lomax backed off and relaxed, getting into the expansive spirit of McTell's music. Now and then, he and his wife interjected comments, including questions about where McTell came from and where he had been. The archivists wanted to find out all they could about the blind, roundish, clear-toned man who picked his guitar superbly.

Lomax dutifully took it all down in the notes for his archive field report, praising McTell's "excellent" guitar playing but sounding unenthusiastic about his singing. That report, along with the Lomaxes' recording, lodged Blind Willie McTell's music in an inconspicuous corner of the official world of folk-song collecting. Yet even though he would never be completely forgotten, McTell would have to be rediscovered by blues enthusiasts, again and again, over the next twenty years. The full importance of his session with the Lomaxes would only begin to become clear during the 1960s. By then, McTell himself was dead.

During the second week of April 1983, Bob Dylan joined the Dire Straits guitarist and vocalist Mark Knopfler, the former Rolling Stones guitarist Mick Taylor, and three other top musicians to begin recording his new album at a reclaimed Con Edison facility, the Power Station, on the far West Side of midtown Manhattan. Nearly two years had passed since Dylan's last album recording session, for the undeservedly ill-fated *Shot of Love,* and having moved on from what would be remembered as his Christian phase, he had a good deal riding on this new effort. He devoted almost all of the first day to one of the new songs that loomed largest, "Blind Willie McTell," sometimes called just "Blind Willie." After several false starts and eight instrumental run-throughs (one of them complete), the group started working in earnest—yet even though two complete takes resulted, they were unsatisfactory. "Blind Willie McTell" got shelved temporarily, to be attempted again at later sessions.

Dylan had entered his Christian phase in 1979, when he experienced what he called a profound spiritual awakening in Jesus Christ with the Vineyard Christian Fellowship in California. His marriage with Sara had finally ended in divorce two years earlier, although a nasty legal fight over custody of their children continued. One of Dylan's girlfriends, the black actress Mary Alice Artes, was drawn to the New Age evangelical sect, and having rededicated herself to the Lord, she arranged for a pair of Vineyard pastors to pay Dylan a visit at his home in Malibu. (Earlier, the former Rolling Thunder Revue band members T Bone Burnett, Steven Soles, and David Mansfield had also entered the Vineyard's orbit.) Dylan told the pastors that, yes, he wanted Christ in his life. He privately received the Christian Messiah in his heart at some point over the next few days.

Dylan's conversion hardly marked his first adult contact with religion or religious themes. Some of his earlier songs about justice and morality evinced clear and sometimes strong biblical influence. "When the Ship Comes In," although obviously inspired by "Pirate Jenny," also contained unmistakable scriptural elements of apocalypse, whether borrowed from the Bible or folk-song prosody. So did "The Times They Are A-Changin'" and, in a very different way, "A Hard Rain's A-Gonna Fall." Some of the songs on *John Wesley Harding* sounded like a fresh take on Woody Guthrie's ballads; others (especially "As I Went Out One Morning") had overtones of William Blake; but still others—"All Along the Watchtower," "The Wicked Messenger," "I Dreamed I Saw St. Augustine" (Dylan's revision of "Joe Hill"), and even the riddle "The Ballad of Frankie Lee and Judas Priest"—were reworkings of scriptural parable, in style and substance. The religious sentiments in songs such as "Oh, Sister" from *Desire* were surprising only because they suggested that Dylan might be taking religious injunction, or the spirit of injunction, more seriously than anyone had thought.

Dylan's turn to Christ after 1979 at once reinforced his religious seeking and style and transformed it utterly. The Vineyard fellowship, like every evangelical Christian sect, emphasized universal access to redemption in Christ from original sin through intense prayer leading to spiritual rebirth. Like other evangelicals, Vineyard Christians fortified their discipleship with concentrated Bible study, then devoted themselves to spreading the Gospel and winning new converts to the Lord. But the Vineyard fellowship also had its particularities, above all an attachment to the premillennial view that Christ's second coming was imminent. After the battle of Armageddon, which was about to start, the wicked would be damned, the godly saved, and a thousand-year reign of peace would commence.

In Dylan's case, the Vineyard's premillennialism came heavily inflected by the best-selling book by the Christian Zionist and former Vineyard devotee Hal Lindsey (*The Late Great Planet Earth,* published in 1970). The fellowship had a joyous side, expressed chiefly in musical performances in church services. But it made no room for the do-gooder reformism associated with most postmillennial sects and denominations, which held that Christ would return only *after* the redeemed had created a heavenly millennium on earth. Taking as their essential biblical scripture the New Testament book of Revelation (which many of them connected to contemporary political and cultural events, as decoded by Hal Lindsey), the New Age premillennialists believed that doomsday truly was impending, that Christ was almost certainly among us now, and that His final judgment would be upon the world before we knew it.

The apocalyptic themes in Dylan's early songs had appeared chiefly as metaphors of social redemption, depicting the revolutionary moment when the oppressors would be undone and the oppressed would take their place.* Now the theme appeared as foretold by the eschatological prophets of the Old Testament, Isaiah, Jeremiah, and Ezekiel, and as described by Saint John of Patmos in Revelation—earth's ruin in the great tribulation, which would bring Satan's destruction and engulf unbelievers in eternal fire, while the paradise of the New Jerusalem opened to the Christ's saints and servants. Faith was the only way to redemption; neither mere goodness, nor wretchedness, nor unearned suffering saved any souls. And there was nothing metaphorical about it. "I told you 'The Times They Are A-Changin' ' and they did," Dylan preached to a concert audience in 1979, in one of what became known as his gospel raps. "I said the answer was 'Blowin' in the Wind,' and it was. I'm telling you now Jesus is coming back, and He is! And there is no other way of salvation . . . There's only one way to believe, there's only one way—the Truth and the Life."

These were frightening things to hear at first, and they even frightened Dylan, not least in the lyrics to "When He Returns," the final song on the first of his three Christian albums, *Slow Train Coming:* "Truth is an arrow and the gate is narrow that it passes through / He unleashed His power at an unknown hour that no one knew." It was no wonder that many of Dylan's fans, having caught up long ago with his emergence as a rock and roller, felt betrayed all over again. Not only had a secular Jew committed the ultimate apostasy; a poet of quicksilver ambiguity was now expounding absolute doctrine that came wholly received from others. The author of "My Back Pages," who sang of becoming his own enemy

---

* "A Hard Rain's A-Gonna Fall," although in part apocalyptic, is also a song of a quest that leads through sights, sounds, and scenes of everyday misery as well as of a blasted, scorched, and bleeding earth. And unlike Dylan's other early songs of destruction, it concludes not with justice or redemption but with the singer vowing to sing to all the world of what he has seen and heard.

"in the instant that I preach," had become a preacher. All of Dylan's old questions—"How many years can a mountain exist?" "Should I leave them by your gate?" "How does it feel?"—now had simple answers, and every answer was the same. The music did flash, sometimes, and the

The Third Gospel Tour: Bob Dylan, Jim Keltner (drums), Tim Drummond (bass), Regina Havis, Mary Elizabeth Bridges, and Mona Lisa Young, Massey Hall, Toronto, April 1980.

songs sounded much better in concert than they did on record; in fact, onstage, they were overpowering, as the bootleg recordings of the shows attest. But with a few outstanding exceptions, Dylan's songs came to have two predictable themes: warning the unrepentant of imminent apocalypse and the Second Coming; and affirming his personal redemption and gratitude to the Lord. By 1981, the sheer repetitiveness of his piety had drained away the sense of dread.

There were, though, those exceptions. On *Slow Train Coming,* "Gotta Serve Somebody" attacked the sins of envy and pride and blasted through dozens of pasteboard masks, including Dylan's own. "Do Right to Me Baby (Do unto Others)" was an interesting revision, lyrically and musically, of sentiments about sincerity in early Dylan songs such as "All I Really Want to Do," but now rendered in light of the book of Luke 6:31. The title track of the uneven but badly underrated *Shot of Love* opened with a two-note guitar burst followed by a three-part a cappella gospel line lightly augmented by studio reverb, and then it slipped into glorious rock and roll about suffering and redemptive love. Two songs recorded for *Shot of Love* but omitted from the original release blended presentiment of doomsday with confusion about love affairs gone bad. The first, "The Groom's Still Waiting at the Altar"—inserted on the LP's second pressing and then the compact disc version, after it received heavy airplay on independent radio stations as the B side of the 45 made of "Heart of Mine"—was another rocker, its sound recalling that of *Highway 61 Revisited.* The other, "Caribbean Wind," composed while Dylan was sailing through the islands, described the destructive tangle of desire and liberty as well as anything he had written since *Blood on the Tracks.*

Above all, there was "Every Grain of Sand," a beautifully wrought composition, tenderly performed as the final track on *Shot of Love,* a summary of Dylan's search for redemption. With no desire "to look back on any mistake," the singer still beheld the events that had caused ruin— "the flowers of indulgence and the weeds of yesteryear." Yet the singer also saw the hand of the Master in every trembling leaf and had come to understand the power and necessity of faith—faith not in fame, influence, a woman's love, or anything other than God. At one level, the song and its images came directly from passages in Matthew and Luke where Jesus speaks of the salvation of the faithful—but its wording, as well as its odd, steady, seven-beat meter lines, also echoed certain of William Blake's poems, including "Auguries of Innocence." In a compact, sharply crafted, unbombastic song, graced, on the record, with a moving harmonica solo, Dylan described a gentle vision of heavenly order and earthly responsibility that he had wrenched out of the chaos.

By the time he had completed *Shot of Love* in 1981, Dylan's writing had begun to turn again, becoming much less preachy than on the preceding two albums. He had hardly abandoned his apocalyptic faith: the thunder of the coming doom is there in "Caribbean Wind" and "Groom," and in later interviews he would affirm his belief in the literal truth of Revelation. Yet clearly something else was growing. There were reports that he had turned his back on Christianity, returned to Judaism, and even taken up studies with the Hasidim Lubavitch, some of which was true: Dylan's evolving spirituality was proving broad enough to embrace the Torah and the New Testament. More important, he had assimilated spirituality to imagination, using faith, and the testing of faith, as a frame or template but no longer as the chief subject of his art. *Shot of Love* included an endearing, completely secular song with a lovely melody ("Lenny Bruce"), driven by Dylan in fine voice and playing a clutching, churchy piano, and it included a booming sacred song ("Property of Jesus") with a put-down, "how dare you?" verve more reminiscent of "Positively 4th Street" than of anything on *Saved*. Once again, Dylan was moving on.

Still, Dylan's Christian phase—his latest explosive confrontation with himself as well as his listeners—had deeply affected his art, and in ways that reached above and beyond the lyrics and melodies. By choosing to record the first two Christian albums with the legendary soul music producer Jerry Wexler, and at Wexler's favored Muscle Shoals Sound Studio in Sheffield, Alabama, Dylan returned to the sounds and surroundings of the South as he had not since *Nashville Skyline*—and this time, he journeyed to the Deep South, the South of black gospel and rhythm and blues. (*Shot of Love* was recorded mainly at Clover Recorders in Los Angeles, but the lead track was coproduced by Little Richard's former producer, Bumps Blackwell.) Dylan's links to black spirituals and gospel—evident in his early recording of "Gospel Plow" and his transforma-

The *Saved* sessions with Mona Lisa Young, Regina Havis, Bob Dylan, Clydie King, and Terry Young at the Muscle Shoals Sound Studio, Sheffield, Alabama, 1980.

tion of "No More Auction Block" into "Blowin' in the Wind"—went back far, at least as far as Odetta, and then the Freedom Singers of the Student Nonviolent Coordinating Committee, and then, maybe most of all, to the Staple Singers, the first African-American group to record

Dylan's songs. (The group's lead singer, Mavis Staples, who, on her own testimony, had a long and intense romantic involvement with Dylan, had been a continuing influence, with a voice, Dylan once remarked, that "just made my hair stand up.")* Now those links were amplified and obvious to everyone, especially on songs like "Saved" and "When You Gonna Wake Up?"

The gospel period also led Dylan to revamp completely his stage show, featuring a revolving cast of black female singers who would open the concert and then provide backup for a set list that, from the autumn of 1979 until the autumn of 1980, consisted entirely of Christian songs. (Dylan would become romantically linked with at least two of the singers, Helena Springs and Clydie King, and would eventually marry a third, Carolyn Dennis, who bore him a daughter, Desiree, in 1986.) As performance, the gospel concerts were as defiantly provocative as the raucous second-half rock shows of late 1965 and early 1966, when frenzied disgust caused one British fan in Manchester to scream "Judas"—odd premonition!—at Dylan from the audience. The format was as unconventional for a mainline rock concert in 1979 and 1980 as the Rolling Thunder Revue had been in 1975. Yet the gospel concerts, like the revue, were very much in the American grain—not a traveling medicine show, but another kind of spectacle beneath the big top. Dylan reinvented the southern tent-show revival, starring himself as the singer and hellfire preacher.

During the quiet, concertless year that followed the end of the *Shot of Love* promotion tour late in 1981, Dylan recorded some duets with Clydie King at the Rundown Studios that went unreleased because, according to Dylan, they didn't "fall into any category that the record company knows how to deal with." By the end of 1982, Dylan was asking various musical notables, ranging from Frank Zappa to Ric Ocasek, about possibly producing his next record. (Dylan himself, along with Mark Knopfler, ended up doing the job.) The changes were now dramatic: the gospel backup singers were gone, and Dylan's thinking had turned to such issues as economic globalization as well as to the modern state of Israel. Dylan told an interviewer he had originally wanted to call the new album *Surviving in a Ruthless World,* but he eventually named it, with his old ambiguity, *Infidels.* Yet there would also be undeniable continuities that connected

---

* The lyrics manuscripts in the George Hecksher Collection at the Morgan Library include a song, "Gospel News," written by Dylan sometime in the early 1960s.

the gospel records to the new one. Knopfler, who had performed on *Slow Train Coming*, would appear once again. Biblical allusions still filled Dylan's head. Although the lyrics were much more concerned with exposing false prophecy than with chastising nonbelievers, the Bible and Satan were very much there, and a religious feeling suffused the songs. Yet the very best song of all, one that marked a leap in Dylan's American art, would, strangely, not appear on the album—the song he had carried with him into the very first *Infidels* recording session, named after the dead blues singer Willie McTell.

McTell was in his late thirties, and had not recorded a song for four years, when John and Ruby Lomax found him at the Pig 'n' Whistle. Dating back to 1927, though, he had made more than twenty 78 rpm records that were released commercially either under his own name or under various pseudonyms, including Blind Sammie and Georgia Bill. He had also played backup guitar on sessions with the husband-and-wife vaudeville duo Alfoncy and Bethenea Harris and the vocalist Mary Willis, and he had recorded four 78s (three of which were released) with his wife, Kate, backed by his Atlanta guitarist friend Curley Weaver. Although McTell never achieved a major hit in the race-record market, his recordings usually enjoyed respectable sales, which allowed him to command an impressive fee of a hundred dollars per recorded side at the height of the Great Depression in the mid-1930s—nearly eight times the average weekly wage for a black workingman in Atlanta. He had a special knack for persuading different recording companies to sign him up, which led to four days of sessions in New York for the Vocalion label in 1933 and two days recording in Chicago for Decca in 1935.* He was also highly resourceful at booking his own appearances around the South—where he performed in every sort of venue, from vaudeville halls to medicine show tents, as well as for private parties and dances—and then picked up extra money playing in the bus stations as he rode from town to town. All of this recording and touring merely supplemented his chief source of income, which came from his regular stands at hotels and eateries in his home base of Atlanta.

---

* Although the sessions rarely lasted more than a day or two a year, between 1927 and 1936, McTell would fail to record only in 1934.

Atlanta's popular black music, from the 1920s through the 1940s, should not be confused with the heavy and sometimes blistering styles of the Mississippi Delta and Chicago that have become the best-known versions of the blues. By the mid-1920s, a new generation of musicians dominated the Atlanta scene, playing idiosyncratic variants of the gleaming, bouncier style common to the southeastern seaboard and Piedmont regions. They included Curley Weaver and two of Weaver's friends, the brothers Robert and Charley Hicks from nearby Walton County. Around 1918, the trio, all of them still in their teens, gained a good deal of attention at fish fries and country balls playing bottleneck-slide style on open-tuned guitars and featuring rapid bass runs fretted with the thumb—thereby concocting a sound much larger than that of most country combos. They duly relocated to Atlanta in search of regular music work; Bob Hicks switched to playing a twelve-string guitar, which created a still larger sound; and in 1927, after a talent scout spotted him performing at Tidwell's Barbecue in the northern Atlanta suburb of Buckhead, Hicks signed a recording contract with Columbia Records.

Under the name Barbecue Bob, Hicks had a big hit with his very first record, "Barbecue Blues," and then enjoyed an unprecedented success with "Mississippi Heavy Water Blues," recorded in June 1927—one of the biggest sellers in a string of quick releases about the floods which had devastated Mississippi and Louisiana that spring. The new, clanging Atlanta sound had broken through, and record companies instantly dispatched scouts and record producers to Georgia. On October 21, 1927, their most talented new discovery, Blind Willie McTell, recorded four songs for the Victor company in Atlanta, two of which became his first 78, "Stole Rider Blues," backed with "Mr. McTell Got the Blues." McTell linked up with the Hicks brothers and in time became Curley Weaver's close friend and collaborator, but his virtuosity, cleverness, and peculiarly melodic style made him special.

McTell had emerged out of a southern tangle of history, speculation, and innovation. One of his great-grandfathers on his father's side, Reddick McTyeir, was a white man, born in 1826, the owner of a small farm outside Augusta, who conceived a son with his slave girl Essie on the eve of the Civil War and then saw heavy combat serving the Confederate cause. McTyeir survived the war and would live until August 1905—about two years after Minnie Dorsey, the teenage lover of his no-account black grandson, Ed McTier, gave birth to a boy in Happy Valley, nine and a half miles outside the town of Thomson.* (The McTyeir spelling had changed two generations earlier.) Named William Samuel McTier, the child was blind from early babyhood if not from birth, possibly as a result (his biographer, Michael Gray, conjectures) of contracting neonatal gonorrhea from his mother while still in her womb—an affliction disproportionally common in the early-twentieth-century rural South and, at the time, by far the chief cause of infant blindness nationwide. Ed McTier, a common field laborer, gambler, and roustabout, drifted off before his boy was seven; Minnie moved with Willie, first to the town of Spread (now Stapleton), with her stepfather and his wife, and then, when Willie was about eight, to Statesboro, the seat of Bulloch County, where she found work as a cook and domestic.

Brannen & Smith Statesboro Ginnery, cotton gin, Statesboro, Georgia, 1913 or 1914.

Compared with rural Thomson or Spread, Statesboro bustled—a major center for the sale of Sea Island long-staple cotton, and connected to the wider world by the Central Georgia and the Savannah and States-

---

* The precise date of McTell's birth is uncertain, but the most exacting study, by Michael Gray, proposes May 5, 1903, as the most likely of all the possibilities.

boro railways. But young Willie was restless, prevented by his blindness from attending school. About the time he was twelve—or so he later claimed—he began periodically running away from home to join one or another of the circuses and road shows that came through Statesboro. "I run away and went everywhere: everywhere I could go without money," he recalled decades later. "I followed shows around till I began to get grown." Yet Willie always returned to one family member or another, and once he did "get grown," by his own account, he settled down and turned to making bootleg whiskey, probably assisting his family members in Happy Valley—steady work for a poor man, and worth the risks.

"My mother died and left me reckless, my daddy died and left me wild, wild, wild," Blind Willie McTell later sang in what would eventually become his best-known song, "Statesboro Blues." How much truth there actually is, though, to the stories about his wild and reckless youth is far from clear. Like the young, dissembling Bob Dylan many years later, McTell could be unnervingly precise when he spun his stories about his boyhood circus days, skillfully dropping names and dates like any sharp confidence man. But Michael Gray casts doubt on all of this and presents evidence that young Willie may have lived quietly at home in Statesboro with his mother (whose boyfriend continued to live with his actual wife and family), working part-time doing odd jobs for a grocery store. It is also unclear who taught Willie about music and guitar playing.* But no matter whether he was homebound or hell-bent, Willie's life changed dramatically during his late teens. In 1920, his mother died of a miscarriage, which may have been the result of a self-induced abortion. McTell later said he became an even wilder wanderer then, which is certainly plausible. But in 1922, a white benefactor in Statesboro—his identity remains unknown except for his last name, Simmons—intervened and arranged for the boy, now nineteen, to be sent for three years of schooling at the Georgia Academy for the Blind in Macon. And by the time he left that academy in 1925, Willie McTier had developed into a superb

---

* Kate McTell, Willie's widow, said many years later that he had learned from his mother, who could "really tear up a guitar, work with it." But as Kate McTell also suggested that many listeners thought that Minnie Dorsey was none other than the blues recording great Memphis Minnie—a patent falsehood—her testimony is, to say the least, suspect on these matters. There are some hints that Willie's father, Ed, and his uncle Harley McTier may have fooled around with him on the guitar when he was very young—but those lessons, if that is what they were, would have ended when his father took off and Willie still was a small boy.

young guitarist and singer, his talents honed by the academy's strong music department, which taught him, among other skills, how to read and write musical notation in Braille.

Inside of two years after leaving Macon, McTier moved to Atlanta, the new hot spot for record company scouts—and no later than October 1927, when he made his first records for the Victor company, Willie McTier had become Blind Willie McTell. Allegedly, the similarities in the surnames, when pronounced with a Georgia inflection, had caused an official mix-up at the Macon academy; alternatively, McTell may simply

Atlanta, Georgia, 1940.

have seemed more felicitous for a professional singer. In any event, over the ensuing two decades, McTell built a singular career as a performer, sharply at odds with the stereotype of southern bluesmen as poor, illiterate geniuses, living on the edge of despair.*

---

* A concise statement of this typical view, especially prevalent among northern enthusiasts after World War II, appeared in the liner notes by the energetic blues collector and producer from the 1940s and 1950s Fred Mendelsohn on a compilation album, *Living with the Blues,* released by his Savoy Records in 1964: "In the beginning there was the blues, born of despair and with no other purpose but to express the feelings of futility."

Despite his physical handicap—and in some respects because of it—McTell was clever, educated, well-spoken, and upbeat, and he was far from lonely or propertyless. Having developed acutely sharp senses of hearing, touch, and direction, he could navigate Atlanta, unassisted, with remark-

Robert Fulton Hotel, circa 1940s, postcard. Blind Willie McTell met John and Ruby Lomax here and recorded his Library of Congress sessions in their room on November 5, 1940.

able ease, and on a good weeknight he could earn as much as a hundred dollars playing regular gigs at places such as the Pig 'n' Whistle (his steadiest earner) and at a small club called the Silver Slipper. Saturday usually found him at one of his choice regular locations or playing either at the matinee or on the evening underbill at the 81 Theater on Decatur Street (where Gertrude "Ma" Rainey, when she was passing through, had performed with the pianist Thomas "Georgia Tom" Dorsey before she relocated her base to Chicago in 1923, and where Bessie Smith and Ethel Waters, among others, were headliners in the 1920s). When he was in his prime, McTell also plotted out the schedules that would take him far and wide on the road, sometimes alone, sometimes with companion musicians (including McTell's wife, Kate, and Curley Weaver), and sometimes with traveling troupes and medicine shows.* His regular routes took him up through Georgia and the Carolinas at the height of the tobacco harvest season in July and August, when dealers and salesmen were numerous and flush; in winter, he headed east and then south to the Sea Islands and to Miami, to play for wealthy white tourists. Occasionally, he also visited northern big cities as distant as New York and Chicago. McTell wandered—"Baby, I

---

* The ubiquity of blind men among the great southern black performers of the era owed partly to the element of sideshow curiosity. But performing music—whether as a sidewalk beggar or stage-show attraction—was one of the few options left open for southern blacks with ambition and musical talent.

was born to ramble," he told his wife—but not aimlessly or impulsively; he was highly methodical. He was likewise exact in his financial dealings with record companies and theater managers. "He always had him a contract," Kate McTell recalled. "He'd say, 'I'm not going to pick my fingers off for nickels and dimes.' "

McTell earned enough money from his music to support himself quite well—and after he married Kate, then a nursing student, early in 1934, the couple resided in a series of rented apartments in northeastern Atlanta not far from the Sweet Auburn district, the commercial hub and most fashionable residential area for black Atlantans. (The couple's first residence in 1934, at 160 Hilliard Street, was about four blocks from the home of the Martin Luther King family, whose boy Martin Jr. was five.) The neighborhood was close enough to the dives and "trick" houses of downtown Decatur Street and to the Black Bottom area around South Bell Street to allow McTell to congregate easily with his fellow Atlanta musicians in some of their low-end haunts, yet McTell's own domicile was eminently respectable. (Musicians would also visit McTell at his home, among them the great blues singer from South Carolina Josh White, who stopped by going to and from concert dates before heading back to his adopted home in New York City.) "They lived a very normal life," Kate's younger brother, Andrew, recalled of the McTells many years later. McTell was also fastidious in his personal appearance, sporting a carefully groomed mustache and wearing an everyday wardrobe of a suit and tie and a fashionable billed cap. "He never allowed himself to believe that he was dressed," Andrew said, "until he put on his necktie." Fleeting acquaintances and close friends alike described him as a warmhearted, generous man, curious about people and the world at large, and devoted to his art.

McTell's decorousness and work ethic marked him, at least outwardly, as an orderly, even straitlaced striver. So did his spiritual life: McTell was not just a believing Christian, but had what his brother-in-law called "a keen sense of scripture" and read the Bible in Braille just as he read many secular books. (For a time, late in his life, he would perform only sacred music under his own name.) Yet through the 1940s, McTell also remained attached to the barrelhouse world of hard drinking, gambling, and prostitution, in Atlanta and on the road—and none of this was contradictory to McTell, at least until he grew older. An unusually intelligent, up-from-under country boy, he became neither rich nor (in his own time) famous—but by the mid-1930s, he had made himself into a successful, consummately professional entertainer and something of an urban sophisticate. That urbanity, and the shrewdness that lay behind it, molded his music.

When he first turned to performing folk music in 1959 and 1960, Bob Dylan immersed himself in the blues but could not have known too much, if anything, about Blind Willie McTell. Unlike John and Alan Lomax's premier discovery, Leadbelly, McTell had had no great promoters and devotees among the nation's leading folklorists or in the overlapping world of the folksy Popular Front Left. None of his songs had appeared on Harry Smith's influential *Anthology of American Folk Music* LP collection in 1952. Other blues veterans of the 1920s and 1930s, rediscovered in the 1960s, would get to enjoy a last taste of acclaim, including McTell's Atlanta friend the guitarist and harmonica player Buddy Moss, but McTell did not live to see the folk revival. Were it not for the English émigré and tireless blues collector Samuel Charters, McTell might have been forgotten by the younger generation far longer than he was, and might have been forgotten altogether.

Charters reissued three of McTell's most striking early recordings, "Statesboro Blues," "Mama, 'Tain't Long Fo' Day," and "Southern Can Mama," on two compilation recordings whose quality and influence deserve more recognition than they have received: *The Country Blues,* released in 1959, and a double LP, *The Rural Blues,* released a year later. In his groundbreaking book, *The Country Blues,* which accompanied his record with the same title, Charters offered little solid information on McTell but did describe him as a "brilliant but elusive blues singer, with an almost indestructible quality about him"—a mixture of reticence and praise that created an alluring aura of obscurity. "On Blind Willie McTell, our imaginations really went to work," the distinguished music historian Peter Guralnick recalls of his high-school years as a blues fan in Boston at the start of the 1960s. "A sensitive, oddly wistful singer, he was, to us, a figure of mystery and determination." Bob Dylan almost certainly listened to "Statesboro Blues" and "Southern Can Mama," on Charters's compilations, from which he took two songs for his own first album, Bukka White's "Fixin' to Die Blues" and Tommy McClennan's "New Highway 51." Still, Dylan showed no signs that McTell's music had yet touched him very deeply or that he had been caught up by McTell's mystique.

In 1960, the small Prestige/Bluesville label released, with little obvious impact, McTell's *Last Session,* a selection of fourteen songs taken from a tape recording made in 1956, three years before McTell's death, by an Atlanta record store owner, Ed Rhodes. Soon thereafter a handful of McTell's commercial recordings appeared on some obscure blues reissue compilations. Then, in 1966, thanks to the rising musicologist Dick Spottswood, the short-lived Melodeon label issued a slightly clipped version of the Lomaxes' Library of Congress tape of McTell from 1940, and two years after that the young, intense (and later legendary) Greenwich Village record collector Nick Perls issued an album on his new Belzona label consisting of fourteen of McTell's early recordings, dubbed from the original 78s. A new cohort of big-city blues enthusiasts—they called themselves the blues Mafia— had fixed its seal of approval on McTell's reputation. And soon thereafter, thanks largely to performers in

Album sleeve of *Last Session* with Blind Willie McTell, Prestige/ Bluesville Records, 1956.

Bob Dylan's ambit, McTell's music would find an audience far larger than even his greatest admirers could have possibly imagined.

In 1964, the offbeat East Village folk duo of Peter Stampfel and Steve Weber, recording as the Holy Modal Rounders, included "Statesboro Blues" on their second album, and two years later the Boston-based singer-songwriter Tom Rush recorded the song on an album for Elektra. Dave Van Ronk (who was a good friend and collaborator of Sam Charters's as well as one of Dylan's mentors) also took a liking to "Statesboro Blues" and recorded his own powerful version of it for Verve Records in 1966. Schooled, in part, by Charters and the young blues aficionados, the singers had prepared the way for the complete recovery of McTell's music. Two years after Van Ronk, the evolving folk and blues musician Taj Mahal's first album included a rock rendition of the song with a bottleneck electric guitar line, which riveted and inspired an up-and-coming guitarist from Macon, Duane Allman. Leading off the Allman Brothers Band's blockbuster album, *At Fillmore East,* in 1971, "Statesboro Blues" almost immediately entered the rock-and-roll canon—and soon the bulk of McTell's original recorded work began appearing on LP reissues. Through the end of the 1970s, hardly a year passed without the appearance of a new album of McTell recordings or of a compilation that included at least one of McTell's originals. In 1977, the British magazine *Blues Unlimited* featured an extensive interview with Kate McTell about her husband, which, although not always trustworthy, filled in some of the large holes in his biography. The last remaining original McTell tracks finally appeared in LP form in 1983—the same year that Dylan recorded "Blind Willie McTell."

With virtually all of McTell's recordings now easily accessible, Dylan, like the rest of the world, could hear him in full as a guitarist, singer, and writer of singular talent. (Five years earlier, Dylan had included McTell among a select group of blues and country artists to whom, he told an interviewer, he most enjoyed listening.) And although a great deal about McTell remained to be revealed as of 1983, enough was known for Dylan to have been able to notice some curious convergences with his own life—and, more important, with his art. To be sure, until the early 1980s, McTell and his music appeared to have had little direct influence on Dylan's work, no matter how much Dylan had come to enjoy McTell's recordings. Even when his song "Blind Willie McTell" finally surfaced in 1991, long after *Infidels* appeared, the title seemed to pop out of nowhere. Dylan might have been expected to write a song that honored Muddy Waters, Big Joe Williams, Mance Lipscomb, Robert Johnson, Sleepy John Estes, or any other of his obvious and long-acknowledged influences, but choosing McTell seemed a little odd. Perhaps it really was no big deal; perhaps McTell's name simply fit Dylan's lyrical needs, in rhyme and meter, better than any of the others. But the way that Dylan's song beckoned to McTell—invoking him over and over as a blues singer like no other—indicated a much deeper personal engagement. For Dylan, McTell's music had become a touchstone, a standard of excellence for comprehending the world.

Although McTell could playact the folklore historian, he was, as Dylan would later be, a musical modernist with strong roots in traditional forms. Here and there McTell tipped his hat to older blues musicians. His partiality to the twelve-string guitar was in keeping with the Atlanta blues associated with Barbecue Bob. But McTell was beholden to no particular performance or composing style (including that of his far less melodious Atlanta friends), and he excelled in numerous genres, including amalgamated genres of his own devising. It is misleading, in fact, to think of McTell narrowly as a blues musician. Like some other southern singers of his time—including Blind Blake, Mance Lipscomb, Leadbelly, Mississippi John Hurt, and (among whites) Charlie Poole and Jimmie Rodgers—McTell is better described as a songster. Working in a tradition, indebted to minstrelsy, that dated back to the vagabond musicians of the Reconstruction years, the songsters mastered all kinds of popular forms, from spirituals to the latest hits from Tin Pan Alley. They certainly played the blues, in part because the blues were popular, and in part because the name became attached, in the 1920s, to most black music that was not labeled jazz. But the songsters did not define themselves as bluesmen.

McTell was one of the geniuses of the blues-singing songster style, a well-traveled performer who provided his customers and the record companies with what they wanted, but also an artist who made his own brilliant musical innovations. And unlike most of the songsters, McTell, from the very start of his professional career, was a city entertainer who heard every conceivable sort of music and sang to all sorts of people. At the simplest level, he was adept at rewriting blues standards and thoroughly transforming them, in seemingly endless variation. Thus, the old slide-guitar standby "Po' Boy" served as the foundation for one of McTell's most startling early songs—and most beautifully performed recordings—"Mama, 'Tain't Long Fo' Day." (The song is also notable for its vivid imagery, one of McTell's other strong points, in lines like "The big star fallin', mama, 'tain't long fo' day.") But "Po' Boy" also inspired the music for two other, very different McTell songs, "Three Women Blues" and "Love Changing Blues." Alternatively, McTell might play an entirely different melody, then jump to one of the blues standards—as in his semi-talking blues narrative "Travelin' Blues," where a rapid virtuoso accompaniment suddenly gives way, for one verse, to "Po' Boy." The inventiveness and spontaneity of McTell's rearrangements required exceptional dexterity, mental and physical, but it also required his songster's mastery of numerous popular forms, including vaudeville hokum (with its spoken repartee), jug band romps, ragtime, country folk songs, modern spirituals, and pop songs.

McTell was a sponge—the word would later be applied to Dylan—

who soaked up every kind of music he heard and then expressed it in his own way. Although not always punctilious about giving due credit, McTell made no bones about being a borrower, while he also insisted upon his musical integrity. "I jump 'em from other writers," he said of his songs shortly before he died, "but I arrange 'em my own way." McTell's touring stints affected his style, and listening to phonograph records gave him even more material, including some lines and sequences that have come to be regarded as his own.

Blind Willie McTell, 1927.

Consider McTell's best-known song, "Statesboro Blues." For four verses, the song follows the standard twelve-bar form but then moves into unfamiliar turf as McTell, singing and playing in a jumpy double time, instructs various family members—"Sister, tell your brother, brother, tell your auntie"—to get out the word: "Goin' up the country, mama, don't you want to go?" The hybrid musical arrangement is pure McTell—yet virtually the same lyrics had appeared on earlier records by the popular Chicago-based blueswomen Sippie Wallace and Lucille Bogan. Other elements of "Statesboro Blues" came from recordings by Bessie Smith and the lesser-known Ivy Smith.

McTell's own commercial recordings, meanwhile, barely began to describe his musical range and ambitions. Playing to whites and blacks for nickels and tips, in Atlanta's drive-in restaurants, taverns, and clubs, as well as on the road, demanded that McTell become not just a songster but a human jukebox—a performer who could provide, on demand, what people on both sides of the color line, affluent and poor, and in the countryside as well as the city, wanted to hear, including the latest hit records. And if McTell was best known, on records and off, for his secular music, he also played gospel songs such as "The Little Black Train" and more jazzy sacred music such as "When the Saints Go Marchin' In," at revivals and in churches, much as he had when he was a boy. Some of his secular rags, folk songs, and hybrids did appear commercially in the 1930s; they included a breathtaking, sped-up, fingerpicked version of Blind Blake's "Wabash Rag" (which he renamed "Georgia Rag") and "Hillbilly Willie's Blues," a reworking of the country tune "This Train"—the popular song that Woody Guthrie would later make famous as "This Train Is Bound for Glory"—that featured references to President Roosevelt ("a mighty fine man"), the rich and the poor, moonshine, a bottle of beer, and Arkansas. But McTell concentrated on recording his religious songs for commercial release only once, during a few days of sessions for Decca Records in Chicago in 1935.

McTell's broad musical interests and talents actually came across best in his hastily arranged two hours of recording for the Lomaxes and the Library of Congress. McTell's tenor pitch had deepened slightly by 1940, but his voice's timbre was as round as ever. If his right hand no longer fingerpicked with quite the ferocity he'd shown on "Georgia Rag," his bottleneck-slide technique had mellowed to become at once more delicate and more resonant. The diversity of his material, meanwhile, was spectacular. Along with an assortment of spirituals, he performed folk songs and ballads ("Boll Weevil," "Delia," "Will Fox," and a bowdlerized "Chainey"), a blues ("Murderer's Home Blues"), a rag ("Kill-It-Kid Rag"), and a pop song ("Baby, It Must Be Love," which he told John Lomax he had written himself, but which had been recorded in 1937 by the Harlem singer Sally Gooding, accompanied by the Three Peppers jive combo). Most impressively, he performed a deathbed frolic, filled with some of his most strikingly visual lyrics, which he said he had put together by himself out of three different songs (one of which, certainly, was "St. James Infirmary") as the dying request of a friend who had been gunned down in 1929, Jesse Williams—"The Dyin' Crapshooter's Blues."

Sung to a dirgelike melody, the song is the exact opposite of a dirge, in its lyrics as well as its tempo, as it relates Williams's riotous last requests:

> *Little Jesse was a gambler, night and day*
> *He used crooked cards and dice,*
> *He was a sinful boy, good hearted but had no soul,*
> *His heart was hard and cold like ice.*

The police have shot Jesse, he knows he's going to die, and with a gang of crapshooters and gamblers gathered at his bedside, he plots his own funeral. Eight crapshooters will serve as pallbearers; behind them will be a motley procession of mourners that includes a contingent of policemen, judges, and court solicitors, sixteen bootleggers, sixteen racket men, and seventy-seven women from what appear to be some of Atlanta's most notorious brothels and gambling dens—all headed to Jesse's grave, freshly dug with the ace of spades, his tombstone a deck of cards.

Once Jesse finishes listing the women, his heart suddenly starts thumping and he goes down "bouncin' and jumpin'," but no tears are to be shed for the crapshooter. "Folks, don't be standin' around Jesse cryin'," McTell sings in an aside, "he wants everybody to do the Charleston whilst he dyin'." The song concludes with a deadpan mixture of the comic, the frivolous, and the grotesque:

> *One foot up, a toenail dragging*
> *Throw my buddy Jesse in the hoodoo wagon*
>
> *Come here, mama, with that can of booze*
> *He got the dyin' crapshooter's blues,*
> *Passin' out,*
> *With the dyin' crapshooter's blues.*

The song, which had started in a mournful E minor key, ends with a G major chord, and the crapshooter Jesse's blues winds up laughing at death and even damnation.

McTell added a great deal of Atlanta detail, but his rewrite of "St. James Infirmary," supposedly a true story, resembled a version of the song that Cab Calloway recorded late in 1930, and which may have been one of the three tunes from which McTell said he borrowed:

> *An' give me six crap shooting pallbearers,*
> *Let a chorus girl sing me a song,*
> *Put a red hot jazz band at the top of my head,*
> *So we can raise Hallelujah as we go along.*

But McTell's source (and possibly Calloway's) is more easily identifiable, and McTell's pilferage was greater than he suggested. In 1927, the second-string jazz and blues pianist and composer Porter Grainger pulled together a number he called "Dyin' Crap-Shooter's Blues," and that same year the prolific blues singer Martha Copeland, backed by a jazz combo, recorded it for Columbia:

Jim Johnson gambled night and day,
  With crooked cards and dice,
A sinful man without a soul,
  His heart was cold as ice.

Half of the lyrics in McTell's song repeat Grainger's word for word, or nearly so, including the lines about the dragging toenail and the hoodoo wagon. All of whatever tunes McTell exploits, including "St. James Infirmary," also appear in Grainger's version. Indeed, there is virtually nothing in Grainger's lyrics and melody that does not appear in McTell's song—a song he told the Lomaxes that he had "made myself."

McTell did not lie here, as he did over "Baby, It Must Be Love"— "making" a song is not the same as writing one—and he acknowledged that he borrowed, though the recording has misled later generations.* And the song that McTell sang to the Lomaxes, although recorded under primitive conditions, is far superior to Martha Copeland's recording of Porter Grainger's "Dyin' Crap-Shooter's Blues." About half again as long as Grainger's version, McTell's turns a novelty number into a three-part tale, depicting Jesse's decline and shooting, followed by the strange, slightly zany funeral procession that Jesse requests, and concluding with Jesse's death. Grainger's smooth musical forms are self-consciously soldered together, as if intended for a stage revue; McTell's performance, by contrast, is jagged, played at slightly uneven tempos, sounding (perhaps deliberately) as if McTell were figuring out, line by line, where he is headed. Grainger's song consists almost entirely of the crapshooter's words as he contemplates his own death. (The lyrics suggest it will be a suicide; there is nothing mentioned about a police shooting; indeed, when the song ends, the crapshooter is still alive.) In McTell's song, the perspective of the lyrics shifts, switching from the voice of the singer to that of the mortally wounded man and finally back to the singer, and time shifts as well, moving from the past to the present to the future to the present again.

One of McTell's masterpieces, "The Dyin' Crapshooter's Blues" marked him as a composer and performer like no other songster bluesman, with an unusually rich, descriptive imagination and a striking ability to bend

---

* No newspaper or official police evidence has been brought to light to corroborate McTell's story about the shooting death of a Jesse Williams in Atlanta in 1929— although given the circumstances at the time, Michael Gray surmises, such an incident may not have left behind an official record.

both time and prospect—an ability that was remarkable in virtually any artistic context in the 1920s and 1930s. It would take two decades for the song to appear, first on the *Last Session* album in 1960, and then, six years later, on the LP of the Library of Congress recording. (McTell also recorded the song for Atlantic Records in 1949, but that rendering was not issued until 1972.) There is no evidence that, more than forty years after McTell first recorded it, Bob Dylan (who was also known to jump songs from other writers and arrange them his way) had the song on his mind, although he'd certainly heard it many times. But when he started recording *Infidels* in 1983, he plainly was thinking about sin, God, America, the blues, and Blind Willie McTell, and he was also thinking about "St. James Infirmary."

The Power Station studio is hushed; there is a barely audible footfall, then Dylan strikes a single piano key. It is a quiet but stark call to musical order. Mark Knopfler softly, exquisitely picks an acoustic guitar in the background, then joins in; Dylan hits a quick pair of somber E-flat minor chords, sketches two measures of melody, and begins to sing, wearily: "Seen the arrow on the door po-ost, sayin' this land is condemned." Twenty years after "A Hard Rain's A-Gonna Fall," he has written another of his many songs that traverse appalling sights and sounds. Almost right away, it is obvious that the melody of "Blind Willie McTell" comes from "St. James Infirmary"—the same melody that dominates Blind Willie McTell's own "The Dyin' Crapshooter's Blues"—with possibly just a touch of Frédéric Chopin's *Marche Funèbre*.

Recording the song has been giving Dylan difficulty. Three complete takes from the first day of work on the album, with his entire ensemble, don't work, and neither do two complete takes from the seventh *Infidels* session. Now, after a grueling three weeks of recording sessions, working six days a week, Dylan returns to "Blind Willie McTell" and attempts to rediscover it at the piano, much as he attempted in 1966 after he lost "She's Your Lover Now." With Knopfler playing beside him, his foot quietly tapping out the time, Dylan runs through the entire song, slowly, but fails to reconnect: whatever he had once heard in his head is gone. *Infidels* would appear later in the year without "Blind Willie McTell," and the recording of Dylan and Knopfler's studio run-through would circulate as a demo tape for possible use by other performers, until it finally appeared in 1991 on an official three-CD retrospective of rare Dylan performances and outtakes. Only then did listeners learn that Dylan had recorded a masterpiece.

The arrow on the doorpost that the singer sees when the song begins is a sign. It might protect the home inside, much as doorway signs of lamb's blood protected the enslaved Israelites in the Passover story. It might mark the household as righteous and observant, like the Jewish mezuzah, affixed to the doorposts of the pious in accord with the holy injunctions in Deuteronomy. But it certainly signifies that the land as a whole is condemned. Which land? "All the way from New Or-*lee*ans to Je-*ru*-sa-lem," Dylan sings. The land where blacks were enslaved; the land where the Israelites ruled only to be cast out and oppressed, and where Herod, in trying to kill the Christ child, massacred the innocents: these lands and all the lands between them, the whole world over, are damned.* The singer suddenly tells of traveling through East Texas—home to Blind Lemon Jefferson, though not to McTell—"where many martyrs fell." The martyrs could be, as the word normally connotes, holy victims, or they could be broken slaves and lynched freedmen, or even Confederate and Union soldiers, or soldiers from the war against Mexico, or the fallen fighters at the Alamo. Or they might include John F. Kennedy. Or they could be all of these. And what does the singer know from these sights and travels? That "no one can sing the blues like Blind Willie McTell."

The next verse thrusts us into Willie McTell's world. The singer recalls hearing a hoot owl singing late at night, after some sort of show had ended and the tents were being struck and folded. (They could be revival show tents or medicine show circus tents; McTell had connections to both.) Yet even though the singer heard the owl—symbol of wisdom and

---

* There is another way to read this, given that all of the song's other obvious references are to the American South. There are more than a dozen towns in the United States named Jerusalem, half of them in the states of the old Confederacy. And what is now Courtland, Virginia, used to be the town of Jerusalem—where the slave rebel Nat Turner was hanged, flayed, drawn and quartered, and beheaded after his capture and trial in 1831. Dylan is a student of the Civil War era, so this reference is plausible—making "Blind Willie McTell" even more a song of the South, though with vaster implications. To complicate matters even further, Dylan has taken, in concert, to singing "New Jerusalem," which might be the city of God as described in Revelation, or one of any number of cities and towns in the United States, or even the New Jerusalem that Joseph Smith, the original prophet of the Church of Jesus Christ of Latter-day Saints, said would arise in Missouri.

victory in ancient Greece, although in other cultures a symbol of bad luck and evil—nobody else did; the owl's only audience was the stars above the barren trees.* By contrast, one can only imagine that an enthusiastic crowd cheered the charcoal gypsy maidens, strutting their feathers, whom the singer recalls next. It seems that the tent show was a lusty one, with swaggering black chorus girls who might have stepped out of "The Dyin' Crapshooter's Blues"—although Dylan himself had performed with his own soulful black maidens, who were also, at various times, his lovers. In the American South, the lines between one kind of show and the other—Holy Rollers and hoochie-coochie—had always been blurry; indeed, one sometimes followed the other on the same night. But no matter because, finally, Dylan sings, "*No*-bu-dee can sing the blues like Blind Willie McTell."

Now sunk in deepest Dixie, the song moves backward in time, not forward through space, and the singer doesn't just relate what he finds, but calmly bids us to look for ourselves:

> *See them big plantations burnin'*
> *Hear the cracking of the whips*
> *Smell that sweet magnolia bloomin'*
> *See the ghosts-uuuuuuuuuvv slavery ships.*

From the Civil War and slavery's Armageddon back to slavery times, cruelty cracked while lush beauty bloomed, and in back of it all stood the shades of the deathly Middle Passage. Suddenly, though, time has slipped again: these are ghosts, not the ships or slaves themselves, and the singer tells of how he can still "hear them tribes a-moanin' " and hear the undertaker's bell ringing. The moaning tribes are the tribes of Africans being sold into slavery, but they could also be the moaning Africans of today, or the ancient enslaved tribes of Israel, or any suffering tribe you choose, at any time you choose. And though the undertaker's bell tolled all over the slave South, that bell has tolled forever, and it tolls for everyone. And still—still—the singer repeats, "Nobody can sing the blues like Blind Willie McTell."

---

* Given that the song has just invoked McTell's name for the first time, it's possible to get confused and think that it is Blind Willie who is singing after the show. It depends on how one hears the lines "The stars above the barren trees / Were his only audience" and takes "his" to mean. Either way, something important is going unheard, unheeded.

Now the song flashes on other southern scenes, and Dylan's voice rises in revulsion. A woman, who seems to know exactly what's up, is down by the riverside with a fine young man, dressed to the nines, who is carrying a bottle of bootleg whiskey. (The song does not say whether they are black or white, because they could be either.) Up on the highway, a convict chain gang toils and sweats. The singer can hear rebel yells. And now he *knows* no one can sing the blues like Blind Willie McTell.

An instrumental break sets off the singer's tale of his journey from his final reflections. Atop Knopfler's strums and liquid licks, Dylan plays a jumpy piano, banging out the chorus with doubled-up, backbeat chords. Then he sings: "Well, God is in His heaven / And we all want what's His." As performed on the session tape, the lines echo the famous conclusion of the poet Robert Browning's "Pippa's Song"—"God's in His heaven— / All's right with the world!"—by which Browning really meant that despite all of the evil and vicious injustice in the world, it is still possible to have faith in God. But as rendered in Dylan's official book of lyrics—"Well God is in heaven"—the lines echo the Bible and convey a darker message. "God is in heaven, and thou upon earth," reads Ecclesiastes 5:2. Dylan's revision of the second line describes a yearning for life everlasting—but also humankind's blasphemous disregard for the separation of heaven and earth. Continuing in a biblical vein, the song explains that in this world, all is vanity, and "power and greed and corruptible seed / seem to be all that there is."* And there is still another possibility, just as close to Dylan's preoccupations and the historical themes of "Blind Willie McTell": "But God is in Heaven, and Grant in the Town, / And Right through might is Law— / *God's way adore*," Herman Melville wrote in one of his poems in *Battle-Pieces*, describing the fall of Richmond, the Confederate capital, and the conclusion of the Civil War.

The singer has seen, heard, and smelled unspeakable things, in the past and in the present. He reports no redress and no redemption, even in Jesus Christ; the only sign he sees of the Lord's true and righteous judgment is an arrow marking condemnation of a heedless world riddled with greed, corruption, and the lust for power. And with that the singer concludes, gazing out a hotel window, his voice rising again, as if to give himself and

---

* Dylan here alludes to an evangelical Christian biblical mainstay, from the letters of Peter, in which the apostle assures the faithful of salvation: "Being born again, not of corruptible seed, but of incorruptible, by the word of God, which liveth and abideth for ever" (I Peter 1:23).

his listeners something to hold on to, proclaiming one last time the one thing that he really knows, that "*no* one can sing the blu-*oo*-ues like *Blind Will-ah-ee McTe-uhl*."* All he has left is the song and its singer.

Dylan and Knopfler play two more verses of instrumental, slowing and swelling at the end, and the performance concludes with a softly ringing harmonic and quick single note from Knopfler's guitar.

There the studio life of "Blind Willie McTell" ended for Dylan. It was May 5, 1983—which, as best anyone can tell, but unknown to everyone at the Power Station, would have been Blind Willie McTell's eightieth birthday.

---

* The song specifies that the singer is in the St. James Hotel, and there has been speculation over the years about the reference, above and beyond the obvious allusion to "St. James Infirmary." Yet that mystery in itself marked Dylan's return, in 1983, to layers of allusion largely missing during his Christian phase. Rather than assume that this is some recondite metaphysical, symbolic, or religious reference—having the hotel named for Christ's apostle Saint James makes no sense—I've preferred to think the song must be talking about a real hotel, just as "Highway 61 Revisited" refers to a real highway. And there are a few possibilities. Unfortunately, of all the St. James hotels, the one that best fits the song could not have been gazed out of by Dylan or anyone else, as it was closed for more than a century until it reopened, restored, in 1997. Built in 1837, the St. James Hotel in downtown Selma, Alabama, welcomed generations of plantation owners and cotton factors; Frank and Jesse James are reputed to have stayed there after the Civil War; and it is located only a short distance from the Edmund Pettus Bridge, site of the momentous "Bloody Sunday" civil-rights march in 1965 that helped secure voting rights for blacks. Still, even if the hotel was empty, the building did stand all those years, a mute witness to scenes right out of "Blind Willie McTell." Another possibility, the original St. James Hotel of New Orleans, was a grand place that opened on Magazine Street in 1859 and closed when the Union army occupied the city during the Civil War and converted the hotel into a military hospital. A thoroughly apocryphal local story calls this the original St. James Infirmary. Partially demolished in 1967 due to structural damage, the New Orleans St. James reopened in a new location nearby in 1999. Since 1875, there has been a St. James Hotel in Red Wing, Minnesota, alongside the Mississippi River—the site of the juvenile penitentiary about which Dylan wrote one of his earliest songs. Unfortunately, though, for listeners who revel in allusion, what seem to be the most likely possibilities have no obvious connection to the American past—although they do carry powerful meanings. One is the luxurious St. James Hotel and Club in London, a favorite of affluent musicians and actors—which would make the last verse cuttingly ironic. The other, the once-rundown St. James Hotel near Times Square in Manhattan (since renovated), would have offered views of the seamy as well as the spectacular side of American entertainment's "crossroads of the world."

"Perhaps the most entrancing challenge in 'Blind Willie McTell,' " Greil Marcus writes, "is to hear in its namesake's music what Bob Dylan heard." One thing Dylan certainly heard was a touch of grace in a ruthless world.

St. James Hotel, New York City, in the early 1980s.

It's not that Blind Willie McTell was the best blues singer ever. Dylan's song makes no such claim, although some listeners have thought it does. McTell was, rather, at least to the singer in the song, unique, unmatched—in the sweetness of his voice, the clarity of his singing, the shimmer of his guitar playing, and the range of his mastery. He was a rambler who lived by his wits and his talent, earned good money, and lived nicely in Atlanta; an unassuming character who was a thoroughgoing professional and nobody's fool; a musical collector and stasher and reinventor; a blind man who wrote intensely visual lyrics that could bend time and space like magic. He was also a godly man whose bottleneck-guitar spirituals were enough to make you shiver; who concocted knowing songs about outlaws and hustlers and painted ladies that described sin but did not judge; and who cut through the racist presumptions of his times with the equalizing spiritual wisdom that, as he told John Lomax, the world was a mean place to live in for whites and a mean place to live in for blacks.

Despite various fresh travails, McTell continued his singing and (occasionally) recording career until the end of his life. His marriage to Kate, racked with tension worsened by his long absences from Atlanta and repeated infidelities, fell apart not long after he recorded for the Lomaxes. Never lacking charm, he very quickly settled into a new relationship with a twice-divorced mother of two, Helen Broughton, which would last until she died in 1958. But the dislocations of World War II, and a ban on recording by the American Federation of Musicians from 1942 to 1944, badly hurt what remained of the southern race-record industry. McTell got by by continuing his sidewalk singing while devoting himself more to performing in churches.

In 1949—two years after he and his brother had founded Atlantic Records, and three years before he signed up a new talent, Ray Charles—the young Turkish-born blues enthusiast Ahmet Ertegun brought McTell back into the studio, after he had stumbled across the singer in Atlanta during a talent-scouting trip. McTell recorded fifteen songs, a mix of secular and religious material, but Atlantic released only a single 78 of "Kill It Kid," backed with "Broke Down Engine Blues." (Now reluctant to be associated publicly with nonreligious music, McTell required that Ertegun issue the record with a pseudonym; they settled on "Barrelhouse Sammy.") A year later, another small company, Regal Records, released two McTell 78s under the name Blind Willie, and another 78 of McTell and his old friend Curley Weaver, performing as the Pig 'n' Whistle Band, named for the drive-in where McTell was still performing, wandering among the parked cars.

By 1956, McTell had moved his act to another drive-in, the Blue Lantern, which is where the record store owner Ed Rhodes, alerted to who he was, persuaded him to make a tape recording in his shop. McTell's health, though, was already failing; in the spring of 1959, he suffered a minor stroke that slurred his speech; and on August 19, after a second stroke hit while he was visiting family relations, he died in Milledgeville State Hospital, at the age of fifty-six. Because of a mix-up, since corrected, his tombstone, in the Jones Grove Baptist Church cemetery outside Thomson, bore the name of one of his cousins, Eddie McTier. McTell's request that he be buried with his twelve-string was overlooked.

Instead, a brother-in-law took the guitar, his grandchildren tore it up, and the pieces were thrown in the garbage.*

In 1981, the Blues Foundation in Memphis named McTell to its Hall of Fame. And had it appeared when it was recorded, Dylan's "Blind Willie McTell" would have capped his posthumous emergence as a musical icon. Yet the song had its own curious history. After Dylan decided to drop it from *Infidels*, his management urged him to include it on subsequent albums, but to no avail. Meanwhile, the Dylan-Knopfler run-through tape circulated among other artists—and finally, the members of a reconstituted version of the Band, without Robbie Robertson, decided to include it on an album they hoped to record. But that project took time to get off the ground, and in 1991 the Dylan-Knopfler version appeared on *The Bootleg Series, Volumes 1–3: Rare and Unreleased, 1961–1991*. Dylan still seemed indifferent. Only during the summer of 1997, four years after the Band's version, sung by Levon Helm, appeared on the album *Jericho*, did Dylan first perform the song in concert.

Dylan had turned forty-two the year he recorded "Blind Willie McTell" and *Infidels*—the same age that McTell had told John Lomax he was in 1940 and that Lomax duly reported on the acetate.[†] *Infidels* received positive reviews; the critics were relieved that as far as they could see, Dylan had forsaken his religious dogma, and the Dylan they were comfortable with—the Dylan they thought they *deserved*—had returned. The Dylan on the record is, for the most part, reflective and tender, especially in his songs of the heart. He is the master of many forms, including rip-roaring rock and roll (although the album's best rock song, "Neighborhood Bully," upset some narrow politically minded critics as a "conservative" defense of Israel). And the songs are wistful and even rueful about the past. At one point, the singer wishes he had become a doctor and saved a life that would have been lost: "Maybe I'd have done some good in the world / 'Stead of burning every bridge I crossed."

Yet *Infidels* without "Blind Willie McTell" is a much diminished album. (Dylan has said that he didn't think the recording sessions captured what

---

* At his death, McTell also owned a six-string acoustic and an electric guitar, but they disappeared and their whereabouts are unknown.

[†] In fact, McTell was in his late thirties. It is unclear why he misinformed Lomax. But the Lomax recording is the source for the common mistaken claim that McTell was born in 1898.

he wanted in the song. Knopfler was upset at its exclusion and argued strongly that it be left in, and Dylan finished work on the album without Knopfler.) Some of the album's other songs contained similar themes, but stated them not nearly as powerfully. ("Oh, man is opposed to fair play, / He wants it all and he wants it his way," in "License to Kill.") A few lines from the lyrics, especially on the lead track, "Jokerman," could have been adapted from Dylan's stronger songs of the mid-1960s ("Distant ships sailing into the mist, / You were born with a snake in both of your fists while a hurricane was blowing"). But in paying his tribute to Blind Willie McTell, Bob Dylan, a man on the move, described a more profound retrieval, in a meditation on good and evil, history and the present. "The past is never dead. It's not even past," William Faulkner wrote—a line that is cited so often, and as often as not inaccurately, that it threatens to become a cliché. "Blind Willie McTell," in its own way, says it just as well, in gloom but with a glimmer of consoling beauty.

In "A Hard Rain's A-Gonna Fall," the blue-eyed son, having traveled through hell on earth, returns home and vows that he will "know my song well before I start singing." In "Blind Willie McTell," in many ways a laconic reprise of "Hard Rain," the singer, now wiser, knows his song much better, maybe even better than well. Yet at the end of this grim passage from the present to the past and back, the singer is gazing out a hotel window through which he has seen it all—on the road, far from home, his thoughts on another singer's singing.

PART IV: INTERLUDE

7

ALL THE FRIENDS I EVER HAD ARE GONE:

"Delia," Malibu, California, May 1993

The years from 1984 through 1991 were eventful ones for Bob Dylan. He released eight albums, including five studio recordings of original material; he toured relentlessly (including stints teamed up with Tom Petty and the Heartbreakers and the Grateful Dead); and he appeared at several high-profile charity benefits, including Willie Nelson's inaugural Farm Aid concert in 1985 to help financially beleaguered small farmers. As a jape, Dylan joined with Petty, George Harrison, Roy Orbison, and Jeff Lynne to form the Traveling Wilburys in 1988 and went on to record two albums. (The first of them, preceded by the hit single "Handle with Care," reached number three on the *Billboard* Top 200, stayed in the best-seller charts for forty weeks, went double-platinum in overall sales, and won a Grammy for Best Rock Performance by a Duo or Group with Vocals.)* Dylan dabbled in various forms of songwriting, including children's songs. He starred in a feature film for Lorimar Productions, playing a crusty, aging rock star. His official distinctions began to pile up, including induction into the Rock and Roll Hall of Fame in 1988 and winning

---

* The second Wilburys album, released two years later and titled *Volume 3* as a joke, was less successful artistically, chiefly because it did not include Orbison, who had died in the interim—yet it still reached number eleven in the U.S. best-seller charts and went platinum.

a Grammy Lifetime Achievement Award in 1991. Dylan also married his second wife, Carolyn Dennis, in 1986, a few months after Dennis gave birth to their daughter, Desiree Gabrielle Dennis-Dylan, although Dylan hid the marriage from the public.

Artistically, however, these years marked a prolonged, depressing setback for Dylan, despite some brief interruptions. Each of his original albums included one or two cuts that were at least interesting, but most of his songs, including such duds as "You Wanna Ramble" and "Ugliest Girl in the World," were uninspired, the thrashing of a tired writer searching for his old spark. (Sometimes there wasn't even all that much thrashing: the album *Down in the Groove,* which appeared in 1988, included only thirty-three minutes and ten seconds of music, Dylan's shortest album by far since the Columbia Records "revenge" release, *Dylan,* in 1973.*) Dylan's stepped-up schedule of concert appearances—including 364 dates from 1988 through 1991, the first four years of what fans dubbed the Never Ending Tour—included far too many shows that were strangled or halfhearted, and by the end of the 1980s reviewers and fans had begun calling Dylan's look onstage his "Death Mask." Apart from one of the songs on the first Traveling Wilburys album, "Tweeter and the Monkey Man"—which was in part a modern-day gunslinger ballad, and in part a send-up of Bruce Springsteen—Dylan made little effort at serious songwriting on either of the Wilburys albums. The film he appeared in, *Hearts of Fire,* was a disaster from start to finish.

Looking back on it all a decade later, Dylan remarked that by 1987, "I'd kind of reached the end of the line." Later, writing in *Chronicles: Volume One,* he affirmed that he had "felt done for," like "an empty burned-out wreck . . . in the bottomless pit of cultural oblivion." Dylan did experience some sort of epiphany in October 1987, performing an open-air concert in Locarno, Switzerland, when he felt his vocal powers suddenly reappear, and he also retrieved a musical system of chords and cycles first taught him when he was starting out in the 1960s by the veteran blues

---

* This is not to say that length is everything. *Nashville Skyline,* with its ten brief tracks, clocked in at twenty-seven minutes and fourteen seconds, the briefest of all of Dylan's studio albums. Still, that album consisted of ten snappy original tracks, whereas more than half of *Down in the Groove* consisted of cover versions, leaving only about fourteen minutes of original material. This included one song held over from *Infidels* ("Death Is Not the End") and the album's best song, "Silvio," which Dylan wrote in collaboration with the Grateful Dead's lyricist Robert Hunter. Clearly, Dylan's songwriting muse was on the lam.

and jazz guitarist and singer Lonnie Johnson. But soon after, he relates a bit mysteriously in *Chronicles,* a sudden, terrible accident mangled one arm and sidelined him.

Four years later, after he performed a rumbling, difficult-to-decipher version of "Masters of War," Dylan accepted his lifetime achievement Grammy Award with an unmistakable cry of self-loathing and despair, mixed with a stubborn faith in recovery: "My daddy once said to me, he said, 'Son, it is possible for you to become so defiled in this world that your own Mother and Father will abandon you. If that happens, God will believe in your own ability to mend your own ways.' " Dylan's biographers describe this period of his personal life as a constant turmoil, filled with sexual affairs (some brief, others very long-term) and chronic alcohol abuse. In 1990, Carolyn Dennis filed for divorce, and the marriage was formally dissolved two years later.

The best of Dylan's albums in these years, musically and poetically, were a pair of multi-record, boxed-set retrospectives. *Biograph,* released in 1985, included a dozen heretofore unreleased or rare tracks along with an extended overview of Dylan's entire musical career. The first three volumes of the Bootleg series, packaged together and released in 1991, contained dozens of outtakes of previously unreleased songs (including, at last, "Blind Willie McTell") as well as some alternate takes of familiar material—but only two tracks (out of nearly sixty) came from the years after 1984. Both collections sold well, kept Dylan's name before the public at large, and delighted his hard-core fan base from the 1960s and 1970s. But they also were a distraction from—and in some ways a rebuke to—much of what Dylan had been writing and performing in the 1980s. *Biograph* in particular, although its title was a pun on both an old record label and the legendary Chicago movie theater where the bank robber John Dillinger was finally gunned down by the police in 1934, could also be taken as a strange epitaph for a continuing career that had careened off the rails—a career that Dylan himself, more than once, said he was considering quitting.

Fitfully, at the end of the 1980s, signs came that Dylan had righted himself. Loosened up by his collaboration with Harrison, Orbison, Petty, and Lynne (which had begun informally at his own home in Malibu), Dylan began composing what he would call "stream-of-consciousness songs," heedless of lyrical or melodic convention. At the urging of his friend Bono, the lead singer for the Irish group U2, Dylan arranged a meeting in New Orleans with the producer Daniel Lanois in September

1988 and agreed to link up with Lanois again the following spring. Right on time, Dylan returned to New Orleans with a batch of new songs in March, and over the ensuing four months, with local musicians recruited by Lanois, he recorded what would become the album *Oh Mercy.*

With Lanois adding his complex voodoo production effects, *Oh Mercy* had a rich, layered contemporary sound unlike any previous Dylan album. It also contained some very strong songs and a few excellent ones. The themes ranged from cutting commentary on the contemporary scene ("Political World") to laments about personal unsteadiness, loss, and resignation ("Most of the Time"). "Ring Them Bells," although quietly scary, was the most noble and moving Christian hymn that Dylan had yet composed. "Shooting Star," the album's final track, beautifully combined Dylan's religious faith with his latest reflections on love's vicissitudes. Above all, there was "Man in the Long Black Coat," a ballad of false prophecy and seduction in the old Anglo-American tradition, yet with overtones of the frightening Charles Laughton–James Agee film from 1955, *The Night of the Hunter,* in which Robert Mitchum played a black-coated fanatical preacher. With its rendering of a blaspheming sermon about abandoning conscience, it was a song of and for the 1980s as well.

Reviewers praised *Oh Mercy* warmly, calling it Dylan's latest comeback. Less than a year later, though, an energized Dylan released *Under the Red Sky,* and the critics once again bemoaned his continuing decline. *Oh Mercy,* it seemed, was a fluke; its successor supposedly proved that Dylan was truly a has-been. The sour reviews translated into disappointing sales.

It was easy enough to ridicule *Under the Red Sky.* Song titles such as "Wiggle Wiggle" and lyrics like "The man was saying something 'bout children when they're young / Being sacrificed to it while lullabies are being sung" (from "T.V. Talkin' Song") sounded risible. In fact, though, the detractors went overboard. Listened to as the children's song that it is, "Wiggle Wiggle" is not silly but charming. (Dylan had dedicated the album to "Gabby Goo Goo," his playful nickname for his four-year-old daughter.) The album's title track, written in the style of a fairy tale, is an equally charming evocation of Dylan's own childhood in Hibbing. On "Unbelievable," Dylan conjured up an abiding outrage at the world's ways and how his life was turning out, both of which were "unbelievable like a lead balloon." "Cat's in the Well" effectively combines a nursery rhyme with social commentary and old-time songster images—"Back alley Sally is doing the American jump"—before ending as a bedtime prayer. A few reviewers understood the album's strengths; one, Paul Nelson, writing in *Musician,* even called it a curious kind of masterpiece. Yet the commercial and critical failure of *Under the Red Sky* led Dylan to step back from songwriting as well as from recording, though not from touring. He would not produce another album of original material until 1997.

A look over Dylan's work in the mid- to late 1980s reveals changes and continuities that were not so evident at the time. Reflections about fatherhood, evident in compositions dating back to "Man Gave Names to All the Animals" on *Slow Train Coming,* reappeared in the nursery songs on *Under the Red Sky.* Tracks such as "Death Is Not the End" on the lackluster album from 1988, *Down in the Groove,* followed by "Ring Them Bells" on *Oh Mercy* and "God Knows" on *Under the Red Sky,* showed that, contrary to widespread assumptions, Dylan had hardly abandoned his apocalyptic Christian beliefs. The hectoring was gone, but his faith in Jesus and his certainty of Christian redemption were still there, in jarring counterpoint to his disordered personal life.

Both Dylan's recordings and his concerts also revealed his continuing, and even deepening, connection to older songs, traditional and commercial, and in a wide range of genres. Dating back to the Rolling Thunder Revue, Dylan's concerts had often featured at least one or two cover versions of folk-music classics; by 1986, old country hits such as Hank Snow's "I'm Movin' On" had begun taking up a large portion of each show; and through the end of the decade, Dylan's set lists included songs like the Irish air "Eileen Aroon," the ancient Anglo-Scots ballad "Barbara Allen," and two American mountain tunes, adapted from the British, that he had sung on his first album, "Pretty Peggy-O" and "Man of Constant Sorrow." Dylan's studio album *Knocked Out Loaded* included a new version of Bill Monroe's "Drifting Too Far from the Shore," and *Down in the Groove* included four cover versions of songs by others—including Hal Blair and Don Robertson's "Ninety Miles an Hour (Down a Dead End Street)," first recorded by Hank Snow, and closing with "Shenandoah" and "Rank Strangers to Me."

Dylan's musical thinking, meanwhile, also ranged far beyond the folk and country music with which he was most closely associated. "Sinatra, Peggy Lee, yeah I love all those people," he informed an interviewer in 1985. "But I tell you who I've really been listening to a lot lately—in fact, I'm thinking about recording one of his earlier songs—is Bing Crosby.

I don't think you can find better phrasing anywhere." Dylan's loyal fans may have taken his praise of "Der Bingle" as a goof, but he was deadly in earnest.* And although it would be a long time before Dylan seriously took up singing Crosby, his attachment to older traditional music,

Bing Crosby, 1940.

the music he had reinvented in the 1960s, would lead him into a new and better phase of his career.

The turnabout began in 1992. Depressed by the failure of *Under the Red Sky*, with the formal ending of his second marriage nearing, and with contractual recording obligations looming, Dylan linked up in June at the Acme Recording Studio in Chicago with an old collaborator, the blues singer and extraordinary instrumentalist David Bromberg, and Bromberg's band, which included trumpet, trombone, tenor saxophone, and clarinet, as well as the usual complement of guitars, fiddles, mandolins, bass, and drums. In three days of work,

Dylan, Bromberg, and the band produced sufficient material for a brief album, mixing traditional folk songs, contemporary folk songs, a blues by Blind Willie Johnson, and Jimmie Rodgers's "Miss the Mississippi and You." Then Dylan shifted to his home garage studio in Malibu, armed only with a guitar and harmonicas, just as he had been at the start of his career, and began turning out more traditional songs to flesh out the Bromberg recordings. Quickly, though, the solo material that

---

* Those fans, and virtually the rest of the world, had no way of knowing it, but at least as early as the *Infidels* sessions in 1983 Dylan played around in the studio by recording several takes of Louis Jordan's jump-blues hit from 1946 "Choo Choo Ch'Boogie" and a Jim Harbert song, "This Is My Love," which Frank Sinatra recorded in 1967 on his album *The World We Knew*. At one session, Dylan also played and sang Mel Tormé's "Christmas Song" and the carol "Silent Night," anticipating by more than a quarter century the release of *Christmas in the Heart* in 2009.

came pouring out of Dylan added up to more than was necessary for an entire album of its own. For reasons never entirely explained, the Dylan-Bromberg recordings were quietly shelved, and instead Dylan released the first of two solo acoustic albums, *Good as I Been to You.*

Even when he turned his back on the 1960s folk revival, Dylan had explicitly honored the traditional folk music, with its myth, contradictions, and chaos; indeed, insofar as the folk revival prized old-time music for its supposed simplicity as well as purity, Dylan's break, and even his turn to surrealism and electricity, can be seen as an effort to preserve the wilder spirit of folk music. "Folk music is the only music where it isn't simple," he told a pair of interviewers in 1965, contrary to the assumptions of many folkie purists. "It's never been simple. It's weird, man, full of legend, myth, Bible and ghosts. I've never written anything hard to understand, not in my head

Bing Crosby in blackface for the film *Dixie*, 1943.

anyway, and nothing as far out as some of the old songs. They were out of sight."

Now that Dylan was feeling as if his creativity, if not exactly shut off like a faucet, had severely slowed—once "the songs would come three or four at the same time," he said in 1991, "but those days are long gone"— he returned to his musical roots, continuing to add traditional material to his concerts and listening to fresh collections of blues, mountain songs, contemporary folk music, and more. Feeling as if he had nowhere to go, he knew very well where he should head: "If you can sing those [folk] songs, if you can understand those songs and can perform them well, there's nowhere you *can't* go."

Recorded in July and August, the tracks on *Good as I Been to You* form a miscellany of old songs that included a turn-of-the-century blues, "Frankie and Albert" (in a mélange of different collected versions); an old English tune, "Canadee-i-o," and an old Irish ballad, "Arthur McBride and the Sergeant," recently given excellent new life on recordings by, respectively, Nic Jones and Paul Brady;* songs made famous by Ramblin' Jack Elliott, the Stanley Brothers, and Mance Lipscomb (including the latter's "You Gonna Quit Me, Baby," which also supplied Dylan with the album's title); Stephen Foster's heartfelt "Hard Times"; plus "Froggie Went A-Courtin'."

The simplicity of the arrangements, the pathos in the new cracking of Dylan's fifty-one-year-old voice, and the retreat from any hint of studio excess impressed the critics, one of whom, David Sexton of the *Sunday Telegraph* of London, likened the album to the work of a ghost, inward rather than nostalgic. Yet the album, in retrospect, was an interesting but uneven warm-up. On some of the renditions—especially of the song "Tomorrow Night," which had been a hit for Lonnie Johnson in 1947 and, much later, for Elvis Presley—Dylan showed he had entered the song and understood it anew; others—such as Ramblin' Jack Elliott's "Diamond Joe"—owed more to other performers' interpretations, but still bore Dylan's personal stamp; but still others, notably "Canadee-i-o" and "Arthur McBride," sounded like run-throughs of beautiful songs in the same versions that other, younger folksingers had recorded far better than Dylan ever could.

Dylan only came into his own a year later when, spurred by the critics' response, he returned to his Malibu studio with his guitar and harmonicas. There had been some complaints that *Good as I Been to You* failed adequately to credit Dylan's sources, and in some cases (notably "Tomorrow Night") completely snubbed the actual writers by calling the songs traditional, arranged by Bob Dylan. Dylan responded by composing his own liner notes, which, in an idiosyncratic, elliptical, at times cryptic style, stated exactly the source for each song and, less exactly, what each song meant to him. The track list was also darker and more coherent, grouped around American rural blues of the early twentieth century about aging, love gone wrong, and murder; a Civil War army ballad and a British navy ballad; two songs, back-to-back, that Blind Willie McTell

---

* Dylan seems to have been especially pleased by Brady's superb work, recorded on *Andy Irvine and Paul Brady* (1976) and *Welcome Here Kind Stranger* (1978), and performed it even though he could never replicate Brady's guitar playing or sweet tenor. Numerous concerts on the Never Ending Tour included Dylan's rendition of Brady's rendition of "The Lakes of Pontchartrain." He would also record, but release only many years later, a version of Brady and Irvine's arrangement of "Mary and the Soldier."

had recorded; and, as a sudden final blessing, an old Sacred Harp ballad hymn he had learned from a Doc Watson record.

Eventually given the title of its lead track, *World Gone Wrong* was varied but hardly random; as placed on the record, the songs formed a logical progression, moving, in the album's middle portions, from a song about hot-blooded love and prostitution to a McTell song about aging and eros, to another song that McTell recorded about passion and murder, to "Stack A Lee" (otherwise known as "Stagolee"), a classic of street honor and murder, to the army and navy songs, and then to the concluding hymn. And Dylan entered each song and possessed it, as he had only begun to do in his recording the previous year. In sorrow, and in consolation, he discovered new things in some old things—not as old as some of the traditional songs on *Good as I Been to You,* but old enough to be of another era.

What was new were the elements of a mature sensibility for Dylan's music, no longer Dylan the young growling rebel of the 1960s, but a darkling survivor who, though wiser, still had attitude and understood it—attitude that was of the moment but also as old as the hills, deeply implicated in the American past but also timeless. Any of the album's unsimple songs, and Dylan's performance of them, reward a much closer listen, both for their own sake and for understanding the terrain Dylan had decided to traverse. None of them is sadder or more haunting than "Delia," which has come down in many versions, including the one recorded by Blind Willie McTell—a song that originated in Savannah, Georgia, at the dawn of the twentieth century, but whose full story goes back a little bit earlier, and to a killing near the banks of the Mississippi River.

After midnight on October 16, 1899, at 212 Targee Street, in a rowdy section of St. Louis, Frankie Baker, a black prostitute, got into a fight over another woman with her lover and pimp, Albert Britt, and shot him. Three days later, Albert died. Frankie was arrested right after the shooting, but the coroner's jury decided that Albert had physically menaced her, and ruled it a case of justifiable homicide. Required to stand trial, Baker appeared in court and faced Judge Willis Clark, who went through with the formalities and duly acquitted her. "Why, the judge even gave me back my gun," she later recalled.

Nearly two years later, on September 6, 1901, at the Pan-American Exposition in Buffalo, a young anarchist named Leon Czolgosz, after waiting patiently in a greeter's line at the Temple of Music, thrust a hand wrapped in a fake bandage at President William McKinley and fired two shots from virtually point-blank range. At first it looked as if McKinley would survive his wounds, but complications set in, and he died eight days later. After a hasty trial, Czolgosz was convicted and electrocuted at Auburn State Prison on October 29. "I killed the President for the good of the laboring people, the good people," were the assassin's last words. "I am not sorry for my crime but I am sorry I can't see my father."

Utterly different by any conventional historical standard, as well as in their outcomes, the two murder-and-trial stories ended up having a good deal in common. Britt's killing became the source for "Frankie and Albert"—one of three homicides in St. Louis in the 1890s that inspired such songs. (The other two were the killing of the patrolman James Brady by Henry Duncan in a barroom battle in 1890, which led to "Duncan and Brady," and the killing, also in a saloon, of William "Billy" Lyons by a local pimp with local ward-heeler connections, Lee "Stack Lee" Shelton, over a Stetson hat, on Christmas night 1895, which led to "Stagolee.") President McKinley's assassination also inspired a song, "White House Blues," which was serious enough in its early versions but became almost comically nonsensical on the recordings that made it famous more than twenty years later by the white country artists Charlie Poole and Ernest Stoneman. Even then, the song about the president would never be as popular as any of the others, least of all "Frankie and Albert" (which is even better known in its commercial pop-song incarnation, "Frankie and Johnny").*

"Stagolee," "Frankie and Albert," and "White House Blues," composed within roughly six years of each other, shared some strong lyrical and melodic elements, and they shared them with yet another song about yet another murder—the shooting of Delia Green by her lover, Moses "Cooney" Houston, in Savannah, Georgia, on Christmas Eve night 1900. Like the other three ballads, "Delia" would be recorded by numerous well-known artists over the ensuing decades—including Dylan, who sang both "Delia" and a version of "Stagolee" on *World Gone Wrong*, and sang

---

* Bill Monroe and His Bluegrass Boys later performed "White House Blues" as a bluegrass breakdown, its lyrics somewhere between straight and comical.

"Frankie and Albert" on *Good as I Been to You.** Like the other three, "Delia" was a musical milestone. Blind Willie McTell, in his session with John and Ruby Lomax—when he sang his own version of "Delia"—dated the blues as a popular musical form back to (roughly) between 1908 and 1914. Other bluesmen who were old enough to know more or less concurred—and included "Delia" among the earliest blues songs.

Around 1910, a blind teenager in rural South Carolina, Gary Davis, who had been teaching himself to play the guitar, heard, for the first time, someone playing in a style called the blues. These were worrying songs, Davis later explained: "got worried about a woman, or worried about a man, something like that. Get all stirred up in a cauldron. Thing like that is the blues." The emotions were timeless, but the label was new, attached to songs that told a story and led to a point where someone is deeply unsettled or depressed about something. That first blues song that Davis ever heard was played by a man named Porter Irving who came to Davis's town one day, out of nowhere, in around 1910, and performed, Davis recalled, "that song about Delia":

> *Oh, Delia, why didn't you run,*
> *Here comes that sheriff with a 44 Gatlin' gun*
> *All the friends I had are gone.*

Over the decades to come, the Reverend Gary Davis made his own mark as a blues and spirituals singer and included a version of the old song in his repertoire (sometimes calling it "All My Friends Are Gone"), while he served as teacher, friend, and inspiration to a succession of performers, including Furry Lewis, Dave Van Ronk, and Bob Dylan. Dylan first tape-recorded "Delia," informally, as early as May 1960, at his friend Karen Wallace's apartment in St. Paul, yet because the relevant portion of the tape has never circulated, above- or underground, it is impossible to know which of the many versions of "Delia" he played. The version he recorded in 1993, though, came indirectly from Davis's.

Formal credit for inventing the blues usually goes to the educated black bandleader and composer W. C. Handy, and not to country pickers like the obscure Porter Irving. Handy's name, and his refined later career,

---

* "Duncan and Brady" would also prove popular, and Dylan sang it often in concert between 2000 and 2002.

Rev. Gary Davis (extreme left) and Bob Dylan (extreme right) at Gil Turner's wedding, 1962.

come as a surprise to modern listeners who identify the blues with Robert Johnson, Muddy Waters, and the other Delta-born musicians who contributed to the rise of rhythm and blues and of rock and roll. (The name came as a surprise to some of the old bluesmen as well: when the up-and-coming blues guitarist and singer Stefan Grossman asked Davis about Handy in the 1960s, Davis replied simply, "No, I ain't never heard of him.") Yet Handy, who in 1892, at the age of nineteen, briefly knocked around St. Louis, tasted the gaslit world inhabited by Stack Lee Shelton, Billy Lyons, Frankie Baker, and Albert Britt. "I wouldn't want to forget Targee Street as it was then," he wrote in his autobiography. "I don't think I'd want to forget the high-roller Stetson hats of the men or the diamonds the girls wore in their ears . . . [t]he prettiest woman I've ever seen." Handy's memories of these women later roused him to write his famous line about the "St. Louis woman" with her diamond rings, powder, and store-bought hair, in "St. Louis Blues," composed in 1914.

There were also other important, if less celebrated, songwriters who were actually based in St. Louis. One, a bar owner and deputy constable named Tom Turpin, wrote, copyrighted, and published in the 1890s some of the first ragtime songs, including "Bowery Buck" and "St. Louis Rag." Like Handy, Turpin expected his compositions would end up being performed in the parlors of respectable middle-class homes. Another St. Louis songwriter, Bill Dooley, was very different, an untrained musician who sang and played on the city's street corners. As near as can be determined, Dooley composed what came to be known as "Frankie and Albert" (originally titled "Frankie Killed Allen," because of a newspaper reporter's mix-up) even as Britt lay dying in City Hospital. It is likely, given the proximity of the events and the musical similarities, that Dooley also wrote "Stagolee." Handy deserves a great deal of credit, but the blues had more than one parent, and long before "St. Louis Blues" appeared, blues music was traveling down countless musical paths all across the South and, in time, the nation.

The identities of the bards who wrote "Delia" and "White House Blues," as well as when, precisely, they wrote them, remain unknown—although both songs sound as if they could be rearrangements of "Stagolee" and "Frankie and Albert." (One field recording of "Cooney and Delia" from 1935, by the Florida duo Booker T. Sapps and Roger Matthews, actually bears the title "Frankie and Albert.") All four songs tell stories of shootings and trials, involving a range of victims that included a young black girl, two pimps, and a president of the United States. "Delia," like "Frankie and Albert," concerns a murder that grew from an impassioned lovers' quarrel. Which song influenced the others and when, and how those influences have continued to unfold, will never be fully untangled. But no matter how the songs came to be the way they did, when Dylan reached back to record "Delia," along with "Frankie and Albert" and "Stagolee," he did more than revive some traditional material. To reclaim his own art, he recovered the songs that did the most to give birth to the blues.

Son of a bitch.

The curse is ubiquitous and supple, mild enough today for prime time. It can connote a bad turn of luck. It gets said in commiseration or as a shout of glee. In the white South, slurred—"*sum*-bitch"—it passes as a mild obscenity, more emphatic and vulgar than "jerk," yet less offensive than the usual four-letter words. But in the poor, rough, and black Yamacraw district in the west end of Savannah on Christmas Eve night in 1900, it was a curse so "wicked"—according to one version of "Delia"— that when fourteen-year-old Delia Green called her fourteen- (maybe fifteen-) year-old lover, Moses "Cooney" Houston, a son of a bitch, he shot her dead.

That version of the song does not reveal why Delia cursed Cooney, what the curse was, why Cooney's outrage turned lethal, and why any-one should care enough to write a song about it. Most of the other versions are equally elliptical, including the one that Dylan sings on *World Gone Wrong*. In his liner notes to the album, though, Dylan offers an interpretation of the song that fairly accurately evokes the actual event: "The song has no middle range, comes whipping around the corner, seems to be about counterfeit loyalty."

The Yamacraw district, Savannah, Georgia, circa 1909. This photograph, from the Christian reformer and scholar H. Paul Douglass's book *Christian Reconstruction in the South* (1909), was obviously shot to show the neighborhood in its best light.

Dylan's understanding, even with its tentative note, comes closer by far to what happened than the most widely listened to "Delia" to date, by the late Johnny Cash. "Delia's Gone"—a common alternate title for the song—is the overpowering first track on Cash's superb album *American Recordings,* which, when released in 1994, a year after *World Gone Wrong,* won Cash a new following among music fans of the rap-and-grunge generation. Cash sings in the first person as an unnamed, scheming killer dealt some unmentioned hurt that is almost certainly infidelity, who has tracked the "low-down, triflin'" Delia to Memphis, tied her to a chair, and blasted her to a pulp with a submachine gun. The killer's conscience bothers him after he lands in prison, but the song ends remorselessly, with a passive-voice line that shifts the blame back from the murderer to his victim.

It's all very different from what Dylan sings and writes—and from the version of "Delia" that Cash recorded in 1962. Although also sung in the first person, Cash's earlier rendition leaves the killer's motive unclear and ends with him shackled to a ball and chain, dogged by guilt and Delia's ghost. Here, the killer cannot escape his shame, even for one defiant moment. According to Cash, he found the new "Delia's Gone" in the same part of his imagination where he found "Folsom Prison Blues"—a revision by an artist "older and wiser to human depravity" than he once was. Whether out of wisdom or vicarious, playacting evil, a young 1990s public, on the verge of the gangsta boom, loved it. Or perhaps the young public loved another, even more fanciful version of the song, as presented in the video that accompanied Cash's song and that got heavy airplay on MTV and CMT. There, the heroin-chic Calvin Klein model Kate Moss played Delia, the perfect white woman-child victim for a certain kind of modern American ballad psychosis.

Delia Green was also a woman-child, but even if we know almost nothing about what she looked like, it's obvious that she was no Kate Moss. And Cooney Houston, the truly disturbing character in the original story, was not exactly the character that Johnny Cash inhabited—although at the time, some people thought that Houston was deeply if deceptively cool, calculating, and ruthless.

Thanks to the research of John Garst, we know more about the facts behind "Delia" than we do for most American blues ballads. At around 3:00 a.m. on Christmas Day, Delia Green, "a colored girl," one newspaper reported, died of a gunshot wound to the groin at her home at 113 Ann Street in Savannah, where she resided with her mother. The police arrested a light-skinned Negro, Moses Houston (most commonly called Cooney, but also referred to as Mose), and booked him for murder. There was never any question about who pulled the trigger, only about why.

The shooting occurred at the home of Willie West and his wife, Emma, one block from where Delia lived. There is conflicting testimony about what happened at the Wests'. Some witnesses said that the place was filled with drunken carousers, most of them women. Others said the group was small, everyone was sober (or that everyone was sober except Cooney Houston), and the assembled were standing around the Wests' organ singing "Rock of Ages." As it was Christmas Eve, an occasion for special celebration and feasting for southern blacks since slavery times, perhaps there was some truth to both accounts—in which case the singing of "Rock of Ages" may have been more profane than pious. In any event, Cooney Houston appears to have been what one witness at the trial called "full," which today would be "loaded," as in drunk.

After the shot rang out, Willie West chased Houston, caught him, and handed him over to the patrolman J. T. Williams. Officer Williams later testified that Cooney immediately confessed to shooting his girlfriend, saying that they had argued and that she had called him a son of a bitch and so he shot her, and he would gladly do it again. For Cooney, it seemed, getting cursed at by a woman was an exculpating circumstance.

Houston stood trial, charged as an adult with murder. (There was no juvenile justice system at the time in Georgia.) On the stand, Houston, backed up by a witness named Willie Mills, told a different story from the one reported by Officer Williams. In the midst of a drunken party, supposedly, Willie West bade Cooney to retrieve his pistol from a repair shop, which Cooney did. Cooney then placed the gun under a napkin. After Cooney returned from a second errand to get more beer and whiskey, he and a friend named Eddie Cohen got in a friendly tussle over the gun, which went off. The bullet accidentally hit Delia.

Houston's courtroom story convinced nobody. Another witness testified that Willie Mills, Houston's corroborating witness, was not even on the scene at the time of the shooting. Eddie Cohen, identified as Emma West's second cousin, swore that he had already left the house when the killing occurred and that he had not struggled with "this boy" over a pistol. The jury found Houston guilty but recommended mercy. The judge, Paul F. Seabrook, sentenced him to life in prison instead of death.

So much for the basic facts. Some surrounding events, and the coverage in the newspapers, made that story much more interesting—and help account for both the power and the eeriness of "Delia."

Reports of Delia Green's murder made it into the two leading local newspapers, the *Savannah Morning News* and the *Savannah Evening Press*. Even though the victim as well as the perpetrator was black, the news was big enough for white editors and reporters to cover the event. The reports affirmed to white readers that drunkenness and violence were endemic to the Yamacraw district. But what made the story more than just another black-on-black murder was the ages of those involved. The first dispatch, in the *Morning News,* noted that Delia was a mere girl "but 14 years old," yet said nothing about Cooney's age. The *Evening Press,* published hours later, got the full story. "Boy Killed Girl," it reported on page 5. It was not simply a crime of passion arising from a lovers' spat; it was a crime of passion involving two lovers barely out of puberty. It was a childish murder. It was precisely the opposite of Johnny Cash's deliberate mayhem, carefully plotted and cruelly executed by an evil man.

The trial transcript affirmed the impulsiveness of the attack. Here, according to the transcript, is roughly what transpired between Delia and Cooney:

> *Cooney:* My little wife is mad with me tonight. She does not hear me. She is not saying anything to me. (To Delia): You don't know how I love you.

Mutual cursing followed.

> *Delia:* You son of a bitch. You have been going with me for four months. You know I am a lady.
> *Cooney:* That is a damn lie. You know I have had you as many times as I have fingers and toes. You have been calling me "husband."
> *Delia:* You lie!

About fifteen minutes after the argument ended, Cooney started for the door, turned, pulled out a pistol, and fired at Delia. He had boasted of a grown-up fantasy about informal wedlock. (It sounds as if the sex was real, although boys in their early teens are known to lie extravagantly about far more equivocal sexual encounters. But the "husband" and "wife" part was not real, or so Delia insisted.) Delia broke up whatever was between them and verbally cut him dead. She was not his "little wife," at least not anymore. She was a lady. He was low, a son of a bitch. Cooney turned hot, saying in so many words that he had fucked her twenty times, and that this meant she was no lady and, what's more, that she was his. But Delia's curse still burned in Cooney's brain, and when he tried to one-up her, Delia hit right back, treating him (as one account put it) with "supreme contempt." Minutes later, she was bleeding to death and Cooney was out the door.

It is a commonplace that in passionate conflicts, women are agile with words, whereas men get frustrated and violent. Something like that seems to have happened here. Add the strong possibility that Willie and Emma West's place, later described by Houston's lawyer as a "rough house," was actually a brothel, and that Delia Green may have been one of the Wests' prostitutes, and the scene looks familiar enough. Yet Delia's words painted a different picture: she was neither a common whore nor Cooney's fictive spouse, she said, she was proper. Saying so with a curse got her killed by her disgruntled boyfriend, who may have been jealous of her johns.

Whatever the case, these two were children. Even by the hard standards of the Jim Crow South of 1900, most people saw Delia Green and Cooney Houston that way, which is why the newspapers took immediate note of the murder as sensational. Albert Britt and Frankie Baker had a similar tussle, but it came after a series of events and by mature if maddened design. (Although Britt was barely older than Cooney, Baker appears to have been in her twenties.) With the adolescents Delia and Cooney, the words cut deeper and the killing came quicker.

"Boy Charged with Murder," blared the front-page headline of the *Savannah Evening Press* on the eve of Houston's trial, three months after the shooting. At the trial itself, age made all the difference, and so did, more subtly, race.

The defense made a great deal of Houston's youth. Cooney, having by now certainly turned fifteen, showed up for his arraignment dressed in short pants. The *Morning News* reported that he had "the round cheerful countenance of many mulattoes" and that he "seemed to be rather above the average of negro intelligence." He "gave no outward indication of being possessed by the 'abandoned and malignant heart,' which the law says shall be inferred to exist" in cases of murder.

In a later petition of clemency, Houston's white attorney, Raiford Falligant, an eminent young member of the Georgia bar, laid out the case for the defense. Houston, Falligant said, was "a mere child" at the time of the killing. He had "got into bad company and so unfortunately committed the act that he now suffers for." It was all a tragic accident. Cooney "was crazed by drink in boisterous company for the first time in his life and . . . the crowd he was with and in got him drunk."

The truly disturbing part of the proceedings, though, at least to the reporters, came immediately after the jury delivered its verdict of guilty. Houston's mother, described by the *Morning News* as "an old black woman of respectable appearance," broke down and sobbed, which was natural enough. Cooney stood up, emotionless, at Judge Seabrook's command.

Seabrook noted the jury's recommendation for mercy, and he followed through with mercy, sentencing Houston to life imprisonment. "In doing so," he concluded, "I exhort you to be a man, even in confinement, to repent of your past evil deeds and strive to earn the confidence and respect of those placed in authority above you." But Cooney did not cooperate with the courtroom theater. Gaily, he thanked the judge and pranced out in a bailiff's custody, "calm and as debonair," the *News* dispatch said, "as if the experience through which he had just passed was a matter of every day occurrence and of no particular importance."

As the convict waited to be taken to prison, a sheriff's deputy asked him how he liked the verdict and sentence. "I don't like it at all," he replied, "but I guess I'll have to stand it." The next day, the *News* reported that Houston's age had "saved his neck" and that he had endured the ordeal "without turning a hair."

What actually happened may have been more pathetic. Cooney, scared out of his wits, could easily have been mustering some teenage bravado. Or maybe, dazed and confused, he simply tried, too late, to show a last bit of respect to the judge, as he'd been instructed to do by his lawyer. ("Thank you, sir," is what Cooney said.) But that is not how it came across in the papers. Instead, it seemed as if a young black—literally a boy—made light of the grimmest of circumstances, sassed a white judge, and showed not regret but a twinkle of triumph. He was a killer, no matter what his age—and by cheating the gallows, he had beaten the system. He was not ashamed. He was not pitiable. And he'd fooled the judge and jury.

Sometime between 1906 and 1908, the folklorist and sociologist Howard Odum first heard a song about the Delia-Cooney case, under the title "One More Rounder Gone," while doing fieldwork in Newton County, Georgia—not far from where Barbecue Bob Hicks and his compatriots would start to gain notice ten years later.* In 1911, Odum published that version in the *Journal of American Folk-Lore*. But Odum's findings were insufficient for Robert Winslow Gordon, the folklorist who was John Lomax's predecessor at the Archive of American Folk Song at the Library of Congress. Fascinated by the song, Gordon traced its origin

---

* According to *The Oxford English Dictionary*, "rounder" is an American term dating to the late nineteenth century that refers to a person "who makes the round of prisons, workhouses, drinking saloons, etc.; a habitual criminal, loafer, or drunkard." In the version Odum collected, the rounder was Delia, not Cooney. Although unusual to find in a song, Odum observed, "the term 'rounder' is applied not only to men but to women also."

to Savannah, where, he said, it was sung as early as 1901 to the same tune as a song he identified as "McKinley (White House Blues)." Given where the actual events transpired, Gordon was almost certainly correct about the place and date—although given that Cooney shot Delia nine months before Czolgosz shot McKinley, it is not entirely certain whether the melody of "Delia" came from "White House Blues" or vice versa. (One version of "Delia," collected in South Carolina in 1923 under the title "Delia Holmes," contains the refrain "Buffalo, sweet Buffalo," which suggests that "White House Blues" was, indeed, the model for "Delia," and not the other way around.)

Also, in 1927, the song collector Newman Ivey White published three variants of "Delia," obtained between 1915 and 1924 in North Carolina, Georgia, and Alabama. Zora Neale Hurston found another version in Florida, and three more appeared under the title "Delia Holmes" in an article by Chapman Milling published in the *Southern Folklore Quarterly* in 1937. By 1940, there were at least two commercially recorded variants: Reese Du Pree's "One More Rounder Gone," released on OKeh Records in 1924; and Jimmie Gordon's "Delhia," released on Decca Records in 1939. And in 1940, Blind Willie McTell played his version of "Delia" in his session with John and Ruby Lomax.

By 1940, though, "Delia" had already begun to mutate. At some point before 1927, the song migrated to the Bahamas, where new versions appeared. The original refrain had been some approximation of the line "Well, it's one mo' rounder gone," or "All I had is gone," but the Bahamians substituted a new line—"Delia's gone, one more round, Delia's gone"—which seems to have been a reworking of "one more rounder gone," possibly from Du Pree's record. In 1935, Alan Lomax and the folklorist and New York University professor Mary Elizabeth Barnicle made a field recording of what they called "Delia Gone" in the Bahamas. Several more Bahamian variants turned up on local field recordings and commercial releases before 1952.

The song's contemporary history began in 1952, when the Bahamian calypso-style lounge singer Blind Blake Alphonso Higgs (not to be confused with the American ragtime guitarist and singer Blind Blake), accompanied by his band, the Royal Victoria Hotel Calypso Orchestra, recorded "Delia's Gone" as "Delia Gone" on his third album for the small Art Records label. Until then, no American recording of the song bore that title, but that suddenly changed, beginning with the versions released by Josh White and the young Jamaica-born calypso singer Harry

Belafonte in the 1950s. Since then, Higgs's rendition has nearly edged out the "Delia" that had emerged from Savannah around 1901. Versions recorded by Pat Boone and the Kingston Trio were based on Higgs's or on some version derived from Higgs's. So were those recorded by Johnny Cash (twice) and Waylon Jennings, Will Holt and Happy Traum, the ex-Byrd Roger McGuinn (with a calypso lilt) and the young rock group Cordelia's Dad. There have, though, been some important exceptions, including the versions recorded by Paul Clayton, David Bromberg, Stefan Grossman—and Bob Dylan.

Blind Blake Alphonso Higgs album cover, Art Records, 1951.

The melodies of the American and Bahamian versions are as different as their refrains, but the stories are generally the same. Many of the American versions of "Delia" have, to be sure, two distinct elements in their narratives not to be found in the Bahamian versions. They often begin with some basic fanciful description of Delia, as in Blind Willie McTell's: "Delia was a gambler, gambled all around / She was a gamblin' girl, she laid her money down." (Here the similarity with "Frankie and Albert" comes in focus; compare McTell's with the first line of "Frankie," recorded to almost the same tune by Mississippi John Hurt in 1928: "Frankie was a good girl, everybody knows / She paid a hundred dollars, bought Albert a suit of clothes.") By contrast, the Bahamian "Delia Gone," sung by Blind Blake Higgs (in an odd Brooklyn accent, vaguely reminiscent of George Jessel's), immediately cuts to the action, quite true to the actual events, even though Higgs changes Cooney's name to Tony:

Delia cursed Tony, it was on a Saturday night,
Cursed him such a wicked curse he swore he'd take her life.

The American versions also commonly add a verse or two about Delia's parents sobbing and moaning; or about how Delia's mother said it wouldn't have been so bad had Delia died at home; or about how Delia's mother returned from a trip west to find her daughter dead. (The last of these resembles a line in "White House Blues" and adds further weight to the idea that the song about McKinley was the main source for the one about Delia and Cooney.) The Bahamian "Delia Gone" leaves out all of these family references.

Many versions of both "Delia" and "Delia's Gone" try to avoid racial connotations by giving Cooney one of a wide assortment of other names—Tony, Cutty, Curtis, or something else—thereby eliminating any allusion to "coon." Otherwise, "Delia" and "Delia's Gone" both cover the same four basic narrative elements in a variety of ways. First, there is the shooting, most often committed with a .44-caliber gun (and sometimes, as in "Frankie and Albert," a "smokeless 44"). Sometimes the song omits any mention of the killer's motive; other times it talks of how he became furious when Delia cursed him; and in still other instances the story is more complicated, as in this version, collected in 1937:

> Now Coonie an' his little sweetheart,
>   Settin' down talkin' low;
> Axed her would she marry him,
>   She said, "Why, sho',"
> Cryin' all I had done gone.

> When the time come for marriage,
>   She refuse' to go.
> "If you don't marry me
>   You live no mo'."
> Cryin' all I had done gone.

Plainly at odds with what actually happened, though, even this version echoed, albeit in a distorted way, some key facets of the true story, particularly Cooney's insistence that Delia was his wife and her fatal denial.

Second, there comes the killer's trial. In McTell's version, the verdict and the sentencing of Cooney Houston (whom he calls Cutty) are straightforward, although there is a hint that Houston was playfully impudent. When he asks the judge "What may be my fine?"—as if he expected such a light sentence—the judge says, "Poor boy, you got ninety-nine." In another rendition, the killer confesses and asks about posting bond; the judge replies that although he could have "Connie" hung, he will sentence him instead to ninety-nine years in prison. The Bahamian Blind Blake keeps the ninety-nine-year sentence, but is more pointed about how "Tony" mocks the court; indeed, the defiance displayed by the killer in Blake's song is so bold and pithy that it sounds amusing, and suddenly (though only for an instant) it switches the song's emotional direction in the killer's favor:

> Judge said "Sixty-four years in prison."
> Tony told the judge "That is no time;
> I have a younger brother who's servin' nine hundred and ninety and
>   nine."

At all events, the trial element in the songs conveys that something disturbing happened—either the killer outrageously expected a light sentence only to receive the heavy one he deserved; or the judge gave the killer a break by sending him to jail rather than the gallows; or the killer, convicted and facing his jail sentence, reacted with mocking contempt. Each version replicates a variant of what actually happened, or of what people might have perceived had happened—but in each variant, the killer looks bad.

Next comes Delia's funeral, which is almost always the same, along the lines of an early version of the song from Georgia that dates from before 1910, in a line that would become a standard blues description of going to and coming back from a cemetery: "Rubber-tired buggy, double-seated hack / Well, it carried po' Delia to graveyard, failed to bring her back."

Finally, there is the killer in prison. The different versions almost always note the injustice of his living while Delia is dead, in lines very close to the ones in "White House Blues" that describe McKinley in his grave and his successor, Theodore Roosevelt, in the White House, drinking from a silver cup. In his session with the Lomaxes, Blind Willie McTell put the killer—"Cutty" in his version—in a barroom rather than in prison, but otherwise the line was typical, with the added twist that most versions gave the killer a cup of tin, not silver:

> Cutty he's in the barroom drinkin' out of a silver cup,
> Delia she's in the graveyard, she may not never wake up.

Blind Blake Higgs's "Delia Gone" basically preserved the line, in its usual form:

> Tony he's in prison, drinking from an old tin cup,
> Delia she's in the graveyard doing her level best to get up.

In some cases, Cooney, or Cutty, or Tony, or whatever his name happens to be, is tortured by his crime. Sometimes he tells the jailer he cannot sleep, since all around his bed at night he can hear little Delia's feet. But the bottom line, in most versions, is harsher—for the killer's remorse is useless as far as poor Delia is concerned. Delia is dead, Cooney is alive, and all the penitence in the world cannot change that cold fact.

It is a sad song, one of the saddest blues ever written. Yet even then, neither "Delia" nor "Delia's Gone," in any of the versions yet recorded or brought to light in print—including Bob Dylan's—mentions the saddest facts of all in the original case: the tender ages of both Delia and Cooney, and the utter waste of their young lives. Were those facts added in, the desolation might be unbearable.

Still, if Dylan's version of the song, like all of the others, falls short of telling the whole sorrowful story, it is sorrowful enough. And by adding pathos to one of the very oldest blues songs, Dylan also took another step out of his own distress and toward a newfound creativity.

Having given "Frankie and Albert" pride of place as the first track on *Good as I Been to You*, Dylan placed "Delia" and "Stack A Lee" (his version of "Stagolee") back-to-back on *World Gone Wrong*. The earlier album contained a good number of folk songs, including two beautiful ballads from and about other lands whose endings were anything but sad or tragic (though in the case of "Arthur McBride and the Sergeant" a kind of rough justice does get meted out to the two British soldiers and their "little wee" drummer boy). *World Gone Wrong*, by contrast, was all-American, and the selection was much darker, distressing, and poignant. There is one killing, a justified homicide, on the first album; there are four on the second, two murders and two deaths in combat (both Union soldiers killed in the same Civil War battle).

Dylan wrote that his "Delia" "is one sad tale—two or more versions mixed into one." The melody line is straight from the Reverend Gary Davis, as transcribed by one of his devotees, Stefan Grossman. The lyrics come, almost word for word, from the track called "Dehlia" on David Bromberg's first album, which appeared in 1971. (Many of Bromberg's lyrics, in turn, were the same that Blind Willie McTell sang on his Library of Congress recording, the verses scrambled in a different order.) Dylan made two tweaks, seemingly minor at first. Instead of describing Delia's funeral, he substituted a verse (which Grossman had taken from Davis) that, out of nowhere, brought up race—marking the song as black—while also lamenting Delia in her grave:

> *Men in Atlanta, tryin' to pass for white,*
> *Delia's in the graveyard, boys, six feet out of sight.*

More important, Dylan substituted the somewhat strange Davis/Grossman refrain—"All the friends I ever had are gone"—for McTell and Bromberg's line, which is easier to make sense of from the very start of the song, "She's all I've got is gone."

The song begins with Dylan strumming, then hitting a solid three-note bass run—a progression familiar from Davis's (and, later, his younger friend and student Dave Van Ronk's) "Cocaine Blues" that is also one of the hallmarks of this particular melody for "Delia." ("Cocaine Blues" is another song Dylan has enjoyed performing from time to time since the 1960s.) Dylan sings the very first line with a deliberateness that immediately creates an ambiguity: "Delia was a *gam*-bol-ing girl, gam-boled all around," which might mean she was a good timer, something of a tart, a run-around—a gamboler. Two verses follow about Delia's parents, and Dylan's voice, softer now, splinters with weariness and pain; the phrase "Delia's daddy weeepp'd" drops like a tear. After a guitar break, the song switches to Curtis (his and Bromberg's name for Cooney), who

Bob Dylan, 1993.

is looking high, looking low, having shot poor Delia down with "a crew-el 44." And what is Curtis looking at? "Them rounders / looking out for me," Dylan sings, in Curtis's voice.

After another guitar break, we are in the courtroom, and the judge is asking Curtis what this noise is all about. "All about them rounders, Judge," he replied, sounding like a tough guy, "tryin' to cut me out." Not

a word about Delia or her gambling (or gamboling); in court Curtis is fixated on the rounders, who are nameless and may just be delusions, existing only in Curtis's mind. Neither does the killer display even a trace of
regret or apology over his crime. And before the judge can ask the logical
question—so, why did you shoot *her* instead of one of *them?*—the song
has Curtis, freshly convicted, asking about his fine and being told, "Poor
boy, you got ninety-nine." Dylan then jumps to the jailhouse, where Curtis is drinking from an old tin cup, while Delia, in the graveyard, may not
ever get up. Another guitar break then divides act 3 from act 4 in Dylan's
little drama.

The final act features Curtis—we can picture him in his jail cell—now
utterly alone, crying out in selfish anguish that borders on agony: "Delia,
oh Delia, how can it be? / You loved all them rounders, never did love
me." And again, a little more to the point: "Delia, oh Delia, how can it
be? / You wanted all them rounders, never had time for me."* Curtis—
who Dylan's liner notes say "sounds like a pimp in primary colors"—shot
Delia not because she had loved and left him but because she had never
given him the time of day, because she loved those no-good other guys,
because she *wanted* them, not him, with her body if not her soul. Curtis's
deed is beyond criminal; he is something of a fiend of egotism. But the
song is a tragedy, not a melodrama. Curtis is the author of his own righteous undoing as well as of Delia's unmerited death. And then, finally, as
the song ends with the imprisoned killer's obsession and grief, the refrain
that Dylan took from the Reverend Gary Davis, and that has been a
little puzzling throughout the song, falls in to make perfect, terrible sense.
Curtis is reviled; he will never recover, and it sounds as if he will not be
redeemed. All the friends he ever had are gone.

Few versions of "Delia," if any—including McTell's classic and the
astonishing version by David Bromberg—display more emotional and
psychological acuity, and better dramatic pacing, than Dylan's. That
achievement, coming nearly a century after the song first appeared, is
impressive enough, but even more so given that Dylan pulled it off by
rearranging words and music that had already been out there for a very
long time. Turning back to the old songs—and, with "Delia," reaching

---

* A musical aside: this line echoes the very first line in one of the many versions of
  "Stagolee," as recorded by Mississippi John Hurt in 1928, further suggesting the two
  songs were connected: "Police officer, how can it be? / You can arrest everybody but
  cruel Stagolee."

to the very taproot of the blues—Dylan began relearning the lessons he had learned when he was just starting out, when his enthusiasm for those songs was feverish. The only drawback was that, because the existing words and music said nothing about Cooney and Delia's ages (which Dylan could hardly have known independently), his "Delia" is still not as affecting as the actual events.

The full musical effects of Dylan's rediscoveries in ancient songs would not begin to come into view for nearly a decade. But in other ways, Dylan's "Delia" marked a leap forward in how he conceived of himself and his art. The critic Bill Flanagan, in the finest review of *World Gone Wrong*, hit the point beautifully. "When Dylan sings, in this version of 'Delia,' 'All the friends I ever had are gone,' " Flanagan wrote, "it breaks your heart. His world-worn voice reveals the cracks behind his stoicism in a way that this most unsentimental of singers would never allow in his lyrics. The weight of nobility and loss are as appropriate to this older Dylan's singing as anger and hunger are to the snarl of his youth."

That weight, and the gallantry with which Dylan expressed it, had belonged to the blues from the start; it just took Dylan a half century of living his own life for him to be able to express it this way. And alongside nobility and loss were other realms of the spirit and the body, including the tender mercies of salvation that the older Dylan wanted to put across anew. For those, he looked to other venerable songs, including a hymn little known among his fans but sung often by others, honored by the faithful as one of the beloved reliables from the old good book called *The Sacred Harp*.

But what of the dead? Moses "Cooney" Houston served just over twelve years of his life sentence. On October 15, 1913, the Georgia governor, John M. Slaton, signed an order approving his parole. Subsequent unconfirmed reports say that Houston got in trouble with the law again after his release, that he moved to New York City, and that he died in 1927, which would have made him a little over forty.

The merciful governor Slaton soon found himself in trouble of a different kind. Five months before Houston's release, the dead body of a thirteen-year-old white girl, Mary Phagan, was found in a pencil factory in Atlanta. In a controversial and still notorious trial, Leo Frank, the factory supervisor and a New York–raised Jew, was convicted of the crime on the basis of tainted evidence and sentenced to death. The anti-Semitism that surrounded the case was unmistakable, and the verdict caused massive civil-rights protests, which led to an unsuccessful appeal to the U.S. Supreme Court. Governor Slaton, believing that Frank had been railroaded, commuted the sentence to life imprisonment. Hounded by an irate public, his effigy burned and cursed, Slaton was soon voted out of office and forced to leave the state. On August 17, 1915, an armed mob lynched Leo Frank, and Georgia authorities filed no charges in connection with the killing—which sparked new protests and which today remains a subject of outrage and shame.

No one has discovered who Houston's friend Eddie Cohen was and why someone with that name was Emma West's second cousin. Nor is it clear how Raiford Falligant came to be Cooney Houston's lawyer.

Laurel Grove Cemetery South, Savannah, Georgia.

Delia Green is buried in Laurel Grove Cemetery South, in Savannah, long the city's traditional burying ground for blacks, amid trees covered with Spanish moss. The exact location of her unmarked grave was forgotten long ago.

8

DYLAN AND THE
SACRED HARP:

"Lone Pilgrim," Malibu, California, May 1993

I n his quirky liner notes to *World Gone Wrong,* Dylan described "Lone Pilgrim" (he slightly clipped the song's original title, "The Lone Pilgrim") and said what he thought the song meant: "the lunacy of trying to fool the self is set aside at some given point. salvation & the needs of mankind are prominent & hegemony takes a breathing spell." It's a very modern reading of a very old song—and an unsettled reading. Hegemonic technology has reached the point, Dylan went on to say, where virtual reality can wipe out and supplant the truth; and, sooner or later, it will. When that happens, "look out!" Dylan wrote, "there wont be songs like these anymore. factually there aren't any now."

A decade after he recorded "Blind Willie McTell," Dylan was still thinking about salvation, humanity, and old songs, but now with a sense that those songs—which could keep the world's power and greed at bay— were doomed; and that he might be one of the dwindling last generation of singers to remember and sing them; and that all he can do in the face of that knowledge is to sing them anyway.* And for the conclusion to

---

* The sense of doom had been building in Dylan's mind for some time. A few years earlier, in June 1989, he performed at the Royal Dublin Society and sang the haunting Irish folk air "Eileen Aroon." (He had added it to his concert song list a year earlier in Denver.) Dylan had learned the song in Greenwich Village in the early 1960s from the

World Gone Wrong, Dylan chose an old song of death, spiritual rebirth, and consolation that appeared in the most venerated collection of Anglo-American songs.

The history of *The Sacred Harp,* the legendary American hymnal, started with a fight.

Sometime in 1835, a Baptist singing master and song collector named William Walker journeyed north from his home in Spartanburg, South Carolina, carrying with him a selection of what he called "Tunes, Hymns, and Anthems" as well as "a number of excellent new Songs." The music was transcribed in the popular form of shaped notes on musical staves. According to a much later, not wholly trustworthy account, Walker had collected the melodies and lyrics with the help of his brother-in-law Benjamin Franklin White, and Walker agreed to set out alone in order to get the collection published for the both of them. Yet once Walker arranged for publication, it looks as if he completely forgot about White.

Later that year, when *The Southern Harmony and Musical Companion* appeared—one source says in New Haven, Connecticut, although the earliest extant edition was printed in Philadelphia—Walker's name alone appeared beneath the preface, which he dated "Spartanburg, S.C., September 1835." The book was an oblong rectangular hymnal of more than two hundred pages, with about half its songs credited to well-known earlier writers, above all the early-eighteenth-century British Nonconformist Isaac Watts, later celebrated as the father of English hymnody. Many of the other songs were credited to no one; still others were credited to disparate authors ranging from Walker's brother, David, to a late-sixteenth-century writer known by the initials "F.B.P." Three songs were partly credited to American Indians, and Walker claimed quite a few of the best selections for himself, including the peculiarly fatalistic, haunting, and encouraging "Hallelujah!":

---

balladeer Liam Clancy of the Clancy Brothers and Tommy Makem. Shortly before his recent death, Clancy told me about the RDS show's after-party, where he and Dylan huddled together and Dylan gloomily lamented, over and over, that his audiences, even in Dublin, no longer knew the wondrous old songs—even "Eileen Aroon."

And let this feeble body fail,
*   And let it faint or die;*
My soul shall quit this mournful vale,
*   And soar to worlds on high.*
And I'll sing hallelujah,
*   And you'll sing hallelujah,*
And we'll all sing hallelujah,
*   When we arrive at home.*

Walker, who said he wanted to include only the best songs in his book, appropriated freely, and he feigned utter candor about it. Given the existence, he wrote, of a "great many good airs (which I could not find in any publication nor in manuscript)," he conceded that he had sometimes thought up lines of his own and called himself the song's author. In fact, he borrowed more of the lyrics than he let on.

NEW AND MUCH IMPROVED AND ENLARGED EDITION.

THE

SACRED HARP,

A COLLECTION OF PSALM AND HYMN TUNES, ODES, AND ANTHEMS,

SELECTED FROM THE MOST EMINENT AUTHORS:

TOGETHER WITH NEARLY ONE HUNDRED PIECES NEVER BEFORE PUBLISHED;

SUITED TO MOST METRES, AND WELL ADAPTED TO CHURCHES OF EVERY DENOMINATION, SINGING SCHOOLS, AND PRIVATE SOCIETIES.

WITH PLAIN RULES FOR LEARNERS.

BY B. F. WHITE & E. J. KING.

TO WHICH IS ADDED APPENDIX I.,

CONTAINING A VARIETY OF

STANDARD AND FAVORITE TUNES NOT COMPRISED IN THE BODY OF THE WORK,

COMPILED BY A COMMITTEE APPOINTED BY

"THE SOUTHERN MUSICAL CONVENTION."

ALSO,

APPENDIX II.,

CONTAINING

77 PIECES OF NEW COMPOSITION BY DISTINGUISHED WRITERS NEVER BEFORE PUBLISHED.

PHILADELPHIA:

PUBLISHED BY S. C. COLLINS, N. E. CORNER SIXTH AND MINOR STREETS,

FOR THE PROPRIETORS, WHITE, MASSENGALE & CO., HAMILTON, GA.

1860.

Title page to an early edition of *The Sacred Harp*, 1860.

As soon as Ben White learned that he had been denied the credit due him for helping to compile *The Southern Harmony*—so the story goes— he ceased speaking to Walker for the rest of his life. What is certain is that in 1844, White (having since relocated to Harris County, Georgia, and having found a new collaborator, the young tunesmith E. J. King) saw his own book appear in Philadelphia—*The Sacred Harp,* presenting more than 250 songs, including, its title page proclaimed, "nearly one hundred pieces never before published." The two hymnals, drawing on many common sources, then battled against each other and several other collections for public favor. White and King's book eventually prevailed. Published today in two separate editions (one of which has been through seven major revisions atop three that White himself made during his lifetime; the other edition has seen six revisions), *The Sacred Harp* remains the predominant hymnal for sacred singing groups in large parts of the American South. The only known occasion when *The Southern Harmony* remains in regular use appears to be at an annual conclave known as the Big Singing in Benton, Kentucky, which, having been held since 1884, does give Walker's book a smaller but undeniable distinction.

The success of *The Sacred Harp* has led many writers and listeners to lump together all shape-note (or *fasola*) singing as Sacred Harp music. It has tied that singing style closely in history to the eruption of religious revivalism before the Civil War described as the Second Great Awakening. The so-called Sacred Harp tradition is also known primarily as an American southern hymnody—what the pioneering folklorist George Pullen Jackson called "white spirituals in the southern uplands."

Each of these propositions contains some justice but is also misleading. Although *The Sacred Harp* greatly helped to spread and popularize the shape-note form, neither it nor *The Southern Harmony* was the first important collection of its kind. The songs performed by shape-note-singing assemblies over the decades have included many with texts dating back to the seventeenth century and in a few cases even earlier, and with melodies as old as Gregorian chants. Likewise, shape-note melody, far from being a distinctly American form (let alone southern regional form), blends styles from the British Isles and the European continent as well as from various parts of what has become the United States. Indeed, by traveling north to get *The Southern Harmony* published in 1835, William Walker carried an American sacred hybrid closer to where it had originated more than a century earlier, in Massachusetts.

Although colonial New Englanders were long used to the recitation and singing of psalms by the early eighteenth century, ministers had become alarmed at the poor quality of vocalizing in church, which they blamed on a shortage of both printed music and ordinary parishioners who could read it. Drawing on the existing model of the evening literary

schools, they founded singing schools for instructing large numbers of
Yankee farmers and artisans in the basic elements of music. Harvard-
trained clerics duly supplied the required hymnals. The first sacred songbook published in the American colonies, John Tufts's *Introduction to
the Singing of Psalm-Tunes,* dates to 1715. Instead of using the standard
note head in his scores, Tufts inserted the first letter of the easily learned
syllabic mnemonic for each note in the musical scale: *fa, sol, la, fa, sol,
la, mi.* Thus simplified, the music became extremely popular during the
colonial period through the American Revolution, as taught in singing
schools that spread westward with the white population. The music in

Paul Revere, "A Music Party," engraving, frontispiece for William Billings, *The
New-England Psalm-Singer* (Boston, 1770).

turn inspired numerous songbook composers from outside the ranks of
the ministry, including the Boston tanner William Billings. In 1770, at
age twenty-four, Billings published the first of his six major sacred song
collections, *The New-England Psalm-Singer.* Musicologists would eventually regard him as the greatest master of choral music in early America.

In the 1790s, just as Billings's career was ending, John Connelly, a
Philadelphia storekeeper, devised a new system of notation, replacing
geometric shapes for the syllables: a triangle for *fa,* a circle for *sol,* a square
for *la,* and a diamond for *mi.* The use of shapes in musical notation dated

back at least to the Middle Ages, but Connelly's was the first system to denote the individual notes of the scale in this way. First utilized in a collection by William Smith and William Little, *The Easy Instructor; or, A New Method of Teaching Sacred Harmony,* which first appeared in Albany, New York in 1798, the shape-note system caught on immediately and became the standard for singing classes around the country. Both *The Southern Harmony* and *The Sacred Harp* adopted its shape-note scheme, as did numerous other new songbooks.

The opening decades of the nineteenth century brought additional developments, liturgical and theological, that altered the geographical locus of *fasola* singing. Beginning in the 1820s, in New England and the Middle Atlantic cities, a so-called better music movement, led by the Presbyterian banker, organist, educational reformer, and music instructor Lowell Mason, displaced the eighteenth-century singing-school curriculum in churches and public schools with music drawn from the European classical masters, including Mozart and Haydn. In place of a hard-edged but harmonically complex tune such as "Prospect," with lyrics taken from Isaac Watts—"Why should we start, or fear to die? What tim'rous worms we mortals are"—the "better music" advocates substituted genteel fare such as "Joy to the World," its lyrics also written by Watts yet with music that apparently was written by George Frideric Handel and arranged by Lowell Mason. *Fasola* singing retreated into the rural backcountry, especially the relatively remote upland South, where northeastern gentility carried little force.

Over these same decades, the rural camp-meeting evangelicalism of the Second Great Awakening, originating in the great revival at Cane Ridge, Kentucky, in 1801, crested. Alongside the major evangelical churches—Baptists, Methodists, and so-called revival Presbygationalists—arose a dizzying array of new Protestant denominations, cults, and sects, in the greatest outbreak of Anglo-American religious invention since the English Puritan revolution of the seventeenth century. The demand for new songbooks rose accordingly, not simply for use at the camp meetings and in proliferating singing societies, but for private domestic worship, in the rural South as well as the more dignified, Eurocentric Northeast. The former provided the spiritual hunger and commercial market that William Walker, Benjamin Franklin White, E. J. King, and other *fasola* songbook writers aimed to tap, aided by recent innovations in printing technology that made the issue of mass editions more efficient and inexpensive than ever before. Precise numbers are impossible to determine, but Walker claimed that *The Southern Harmony* sold about 600,000 copies in its first half century on the market. One observer noted that in the years just preceding the Civil War, the only book more likely to be found in a southern household other than *The Sacred Harp* was the Holy Bible.

The *fasola* compilers, especially Walker, White, and King, were driven by more than a desire to cash in. "I have endeavoured to gratify the taste of all," Walker wrote in his introduction to the first edition of his book. This meant supplying the entire array of evangelical churches "with a number of good, plain tunes" suited to the meters of their different existing hymnals—but also including older, contrapuntal "fugued" compositions at which Billings had excelled, as well as newer melodies picked up from hither and yon, often credited to one of the compilers. Eclecticism as well as excellence dominated the selection process. "Those that are partial to ancient music, will find here some good old acquaintances," *The Southern Harmony* claimed, while "youthful companions, who are more fond of modern music," would find enough to satisfy them. (The former included selections from Billings, as well as from European sources as old as John Calvin's Genevan Psalter; the latter included music by Mozart and Carl Maria von Weber.) Across the abundance of sects and denominations, the hymnals would spread the lessons and pleasures of musical fellowship, open to all believers just as God's grace was open to all sinners who sought it. And musically, the songbooks proved flexible to adapting all sorts of influences—including those aimed against the supposed vulgarities of *fasola* singing. The third edition of *The Southern Harmony,* published in 1854, took note of Lowell Mason's collection *Carmina Sacra,* which had appeared thirteen years earlier—and Walker included a shape-note version of "Joy to the World."

As its influence spread in the 1840s and 1850s, *fasola* singing remained firmly participatory rather than grandly performative. The major singing sites became gatherings known as conventions, including the Southern Musical Convention (organized in Upson County, Georgia, in 1845, with *The Sacred Harp* as its official book) and, after the Civil War, the Tallapoosa Singing Convention (organized in Haralson County, Georgia, in 1867), along with countless others located in towns from the Carolinas to Texas. Although reputed to be uniquely popular among Baptists (especially Primitive Baptists or those who preferred to be known simply as "plain old Baptists"), the *fasola* conventions admitted of no distinctions other than the desire to sing of and to the Lord, a cappella, with the assembled faithful seated in a square, arranged section by section—

trebles, altos, tenors, and basses—and with a group leader conducting from the square's center. The basic layout survives at the scores of *fasola* singing conventions still held today chiefly in the Deep South.

Musically, the *fasola* tradition is most readily identifiable by its insistent modality, reinforced by the frequent absence of a fifth in the chordal structure. Harmonies are present, but they are odd, with each vocal part sounding as if it follows its own line only to converge at climactic moments. The style, known to musicologists as dispersed harmony, was typical of the early American singing-school idiom; it also retained vestiges of Renaissance polyphony. Apart from Native American chants, it remains the most ancient form of popular music sung in the United States.

Lyrically, the hymns, psalms, and odes strongly reflect the nonconformism of the early eighteenth century and after, both in their theology and in their poetry. The songs chiefly concern human frailty and death (the essence of American secular balladry) as well as faith and redemption. But there are many *fasola* songs that, while pursuing these themes, break out in a strange beauty all their own. Consider the *Sacred Harp* psalm tune "Africa," its melody composed by Billings, who lifted the lyrics from Watts in 1778. The song has nothing explicitly to do with Africa. (Billings freely chose the names of New England towns and foreign continents as titles for his songs.) It begins with a leap of joy at the solemn oaths that have turned God's mercy drops into a shower of salvation upon Sion-Hill (which in the patriot Billings's compositions often means America). Sion would dwell on the heart of everlasting love, says the Lord, even "should nature change / And mothers monster prove." But the final verse, carried along by Billings's majestic musical cadences, suddenly describes a painful act of human redemption, with blood gushing in a Sion that has fallen to pieces:

> *Deep on the palms of both my hands*
> *I have engraved her name;*
> *My hands shall raise her ruin'd walls,*
> *And build her broken frame.*

Perhaps Billings thought he was updating Watts in order to refer to wartorn America; or perhaps the choice of "Africa" was a deliberate reference to slavery; or perhaps the composer was simply struck by Watts's startling image. No matter: the amazing lines would resound over hills and valleys across the South for a century and a half.

A full accounting of Sacred Harp singing's effects on American literature as well as on American music has yet to be written. Only when George Pullen Jackson published the first major study of the genre in 1933 did it come to broad notice as a popular art form. Beyond Joe Dan Boyd's fine biography from 2002 of Judge Jackson, who produced *The Colored Sacred Harp* in 1934, much remains to be learned about the distinctive African-American renditions of *fasola* music. The form seems to be enjoying a new lease on life, decades after the 1960s folk revival, as shape-note assemblies gather regularly in such unlikely places as Waldoboro, Maine, and Brooklyn, New York. And those with a taste for the weird revenants of American culture need only listen to Bob Dylan's rendition, on *World Gone Wrong*, of a hymn that appeared in *The Sacred Harp*, "The Lone Pilgrim."

The first song that Dylan describes in the notes to *World Gone Wrong* is Willie McTell's "Broke Down Engine," from the middle of the album's track list—a blues in which the singer cries out to the Lord, not for religion, but to "give me back my good gal, please." Dylan calls it "a Blind Willie McTell masterpiece" that is "about trains, mystery on the rails— the train of love, the train that carried my girl from town—The Southern Pacific, Baltimore & Ohio whatever—it's about variations of human longing—the low hum in meter & syllables." The last song that Dylan describes, and the last song on the album, is "Lone Pilgrim," which, although Dylan doesn't note it and may not have known, was among the hymns included in both *The Southern Harmony* and *The Sacred Harp*.

Dylan performs the song as a hushed devotional. He begins with some jagged strummed guitar chords outlining the melody (slightly muffing a couple of them, which is in keeping with the record's informal mood), then, settling down in a voice that is calmly comforting, he sings of coming to the grave site of the Lone Pilgrim, contemplating his tomb, and hearing someone say in a soft whisper: "How sweetly I sleep here alone." The aural mood is placid, but the lyric is unnerving, or should be—for just as in the haunting ballad "Long Black Veil," a dead man is speaking from the grave to the living. (Written in 1959 by Danny Dill and Marijohn Wilkin, and first recorded by Lefty Frizzell, "Long Black Veil" only sounds as if it is as old as, or even older than, "The Lone Pilgrim.") The whisper is not the blowing of the wind, or a magician's illusion, or the singer's imagination playing tricks on him: the singer doesn't *think* he hears something say something, he hears. The buried corpse, or maybe the dead man's invisible spirit, actually speaks, and the rest of the song belongs to that voice.

The song's lyrics date to 1838. Brother John Ellis, a twenty-six-year-old itinerant preacher for the anti-denominational Christian Connection—and a sometime poet—had been converting souls in Pennsylvania. His sect had originated in the merger, thirty years earlier, of three groups of dissidents: the Republican Methodists of Virginia and North Carolina; the self-styled Christians of New England; and some of the followers of the former Presbyterian evangelist Barton Stone. (Stone had been the leading force behind the momentous Cane Ridge, Kentucky, revival meetings in 1801, which are often seen as the spark that touched off the Second Great Awakening.) Eschewing creed as well as denominational distinctions, the Christians called themselves, simply, Christians and professed sole reliance on the Bible as the rule of faith and progress. Christian preachers were especially critical of the arcane but vicious sectarian fights that pitted Presbyterians against Methodists, Methodists against Baptists, and even clashing factions within these denominations against each other. Ellis, who had arrived in Pennsylvania from his native New York State to commence his preaching mission five years earlier, took a trip to New Jersey with one of his sisters during the autumn of 1838 and came to the town of Johnsonburg. There he found the grave of another Christian, dead for more than three years—the wandering preacher Joseph Thomas, better known as the White Pilgrim.

Joseph Thomas, "The White Pilgrim," circa 1835.

Thomas was one of the more interesting seekers and holy men of the awakening. Born in the North Carolina backcountry shortly after the American Revolution, he was orphaned at age seven, then raised by an older brother who lived in Virginia and who arranged for his schooling. At age sixteen, after a camp-meeting revival caused him to undertake a year of intense private prayer, Thomas was convinced of his salvation and received the Lord's call to preach the gospel. Baptized soon after as a Christian, he was also licensed to preach, having already displayed what he later called "my gift in speaking among the brethren." The boy preacher was an immediate sensation.

Over the ensuing decade, Thomas sermonized throughout North Carolina and Virginia, traveling as far north as Philadelphia, and he completed an eighteen-month, seven-thousand-mile tour of the western states, appearing in Methodist, Baptist, and Presbyterian churches as well as before his fellow Christians. Especially in the West, he later remarked, he found that popular religious devotion had achieved an "uncontrollable power." Thomas married in 1812 and started a family, settling his household first near his North Carolina birthplace and a year later in a home he purchased in the Shenandoah Valley near Winchester, Virginia.

By then, Thomas had grown to become an impressive figure—nearly six feet tall, with an athletic build, mild countenance, and friendly disposition. He was also exceptionally energetic, finding the time, despite his journeys, to work on far more than his preaching. In 1812, he published the first of two editions of his autobiography. And as he traveled about, Thomas collected the lyrics to liturgical music from every Protestant denomination, which he published in 1815 as *The Pilgrim's Hymn Book, Offered as a Companion to All Zion Travellers,* a pocket-sized compilation of 169 hymns and sacred songs. The contents, Thomas wrote, were inclusive, "purely calculated for holy praise, and not partly to promote the opinions of a particular sect." The hymnal lacked musical notation, yet it foreshadowed, in its breadth, the works of William Walker and Benjamin Franklin White. More than twenty of Thomas's selections, including "New Britain" (known today as "Amazing Grace") and William Billings's "Rochester" ("There is a land of pure delight"), later turned up in *The Southern Harmony, The Sacred Harp,* or both.

By the time the first edition of *The Pilgrim's Hymn Book* appeared, Thomas had transformed his ministry, following an intense personal reconsideration of religion in 1814. Now convinced, he wrote, that he had been called to provide an example of Jesus Christ, he would bear "a full and faithful testimony against Anti-Christ, and against the pride and fashion of this world." He considered clothing especially important to his efforts; henceforth, he would spurn "the present fashion of dress" and wear a white robe, "indicative of the bride, having made herself ready

for the marriage, and the innocency and purity which should character-
ize every minister of Christ." He sold his Virginia home, as well as all of
his other earthly possessions, relocated his family twenty-five miles to
the south, and, the following year, commenced (initially on foot) a new
ministry that would take him from his growing family for months at a
time, preaching the word of God in his new white raiment. Thomas also
carried and passed out copies of his hymnal, a service that forced him to
bow to necessity and ride on a horse. Initially disparaged for abandoning
his family and mocked (especially in his own neighborhood) as "Crazy
Thomas," he relocated his household to more hospitable ground in central Ohio around 1820. Over the ensuing decade and a half, though, he
earned more fame than notoriety as the White Pilgrim.

Except for his very last preaching tour, the details of the White Pilgrim's travels after 1820 are sketchy, but he is supposed to have spoken to
many thousands and converted many hundreds of souls, with what one
eulogist called "the sweetest strains of eloquence" delivered in a melodious voice. His surviving sermons and more than two score poems contain
an interesting mixture of Christian Connection precepts with social and
political reflections. The White Pilgrim preached a gospel of simplicity,
of the basic equality of humans before God, and of the primacy of com-
passion and charity among all the godly virtues. He argued a form of
pacifism as well, describing war not as a holy scourge in retribution for
men's sins but as an unleashing of ungodly, hellish passions. Thomas for-
swore any political activity, but he paid enough attention to politics to
write an extended poem on the debates in Congress over the expansion
of slavery that led to the Missouri Compromise in 1820. And although,
in that instance, he called for sectional comity, Thomas was a sincere
hater of slavery and what he called its "bloody whips." An egalitarian, he
lauded in his poetry what he saw as the democracy of his new home in the
North, where "the poor are rich, the rich are brought to see / Mankind
are one beneath this blessed tree."

In 1835, Thomas—astride a white horse, its tack bleached in lime—
took his message to the northern middle states of New York and New
Jersey, with plans eventually to head up to New England, but he never
made it all the way. Apparently, while walking the streets of Manhattan,
he contracted smallpox and succumbed shortly thereafter in the village of
Johnsonburg, New Jersey, about sixty miles west of the city, where he had
just delivered a sermon. After a few days of suffering, he died, attended

to in his final hours, one source claims, by a lone Negro nurse. According to several accounts, Thomas was originally buried in a disreputable old graveyard, set aside for gamblers and criminals. Popular belief held that the corpses of smallpox victims could somehow contaminate those already buried, and supposedly, despite the love and respect they had for the White Pilgrim, the elders of Johnsonburg decided to play it safe. By these same accounts, eleven years passed before Thomas's body was relocated to where it still rests, beneath a small, engraved marble obe-

Obelisk at the grave of the White Pilgrim, constructed in late 1850s at the Johnsonburg Christian Church cemetery, Johnsonburg, New Jersey. Inscription on the obelisk at the grave of the White Pilgrim.

lisk, in the Johnsonburg Christian Church cemetery. If these accounts are reliable, the grave that Brother John Ellis saw in 1838 was not the one that we see today. Certainly Ellis did not see the obelisk, which was not erected until the late 1850s.

Ellis wrote his poem—which he entitled "The White Pilgrim" and which made direct reference to "Joseph"—soon after he visited the grave, and was later chagrined to hear it credited to others. The poem's key elements and basic structure are contained in the song that eventually ended up as "Lone Pilgrim" on *World Gone Wrong*. But there were some complications along the way with respect to the melody as well as the lyrics. Benjamin Franklin White claimed he wrote the song when he included it in his expanded edition of *The Sacred Harp* in 1850; William Walker also claimed authorship in the third edition of *The Southern Harmony* in 1854. Both assertions were entirely untrue. Ellis wrote the basic lyrics, and substantially the same tune as appeared in both *The Southern Harmony* and *The Sacred Harp* appeared earlier as "Missionary; or, The White Pilgrim" (with most of Ellis's verse, intact, as well as the lyrics) in a collection, *Indian Melodies,* by a Narragansett Indian, Thomas Commuck, published in New York by the Methodist Episcopal Church in 1845. How Commuck (who also claimed credit for the hymn) came upon Ellis's poem is unknown. It is also unknown whether Commuck or the man credited as the book's "harmonizer," Thomas Hastings—the composer who wrote the melody of the classic hymn "Rock of Ages"—actually set the words to the music. But the tune is basically the same as a variant of the Scots air "The Braes of Balquhidder," which the poet Robert Burns took for his song "Bonie Peggy Alison," first published in 1788.

The process of literary revision, from Ellis's poem to the later hymns, was similarly convoluted. Commuck's version added an entire verse that Ellis did not write (or at least did not include in the version he printed in his autobiography in 1895); yet Ellis's and Commuck's versions shared a verse about the White Pilgrim spreading the gospel, which both White and Walker later eliminated. In *The Sacred Harp,* White changed the relevant pronouns so that it is always the visiting singer, and not the departed pilgrim, who speaks, thereby removing the hymn's most haunting feature. Complicating matters further, a broadside, entitled "The White Pilgrim" and published in New York at some point in the 1840s or 1850s, includes the Ellis and Commuck versions, but with an additional eight verses, describing a visit to the White Pilgrim's widow—the first six verses taken from a subsequent poem of Ellis's, "Reply to 'White Pilgrim,' " written in 1843. Two things are certain: the song was highly popular before the Civil War, largely though not simply because of its inclusion in *The Southern Harmony* and *The Sacred Harp;* and "The White Pilgrim" became "The Lone Pilgrim" because of White's and Walker's revisions, probably undertaken to remove any reference to a specific individual or religious body that might cause controversy. Ironically, a tribute to a specific American holy man who despised denominations turned into a generic lyric about a solitary wanderer out of a desire to break through denominational barriers.

In his notes to *World Gone Wrong,* Dylan wrote that he took "Lone Pilgrim" from an old Doc Watson record, and the version that Dylan sings is identical to the one Watson sings on the album *The Watson Family*, first released in 1963.* (Watson's version, which he states was one of his father's favorite hymns, is in turn a slightly shorter replication of the version in *The Sacred Harp,* except with the ghostly original pronouns restored.) Several recordings of the song appeared between Watson's and Dylan's, but either Dylan didn't know them or they had no effect. The Watson family album, produced in 1963 by Dylan's Village friend Ralph Rinzler of the Greenbriar Boys, is drawn from genuine field recordings made between 1960 and 1963 in Tennessee, Virginia, and North Carolina—and it thus has the spontaneous, homemade, "live" quality that is a key to *World Gone Wrong* (which might be described as a set of Dylan's field recordings of himself).

Watson's rendition is both rich and piercing (the fiddle adds to that), in the peculiar combination that makes Watson's singing so singular and enthralling. There is a charming, slightly clunky quality to the performance, as if Watson is trying hard to merge his tempo and phrasing to fit those of the fiddler (who is Watson's father-in-law, the superb old-time banjo and fiddle player Gaither Carlton). On the second line of each verse, as the melody ascends—"And pensively stood by his tomb"; "And gathering storms may arise"; and so on—Watson's timbre intensifies, placing an almost desperate emphasis on the fifth and eighth syllables ("stood" / "tomb"; "storms" / "rise"). Dylan, in contrast, sings only to his solo guitar strumming, and his voice is muted and tender throughout—melodious yet barely rising above a whisper. His voice becomes the one murmuring at the pilgrim's grave.

---

* Dylan's official lyrics change *The Sacred Harp*'s and *The Southern Harmony*'s wording of the third verse's opening line, as actually recorded by both Watson and Dylan—"The cause of my Master compelled me from home"—to read "the call of my master compelled me from home." The substitution marginally strengthens the song's religious directness. At the same time, by rendering "Master" in lowercase, the official lyrics diminish the religious sense by making the word more ambiguous: as read, the dead pilgrim could be a slave, separated from his family because he has been sold by his master. The official lyrics alter two additional important words, changing the line "pensively stood by his tomb" to "patiently stood by his tomb" and changing "The same hand that led me through scenes most severe" to "The same hand that led me through seas most severe." The first change badly damages the line, indeed, renders it almost unintelligible. (What was the singer being patient for?) The second provides a more vivid image, but is not necessarily an improvement. The version in *The Sacred Harp* excluded an extra verse, composed by one J. J. Hicks of North Carolina, which Walker included in *The Southern Harmony.*

Doc Watson and Gaither Carlton, recording in New York, 1961. Photograph by John Cohen of the New Lost City Ramblers.

Far more successfully than Watson, Dylan enters and inhabits the song's core, offering a breathing spell from what he called inhumane modern technocratic convention—and offering consolation. The itinerant "I," who sings the first three lines, suddenly becomes another "I," the man who died and yet who lives, and who now gently speaks. This second "I" once wandered too, as compelled by his Master (or master), but (and here Dylan's voice swells just slightly) he "met the con-*taaaaa jun 'n'* saannk to the tomb." His far-off "companion" and children should not weep now that he is gone. (Dylan does not sing the word "gone" so much as he exhales it.) "I" is free at last from earthly tempests; his rested soul has achieved the Lord's many mansions and he is calm; and anyway he is not really gone, not completely, at least for the length of this song.

Coming at the conclusion of an album of old ballads and blues about strange happenings, about men no longer able to do their women right because the world is going wrong, about rounders, gamblers, six-gun shooters, a blue-eyed, blue-bellied Boston boy cut down by Johnny Reb, and more, "Lone Pilgrim" is a reprieve, a coming to rest, a ghost note of a different order, and it is also a benediction. Dylan had found a new use for a *fasola* standard from *The Sacred Harp,* a song inspired by a godly, white-robed minister of charity, decency, and redemption—and a compiler of hymns—in an America convulsed by religious awakenings. The song, as he describes and performs it, might even have been a gloss on one of the White Pilgrim's poems:

Let me arise above the fame,
Of riches and renown,
Above in earthly monarch's name,
To an immortal crown.

Hearing Dylan sing "Lone Pilgrim" when my father fell ill in 1994, and then listening again over and over during the months after he died, brought a solace that came from the last place, and the last performer, I'd have expected it from. More than a decade later, it still brings solace, especially in the last two lines and the very last word, which is also the last word on *World Gone Wrong:* "The same hand that led me through scenes most severe / Has kindly assisted me home." For that performance—of a song that few except Dylan's most passionate fans remember—I will always feel a gratitude that is completely personal. But all of that aside, it is clear that with "Lone Pilgrim" and *World Gone Wrong,* Dylan had reached the end of the beginning of his own artistic reawakening and, assisted by the kind Master, had reached a place that at least felt more like home.

World Gone Wrong was the rock-and-roll equivalent of a literary succès d'estime, garnering rich praise and poor sales. A few knowledgeable critics and writers, including the biographer Clinton Heylin, deemed it, along with *Good as I Been to You,* an unfortunate retread of the kind of cover material Dylan was performing in concert. Some detractors even condemned Dylan's liner notes as wordy and incomprehensible. For the most part, though, reviewers agreed with Robert Christgau, who called the album "eerie and enticing" and perceptively noted the non sequiturs and other odd features in the old buried songs, usages that Dylan had long ago absorbed in his own songwriting "because he believes they evoke a world that defies rationalization." The album won Dylan another Grammy, this time for Best Traditional Folk Album. But the recordings meant little to listeners who were not even born when the folk revival of the 1960s arrived, and the ranks of the older loyal folkies had thinned.

The album fared far less well in the U.S. sales charts than had either *Under the Red Sky* or *Good as I Been to You.*

Dylan himself, though, was pleased enough to play a portion of the acoustic material in a block of four important shows at Manhattan's Supper Club in mid-November 1993. Dylan had booked the club with the hope of making a concert film for television as well as a new live album. The film and album projects never materialized. But the soundboard and audience recordings that survived (and have been widely bootlegged) show Dylan in top form, singing and playing acoustic guitar with his band, interspersing strong renditions of "Absolutely Sweet Marie," "Queen Jane Approximately," and other songs from his mid-1960s zenith with traditional songs, including several from *World Gone Wrong*: "Ragged and Dirty," "Blood in My Eyes," "Jack-A-Roe," and "Delia." Heylin has called the shows "exceptional" and remarked that Dylan performed "with all the hurt that inner voice felt when left crying to be heard."

A year later, Dylan and his band recorded a pair of shows in another intimate setting, a special Sony Records concert studio, for inclusion in MTV's *Unplugged* series of taped televised concerts. Dylan would have preferred to play old folk songs with nothing but acoustic instruments— in the true spirit of the series' title—but the programmers decided that traditional music without drums and at least some electric guitar backing would turn off the youthful MTV audience. Instead, Dylan, once again fronting his band on acoustic guitar, performed standards from his personal songbook, with some quirky additions like the heretofore unreleased antiwar song from 1963 "John Brown." Although some of the best performances ended up on the cutting room floor—including a superb rendition of "Absolutely Sweet Marie" and a slow, sexy "I Want You"—the *Unplugged* show, as broadcast, showcased a revitalized Dylan to millions of viewers. As a special sign to those older fans and sometime fans who tuned in—but also to show he had not grown too old—Dylan wore a black-and-white Pop Art polka-dot shirt along with vintage Ray-Ban Wayfarer sunglasses. Both accoutrements were literal throwbacks to 1965—yet far from pathetically out-of-date, Dylan looked energetic and oddly stylish.

Several months later—after a surprising appearance at the Shrine Auditorium in Los Angeles for a grand celebration of Frank Sinatra's birthday, where he sang, at Sinatra's personal request, his old song of parting "Restless Farewell," accompanied by a strong quartet—Dylan found himself snowed in on his Minnesota farm, and he began writing new songs. Contrary to his usual practice, he would hold on to the new material for a while—the entire summer and autumn of 1996—revising lyrics and melodies, before he finally booked studio recording time in Miami in January 1997. "It's a spooky record," Dylan later said, "because I feel spooky. I just don't feel in tune with anything." Hoping to achieve a sound that was neither glitzy nor self-consciously old-fashioned, Dylan turned again to Daniel Lanois to work with him as coproducer. The album would eventually be called *Time Out of Mind*, and it would mark the completion of Dylan's comeback from his travails and turmoil of the 1980s.

On an initial listening, *Time Out of Mind*'s most striking features are its deliberate pace and its muffled, boggy sound. Although the album includes a country jump song, "Dirt Road Blues," and a banging, sinister backbeat rocker, "Cold Irons Bound," most of the songs amble quietly, no matter whether the lyrics convey revulsion or resignation. Lanois's reverberating special production effects—which Dylan later said he regretted—produced an album very much in the mysterious voodoo style of *Oh Mercy*, but much darker and foggier. Whereas the earlier album sounds like New Orleans, *Time Out of Mind* conjures up the deepest recesses of a bayou, with smoke drifting lightly across black-green water, Spanish moss clumped so thick that it seems impenetrable. Neither coproducer would tax Dylan's aging vocal cords unduly, and so, although the cracked-leather vocals of the earlier acoustic albums show up only now and then, on most of the songs Dylan's voice is hushed—sometimes sepulchral, and sometimes spectral.

One of the album's best songs—and the one that now seems likeliest to survive as a canonical Dylan composition—is "Not Dark Yet." Commonly described as a meditation on morality (which in part it is), it is actually more of a song about weary alienation from a world full of lies, where behind every thing of beauty lurks some kind of pain. Dylan sings of receiving a woman's kind and forthright letter, but it is of no account because "it's not dark yet, but it's getting there." Song after song on *Time Out of Mind* conveys a similar sense of loss and estrangement, portraying a world emptied of everything the singer has ever valued, where his loved ones are either gone or no longer his loved ones. The best he can do is dance with a stranger, which only reminds him that he once truly loved someone else.

The album's most brilliant song, the hypnotic, sixteen-and-a-half-minute "Highlands," which concludes the album, takes its opening line from Robert Burns's verse "My Heart's in the Highlands," itself a poem of distance and estrangement, drawn from a traditional Scots air. In Dylan's version, complete with its mention of bluebells and the waters of Aberdeen, the Highlands could be Dylan's own northern Midwest just as easily as it could be Scotland; or it could also be God's heaven, at least in the final verse. But the song quickly shoots into a rat-race urban America where the singer walks past a park, spots a mangy dog crossing the street, and brushes past an earnest voter registrant. The singer is a man who, like Dylan, is nearing sixty or is just past it; he apparently lives alone; and the song describes his meanderings in a tone that is alternately kvetchy, bemused, amused, and bitter. The central episode involves a semi-flirtation with a pretty waitress, the only person that the singer as much as speaks with during the entire song; the talk gets nowhere; and the man departs the diner, "back to the busy street, but nobody's going anywhere." The song is very long, but when it concludes, little has happened and nothing has changed.

One of the things that makes "Highlands" stand out are its quiet jokes, about Neil Young, about women and women writers, about elections. The lines are at most mildly funny when read, but they are hilarious when sung, or at least they can be when Dylan sings them. Just as changing a few pronouns in a song such as "Tangled Up in Blue" can dramatically shift its meaning, so changes in inflection can invest "Highlands," a song of Hopper-esque solitude, with an encouraging laughter and wit. "Highlands" also describes a refuge from the alienation and pain, a place that can be reached, a place where the disconnected singer had already traveled in his own mind. Even on an album as bleak as *Time Out of Mind,* Dylan still manages to sign off with a hopeful "good luck."

On repeated listening, another feature about the album stands out: Dylan's repeated, deliberate, always unacknowledged, but sometimes obvious adaptations from traditional folk and country-and-western music, as well as from high literature. Dylan took the title and some of the words in "Highlands" from Burns, but based its tune on a riff by the great 1930s bluesman Charley Patton. Dylan also lifted the title "Dirt Road Blues" from Patton. The title of the first song on *Time Out of Mind,* "Love Sick," echoes Hank Williams's hit "Lovesick Blues." Bits and pieces of lyrics from songs ranging from the spiritual "Swing Low, Sweet Chariot" to Jimmie Rodgers's "Waiting for a Train" turn up here and there. The album's title—an old phrase, long out of usage, meaning "time immemorial"—may just have come from *Romeo and Juliet,* specifically Mercutio's description in act 1 of the tiny fairy Queen Mab, who would ride over sleepers and induce dreams of wishes fulfilled:

> *Her chariot is an empty hazel-nut,*
> *Made by the joiner squirrel or old grub,*
> *Time out o' mind the fairies' coachmakers.* *

Although it was too early to discern what he was doing, with these pastiches Dylan had begun to revamp his American style.

What was clear at the time was that Dylan had returned to excellent form. And although it was sheer coincidence, it now seems almost symbolic that between the time the studio recording ended and the album's release, Dylan suffered through and recovered from a grave attack of histoplasmosis, a serious heart infection that might well have killed him. After enduring severe pain for much of the month of June, Dylan was back on the road at the start of August. In late September, he played a special performance for Pope John Paul II at the Italian National Eucharistic Congress in Bologna. Four days later, he inserted "Love Sick" on the band's encore playlist—the first song from the new album to be played in concert. Early in 1998, the official accolades began coming in, starting with the Grammy for Best Album of the Year.

Over the next three years, the aura around Dylan was brighter than it had been at any time since the mid-1970s. His touring arrangements affirmed his regained stature. In April 1998, he teamed up with the Rolling Stones for a six-date tour of South American cities. Later tours in 1998 and 1999 included a triple bill with Joni Mitchell and Van Morrison, as well as tours with Paul Simon and with the Grateful Dead's bassist Phil Lesh's new combo, called Phil Lesh and Friends. And by 2000, Dylan was back to his songwriting.

---

* Alternatively, Dylan could have lifted the phrase from Walt Whitman's "Song of the Broad-Axe" (1856): "Served those who, time out of mind, made on the granite walls rough sketches of the sun, moon, stars, ships, ocean-waves"; or William Butler Yeats's "Upon a House Shaken by the Land Agitation" (1910): "How should the world be luckier if this house / Where passion and precision have been one / Time out of mind, became too ruinous / To breed the lidless eye that loves the sun?" But by far the likeliest source is Warren Zevon's ballad "Accidentally Like a Martyr" (1978): "Never thought I'd ever be so lonely / After such a long, long time / Time out of mind."

In 1999, an interviewer for *Guitar World* magazine reflected on Dylan's brush with death and asked him whether, knowing what he now did about *Time Out of Mind*'s success, he would have been satisfied had it been his final album. Dylan demurred: "I think we were just starting with getting my identifiable sound onto the disc. I think we just started. I think there's plenty more to do. We just opened up that door at that particular time, and in the passage of time we'll go back in and extend that. But I didn't feel like it was an ending to anything. I thought it was more the beginning."

PART V: RECENT

9

THE MODERN
MINSTREL RETURNS:

"Love and Theft," September 11, 2001, and the Newport Folk
Festival, Newport, Rhode Island, August 3, 2002

t is May 24, 1966, and at the Olympia in Paris, also known as *"la salle la plus importante d'Europe,"* time slips.

Two years after this night of music, many of the young people in the audience will be rioting in the Paris streets, their heads full of ideas that will drive them to proclaim a revolution of the imagination, fight pitched battles with the police and the National Guard, and try to burn down the Paris stock exchange, in what would become known in Left Bank lore as *"la nouvelle nuit des barricades,"* the most dramatic street fighting of May 1968. Seven hundred and ninety-five rioters are arrested, and 456 are injured.

But now it's exactly two years earlier—to the minute—and the rebels-to-be sit expectantly, waiting for the second half of the show, when the curtain parts, and there they see to their horror, attached to the backdrop, the emblem of everything they are coming to hate, the emblem of napalm and Coca-Cola and white racism and colonialism and imagination's death. It is a huge fifty-star American flag. And Bob Dylan, the emblem of American rebellion and imagination's rebirth, has hoisted it aloft.

What's the joke? But it is no joke. They are here to hear the idol, and know full well that the idol now will play electric (after what turned out to be a frustrating-to-all-concerned acoustic set), which will offend the

Bob Dylan and his band at the Olympia, Paris, May 24, 1966. In the shadows, left to right: Rick Danko, in the background just over Dylan's shoulder, dragging on a cigarette, Mickey Jones, Robbie Robertson.

folk purists in Paris as it has in cities across the United States and Great Britain. But this Stars and Stripes stuff turns a musical challenge into an assault, an incitement, as in-your-face—more so—to the young Left Bank leftists as any Fender Telecaster. In England, the idol had traded insults with the hecklers, but in Paris, on this, his twenty-fifth birthday, he strikes first.

Whether they like it or not, the idol will give them his own version of "America," a place that they have never learned about in books and, if they have, that they do not comprehend. Angry patrons boo and shout, "U.S. go home!"

Not quite five months after this concert, the French pop singer Johnny Hallyday plays the Olympia. He has two young women backup singers, one wearing a miniskirt, the other, vaguely resembling Marianne Faithfull, dressed in trousers and a vest. He also has a backup band that doubles as his warm-up act, a new group, assembled only recently and still a little rough, that is introduced to the audience as hailing from Seattle, Washington, and that performs, among other numbers, a bent-out-of-shape version of the Troggs' Top 40 summer smash "Wild Thing." There is no flag, and by now the Paris audience has caught up, musically—enough to be amazed, not dismayed, by the combo that will later gain fame as the Jimi Hendrix Experience, in its fourth public appearance. Only a year earlier, Hendrix was playing with an ensemble, the Blue Flame, as the obscure house band at the Café Wha? on MacDougal Street, where Dylan had scratched out his first gigs in New York, and in time, after his star began to streak, some of Hendrix's most powerful performances would be his soaring interpretations of Dylan songs. In a time that, looking back, seems impossibly compressed, the early 1960s gave way to the late 1960s, even in Paris, and to the musical counterculture that Hendrix helped invent but from which Dylan always stood at one remove.

Suddenly, it's May 1966 again—except that it's not 1966, it's 2001, and the venue is certainly not the Olympia, and really doesn't look like Paris at all. As expected, an organist and a drummer and a bunch of guitarists take the stage. But the headliner, skinny as a fence rail, has swapped his mod-cut houndstooth suit for a black and silver Nashville number, and he wears a five-gallon hat, and he has sprouted a Dapper Dan pencil mustache. Then the band rips into an up-tempo version of "From a Buick 6," a song off of the album *Highway 61 Revisited*—except the lyrics have completely changed. The headliner rasps the opening lines:

Tweedle-dee Dum and Tweedle-dee Dee
They're throwing knives into the tree.

With "*Love and Theft*," Dylan changed shape once again, not as dramatically or as fractiously as he did in 1966, but emphatically enough. He also played tricks with the past and present, memory and history. The new album was certainly the work of an older and wiser artist, now on the verge of sixty, burdened with a mountain of rue. But, stepping outside the squitchy, boggy gloominess and resignation of *Time Out of Mind*, the singer also sings of brimming desire and is eager to tell about it, though not without irony. He has truly relocated his mark and is ready to step up and cut loose; he has found things he had once thought were lost.

Even more striking than the album's mood is its dense eclectic style—the most varied of any Dylan album before it since *The Basement Tapes*. More explicitly than ever, Dylan travels through time and space at will on "*Love and Theft*," picks up melodies and lyrics from hither and yon (including some wildly unexpected places), and then assembles something new and original for himself and his listeners. He crashes through the deadening domination of up-to-the-minute, on-the-buzz, virtual reality with musical and literary forms (and even recording devices) that are older and truer, without turning in the least antiquarian.* He reclaims the present by reclaiming the past. And he commands his amalgamating American art in wholly new ways in order to express loss and hope, cynicism and wonder, as he had come to feel them at the century's turning.

Love and theft, Bob Dylan has said, fit together like fingers in a glove.

People noticed as soon as "*Love and Theft*" was released that its title is the same as a book by the cultural historian Eric Lott about the origins and character of American blackface minstrelsy. In the 1820s and 1830s, young working-class white men from the North began imitating southern slaves onstage, blacking up and playing banjos and tambourines and rat-a-tat bones sets, jumping and singing in a googly-eyed "Yass, suh, Noooooo, sah" dialect about sex and love and death and just plain nonsense. The minstrels stole from blacks and caricatured them, and often showed racist contempt—but their theft was also an act of envy and desire and love. Bluenoses condemned the shows as vulgar. Aficionados, from Walt Whitman to Abraham Lincoln to Mark Twain, adored the minstrels for their fun, and for much more than that. " 'Nigger' singing with them," Whitman wrote of one blackface troupe in 1846, "is a subject from obscure life in the hands of a divine painter."

Dylan has neither confirmed nor denied that he took his title from Lott's book, although when he placed the words inside quotation marks, he strongly suggested that he did. But there is plenty of theft and love (and divinity) in "*Love and Theft*," some of it obvious, especially in the lyrics. One needn't know much more about the blues than the songs of Robert Johnson, Robert Wilkins, and the rest of the Delta and Memphis players or the versions copped by the Rolling Stones in order to recognize the po'boy prodigal son or the line in "Tweedle Dee & Tweedle Dum" about someone's love being "all in vain." Johnson again, but also the up-country white pickers Clarence Ashley and Dock Boggs provide elements of "High Water (for Charley Patton)," the best song on the album. Patton, who is something of the presiding shade of "*Love and Theft*," also

---

* The album was the first that Dylan decided to produce by himself, under the pseudonym Jack Frost. He was especially interested in using recording techniques and equipment long since displaced in most studios.

An early minstrel sheet music cover, highlighting the supposed differences between the "dandyism" of the northern blackface performers (top) and the strange contortions of southern slaves (bottom), from Boston Minstrels, "The Celebrated Ethiopian Melodies" (Boston, 1843).

wrote and recorded a song about the great 1927 flood in Mississippi, "High Water Everywhere." (Likewise, "Dirt Road Blues," on *Time Out of Mind,* borrows from Patton's "Down the Dirt Road Blues.") "Lonesome Day Blues" was the title of a song by Blind Willie McTell (recorded with Ruby Glaze under the name Hot Shot Willie), although Dylan's song also echoes the Carter Family's "Sad and Lonesome Day." Dock Boggs, among many others, recorded a song called "Sugar Baby." The melody of "Floater (Too Much to Ask)" is the same as the Joe Young and Carmen Lombardo tune "Snuggled on Your Shoulder," recorded by Bing Crosby in 1932; and "Bye and Bye" sounds a great deal like "Having Myself a Time," as recorded by Billie Holiday in 1938.

Charley Patton, circa 1920s.

Dylan had been committing this common kind of theft all of his working life, right down to swiping his own surname. The tune of his tribute to Woody Guthrie, "Song to Woody," on his very first album, comes directly from Guthrie's own "1913 Massacre," which Guthrie appropriated from a traditional song. And Dylan has never simply been a brilliant, deeply knowledgeable, opportunistic folkie; nor has he been, either legally or spiritually, a plagiarist, although some critics and rivals have claimed he is.* He has been a minstrel, or has worked in the same tradition as the minstrels (a tradition that includes vaudeville as well as the southern songster performers, among them Blind Willie McTell)—copying other people's mannerisms and melodies and lyrics and utterly transforming them and making them his own, a form of larceny that is as American as apple pie, and cherry, pumpkin, and plum pie, too. As American as the hybrid music of Aaron Copland or "The Lone Pilgrim." Or as American as Chang and Eng, the original Siamese twins, who, though born in Siam, started touring the United States in proto-carny style in 1829, coming to town right beside the minstrels, before they signed up with P. T. Barnum in 1832, for whom they worked for seven years. They then retired to Wilkesboro, North Carolina, became American citizens, married a pair of sisters, and

---

* For a fuller discussion of these matters, including legal definitions of plagiarism, see below, pp. 308–13.

raised two families; and they show up on *"Love and Theft"* in "Honest with Me."

But even when Dylan has sung or adapted ancient words and melodies, he has been a modern minstrel—a whiteface minstrel. The hard-edged racism taken for granted by the nineteenth-century minstrel troupes is of another age, at least in Dylan's art. The disguises that Dylan has sported onstage—recall him telling his audience in Philharmonic Hall, off the cuff, on Halloween night 1964, "I have my Bob Dylan mask on"—have been more of himself, his time, and his America, even when, since the 1990s, he has worn his Rockmount cowboy shirts. (When Dylan, in recent years, has dipped back sartorially into the nineteenth century, he is most likely to wear a long black coat and a riverboat gambler's hat—looking a bit as I imagine Herman Melville's Confidence Man, or maybe one of his marks, must have looked, churning down the Mississippi aboard the mythic paddle wheeler *Fidèle*.) While he has

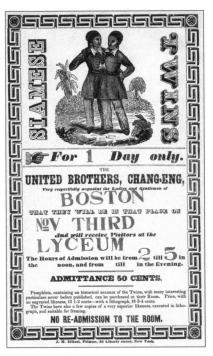

Poster advertising a Boston appearance by Chang and Eng Bunker, the original Siamese Twins, 1829.

tipped his hat to the old-time minstrels, Dylan has inverted their display, as when he actually whitened his face for the Rolling Thunder Revue—turning himself into a classic European Pierrot mime, but also alluding to the old practice of "blackin' up," in reverse.

As a modern minstrel, Dylan has continually updated and widened his ambit, never more so than on *"Love and Theft,"* lifting what he pleases from the last century's great American songbook. Folk songs, as ever: the wonderful tagline of "Mississippi" (a song originally intended for *Time Out of Mind*)—"Only one thing I did wrong / Stayed in Mississippi a day too long"—comes from an old work song called "Rosie." (Rosie herself gets mentioned in the lyrics.) "The Darktown Strutters' Ball" is here, plain as day. But there are also melodies and lyrics reminiscent of, and sometimes taken wholesale from, blues and pop songs of the 1920s through the 1950s. Listen to "Cry a While," then compare its melody with the Mississippi Sheiks' "Stop and Listen Blues" from 1930. Compare "Lonesome Day Blues" with the Sheiks' song's opening line: "Yes, today have been, baby, long old lonesome day." Then compare "Cry a While's" refrain with that of "I Cried for You," written by Gus Arnheim, Abe Lyman, and Arthur Freed in 1923, and later performed brilliantly by Count Basie and Sarah Vaughan, as well as Billie Holiday:

> *I cried for you, now it's your turn to cry for me.*
> *Every road has its turning, that's one thing you're learning.*

As "Cry a While" continues, make a note to check out Sonny Boy Williamson's "Your Funeral and My Trial," from 1958, or to listen to the line "Feel like a fighting rooster / Feel better than I ever felt," on Victoria Spivey's "Dope Head Blues," released in 1927. Then track down a copy of the 1960s East L.A. hot-rod song "Hopped-Up Mustang," by a group called the Pacifics, and listen again to the lyrics of "Summer Days" and "High Water," on *Love and Theft.*

After a while, a listener stops looking for antecedents and sampling and begins to wonder which versions of the quoted songs (and bits of quoted songs) might have been in Dylan's head, not necessarily with the idea of emulating them, but to learn what he could about phrasing and dynamics. "Sugar Baby" contains one line—"Look up, look up, see your maker / 'fore Gabriel blows his horn"—taken word for word, and note for note, from "The Lonesome Road," credited to the 1920s hit makers Nathaniel Shilkret and Gene Austin (though it sounds like a much older African-American spiritual) and recorded by dozens of performers. Did Dylan have in mind Paul Robeson's version of the song, recorded in 1929; or Stepin Fetchit's, released that same year, at the conclusion of an early film version of Edna Ferber's *Showboat;* or a young Sister Rosetta Tharpe's recorded version from 1938 or her movie version from 1941; or perhaps Frank Sinatra's stylish, hipped-up rendition, on Sinatra's album *A Swingin' Affair!* released in 1957?* Sinatra, the original Ol' Blues Eyes,

---

* And this hardly exhausts the possibilities. As of 2009, there were more than two hundred known recordings of "The Lonesome Road," by artists as disparate as Lonnie Johnson, the Boswell Sisters, and Tab Hunter.

should not be discounted: Sinatra also sang "I Cried for You," as part of his starring role in the film *The Joker Is Wild* from 1957.

(In a disarming little story about three jolly kings that became the liner notes to *John Wesley Harding,* Dylan pokes fun at the Dylanologists who search for the great true meaning in his songs: "Faith is the key!" one king says. "No, froth is the key!" the second says. "You're both wrong," says the third, "the key is Frank!" In the story, the third king is right, sort of—but who would have ever imagined that Frank might turn out to be someone like Sinatra?)

Nor does Dylan confine himself to musical sources. "Summer Days" contains a verse that refers to a politician running for office in jogging shoes—when I first heard the album, my mind ran immediately to Bill Clinton—who has "been sucking the blood out of the genius of generosity." The allusion is, in part, political, as Dylan borrowed the line from a little-known speech by Abraham Lincoln, written in 1842, while Lincoln was still an aspiring local politician. But the allusion (if that is what it is) is to something else—for Lincoln's speech, addressed to the Washington Temperance Society of Springfield, Illinois, endorsed the group's nonjudgmental, openhearted approach to getting drunkards to reform; noted that the afflicted seemed, to an unusual extent, to include "the brilliant, and the warm-blooded"; and observed that "the demon of intemperance ever seems to have delighted in sucking the blood of genius and of generosity." That Dylan would have read this particular speech, in whatever context, says something about his outsized reading interests; that he salted the line away in his memory, or wrote it down, and then recycled it on *"Love and Theft"* may mean no more than that he knows a great line when he discovers it.*

And, of course, among the great old last-century songwriters whom Dylan recycles is himself—and not just from his songs or his adaptations of other people's. In New Orleans, there was a streetcar line that had as its destination a street called Desire. Tennessee Williams used it for the title of his play; Dylan appears to have adapted it (or used Williams) for the title of an album. (*Streetcar,* the play, may have turned up in one of Dylan's

---

* The Washington Temperance Society (known familiarly as the Washingtonians) was founded in 1840 by a group of Baltimore workingmen who sought a less preachy and censorious alternative to the existing anti-liquor movement. During its meteoric heyday, the society enlisted untold thousands of members and pioneered some of the principles and practices later refined, with enduring effect, by Alcoholics Anonymous. My thanks to Nina Goss for the Lincoln reference.

early songs, "Love Is Just a Four-Letter Word," echoing Blanche DuBois's immortal line about how her family's "epic fornications" led to the loss of its estate on a called-in mortgage. "The four-letter word deprived us of our plantation," Blanche remembers wryly. More likely, though, Dylan was thinking of the film version of Williams's *Cat on a Hot Tin Roof,* in which the alcoholic Brick Pollitt, played by Paul Newman, tells his father, Big Daddy, played by Burl Ives: "You don't know what love means. To you, it's just another four-letter word.") Well, Desire, the streetcar, is back on *"Love and Theft,"* ridden by Tweedle-dee Dum and Tweedle-dee Dee to their rural retirement. "Tweedle Dee & Tweedle Dum" and "Honest with Me" and "Cry a While" are all variations of standard twelve-bar blues, but listen hard and I think you'll catch the musicality of "Buick 6" (especially the bootleg outtake version) and of "Leopard-Skin Pill-Box Hat" (a standard number in Dylan's live shows in 2001) and of "Pledging My Time." Same thing with the eight-bar blues "Po' Boy" and the eight-bar "Cocaine," yet another concert standard in 2001. The opening guitar lick of "High Water" brings my ear back to "Down in the Flood," and the rest of the song recalls John Lee Hooker's "Tupelo," as rendered on the complete bootleg version of *The Basement Tapes.* Dylan had been singing his own version of "The Coo Coo" (which turns up, fleetingly, in "High Water") at least since his Gaslight days forty years earlier.

There's no message to this modern minstrel style. It is a *style,* a long-evolving and still-evolving one, not a doctrine or an ideology. But that's not to say that Dylan, a craftsman, has ever been unaware of that style and how he has worked with it and altered it, or that we should be either. Several years before *"Love and Theft"* appeared, Johnny Cash released an excellent album of traditional songs that he called *American Recordings.* *"Love and Theft"* could have the same title, though Dylan's musical reach is even wider than the great Cash's was, and his minstrelsy more complicated. He unfurled that American flag once again, the masked man remaking his art out of (mainly) American materials.

In keeping with the seemingly miscellaneous but highly structured randomness of the minstrel shows, *"Love and Theft"* is an album of songs—greatest hits, that haven't become hits yet, Dylan said at the time. And like the minstrel shows (and their successors, the vaudeville shows), the album is funny, maybe the funniest Dylan had produced since he was writing songs like "Outlaw Blues." Some of the jokes, like the minstrels', read flat on the page—"Freddy or not here I come"—but Dylan's delivery of them makes me laugh out loud. Here's another one, a rim-shot pun that could have come right from an old minstrel show or vaudeville sketch—dull to read, but funny when sung:

> *I'm stark naked, but I don't care*
> *I'm goin' off into the woods, I'm huntin' bare.*

When asked who his favorite poets were in 1965, Dylan mentioned a flying-trapeze family from the circus, Smokey Robinson, and W. C. Fields (who through vaudeville had his own connections to minstrelsy); now, in "Lonesome Day Blues," he pays a little homage to Fields's snow-bound gag line in *The Fatal Glass of Beer*: "T'ain't a fit night out for man nor beast!"

Many of the other jokes are high-low literary and operatic. Don Pasquale's 2:00 a.m. booty call in "Cry a While" comes right out of Donizetti's *Don Pasquale*, a farce about a foolish old man who disinherits his own nephew, unknowingly marries the nephew's girlfriend, and comes to misery—a work first performed in Paris in 1843, high-minstrel time in America. Then there are the Shakespearean jokes about shivering old Othello and the bad-complexioned Juliet. All of these high-low jokes, too, are in the updated minstrel style, last heard from Dylan in

Bob Dylan and his "Love and Theft" period band aboard tour bus. Left to right: Dave Kemper, Tony Garnier, Bob Dylan, Larry Campbell, and Charlie Sexton (kneeling).

this humorous way on *Highway 61 Revisited*: the blackface companies regularly performed spoofs of grand opera and Shakespeare (*Hamlet* was a particular favorite)—popular works as familiar to American audiences a century and a half ago as *Seinfeld* and *The Little Mermaid* are today.

Dylan delivers every joke deadpan, like someone out of something by the minstrel show patron Twain. And some of the jokes come close to being sinister. To the steel-guitar background in "Moonlight," all is songbirds and flowers in the heavy dusk, when, lightly lilting, the crooner sings:

> *Well, I'm preaching peace and harmony,*
> *The blessings of tranquillity,*
> *Yet, I know when the time is right to strike.*
> *I'll take you 'cross the river, dear,*
> *You don't need to linger here;*
> *I know the kinds of things you like.*

Ah, the silver-tongued devil. Rudy Vallée turns into someone else—maybe Clark Gable, or, far more frightening, Robert Mitchum. It sounds as if it could be scary—much depends on what the singer means by "strike"— and yet it's also hilarious.

And there is plenty more serious and fearful play on "*Love and Theft.*" More than any old-time minstrel (and much like most of the later song-sters, bluesmen, and country singers), Dylan thinks about the cosmos contained in every grain of sand. All of those floods aren't just floods; they're also the Flood. Why else do Charles Darwin and his ultra-materialist friend George Lewes (lover of the great novelist George Eliot) turn up in "High Water," wanted dead or alive by a snarling Mississippi judge? Lewes tells the believers, the Englishman, the Italian, and the Jew (Protestant, Roman Catholic, Hebrew?), that, no, they can't open their minds to just anything, and for that the high sheriff's on his tail.* "Some

---

* In his revised official book of lyrics, published well after "*Love and Theft*" was released, Dylan spelled the name as George Lewis. Unless he is referring to the jazz clarinetist from the 1940s, 1950s, and 1960s—which makes no sense in this context—the name is perfectly random. My guess is that Dylan originally had Lewes in mind but that, after the fact, he decided to go with Lewis just to keep his admirers and critics alert.

of these bootleggers," Dylan sings on "Sugar Baby," "they make pretty good stuff." He could be sending a little shout-out to the dedicated fans who assiduously (and covertly) record his shows from the audience, night after night, or he could be warning once again about the allure of false prophets, or he could be singing about himself.

"*Love and Theft*" ought to correct any lingering impression that Dylan left his religion or his religious preoccupations behind in the 1980s. At times, the singer becomes the Lord's messenger, who is vengeful. Hear what Dylan does with "The Coo Coo" on "High Water":

> *Well, the cuckoo is a pretty bird, she warbles as she flies*
> *I'm preachin' the word of God, I'm puttin' out your eyes.*

And Jesus isn't any pushover either. Listen to "Bye and Bye," another crooner's tune, and imagine that, alongside Augie Meyers's wickedly goopy organ, the crooner is Christ himself, in some of the verses anyway. The song begins sweetly enough, albeit with a touch of irony, including one of the hokier of Dylan's puns:

> *Bye and bye, I'm breathin' a lover's sigh*
> *While I'm sittin' on my watch so I can be on time*
> *I'm singin' love's praises with sugar-coated rhyme.*

But it ends with lyrics that might have been written by Saint John of Patmos:

> *I'm gonna baptize you in fire so you can sin no more*
> *I'm gonna establish my rule through civil war*
> *Gonna make you see just how loyal and true a man can be.*

Christ comes with peace—and a sword.

And there are other seers and magicians here too, the hoodoo men of the Delta blues—bragging mannish boys with their Saint John the Conqueroo who say if you can do it, it ain't bragging. From "High Water":

> *I can write you poems, make a strong man lose his mind*
> *I'm no pig without a wig, I hope you treat me kind.*

"Cry a While":

> *I don't carry dead weight, I'm no flash in the pan*
>   *All right, I'll set you straight, can't you see I'm a union man?*
> *Feel like a fighting rooster, feel better than I ever felt.*

And this, from "Lonesome Day Blues":

> *I'm going to spare the defeated, I'm going to speak to the crowd*
>   *I'm going to spare the defeated, boys, I'm going to speak to the crowd*
> *I'm going to teach peace to the conquered, I'm going to tame the proud.*

That last verse may just also be a paraphrase from Virgil's *Aeneid.* But they all show Dylan writing about asserting power, especially sexual power—which reaches into the emotional core of "*Love and Theft.*"

A preoccupation with aging and ardor surfaced in Dylan's work as early as *World Gone Wrong,* when Dylan covered Blind Willie McTell's "Broke Down Engine Blues." It reappeared on *Time Out of Mind* in "Make You Feel My Love." On "*Love and Theft,*" Dylan presented songs such as "Summer Days," which portrays an older man boasting that, even though he might be in the September of his years, he's no worn-out star; he's the man that you *really* love, pretty baby, and he knows a place where something's still going on. Yet as the song proceeds, the singer is funnier, more candid, and less certain—he's got eight carburetors, but he's low on gas and starting to stall. His hammer's ringing, but can't drive in the nails. He still has the balls to claim, in a line taken directly from some dialogue between Jay Gatsby and Nick Carraway in *The Great Gatsby,* that it's perfectly possible to repeat the past, but it sounds unconvincing.

Loss and misfortune from long ago and from right now also recur. On "Lonesome Day Blues," the singer sets his radio dial and drops his car (or truck) into overdrive, when out of nowhere he sings, "I wish my mother was still alive." (Dylan's mother, Beatty, died a few months before he recorded "*Love and Theft.*") Sometimes, the past just seems too much, as in "Honest with Me": "These memories I got, they could strangle a man." And sometimes, it's just sad and poignant—as if the singer is talking with one of the unhappy liaisons he sang about in the 1960s. "So many things we never will undo," he sings in "Mississippi," "I know you're sorry, I'm sorry too." But as ever with Dylan, there are streaks of hope amid the darkest melancholy, and also something new, a sense of calm, absolution, fondness, even gratitude, now that he is well past the middle of the journey. (Again from "Mississippi": "But my heart is not weary, it's light and it's free / I've got nothin' but affection for all those who've sailed with me.") And besides, although summer days are gone, the best may well be yet to come. "Stick with me baby, stick with me anyhow / Things should start to get interesting right about now."

There is a mellowness of acceptance mingled with anticipation to these words and melodies that is reminiscent of the older Charles Aznavour as well as Sinatra and Tony Bennett. Just as there is a richness to the musical and literary references in "*Love and Theft*" that was only foreshadowed in "Tombstone Blues," with its glimpses of Ma Rainey and Beethoven. And just as there is a wise gravity to Dylan's silk-cut voice and to his diction, phrasing, and timing, not captured on previous studio albums. (He *had* been listening to Sinatra, and maybe Caruso, and Allen Ginsberg, and surely Bing Crosby, as well as to the old singers whose songs he recorded anew in 1992 and 1993.) He had mastered so much more, including his own performing style, or at least his recorded performing style. Listen to the breakneck opening lines of "Cry a While"—"didn't havta' wanna' havta' deal with"—then the sudden bluesy downshift; or the killer long line about repeating the past in "Summer Days"; the pause in Juliet's reply to Romeo in "Floater (Too Much to Ask)"; the "High Water" judge's creepy, "Either one, I don't care," the last word dropping and landing with a thud like one of the song's lead-balloon coffins.

And with his expert timing, better than ever, Dylan shuffles space and time like a man dealing stud poker. One moment it's 1935, high atop some Manhattan hotel, then it's 1966 in Paris or 2000 in West Lafayette, Indiana, or this coming November in Terre Haute, then it's 1927, and we're in Mississippi and the water's deeper as it comes, then we're thrown back into biblical time, entire epochs melting away, except that we're rolling across the flats in a Cadillac, or maybe it's a Ford Mustang, and that girl tosses off her underwear, high water everywhere. Then it's September 11, 2001, eerily the date this album was released, and we're inside a dive on lower Broadway, and, horribly beyond description, things are blasted and breaking up out there, nothing's standing there, "it's *baaaaad* out there / High water everywhere." It's always right now, too, on "*Love and Theft*."

Dylan, remember, had already been out there a very long time. He spent time with the Reverend Gary Davis, and Robert Johnson's rival Son House, and Dock Boggs, and Clarence Ashley, and all those fellows;

he played for Woody Guthrie, and played for and with Victoria Spivey; Buddy Holly looked right at him at the Duluth Armory less than three days before Holly plane-crashed to his death; there isn't an inch of American song that he cannot call his own. He steals what he loves and loves what he steals.

In August 2002—coming up on a year after the Al Qaeda terrorist attacks and release of "*Love and Theft*"—Dylan performed at the Newport Folk Festival for the first time since he played his famous electric set in 1965, and I drove up to hear him. Much of the talk I heard from other concertgoers had to do with the 1965 appearance and the controversy it caused— yet Dylan was not simply returning to a scene of artistic notoriety.

Dylan first appeared at the folk festival in late July 1963. Peter, Paul, and Mary had hit it big with their recording of "Blowin' in the Wind," but they deferred to the new prodigy of the folk revival. Dylan closed his evening concert finale by bringing to the stage Joan Baez, the Student Nonviolent Coordinating Committee's Freedom Singers (including the later-to-be-famous Bernice Johnson), and Peter, Paul, and Mary, to sing "Blowin' in the Wind," and then, joined by Pete Seeger and Theodore

The finale of the Newport Folk Festival on July 28, 1963.

Bikel, Dylan and his friends, in a hand-clasping formation, ended the entire festival with "We Shall Overcome." The scene, as reproduced in countless photographs, is an icon of the protests of the early 1960s, when Bob Dylan's music helped to fortify the civil-rights movement that overthrew Jim Crow segregation.

Dylan was featured in 1963, though, not only as a singer and songwriter but also as the author of an epistolary prose poem that was printed in the festival's program. "For Dave Glover," composed in the dropped-consonant vernacular Dylan favored at the time, was a catching-up letter to a Minneapolis friend—part reminiscence, part apology (for what, Dylan never said), and part complaint about the false labels and dogmatic authenticity of the folk-song purists. The writer couldn't sing "Barbara Allen" or "John Johanna" anymore, he declared; he must sing "Seven Curses" and "Don't Think Twice," befitting the "COMPLICATED CIRCLE" of his own time, so different from Woody Guthrie's 1930s. But neither did Dylan renounce those older songs, because without them the new ones that he could sing would not exist. Music not busy being born is busy dying, and the writer had to wager on himself and sing for himself and for his friends and his day; yet neither would he disown the heritage that folk-song purists also wanted to preserve:

An I got nothin but homage an holy thinkin for the ol songs and stories
But now there's me an you

Two years later, back at Newport in 1965, Dylan would pay his notorious homage to the old song "Down on Penny's Farm" by changing Penny's name to Maggie, plugging it all in to a primitive sound system, and describing wholly new arcs of complication that nobody, not Pete Seeger, not Joan Baez, and maybe not even Dylan himself, fully understood. Portents, though, of that explosive emotional paradox of old and new—of the collision between holy thinking and Bob Dylan's irrepressible eye—had turned up in Newport in 1963, in "For Dave Glover." And the complicated circles returned to Newport, like a little whirlwind, when Dylan returned to Newport, almost forty years later.

Some notes on Bob Dylan, the 2002 Newport Folk Festival, and the modern folk process:

In advance of the 2002 festival, the *New York Times* (among others) wondered if Dylan would hit the stage the same way he did in 1965, playing electric, and maybe even playing "Maggie's Farm." Although Dylan did, of course, play rock and roll during his set, he did not play "Maggie's Farm," and sticking to his concert format, at the time, he opened with an acoustic number, "The Roving Gambler." Not everybody in the audience recognized the song, but by playing it, Dylan made a point.

In September 1963, shortly after "For Dave Glover" appeared at Newport, Glover, better known to blues fans as the harmonica wizard Tony "Little Sun" Glover, traveled to New York to make his second album of blues, rags, and hollers with his fellow Minneapolis musicians "Spider" John Koerner and Dave "Snaker" Ray. Among the songs they recorded was Koerner's one-man, rap-prefaced version of "Duncan and Brady," the old St. Louis song about a pair of gamblers, which had become a folk-revival standard, recorded earlier by Dave Van Ronk. Koerner would repeat his fractured version of the song (described aptly by Dave Ray as "hyper Zen") at the same Newport Folk Festival where Dylan played "Maggie's Farm." Koerner, Ray, and Glover would continue to team up, in various combinations, over the next thirty-five years. In 1986, with Glover assisting on harp, Koerner released a solo album that included another gambler song, "The Roving Gambler," descended from an ancient English tune.

"The Roving Gambler" had been a favorite in Minneapolis's Dinkytown folk-song circles since the late 1950s. (An eighteen-year-old Bob Dylan sang a version into a tape recorder at his friend Karen Wallace's apartment in May 1960.) It was first recorded commercially, as far as anyone knows, in 1930, by a popular cowboy singer, Carson Robison. Woody Guthrie's sidekick Cisco Houston also sang it, as did the Stanley Brothers, as did, years later, Marty Robbins, Jim Reeves, Frankie Laine, Ramblin' Jack Elliott, the actor Robert Mitchum, and Woody's son Arlo Guthrie, among dozens of others. Alan Lomax included a transcription of "The Roving Gambler" in his definitive 1960 collection, *The Folk Songs of North America.* And by then the song was enjoying another sort of revival in the American mass market. Tennessee Ernie Ford, of "Sixteen Tons" fame, hit the middle of the pop charts with his "Roving Gambler" in 1956. Two years later, the rock-and-rolling Everly Brothers included a slow, reflective version on an acoustic album of old standards called *Songs Our Daddy Taught Us.* And in early 1961, the commercially successful mainstream folk performers the Brothers Four, second in popularity only to the Kingston Trio, released a new album with yet another version of "The Roving Gambler," this one arranged by the group's bass player, Bob Flick.*

The song appeared in many places and in many guises. In 1957, Andy Griffith starred in the Budd Schulberg–Elia Kazan film *A Face in the Crowd,* playing Lonesome Rhodes, a convicted hobo and country singer who, thanks to a shrewd handler and his own frightening manipulative genius, becomes a nationwide TV celebrity and reactionary demagogue— a forerunner of Rush Limbaugh and the fictional Bob Roberts in the movie of the same name. Bob Dylan saw *A Face in the Crowd* in the Village in 1962 and, reportedly, was more shaken by it than by any film he'd seen since *Rebel Without a Cause* or *The Wild One.* At a crucial moment in the film, Griffith's character realizes he's going to make it to the big time in New York—and he starts singing an exuberant and menacing version of "The Roving Gambler."

On August 24, 1997, a friend took me to hear Bob Dylan—who had cheated death weeks earlier and was now on the verge of releasing *Time Out of Mind*—play a concert at Wolf Trap in Vienna, Virginia. (I later also obtained an unusually crisp bootleg recording of the show.) The songs included "The Roving Gambler," which Dylan and his new band had added to their set list a few months earlier. (They would eventually alternate it with "Duncan and Brady.") Three songs later, after "Blind Willie McTell," Dylan introduced his band and acknowledged the presence in the audience of one of the men "who unlocked the secrets of this kind of music," Alan Lomax. (At Newport, in 1965, Lomax along with Pete Seeger led the old guard that objected to the blasts of white-boy electricity, including Dylan's. Now all seemed forgiven.) Then, with a mischievous audible chuckle, Dylan and the band kicked into a roaring "Highway 61 Revisited," a consummate Dylan rocker of the kind that had so enraged Lomax in 1965. "This kind of music," indeed—except

---

* The Brothers Four, although disdained in the snobbier hip folk circles for their frat-house, crew-cut, white-bread style, were and are accomplished musicians, with a knack for recording great songs, old and new. Like Koerner, they came up with their own adaptation of "Duncan and Brady," which they called "Brady, Brady, Brady." In 1964, they were performing a strong version of Pete Seeger and Joe Hickerson's antiwar anthem "Where Have All the Flowers Gone?" as well as Dylan's "Don't Think Twice." In May 1965, only weeks after Dylan recorded "Mr. Tambourine Man," the Brothers Four released their cover version, beating the Byrds by a month.

that "Highway 61" includes the following verse, with ominous under-tones of both ancient folk music and *A Face in the Crowd*:

Now the rovin' gambler he was very bored
    He was tryin' to create a next world war
He found a promoter who nearly fell off the floor
    He said I never engaged in this kind of thing before
But yes I think it can be very easily done
    We'll just put some bleachers out in the sun
And have it on Highway 61.

On July 19, 2002, two weeks before what the press would soon be hyping as Bob Dylan's triumphant return to Newport, Alan Lomax died. But something of his spirit, and that of the recently dead Dave Van Ronk, and also those of Tennessee Ernie Ford, Don and Phil Everly, Robert Mitchum, and Lonesome Rhodes all appeared when Dylan, wearing a cowboy hat, a fake beard, and a wig that made it seem, from five rows back, as if he'd sprouted enormous flowing Orthodox Jewish earlocks, opened his set with the Brothers Four's arrangement of "The Roving Gambler."

Newport had changed mightily in forty years. Once an admixture of Gilded Age mansions and wharf-side stripper bars, the place was now tourist-friendly, its waterfront crowded with up- and middle-scale bars and eateries, fake-scrimshaw curio shops, and the inevitable Marriott. It was no longer Newport; it was "Scenic Newport," the direction signs said, which told you how hard the developers had pushed.

The folk festival was different too, although I knew about the early festivals only from records, books, and films. In 1963, the main concerts took place in town at Freebody Park, while the workshops sprawled out over the grounds of the Newport Casino (no gambling, but an old-line lawn-tennis club) and St. Michael's School, near the park. The crowds were huge (reaching upwards of seventy thousand by the mid-1960s, which forced the promoters to move the event to a large field adjacent to the city); they were white, and young, and earnest; and many thousands of those who came, not just the performers, played some sort of musical instrument, and had brought along their guitars, and harmonicas, and Jew's harps, and bongos. Back then, the folk festival was a place to jam and to learn new licks and to rub shoulders with other amateur musicians, as well as to hear the big- and not-so-big-time acts.

The 2002 festival was much smaller—about fifteen thousand persons over two days—and, perched out at Fort Adams in Newport harbor, harder to get to, at least if you lined up to take one of the water taxis from town. About half of the crowd could have been at Newport forty years earlier. I counted only one family of blacks on the day I was there (that, by all accounts, was much the same). Apart from a trailer set up to hawk Gibson guitars and a booth displaying handmade dulcimers, there was not a single musical instrument in sight offstage. This was an event for listening, not for playing.

A few prominent old-timers were in evidence. Near the front of the main stage, gray-haired David Gahr, one of the court photographers of the 1960s folk revival, waddled about, smiling, in an orange shirt and shorts, camera at the ready. Out among the craft booths, Dick Waterman, another well-known folkie and picture taker—and one of the rediscoverers of Son House, the Mississippi blues great—was selling his prints of young Dylan and Baez and folk festivals past. The really important thing, he was telling an interviewer, wouldn't be so much what Dylan chose to sing as what he might choose to say to acknowledge his return.

Mainly, there was Geoff Muldaur, in fine voice at a side-stage songwriters' group session. Muldaur, who must have been around sixty, looked younger than that, and in his chinos and running shoes he could have been your friendly neighborhood chain-store pharmacist, until he tenderly wailed "Wild Ox Moan" and you realized that, more than ever, he is the real goods, and a beautifully deceptive slow-hand guitarist to boot. Way back when, Muldaur's gifts were hidden a bit by the more outlandish Jim Kweskin, by the jug player Fritz Richmond, by the weird harmonica player and future cult leader Mel Lyman (not to mention Muldaur's gorgeous then-wife, Maria), and by the raucous thump of the Kweskin Jug Band. The man was and is a natural-born blues singer.

And at Newport, he also tended the flame. Apropos of something I've now forgotten, he told the little crowd packed beneath a tent that Dylan had once called him the female Carolyn Hester. "He *did*," Muldaur said, when nobody responded, as if by emphasizing, he could explain to his audience who the formidable Carolyn Hester was and is, and why, therefore, Dylan's long-forgotten (but not by Muldaur!) little put-down, calling him her feminine counterpart, was also amusing. He announced he would sing Mississippi John Hurt's spelling song "Chicken," then asked if anybody had heard of it, and a look of bemused perplexity crossed the face of the pleasant young performer seated beside him, Caroline Herring, herself Mississippi-born. "Back in 19-whatever, when Mississippi John Hurt was here, he'd just keep doing this little thing," Muldaur said, then picked a moment on his guitar, "and we'd all collapse." The line raised a little light laughter. Things had changed.

There was more strong music on that first festival day, including some snappy harmonizing by the Australian trio the Waifs and a set of Cajun zydeco by Rosie Ledet, backed by what looked like half of her extended family. Louise Taylor sang an earthy rendition of her song "Dangerous," and Bob Hillman presented a funny New Yorker's put-down of the all-American booboisie, bringing back a touch of the old post-McCarthyite feeling that, for a couple of days a year, Newport was a subversive place.

But what wasn't there stood out as much as what was. How strange, amid the renewed success of old-timey music thanks to *O Brother, Where Art Thou?* not to have had more of it. No Alison Krauss, let alone Ralph Stanley. Stranger still, no Handsome Family, no Anna Domino or Snakefarm (heck, *Songs from My Funeral* had been out three years already), nor any of the other hugely intelligent cracked balladeers who were remaking the folk and blues traditions in their own edgy, mordant way. Maybe they'd have been just too much, just too strange. Maybe Newport was still playing it more than a little on the safe side.

In any case, a lot was left on the shoulders of the unsafe and unsound Bob Dylan. And he and his band turned in not the very best performance I've ever heard them play, a contrast to the previous night in Worcester, when they peeled more plaster off the peeling walls of a cavernous old vaudeville house turned concert arena. At Newport, some virus seemed to be running loose in the guitarist Charlie Sexton's miking setup, which was distracting. The late-afternoon broiling open-air setting had the effect of diffusing the crowd's appreciation, so that unlike the response blasts that arose in Worcester, it got to sounding almost silent between the songs.

As usual, Aaron Copland's "Hoe-Down" signaled the start of the show. For the very first time, though, I realized that thanks to a television commercial by the National Cattlemen's Beef Association that used "Hoe-Down" as its theme, an entire generation of Americans now instantly connected that music to steak and hamburger. "Beef. It's what's for dinner," one young woman chortled to her companions when "Hoe-Down" commenced. It was a harmless comment, which could have registered a certain surprise and discomfort at hearing classical music during the folk festival. Still, if that's how the young heard Copland's music, how would they, or their children, come to hear Bob Dylan? It certainly would have discouraged the good-natured Copland, and might be a sign that Dylan's ideas about the coming reign of virtual culture may be true. Unhappy thought.

Dylan's fake beard and wig turned out to be much like a costume he would wear in the video of a new song, "Cross the Green Mountain," written on commission for an epic film about the Civil War, *Gods and Generals,* financed by Ted Turner. Focused on the years of fighting before the battle of Gettysburg, and especially on the exploits of the Confederate general Thomas "Stonewall" Jackson, the movie had a decided prosouthern tilt, both in the proportional time it devoted to the two sides and in its heavy-handed efforts to place slavery and antislavery at the margins of the conflict. Dylan's song and the video are much more ambiguous. The video centers on scenes of army camp life; sometimes it is a Union camp and sometimes Confederate. It features Dylan silently acting the role of a mysterious man (wearing the top hat that had been one of his signature accoutrements since the 1960s) who floats around and among the soldiers, witnessing horrible death, laying a daguerreotype at the headstone of one of the fallen. (Two members of Dylan's touring band at the time also appear, the guitarist Larry Campbell as a preacher saying prayers over the dead and the bassist Tony Garnier as a man dressed in civvies, a rifle slung over his shoulder.) The grave Dylan visits happens to be that of a Virginia cavalryman, but otherwise the video depicts the suffering and boredom of war on both sides.

That evenhandedness was another sign of how much had changed since the evening concert in Newport in 1963, when Dylan's encore turned into the equivalent of a civil-rights rally. Dylan has long been fascinated by the Civil War, not simply as a political struggle, but as a human experience, and over the decades he became an expert reader on the war's military history. He had come to see human folly as well as cowardice and courage in both of the contending armies, but mainly he came to see the gruesome evil of a nation at war with itself—both sides praying to the same God, both sides doing ungodly things. It was not how the civil-rights movement had understood the war, and "Cross the Green Mountain" was light-years away from "Blowin' in the Wind" and "We Shall Overcome." Dylan's new song said nothing about slavery but instead spoke of the war as a "monsterous dream" in which something came out of the ocean and swept through "the land of / The rich and the free"—an apocalypse as frightening as any in the biblical books of Daniel or Revelation, but with no hint of salvation. And it is all the more frightening because it is gentle and funereal, made even sadder by Larry Campbell's country mountain fiddle line—a tender song about the corruption of rotting flesh and perverted morals.

In some respects, the song's greatest interest—although not sufficient for Dylan to include it in his collected lyrics—was literary. In thinking over the project, Dylan clearly reimmersed himself in the poetry of the Civil War era, from both sides, and the effects were obvious in the lyrics of "Cross the Green Mountain."

Henry Timrod, 1867.

Some critics—lodging early complaints in what would become a rising chorus of fury—seized on how the song lifted a line from the poem "Charleston" by the almost completely forgotten Confederate poet Henry Timrod. But Dylan's borrowings were actually much more extensive. "Cross the Green Mountain" included lines and images from sources that ranged from Julia Ward Howe's "Battle Hymn of the Republic," Henry Lynden Flash's "Death of Stonewall Jackson," and Nathaniel Graham Shepherd's "Roll-Call," to Frank Perkins and Mitchell Parish's jazz standard from 1934, "Stars Fell on Alabama." In the next-to-last verse, Dylan condensed an entire Walt Whitman poem, "Come Up from the Fields, Father," about the news of a young man's falling in combat reaching home, into a single, compact eight-line stanza, and he took a phrase from Whitman's original to boot. The immediacy of death throughout the song brings to mind works of the time such as Henry Wadsworth Longfellow's "Killed at the Ford," and there is even a line about "Heaven blazing in my head" that echoes Yeats's poem about the onset of World War II, "Lapis Lazuli." The sophisticated borrowing-and-transforming method that Dylan had refined for *Love and Theft* served again for his movie-song project, although he now confined himself largely to the verse of the 1860s.

Knowing about none of this, all that the audience at Newport could see was Dylan's latest disguise, which looked like his most bizarre costume yet—perhaps a parody of his friend Kinky Friedman's Texas Jewboys. Yet despite the high jinks and mishaps, Dylan and the band still gave a singular show, crisscrossing the past and the present with what looked like a carefully chosen collection from Dylan's songbook. "Maggie's Farm" might have struck Dylan as too obvious; in any case, he skipped it. But the first half-dozen songs he played after opening with "The Roving Gambler" amounted to a set list of greatest hits from roughly 1965, starting with "The Times They Are A-Changin'" and "Desolation Row" and including a few numbers he hardly ever played anymore, above all "Subterranean Homesick Blues" and "Positively 4th Street." At times, the music really sounded a little like July 1965, except played with much tighter chops than the barely rehearsed Paul Butterfield band members plus Al Kooper back then, and in new arrangements.

After "Subterranean Homesick Blues," Dylan and the band jumped to the present with "Cry a While." Later, they played "Summer Days." But these were the only two songs that came from "*Love and Theft*"—and the most recent of all the others was "Tangled Up in Blue." On paper, the set, with songs such as "Girl from the North Country," "Mr. Tambourine Man," and "Leopard-Skin Pill-Box Hat," looked like a Dylan golden-oldies show for baby boomers. Dylan knew his audience.

Yet thanks in part to Dylan's rearrangements of his old material—and thanks to the skills of Campbell, Sexton, Garnier, and the drummer, George Recile, possibly Dylan's best touring band aside from the Band—it was possible to hear the show very differently. Just as he did night after night on the road, Dylan took his audience on a tour of the traditions he had been making his own for forty years and more, including whole chunks of American music that had barely shown up during the rest of the festivities, including rockabilly ("Summer Days"), political song ("The Times They Are A-Changin'"), good-time pedal-steel country music ("You Ain't Goin' Nowhere"), slide-guitar blues ("Cry a While"), and whomping, diabolical rock and roll (in a brilliant reinvention of "The Wicked Messenger"). Not all of the performances were up to the occasion—Dylan's harmonica playing was too often uninspired, and many of the instrumental entrances were ragged—but despite that, the music alone lifted the festival out of its narrow confines.

The most powerful and poignant moment came after the regular set ended with "Leopard-Skin Pill-Box Hat," as the unshadowy sun, just starting to set, turned the great granite stonework of Fort Adams from gray to amber. Dylan, his fake locks damp now, looking like one of the diminutive Russian aviators from the Marx Brothers' *Duck Soup,* came back with the band for the encore and lit into one of the most joyous versions of "Not Fade Away" I have ever heard, in the Grateful Dead's arrangement. The ghosts of Buddy Holly and Jerry Garcia started chasing the ghosts of Mississippi John Hurt and Son House and Clarence Ashley, all conjured up by the Prospero onstage, all back in Newport.

At one point, while going through the ritual of introducing the band, Dylan paused for half a second, looking as if he just might say something to mark the occasion, as if the words were coming to him, as Dick Waterman had thought would happen. If he was to say anything, he would say it now, and for a moment, beneath his getup, Dylan seemed to be thinking it over.

But instead he smiled and twitched and went back to playing, letting his masked theatrical speak for itself, an entire festival in just one act.

10

BOB DYLAN'S
CIVIL WARS:

Masked and Anonymous, July 23, 2003, and
Chronicles: Volume One, October 5, 2004

After the critical triumph of *"Love and Theft"* in 2001 and Dylan's return to Newport a year later, he began turning out fresh work like a man possessed. Not a year passed over the ensuing seven when he failed to produce something of significance, including two albums of original music; a large retrospective of previously unreleased recordings; an album of traditional carols and pop Christmas songs; the first volume of his memoirs, *Chronicles;* a full-length feature film; a three-and-a-half-hour television documentary, directed by Martin Scorsese, about his early life and career; a major museum exhibition in Europe of his sketches and gouaches (with clear artistic debts to Norman Raeben); and *Theme Time Radio Hour with Your Host Bob Dylan,* the most original radio show to appear on the air in recent memory. Dylan also received two Grammys, a Prince of Asturias Award, an honorary degree from the University of St. Andrews in Scotland, and a Pulitzer Prize special citation. All the while, he performed, on average, more than a hundred shows a year, and never fewer than ninety-seven—a punishing schedule almost unheard of these days for an artist of Dylan's stature and renown, let alone one who was past sixty.

While he did not come close to the astounding creative intensity of 1962–66—no artist his age could possibly have replicated that experience—Dylan enjoyed the most productive phase of his career since that time, as he extended and explored the inventiveness sparked by his reawakening in the early 1990s. He also consolidated the latest incarnation of his public image, now carefully constructed as a wizened cultural elder statesman, an icon of musical Americana who still had plenty left to say, do, and sing, before it got too late. His new work hardly received universal acclaim. Listeners caught on to his method of writing and playing as, in the critic Jon Pareles's words, "the emissary from a reinvented yesterday," which at once had made him more comprehensible and created new controversies. But Dylan kept moving on, pursuing ambitions old and new, compelled by some combination of forces to push himself as hard as he could for as long as he could.

One of the old ambitions that Dylan rekindled was to make a film to match his musical style and literary visions. The result, in 2003, received one of the worst critical drubbings of his career—a predictable outcome, in retrospect, though one that said something about the state of mainstream film criticism as well as about the manifest shortcomings of Dylan's movie.

Masked and Anonymous is a manic film about the death agonies of one America and a chilling portent of the birth of a new one. The dying America is the one that, briefly, made Bob Dylan famous—and now aging embittered men and women of that era try to do what they once thought would make the world better. They've had that idea of making the world better crushed out of them, but they carry on anyway, without much hope or reason, resigned to futility. Others of their generation keep on hustling, living by their lying wits, talking on because it's the only way they can make sure they're not dead. There are still tendrils of beauty in this America—a battered old guitar, a little girl singing an old song about changing times—but they're not going to make it. The times have changed, they are blasted, and things will get ten times worse.

The film is layered, moves abruptly from one layer to the next, is filled with visual quotations and allusions, and thus is difficult to comprehend on a single viewing. Some of the themes are immediately recognizable to anyone who has attended to Dylan's earlier work: politics, religion, the mass media, celebrity, entertainment, betrayal, and fate. The materials from which it is constructed are also Dylan's materials: circus performers, the blues, vaudeville-style jokes and puns, the Bible, old movies, Gene

Pitney's song "Town Without Pity," the down-and-out, Shakespeare. And it is constructed out of Bob Dylan himself: one layer of *Masked and Anonymous,* shot along some forlorn, lack-love, vagrant avenues in Los Angeles, is a film called *Desolation Row Revisited.*

But there are less obvious themes and layers as well. The film is set, it says, "somewhere in America," but it is a country that looks and feels more like a borderland between the United States and a generic Central or South American dictatorship. A civil war rages between the dying maximum leader's government and a guerrilla insurgency, although the lines between the two are not at all clear and nobody seems to remember anymore what the fighting is all about. Uncle Sweetheart, a hustler played wonderfully by John Goodman, recruits an imprisoned former rock star named Jack Fate—Dylan's character—to play a benefit concert for the vaguest of beneficiaries. But behind the stories that unfold about the concert is an important backstory, developed in flashes. Fate is actually the caudillo's son who has shared a mistress (played by Angela Bassett) with his father, causing estrangement (and, it seems, Fate's incarceration). The path is clear for the leader's adoptive son, Edmund (played by Mickey Rourke), to take over once the old man dies. The fractured references are to *King Lear.* Jack Fate, at this level, is a stand-in for Shakespeare's Edgar, and the caudillo for the Earl of Gloucester, and the film's Edmund, like the Edmund in *Lear,* stands by a new and ruthless code of power. The difference is that, in Dylan's film unlike Shakespeare's play, an unrepentant Edmund appears to triumph outright. An old order that was harsh enough gives way directly to a far harsher new one.

Another literary layer in the film is American and dates from the years that led to the historical Civil War. Almost all of Bob Dylan's work gets scrutinized as a possible allegory, and *Masked and Anonymous,* packed with aural and visual clues, certainly invites such scrutiny. Is it allegorical? The answer is: not exactly. Anyone looking, at any level, for exact and consistent correspondences between characters, things, and symbols, on the one hand and history or current events, on the other, will be disappointed. But the allusions, gestures, and hints all do pile up. In this way, *Masked and Anonymous,* like many of Dylan's songs, operates as pop sensibility in an American tradition of high allegory going back at least to Melville's *Moby-Dick.* (Melville, 1851: "I had some vague idea while writing it, that the whole book was susceptible of an allegoric construction, & also that *parts* of it were.")

Jack Fate, played deadpan by Dylan, has some of Ishmael's detached, fish-eyed, all-observant qualities, and, like Ishmael's in the novel, Fate's inner dialogue—sometimes philosophical, sometimes more like reverie—provides the film with its running narration. The herky-jerky plot of *Masked and Anonymous* touches on things we know happened, from the murder of Martin Luther King Jr. to the Woodstock Music and Art Fair, but just barely, describing a doomed America that is not exactly any America we know, but one that, like the *Pequod,* seems about to be splintered and swallowed up in a vortex.* And Dylan is trying to draw some sort of connection between that time and our own—as if they are more alike than anyone sees.

In composing their script, Dylan and his writing partner, the film's director, Larry Charles, were mindful of numerous historical artifacts from Melville's America during the years and decades that preceded Fort Sumter. Confronted by a pair of official thugs, Uncle Sweetheart greets them as "the dark princes, the democratic republicans, working for a barbarian who can scarcely spell his own name"—lifting a phrase that the antislavery former president John Quincy Adams used to describe the slaveholder Democratic Republican president, Andrew Jackson, in 1833. In the original script, the evil Edmund gives a long speech that repeats, almost word for word, Jackson's warning in his Farewell Address of 1837 about dangerous subversive forces afoot in the land, driven by "cupidity [and] corruption"—the scapegoats, the film says, for justifying repression. Late in the story, as Dylan's Jack Fate prepares to take the stage, Ed Harris appears in full blackface as the strangely solid ghost of a banjo-playing minstrel, who imitates the subversive imitators superbly, and explains to Fate the lethal consequences that can come from performing the truth about the powers that be. In one of the most affecting of the other musical performances that punctuate the film, Dylan's character, asked to play "Won't Get Fooled Again," "Ohio," or some other classic rock protest number, performs "Dixie." It is as if Dylan/Fate is saying, "You want a protest song, a rebel song? Okay, I'll give you one; I'll give you the real thing." Yet the connection runs deeper, because "Dixie" was written by the blackface minstrel Dan Emmett in 1859 and, to Emmett's dismay,

---

* This is not at all to claim that *Masked and Anonymous* is some sort of cinematic equivalent of *Moby-Dick,* or anything close—an absurdity that some normally perceptive and generous friends and critics read into an essay of mine written in early summer 2003 that accompanied the film's release, and from which parts of this chapter are drawn.

Bob Dylan and Larry Charles on the set of *Masked and Anonymous*, Los Angeles, July 2002.

got picked up by the Confederacy and turned into its virtual national anthem. Dylan borrowed from an academic study of black minstrelsy for the title of "*Love and Theft*"; a related study, by the cultural historian Dale Cockrell, describes those who perform "charivari" entertainments like the minstrel shows as "masked and anonymous."

And just as Melville's glancing allegorical style spoke to and about his times, so *Masked and Anonymous*—including its line about an unlettered barbarian president—spoke to the political and cultural circumstances of 2003. Dylan's presentiments from a decade earlier about the victory of virtual reality seemed ever more prescient (they still do), spoofed mordantly in the film's depiction of a projected mass media in which straight journalism is utterly hollowed out and desperate, and where television is dominated by official propaganda and hour-long "reality" shows with titles like *Slave Trade* and *Lava Flow*. In the immediate aftermath of America's invasion of Iraq—an America run by a radical, power-hungry right-wing White House of dubious legitimacy, a supine Congress, and a Washington press corps that was either cowed or complicit—there was also a chilling familiarity to some of the film's dialogue.

The convergence of fact and fiction became almost too close for comfort during the film's convulsive conclusion when the newly elevated president, Edmund, proclaims his new administration, a regime in which all collective memory will be wiped out, real violence will replace manufactured violence, eagles will scream, and great nations will fight large wars. "It's a new day," Edmund declares. "God help you all." Dylan had long before renounced any pretensions to being a political seer, but commentary that was all the more dismaying and even frightening for its obliqueness runs through the film, and it remains dismaying today.

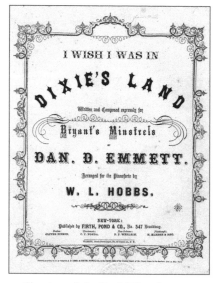

Sheet music to Daniel Decatur Emmett's "Dixie's Land," 1860.

None of this, and nothing else about *Masked and Anonymous,* impressed the film's reviewers at the time, most of whom gave it a reception even more contemptuous than the one accorded *Renaldo and Clara* a quarter century earlier. (Music critics took a very different view of the film's eclectic, cosmopolitan soundtrack.) The few writers who described the film as worthwhile ran the risk of being dismissed as addled Dylan freaks. The critics' complaints about *Masked and Anonymous* were, in fact, remarkably similar to those made about *Renaldo and Clara:* both films, supposedly, were overblown vanity projects undertaken by a rich and pampered star; both were pretentious and incomprehensible; both took a perverse false pride in their willful obscurity.*

The vilification was not simply a collective reaction by the "cool kids" of the movie-reviewing establishment against a bunch of oddball interlopers—a revenge of the nerds against other nerds, one of whom was a

---

* It's worth noting that one of the film's rare defenders in the mainstream press, the *New York Times* rock critic Jon Pareles, said that *Masked and Anonymous* "plays like a feature film, complete with an intelligible plot, vivid professional camera work, and well-known actors," observed that it flips easily between what Pareles called "the death-haunted estrangement of 'Time Out of Mind' and the gallows-humor cackles and shrugs of 'Love and Theft,' " and concluded that "it also plays like a Dylan song: a shaggy-dog story about power, love, show business, prodigal sons, faith and destiny." Pareles, "Film; Bob Dylan Plays Bob Dylan, Whoever That Is," *New York Times,* July 27, 2003.

rock star. Nor was it simply a response to the film's sardonic depiction of critics and reviewers, personified by an obtuse, self-inflated writer played by Jeff Bridges. The film certainly was open to criticism on numerous counts, not least a lack of thematic coherence in its latter stages that worsens until the very final scene, along with an allusiveness that at times was so obscure that it undermines artful intentions. Early on, for example, Dylan strides onscreen as Jack Fate and is greeted by a character named Prospero (played by the comedian and actor Cheech Marin), who reports having just seen two eagles attack and kill a pregnant rabbit—a strange sight indeed, stranger still in the film's blasted urban landscape. Many viewers no doubt caught the Shakespearean reference, and a few no doubt identified the omen of the eagles and the rabbit from Greek myth and Aeschylus's *Agamemnon.* But how many simply would not get it, no matter how many times they heard Prospero's line? In a little scene intended as important and portentous, weren't Dylan and Charles being just a little too clever for the good of their movie?

Part of the difficulty, though, is inherent in what Dylan has always attempted to do, albeit in a variety of ways, with his movie collaborators. When asked at a press conference in 1965 about a rumored film in the works and what it would mean, Dylan replied that it would "just be another song." Larry Charles, in an interview about *Masked and Anonymous,* said he hoped it would be "like a great Bob Dylan song that is listened to over and over." Not surprisingly, though, making a Dylan song, or even the semblance of a Dylan song, into a film turned out to be much more challenging than recording one for an album or CD. Yet instead of taking the film on its own terms and trying to understand its ambitions, the critics declared it unintelligible and turned their backs.

In his early experiments with Howard Alk, Dylan tried to make songs out of documentary footage and semi-scripted "real life" encounters. Those efforts failed badly—in part because as much as these kinds of unrehearsed happenings can serve as raw materials for effective cinematic drama (whether directed by D. A. Pennebaker or John Cassavetes), they are ill suited to the painterly imagination that goes into writing a successful song, no matter how much that song might draw on documented facts. And although any number of great songs, including great Dylan songs, have contained imagery, sweep, sound, and shifting perspective that can be called cinematic, not too many films have contained the wild ambiguities, aural as well as visual allusions, and layered connections of a great song. Without question, *Masked and Anonymous,* written and performed as an unconventional contrivance, came closer to achieving that goal than any film Dylan had previously attempted. But just how successful it actually is will take time to tell. The entire enterprise may prove to have been impossible from the start. Dylan's art is better suited to adapting film to song than vice versa; perhaps lyrics and music are simply more imaginatively numinous than any visual medium. Still, by assembling so much at so many different levels, musically and philosophically as well as visually, *Masked and Anonymous* was an interesting critical and commercial flop, and may yet establish itself as, at the very least, a telling cultural artifact of a nation in confusion at the close of a long conservative cultural and political era—something much more important than a vanity project from Dylan's late-career outburst.

Chronicles is one of the Bible's books of history, not prophecy. It tells of King David, who saw to it that the chiefs of the Levites, appointed as musicians and singers, had free rein in the Lord's house, "for they were employed in that work day and night." Dylan's memoir *Chronicles,* the first volume of whose three projected volumes appeared in 2004, is also a history, recording names now sung and unsung, while it clears away gossip and tall tales. Among many other things, the book tells us how deeply Dylan has immersed himself in books of history, and it reveals he had been something of a historical researcher during his early days in New York, which had an enduring impact on his work. Yet the most immediately striking things about the book are its warmth, straightforward prose, and grateful tone.

"Gratitude, not an easy thing," the literary scholar Christopher Ricks writes: it is "among those human accomplishments that literature lives to realize." For Ricks, as well as for Dylan (who is one of the major writers Ricks has studied meticulously), gratitude means pleasure, the kind of pleasure that comes with love, especially if you take love all the way. In *Chronicles: Volume One,* Dylan takes great care to record old gratitude, even when, because of distance, distraction, or deviousness, he did not go all the way. Dylan is also candid about the limits of his gratitude. The book is honest about goodness, given and received.

Many of Dylan's fans were surprised to learn about the variety of artists whom he has appreciated over the years, and to whom he now tips his hat. He writes, for example, of how, newly arrived in New York in

1961, he listened endlessly to Frank Sinatra's rendering of "Ebb Tide," awestruck by Sinatra's singing and by Carl Sigman's mysterious lyrics. He heard it all in Sinatra's voice—"death, God and the universe, everything."

More than forty years later, and now nearly twenty years older than Sinatra was in 1961, Dylan records his appreciation. Yet he doesn't linger over it. Back then, the action was elsewhere, and that's where he wanted to be. "I had other things to do . . . and I couldn't be listening to that stuff much."

A teenage Ricky Nelson, circa 1955.

Dylan also writes about listening, around the same time, to Ricky Nelson, whom he also enjoyed—up to a point. "He sang his songs calm and steady like he was in the middle of a storm, men hurling past him. His voice was sort of mysterious and made you fall into a certain mood":

> I had been a big fan of Ricky's and still liked him, but that type of music was on its way out. It had no chance of meaning anything. There'd be no future for that stuff in the future. It was all a mistake. What was not a mistake was the ghost of Billy Lyons, rootin' the mountain down, standing 'round in East Cairo, Black Betty bam be lam. That was no mistake.

"Black Betty bam be lam"—that is, the song "Black Betty"—had come from the ex-convict Leadbelly, and also from the violent multiple repeat offender James "Iron Head" Baker, as recorded by Alan Lomax inside Central State Farm prison in Sugar Land, Texas, in December 1933. And in 1961, as Dylan embarked on his career, this, and not the music and singing of Frank Sinatra or Ricky Nelson, was where it was at, or where it was about to be at. Yet Dylan forgot nothing.

Four years later, playing a concert at the West Side Tennis Club in Forest Hills, Queens, Dylan finished his first set with "Mr. Tambourine Man," singing solo of the sea and of escaping sorrow. (It happened to be the second Dylan show I'd ever attended.) During the intermission, as the stage crew finished setting up for the show's second half, Dylan told Robbie Robertson, Levon Helm, Al Kooper, and Harvey Brooks to play his songs calm and steady, come what may. ("Just keep playing *no matter how weird it gets*" were his exact words, Helm recalls.) Then they played in the middle of a summer windstorm: great gusts circled and whistled through the fake-Tudor stadium, whipping the music and the boos and the cheers into a roar nearly as loud as the planes landing nearby at La Guardia Airport. Onstage, outraged men hurtled past the musicians; one protester even knocked Al Kooper off his stool. Yet Dylan appeared to be completely calm, and at the tumult's height he recomposed the crowd by playing on the piano, over and over and over again, the opening chords of "Ballad of a Thin Man," a sinister riff now turned, strangely, into a mass tranquilizer, restoring law and order and even good humor, mysteriously putting everybody in a quieter mood. He won the crowd over by playing an updated "bam be lam," only now it came out as "bam be *bee* bam."

Maybe, if only for an instant, Dylan recalled the performance style of Ricky Nelson, playing calm and steady in the middle of a storm. In any event, he recalled that wisdom forty years later in *Chronicles*.

When *Chronicles* finally appeared, there was palpable relief among people I spoke with who had not known what to expect. More than once I heard: "Thank God, it's not *Tarantula*." This was, I think, unfair to *Tarantula*, Dylan's late 1960s word collage, which for all of its wasted words has some remarkable passages of avant-garde hilarity and serious grace. Dylan had the intelligence to hold out the ten best pages—a long string of vomit, he called it—and turn it into "Like a Rolling Stone." After that, he said, no book or poem he wrote seemed really worthwhile; he'd *done* it. But if you read *Chronicles* closely enough, bits and pieces of *Tarantula* shimmer through, none more so than the particularly gonzo section, "Having a Weird Drink with the Long Tall Stranger":

> back betty, black bready blam de lam! bloody had a baby blam
> de lam! hire the handicapped blam de lam! put him on the wheel
> blam de lam! burn him in the coffee blam de lam! cut him with a
> fish knife blam de lam!

On through:

> fed him lotza girdles, raised him in pneumonia . . . black bloody,
> itty bitty, blam de lam!

And concluding:

> betty had a loser blam de lam, I spied him on the ocean
> with a long string of muslims—blam de lam! all going quack
> quack . . . blam de lam! all going quack quack. blam!

Coming out of 1965–66—the years of Watts, black power, and the shotgun murder by Muslims of Malcolm X, who himself enters into a funny story in *Chronicles*—this bit of *Tarantula* is comedy going berserk, the non sequiturs of "Black Betty" replaced by public service announcements and pain and torture and nonsense, but also crazy like in the song, where Betty's baby gets dipped in gravy. It is a parody of the folk process spinning out of control and spilling more and more blood—blood spouting black, black bloody, blam!

This was Bob Dylan playing around with what in *Chronicles* he calls the artistic and linguistic and spiritual template he discovered in his early months in New York, a timeless yet deeply American template, out of which he was able to speak of his time and out of another simultaneously. It was not an epiphany but a process, and more than we ever knew, Dylan now reveals, it came out of literature and libraries and history books.

Luc Sante has correctly called *Chronicles* a nonfiction bildungsroman, an education or coming-of-age story, although it's a *Bildung* three times over, treating three different moments of transformation—in James Joyce's pun from *Finnegans Wake,* "buildung" and "supra buildung." It starts with two chapters on the New York folk-song scene in the 1960s and ends with a third; in between, it jumps to two other points, in the early 1970s and the mid-1980s, when Dylan, disoriented, had more to learn and relearn. Each of these periods, but especially the first, tells something about how Dylan entered (and then reentered) into history. The entire book is informative as well as grateful, but I find the first two chapters and the last the most compelling, portraying a young artist who, he now writes, felt destiny looking straight at him and nobody else, but who also entered a universe of archaic yet living American archetypes from which, he says, all his songs then sprang—the nation of blam de lam.

It is decidedly not the story of a baby boomer. Although he is stamped as a 1960s troubadour, Dylan, who was born in 1941, is at pains to point out that he is really a product of the 1940s and early 1950s, which he remembers as a long-past era of political giants like Roosevelt, Hitler, and Stalin, unterrified men, including "rude barbarians," who would not be denied. "The world was being blown apart," he says, and the great men "carved up the world like a really dainty dinner." Chaos and fear and smaller leaders came in their wake. A babe in arms when the Japanese attacked Pearl Harbor, Dylan remarks that "if you were born around this time or were living and alive, you could feel the old world go and the new one beginning . . . like putting the clock back to when B.C. became A.D." The changes were local as well as international: an older industrial America was dying—the begrimed factory and sunbaked plantation America of the prewar years, a passing America that included Dylan's Hibbing, the old iron-ore boomtown—and a newer America of suburbs and superhighways and urban ghettos was being born. Yet the change was not always explosive, let alone apocalyptic. And through books as well as music, Dylan was able to reinhabit worlds that had completely disappeared.

Chronicles opens with an evocation of the now-long-gone Broadway and Times Square, still rooted in the prewar metropolis, which Dylan encountered when he finally arrived in New York. The stogie-smoking Lou Levy, just this side of Damon Runyon, is the head of the music publishing company Dylan has signed with, and Levy introduces him to one of the great figures of the Roaring Twenties, the former heavyweight champion Jack Dempsey, amid the maroon leather booths in Dempsey's restaurant. From the very start, Dylan's recollections shuffle time and memory, jumping the line between B.C. and A.D., pulled backward even as he plunges forward. And backward could go back a long way. "It was said that World War II spelled the end of the Age of Enlightenment," he writes, without saying who said it, "but I wouldn't have known it. I was still in it."

The liner notes on the back of Dylan's very first album say that he flunked out of college because he did what he wanted to do—including pore over the works of Immanuel Kant instead of what he should have been studying, *Living with the Birds,* for a science course. Whatever grain of truth there may have been in that, Dylan now says he came to New York with a mind shaped and constrained by postwar commercial and political culture and its touchstones, from James Dean and *I Love Lucy* to Holiday Inns and red-hot Chevys. One of the few models of something different was in the hipster vision and street philosophy of the Beats, and some of that would stick. Another model was in Woody Guthrie and his music, which stuck more. Though Dylan doesn't say much about it, he'd learned enough in Hibbing to appreciate the likes of John Steinbeck and Walt Whitman as well as Hank Williams and Little Richard. And some of the 1950s—like James Dean and the hot rods—never disappeared.

Dylan's biographers tell of the musical education he received once he arrived on MacDougal Street. But *Chronicles* reveals the depths of Dylan's education and self-education from books during his early years in New York. The most exactly rendered scenes of Dylan reading occur in the groaning-shelf apartment of a somewhat mysterious couple who lived even farther downtown than Greenwich Village. (The couple is almost certainly a fabrication, most likely a composite, built out of Eve and Mack Mackenzie, Dave Van Ronk and Terri Thal, Ray and Bonnie Bremser, and a few others.) But Dylan also read at the New York Public Library on Forty-second Street. Although at first his choices of reading had little reason or rhyme—if he didn't connect with a book right away, he says, he'd re-shelve it—the intellectual feast he describes amounted to a pretty fair core curriculum for any college, including Tacitus, Machiavelli, Milton, Balzac, Clausewitz, and Pushkin. It also included, Dylan reports, many books on American history, above all the history of the Civil War. "How much did I know about that cataclysmic event?" he muses. "Probably close to nothing. There weren't any great battles fought out where I grew up. No Chancellorsvilles, Bull Runs, Fredericksburgs or Peachtree Creeks." But he quickly filled in the gaps in his knowledge. Biographies of Robert E. Lee and the antislavery Radical Republican Thaddeus Stevens, he says, made the greatest impression on him; he took inspiration from the gray as well as the blue.

In all of these books were amazing thoughts, contained in personal stories as well as philosophical treatises, set against the backdrop of grander bewildering dramas—and it was all as pliable to Dylan's intelligence, he discovered, as any ballad. ("A political poem about the murder of innocents by the Duke of Savoy in Italy," he recalls of Milton's "On the Late Massacre in Piedmont." "It was like the folk song lyrics, even more elegant.") Here, too, especially in the American past, were unforgettable characters, utter individuals, as mighty as John Henry and as sinister as Diamond Joe. Having, he says, "cast off gloomy habits and learned to settle myself down," Dylan trained his mind to tackle longer and more difficult books: "I began cramming my brain with all kinds of deep poems. It seemed like I'd been pulling an empty wagon for a long time and now I was beginning to fill it up and would have to pull harder. I felt like I was coming out of the back pasture." While pulling that wagon, he began to understand that beyond an affection and talent for music, he had a powerful mind.

Although particularly drawn to history books, Dylan did not think about the past with an eye to tracking dialectical abstractions; nor was he interested in looking backward for pointers about the present or the future. History, he figured, was cyclical: civilizations rose, decayed, and fell, each different from all the others but also fundamentally the same; and there was no telling where America was in its historical cycle; it was too new. What struck him most powerfully, though, was his realization of the closeness between then and now, especially in America: that the distance was so small, it could fit inside an apostrophe, and that the songs on which he'd wagered his heart and voice collapsed the distance automatically. It wasn't just that J. P. Morgan and Teddy Roosevelt would have made great ballad heroes or villains. There was also something in the language of the folk songs, an old but living vocabulary, and a grammar that seemed to be groping for itself—a language, he now writes, that was "tied to the circumstances and blood of what happened over a hundred years ago over secession from the Union—at least to those generations who were caught in it. All of a sudden, it didn't seem that far back."

Many of the ballads Dylan had been singing told old stories of capricious or tragic death, when a lovely scene shattered and the Grim Reaper appeared. Traditional songs like "Pretty Polly" and "Omie Wise" fit that

Irish folk singers the Clancy Brothers with Tommy Makem in the Columbia Records studios in 1963 in New York City. Left to right: Liam Clancy, Tommy Makem, Pat Clancy, and Tom Clancy.

mold, as did Leadbelly's version of "In the Pines" and Woody Guthrie's "1913 Massacre." Listening to the Clancy Brothers and Tommy Makem at the White Horse Tavern on Hudson Street, Dylan heard other kinds of songs drenched in history, where "even in a simple, melodic wooing ballad there'd be rebellion waiting around the corner." Rebellion spoke to Dylan louder than death; he wanted, he now says, "to change over" songs like "The Minstrel Boy" and "Kevin Barry" to have them fit an American landscape. And so, searching for "some archaic grail to lighten the way" for his songwriting, he went uptown to the New York Public Library and read about America during the Civil War era—not just what historians had to say, but the sources themselves, old articles from newspapers with titles like the *Pennsylvania Freeman* that the library made available on microfilm.

For a professional historian, it was mildly thrilling to learn that Dylan discovered the cuneiforms of his art in the microfilm room. Dylan quickly realized, as any novice historian does, that in the 1840s, 1850s, and 1860s there were many issues and stories besides slavery—reform movements, rising crime, religious revivals, riots over whether an English or an American actor should be allowed to perform in a New York theater. Americans worshipped the same God, shared the Constitution and the major political parties, thought of their democracy as the world's best hope; yet increasingly, different groups of Americans eyed each other as enemies. "After a while," Dylan writes, "you become aware of nothing but a culture of feeling, of black days, of schism, evil for evil, the common destiny of the human being getting thrown off course." It felt creepy, reading of an America not at all like the one outside the library walls but that still, in some mysterious ways—not least amid the black struggle for civil rights—resembled it a lot. In time, the stories and the feelings, and the language and the rhetoric of the newspapers, cohered: "Back there, America was put on the cross, died and was resurrected. There was nothing synthetic about it. The godawful truth of that would be the all-encompassing template behind everything that I would write."

Dylan doesn't call this a breakthrough, but that is what it was. He had already, through the folk songs, landed in a parallel universe, "one where actions and virtues were old style and judgmental things came falling out on their heads. A culture with outlaw women, super thugs, demon lovers and gospel truths . . . streets and valleys, rich peaty swamps, with landowners and oilmen, Stagger Lees, Pretty Pollys and John Henrys—an invisible world that towered overhead with walls of gleaming corridors."

The only problem was there was too little of it, and, as lovingly preserved by the folklorists, that universe still felt cut off from the present: "It was out of date, had no proper connection to the actualities, the trends of the time. It was a huge story but hard to come across." But once he had read the history, the gap closed; what had once felt real but antique now was the underground story of the day, as he would relate it in songs he was now ready to write, a mere imitator no more. The more he thought about it, the more the parallel universe was really real and completely visible; in fact, it was all around him, on Seventh Avenue, where he passed a building where Walt Whitman had lived and worked, "printing away and singing the true song of his soul," and on Third Street, where he stared mournfully up at the windows of Edgar Allan Poe's house. The songs were no longer an escape from conformist reality, but reality itself. "If someone were to ask what's going on, 'Mr. Garfield's been shot down, laid down. Nothing you can do.' That's what's going on." Looking for the American version of the Irish "Minstrel Boy," he had found what he needed and more in the public library, a story of biblical proportions, a story that was not over, not by a long shot—the story of the death and transfiguration of a nation.

Bob Dylan's education did not end there, and *Chronicles: Volume One*, always with gratitude, tells how it continued, from collaborating briefly with Archibald MacLeish (which produced the songs on *New Morning*) to stumbling, many years later, upon an unnamed jazz singer in a California bar, who reminded him how to perform. Shortly after that, Dylan relates, he recalled a "mathematical" musical system that the great and now nearly forgotten blues guitarist Lonnie Johnson had taught him decades earlier, and that now helped him get back on track. But Dylan learned something else, important and indelible, around the time he first communed with Johnson, something that unlocked the mysteries of the folk songs Dylan had come to love. It was his first real discovery of America, his greatest great awakening. After that he was ready to clear his throat with "The Death of Emmett Till" and then write "A Hard Rain's A-Gonna Fall," and "The Times They Are A-Changin'," and everything else. He had learned to write about the present out of the past. And in that stuff, there was, and there is, a future.

Over the next few years, however, *Chronicles* also became a focus of controversy. Although consistently grateful to so many of Dylan's past friends, mentors, and muses, the book did not acknowledge the literary sources that had aided its author in the here and now. Two years after it was published, bloggers on various sites, led by one "Ralph the Sacred River" (his own pseudonym a pun on Samuel Taylor Coleridge's sacred river Alph in the epic poem "Kubla Khan"), began reporting on its various borrowings. One small example came from Mark Twain. In *Chronicles,* Dylan describes writing the song "Political World" for *Oh Mercy* in a sudden burst of inspiration after a long drought:

> One night when everyone was asleep and I was sitting at the kitchen table, nothing on the hillside but a shiny bed of lights . . .

In chapter twelve of *Huckleberry Finn,* Huck describes the first days of drifting, with Jim, down the Mississippi River on their raft:

> Every night we passed towns, some of them away *up on black hillsides, nothing but just a shiny bed of lights,* not a house could you see . . . There warn't a sound there; *everybody was asleep* (emphasis mine).

Numerous other passages in *Chronicles* bear similar likenesses to passages from works by authors ranging from Marcel Proust to (most frequently) Jack London. Apparently, Dylan used some of the same techniques in composing his memoir as he had in writing *"Love and Theft,"* lifting no more than a few words a line or two at a time, but always lines that contained striking images or felicitous turns of phrase. Some readers and critics dismissed the revelations as nothing more than examples of one artist picking up fragments from other artists. Others, though, questioned whether what passed as unobjectionable recycling in folk and blues music amounted, in the case of a published memoir, to what "Ralph" described as "pretty close to real plagiarism."

The charges appeared far too late to affect the book reviewers, whose enthusiasm for *Chronicles* led to its being named a finalist for the National Book Critics Circle Award in biography for 2004. Even had the charges arisen earlier, it is likely that the critics would have dismissed them as trivial. By now, chiefly through *Time Out of Mind* and *"Love and Theft"* (and despite the failure of *Masked and Anonymous*), Dylan had come far in reestablishing himself as a musical symbol, a survivor who somehow represented not only the Dylan of the "protest" 1960s and the hipster *Blonde on Blonde* 1960s but every shape he had ever assumed—and along with that every facet of American popular musical history. Discovering a few phrases lifted from Mark Twain and Jack London in a book so engaging, fluid, and generous as *Chronicles* would not have been sufficient grounds for daring to knock a national treasure. Indeed, the discoveries probably would have added to Dylan's mystique.

But when Dylan released his next album of new material in 2006, its title taken from that of a famous film from the 1930s, renewed claims of alleged plagiarism (which had also begun to hover over "*Love and Theft*") became too numerous and angry to ignore. Dylan's continuing artistic comeback had brought him ever-increasing public praise and stature, but there were writers who now declared his new work was, at best, derivative and, at worst, a shill. Even as a senior citizen, Dylan was still getting under some people's skin.

11

DREAMS, SCHEMES, AND THEMES:

Modern Times, August 29, 2006; *Theme Time Radio Hour with Your Host Bob Dylan,* May 3, 2006–April 15, 2009; *The Bootleg Series, Vol. 8: Tell Tale Signs: Rare and Unreleased, 1989–2006,* October 7, 2008; and *Together Through Life,* April 28, 2009

An advance copy of Dylan's *Modern Times* came in a slim jewel case and a plain white cover, listing ten new songs. The song titles made it clear that the music would be in the style that Dylan had been working with since *Time Out of Mind,* self-consciously reclaiming old songs and poems, sometimes explicitly, and giving them his own sounds and layers of meaning. The borrowing began with the album's title.

During his early years as a performer, Dylan's amusing, quirky stage persona had been called Chaplinesque, and one of Dave Gahr's color photographs featured on *"Love and Theft"* portrayed Dylan, in mustache and dark curly hair, like an aging version of Chaplin's Little Tramp, and so the title, *Modern Times,* came as no shock.* At the very least, it delivered a tribute to Chaplin and to the Chaplin film of the same name, in which the much-misunderstood Tramp tries to survive in a harsh new world of heavy industrial mass production. The film ends with the Tramp in a cabaret, pantomiming and improvising a song whose words he has lost—and he makes a big hit. The very last shot is of the hero and his beloved orphan

---

* "If I'm on stage, my idol—even my biggest idol when I'm on stage—the one that's running through my head all the time, is Charlie Chaplin," Dylan remarked in 1961. See "The Billy James Interview Fall 1961," www.interferenza.com/bcs/interw/61-fall.htm.

girl (played by Paulette Goddard), having eluded the police who want to arrest her on a vagrancy charge, walking straight into the dawn, full of doubt but hardly hopeless. ("Buck up—never say die. We'll get along!" the Tramp tells the despairing girl.) It is one of the countless images in

Still from *Modern Times* (1936).

Chaplin's films that could easily have turned up in a Dylan song, especially the last songs on his albums, which almost always seem to contain sentiments of hope or good luck. And, as it happened, Dylan's album had an additional connection to Chaplin's film, but it would become clear only upon listening.

Beneath the album title, the song titles on the white cover showed that Dylan was not only borrowing a great deal but also being more up front about it than ever, even though it lacked any formal credit lines or little explanatory essays as accompanied *World Gone Wrong*. Nearly half the titles came directly or almost directly from well-known blues songs: "Rollin' and Tumblin'" (an old song first recorded by Hambone Willie Newbern in 1929, though most famous in the version recorded in 1950 by Muddy Waters); "Someday Baby" (Sleepy John Estes); "Workingman's Blues #2" (Merle Haggard); and "The Levee's Gonna Break" (Kansas Joe McCoy and Memphis Minnie's "When the Levee Breaks," though best known to rock and rollers in Led Zeppelin's version, from which Dylan apparently took his own title). Another title, "When the Deal Goes Down," strongly resembled that of the old-time country classic "Don't Let Your Deal Go Down" (recorded by Charlie Poole in the 1920s, but also by the New Lost City Ramblers, Doc Watson, Flatt & Scruggs, and numerous others in the 1950s and 1960s). And those were just the easy ones. The title and some of the narrative touches of still another, "Nettie Moore," came from a song I'd never heard of that turned out to be a popular sentimental blackface song from the 1850s.

Blues guitarist and singer Memphis Minnie and her husband, guitarist Kansas Joe McCoy, pose for a portrait, circa 1930.

On first listen, the music and the lyrics were also as expected, only more so. Some of the songs, such as "When the Deal Goes Down," are different in every way from their predecessors—yet even the melody of "Deal Goes Down" reworks an old Bing Crosby hit, "Where the Blue of the Night (Meets the Gold of the Day)." Musically, "Rollin' and Tumblin'" is basically a cover version of the familiar song, with much of the first and last verses intact, except that where the singer in Muddy Waters's version woke up not knowing right from wrong, the singer in Dylan's thinks he must have bet his money wrong. (In the original, infidelity leads to drink; in Dylan's, a sour relationship with a woman leads, finally, to a bid for reconciliation and to "put old matters to an end.") "The Levee's Gonna Break" is even closer to the original, quoting a few lines and mixing scenes of disaster with talk of love. (Just as the original made no hints about the recent floods in Mississippi and Louisiana, Dylan's song made no hints about Hurricane Katrina the year before: given the impact of both events, neither song had to.) The melody, structure, and title of "Shake Shake Mama" come from one of Mance Lipscomb's records. The refrain to one of the more original songs, "Ain't Talkin'," echoes that of an early Stanley Brothers recording, "Highway of Regret."

The additional link with Chaplin's *Modern Times* had to do with the album's sound as well as its lyrical content. Chaplin originally planned to make his film as a talkie, with the dialogue, like everything else, in sound. By 1936, nearly a decade after Al Jolson and *The Jazz Singer*, the use of sound had become universal. But Chaplin decided that his famous Little Tramp character would not translate well in a talkie picture, and he stubbornly kept the dialogue to *Modern Times* silent, run on panels as silent films always had. Dylan, in interviews after *"Love and Theft"*—which he produced himself, under the name Jack Frost, much as Chaplin directed his own movie—discussed his decision to use older forms of microphones and recording equipment that, he insisted, better fit his voice and his music. The same rules applied to the recording of *Modern Times*—as with Chaplin, a deliberate archaism, the peculiar archaism that had become a part of Dylan's style of composition.

With this album, though, Dylan's adaptations of earlier songs intensified a renewed controversy that had fitfully been building for years. Accusations about Dylan plagiarizing melodies had not ended with Dominic Behan's complaints in the 1960s about how he stole "The Patriot Game." It did not take much expertise in the blues to hear similarities such as those between "Pledging My Time" from *Blonde on Blonde* and Elmore James's "It Hurts Me Too." Some folk fans alleged that Dylan had based his arrangement of "Canadee-i-o" on *Good as I Been to You* from the one recorded by the exceptional British folk revivalist Nic Jones (allegations that, though almost certainly correct, also had limited force, as Jones, by far the superior guitarist, played an instrumental line completely different from and better than Dylan's). But the charges had recurred after 2001 and concerned Dylan's lyrics as well as his melodies.

In 2003, an alert reader and listener noticed similarities between a few lines on *"Love and Theft"* and the English-language edition of an obscure oral history of a Japanese gangster, translated as *Confessions of a Yakuza*, written by a physician and writer, Junichi Saga, from a small town north of Tokyo. A closer look, especially at "Floater (Too Much to Ask)," showed that about a dozen brief fragments from Saga's book ended up, without attribution, on Dylan's album. The news became a front-page story in the *Wall Street Journal* and caused the critic Christopher Ricks, normally a defender of Dylan's creative processes, to step back and say that this time the accumulation was "quite striking." The release of *Modern Times* three years later sent listeners scurrying to find more, and they did: numerous lines from the poems of Henry Timrod (following up on the snippet from Timrod in "Cross the Green Mountain"); passages from poetry of Ovid's, written while the poet was in exile on the Black Sea. Dylan's literary references apparently knew no bounds of time and space. Even the much-noted, up-to-date shout-out to the rising star Alicia Keys in "Thunder on the Mountain" (whose title alluded to the voice of God in the book of Exodus) turned out to be a rephrasing of Memphis Minnie's tribute song "Ma Rainey," recorded in 1940. And so, even though *Modern Times* enjoyed huge sales and critical acclaim, and earned Dylan two Grammys, it also brought a renewed clamor, much of it from Internet postings but also from the *New York Times,* that he was not simply a magpie but a plagiarist.

The controversy was, in fact, very much of the digitized Internet age. Thanks to the increased sophistication of general-use search engines such as Google, as well as scanning technology and the appearance of literary and musical concordances online, censorious sleuths could track down the tiniest pieces of Dylan's lyrics without having to spend months at the library. The rapid circulation of information and music on the Internet had also panicked music publishers, record companies, and some artists, who

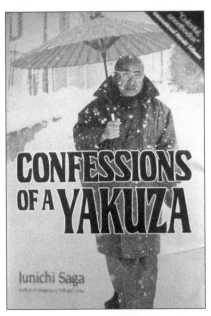

Cover of the translated American edition of Junichi Saga's *Confessions of a Yakuza: A Life in Japan's Underworld* (1991, 1995).

worried whether they would ever again be able to sell their work for profit, and also fretted over how copyrights could be secured for performances as well as songs. The use of sampling techniques by rap artists, which had begun in the 1980s and raised hackles from the start, intensified these worries. Some high-profile cases of plagiarism through Internet downloading at newspapers and magazines, and widely publicized accusations of more old-fashioned forms of plagiarism and fabrication among celebrated journalists, memoir writers, and historians, added to the frenzy. It appeared that the information superhighway, for all of its wonders, had created new opportunities for cultural counterfeiting—and it had also created new ways to track down the most recondite allusions. The discoveries of Dylan's quoting became, in this climate, whipped up into something potentially sensational.

At the most basic legal level, the charges of plagiarism were groundless. Many of the words as well as melodies that Dylan appropriated had long ago passed into the public domain and were free for appropriation by anyone. The exceptions, like the *Yakuza* borrowing, involved isolated lines—images and turns of phrase—that hardly represented passing off another person's memoir as his own. According to American copyright law, as affirmed by the Supreme Court, transforming the meaning of a copyrighted work can constitute fair use.* Obviously, Dylan's songs were not about Japanese gangsters; it came as no surprise when journalists reported that Junichi Saga, when informed about Dylan's use of his words, felt honored, not abused. Much of the literary lifting sounded as if Dylan had simply jotted down little phrases he found compelling in books or in songs, saved them up, then used them for his own very different purposes in his own work. Indeed, Joni Mitchell (years before she accused Dylan of plagiarism in 2010) is reported to have told an interviewer that Dylan had explained to her that this was exactly how he worked in order to spark his ideas.

Yet there remained an uneasy feeling among some detractors that Dylan, whose reputation had derived from his poetic originality, was a faker unless everything he wrote came out of his own imagination, word for word, note for note. And many more charged that if Dylan used the words as well as the melodies of others on an album of supposedly original material, he ought to find some way of acknowledging as much, instead of claiming them under his own copyright. Adaptation, after all, is not simply a matter of law; it is also a matter of ethics.

Dylan's many defenders counterattacked that the critics completely misunderstood what he was doing. Dylan's supposed plagiarism, some claimed, was simply part of the folk process that Dylan had inherited from Woody Guthrie, Leadbelly, Blind Willie McTell, and the centuries of troubadours before them, and that had been central to Dylan's art since he turned "1913 Massacre" into "Song to Woody," and "No More Auction Block" into "Blowin' in the Wind." (For that matter, it was not too different from Robert Burns borrowing from Scots folk songs for his verse, or Aaron Copland adapting cowboy songs and fiddle tunes for his orchestral suites.) Everybody took things from everybody else and made those things his or her own. Dylan was simply, as Pete Seeger had described himself, "a link in a chain" of folksingers.

---

* In the landmark case of *Campbell v. Acuff-Rose Music, Inc.* (1994), the Court ruled that the key factor in determining fair use is "whether and to what extent [the new work] is 'transformative,' altering the original with new expression, meaning, or message."

Much of what sounded, to an unpracticed ear, like lifting amounted to no more than Dylan using commonplace phrases—sometimes known as floaters—that recur in innumerable blues, country, and folk songs, serving the singers as a sort of shorthand. Lines on *Modern Times* such as "couldn't keep from crying," "what's the matter with this cruel world today," "put some sugar in my bowl" are among the standards, about as familiar in various forms of American traditional song as "woke up this morning," "back-door man," and "brown-skinned woman." If these lines made Dylan a plagiarist, his defenders claimed, then the charge could be lodged against practically every American blues, country, and folk artist who ever performed in public.

This all made a great deal of sense, especially regarding Dylan's obvious recycling of the work of Memphis Minnie and of songs like "Rollin' and Tumblin'." But was adapting the melody of "Snuggled on Your Shoulder," a nearly forgotten Bing Crosby tune from 1932, for a song on *"Love and Theft"* an example of the folk process? Without a credit line, was it a silent allusion and tribute to Crosby and the song's composers, Joe Young and Carmen Lombardo? Perhaps not—but two years before *Modern Times* appeared, Dylan told a reporter from *Newsweek* that he was working on a song based on a Bing Crosby melody, which may have been "When the Deal Goes Down," and nobody objected. Dylan's borrowing from older pop music was certainly in the tradition of earlier honored songsters like Blind Willie McTell. (Pop songwriters, meanwhile, regularly borrow from the classics with impunity.) What about, though, the literary sophistication of so many of the uncredited quotations in Dylan's recent lyrics? The Bible had always been common currency for all of American song, Dylan's included—but not until Dylan did folksingers snatch bits from a Japanese true-crime paperback, let alone from shrouded poems by Ovid. There is something impressive about this as a literary marker—but some purists wondered if it was an authentic variation of the folk process.

The suggestion (ventured, but then rejected, by the folksinger Suzanne Vega in an op-ed for the *New York Times*) that it was all unintentional, that Dylan hadn't truly meant to appropriate these lines, that they had just stuck in his mind, did not stand serious consideration, especially given how often Dylan used other writers' lines, and given how often he used certain favorite writers' lines. Closer to the mark was the critic Jon Pareles's observation that all art, and not just folk art, involves conversations with the past, battening on all that the artist can find in culture and history instead of acting as if culture and history don't exist. Pretending to an utterly pristine originality is not just impossible; it is itself the basest kind of fakery. Pareles's term for Dylan's work—one form of "information collage"—was inelegant, but it moved the debate beyond the clichés about the folk process. It also offered a more exact defense against the accusations of plagiarism, calling Dylan's songs "new work that in no way affects the integrity of the existing one and that only draws attention to it."

Yet to locate Dylan's new songs within a more refined understanding of artistic originality—while countercharging, in the words of the poet and critic Robert Polito, that to accuse Dylan of "possible plagiarism is to confuse, well, art with a term paper"—still left Dylan's style and purposes vague. Polito's invocation of what he called "Modernist collages," dating back to Ezra Pound and T. S. Eliot, was more precise. Dylan's borrowed lyrics certainly bumped up against his own words and reverberated with them, as Polito observed—evoking, say, the Civil War America of the 1860s through the odd Confederate verse of Henry Timrod, sentimental yet darkling, and meshing it with the polarized, pained America of 2006 (as suggested earlier in *Masked and Anonymous*). Dylan's preservation of shards from a bygone world—including the world of his younger self, a world being overtaken by virtual reality—while embedding them in a wholly different context recalled Eliot's dictum that "immature poets imitate; mature poets steal; bad poets deface what they take, and good poets make it into something better, or at least something different." None of Dylan's songs are about the modern Tokyo underground, but the strangely historical tough-guy phrases of Saga's *yakuza*—with references to feudal lords and wealthy farmers—are appropriate to some of the things the songs are about, including bullying, fear, and friendship. Dylan makes them new and different.

What about, though, the lack of acknowledgment? When Eliot, Pound, and the modernists spoke of stealing and renewing, the renewing was supposed to be in part an overt allusion to the stolen object: hence, for example, the notes that Eliot appended to *The Waste Land* to explicate the poem. Much of Dylan's borrowing—"Rollin' and Tumblin'," for example—was so obvious that it required no explanation. But Dylan also deployed fragments from poetry and song so obscure that they remained unidentified until some obsessed blogger, using the latest technological wizardry, came along to do so. Literalists concluded that Dylan deliberately chose obscure material in purposeful acts of artistic deception. But that made little sense. Had Dylan's original purpose been to deceive, he made a lousy job of it, and as soon as the first commentaries on *"Love and Theft*" appeared, he would have known he could not succeed for very long. Yet he became more blatant.

Although reminiscent of the modernists' collages, Dylan's method aimed not simply at allusion but at something very different, essential to his recent work—a more emphatic, at times risky dissolution of distinctions between past and present as well as between high art and low, scholarly and popular, exotic and familiar, moving between and among them as if it required no effort. The origins of the technique could have dated back to his discoveries at the New York Public Library in the early 1960s, as described in *Chronicles*:

> The age that I was living in didn't resemble this age, but yet it did in some mysterious and traditional way. Not just a little bit, but a lot. There was a broad spectrum and commonwealth that I was living upon, and the basic psychology of that life was every bit a part of it. If you turned the light towards it, you could see the full complexity of human nature.

Having been instructed about the obliteration of time and space by Norman Raeben, unnerved by the apprehension that soon no one would remember any of the old songs, and convinced that a manufactured, ahistorical virtual reality was becoming omnipotent, Dylan created a new magic zone where it was 1933 and 1863 and 2006 all at once, and where the full complexity of human nature might still be glimpsed. Quoting, without credit, bits of a Henry Timrod poem or adapting a Bing Crosby melody was not, by these lights, an act of plagiarism, and it involved more than recycling the forgotten. It was part of an act of conjuring.

Yet accounting for the poetics of Dylan's form of renewing did not fully describe what he had accomplished on "*Love and Theft*" and *Modern Times,* and how it compared with his earlier work. Merely to say that Dylan had always borrowed did not mean that he borrowed in precisely the same way, or that the balance between what was original and what was not was the same, or that the finished work was of similar, let alone equal, quality. The great producer Phil Spector pointed out in a famous interview in 1969 that "Like a Rolling Stone" took its chord structure from the Ritchie Valens song "La Bamba"; the writer Roy Harris has recently added that Dylan's opening words come from every fairy tale ever told—and it is a far better song than anything on Dylan's recent albums. The same could be said of much of Dylan's work, now and then.

Remarkable as it could be, with its new aesthetic aims, Dylan's work of the 1990s and after certainly lacked the emotional fire of *Bringing It All Back Home, Highway 61 Revisited,* and *Blonde on Blonde.*

Likewise, judged musically as well as poetically, *Modern Times* fell short of what Dylan had achieved on *"Love and Theft."* The sound of the later album suffered because Dylan recorded it with some new musicians who, for all of their talents, sounded as if they were still feeling their way in the recording studio with him, unlike the combination of Garnier, Campbell, and Sexton that grounded *"Love and Theft."* But the songs were not as strong either, and would not hold up as well over the first years after the album's release. The brand-new lyrics to "Rollin' and Tumblin' " did not create a remarkable new composition. The same held for "The Levee's Gonna Break." (As a blurring of old and new, various reprises of Randy Newman's "Louisiana 1927," including one performed by Newman himself on a televised benefit show, proved more powerful than any other musical reflection on Hurricane Katrina. Had Dylan wanted to offer a similar reference, he might have rerecorded "Down in the Flood" or added it to his regular concert set list. But the idea of a televised benefit might have felt a little too much like a theme of *Masked and Anonymous* come to life.) The refurbished Bing Crosby selection, "When the Deal Goes Down," did turn into an effective song of an older man's love, but not into a major piece of work. The dark, brooding "Ain't Talkin' " was an arresting mystery that told of the yearning that does not disappear with age, and that also, to my ear, sounded at one level like a narrative of Christ's last days. (By that reading, the sudden switch to a glowing, hopeful major chord that concludes the song, and the album, might convey the hope that is the Resurrection.) One track, though, stood out as a sublime piece of modern minstrelsy, and later became a highlight of Dylan's concert shows: "Nettie Moore."

The song's title and the opening lines of its refrain come from a minstrel melody that became a parlor song, "Gentle Nettie Moore" (also known as "The Little White Cottage"), written in 1857 by the blackface performer and lyricist Marshall Pike and James Lord Pierpont, the composer (during that same year) of "Jingle Bells." In Pike and Pierpont's original, the singer is a South Carolina slave pining for his departed wife, the gentle Nettie Moore, who has been sold by their master—sold, literally, down the river, to a Louisiana slave trader. The theme of heartbreak intermingled with a Civil War–era story right out of *Uncle Tom's Cabin* fit perfectly with Dylan's masked minstrel patterns of love and theft. But there was a very different Old West connection—for in 1934, backed by a prairie fiddle, a cowboy band, the Sons of the Pioneers (who, at the time, featured the later TV star Roy Rogers), recorded the song for the radio in Los Angeles and then released it on a 33⅓ rpm record. Either version could have been on Dylan's mind; it's likely that both were. And even though the rest of Dylan's lyrics, and his lovely melody, bear no resemblance to "Gentle Nettie Moore," his "Nettie Moore" contains several more appropriations and permutations.

A gentle, syncopated, guitar-and-piano-led setting ascends from an E minor chord to G, then pauses,

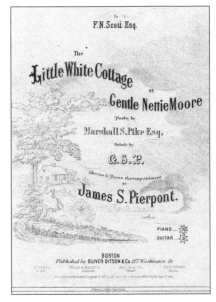

Sheet music for Marshall Spring Pike and James Lord Pierpont's "The Little White Cottage (Gentle Nettie Moore)," 1857.

and then rises again and descends; throughout, without pausing, George Recile's bass drum booms to the rhythm of a heartbeat, in 2/4 time. Except during the choruses, the booming continues, never racing, never quieting, always insistent—the telltale heart that will not stop and that drives the tale that the singer sings. The instrumental introduction gives way to Dylan's leathery voice, supple but also weathered in patches, gently singing the opening lines:

> *Lost John sittin' on a railroad track*
> *Something's out of whack*
> *Blues this morning falling down like hail*
> *Gonna leave a greasy trail.*

There are no doubts about Dylan's borrowing here. The first line is from "Long Gone Lost John," an old song recorded in 1928 by the great, undervalued, risqué medicine show bluesman and banjo player Papa Charlie Jackson, then turned into one of the hits of the 1950s British skiffle craze by the craze's biggest star, Lonnie Donegan. (Later still, the skiffle player turned rock and roller John Lennon recorded the song, as did Lennon's widow, Yoko Ono, as a tribute after Lennon's murder.)

Pat Brady (third from left) and Bob Nolan (far right) with Roy Rogers (center) and the Sons of the Pioneers on the set of *Home in Oklahoma*, 1946.

Dylan's third line, more familiar to American listeners, comes direct from Robert Johnson's blues masterpiece "Hell Hound on My Trail," with the inserted words "this morning" echoing the title of one of the classic blues studies from the early 1960s, Paul Oliver's *Blues Fell This Morning*.

The quotations sound random, but Dylan reconstructs them in a clever and amusing way. Both of the two lifted lines last for two measures, in each case followed by a one-measure pause when only the bass drum beats (just as in the introduction), followed by two measures of what seem to be non sequiturs. At first, it sounds as if Dylan means to sing an old folk song but can't get beyond the opening line: something's out of whack. But then Dylan appears to be playing a parlor game (or maybe a dressing room game): give him a bit of old lyric, he'll think for a second—the pause—and then, boom, he comes up with a rhyming line of his own. "Track" and "out of whack"—why not? And why not take Robert Johnson's own rhyme from "Hell Hound"—"hail" and "trail"—but make the trail into something that's left behind and greasy.

The pattern reappears throughout the song: Dylan supplies either direct quotations from or allusions to numerous blues and country recordings—including no fewer than three snippets from two more Papa

Charlie Jackson songs, "Bad Luck Woman Blues" and "Look Out Papa Don't Tear Your Pants," but also including the standards "Frankie and Albert," "Moonshiner," W. C. Handy's "Yellow Dog Blues," and Hank Williams's "I'll Never Get Out of This World Alive"—and finishes them off according to the rules of what seems to be his little game.* (Hence: "Albert's in the graveyard, Frankie's raisin' hell/[pause/boom]/I'm beginning to believe what the scriptures tell.") Far from plagiarizing, Dylan is in this instance drawing attention to his self-conscious borrowing, and seems to be having fun with it. With his backbeat and his pauses, he is also having fun playing around with rhythm. But the song's refrain about love lost and the world going black—sung with Donnie Herron playing fiddle on a heart-catching tune that, if not reworked from Stephen Foster or one of the other minstrel songwriters from the 1850s, might as well be—keeps "Nettie Moore" from becoming anything like a jest. In an interview that accompanied the release of *Modern Times,* Dylan said he took special pains with "Nettie Moore" to make sure that the song was not simply a free association of verses. And after one listens to the song several times, "out of whack," "Frankie and Albert," and the refrain all do fit together—possibly as a modern form of classic American balladry.

Dylan's game turns out to have layers that are far from haphazard, let alone nonsensical. When he sings of the world of research going berserk with "too much paperwork," he could be talking about efforts to extract deep meaning from his songs. But then he alludes to "Frankie and Albert" as fact, stone cold fact, and the succeeding line, about beginning to believe what the scriptures tell, might mean the Bible but might also mean "Frankie and Albert" and all the other verses that have inspired Dylan and that, for him, require no ponderous exegesis. ("I find the religiosity and philosophy in the music," Dylan told an interviewer in 1997. "I don't find it anywhere else . . . I don't adhere to rabbis, preachers, evangelists . . . I've learned more from the songs than I've learned from any of this kind of entity. The songs are my lexicon. I believe the songs.")

Other hints and provocations begin to add up, without ever becoming directly linked. There, in plain view, is a song of a lover's murder: Albert

---

* The borrowing from Jackson includes the first line of the third verse, "I'm the oldest son of a crazy man"; "Look Out Papa Don't Tear Your Pants" includes the spoken introduction: "Yessir! My pappy's an old man, crazy 'bout young gals. By me being the oldest son, that made me be crazy too. Now I'm gonna tell you all about my pappy getting over that fence."

is dead, and Frankie is raising hell. (Dylan might just as well have sung Delia and Curtis, but the reference would have been more obscure.) There is a singer who has committed a pile of sins, thus far with impunity, who is hounded by the blues, and who loves his departed Nettie hard, with a love so thick even a knife cannot destroy it. There is a faint suggestion that Nettie was unfaithful. ("Don't know why my baby never looked so good before / I don't have to wonder no more.") Suddenly there is a judge who enters the courtroom (and enters the song, only to disappear), and all are bidden to stand: some kind of official justice or injustice is done. It is early spring, the river is on the rise, yet the singer, with no one around him to tell of his continuing love for Nettie, sees the world darken before his eyes. A moment of hope arrives: the singer's grief gives way, he sings of a lifetime with his love, like some heavenly day—in the original "Gentle Nettie Moore," the singer is certain he will meet his wife in heaven—and then the singer stands in the bright sun and the voice of holy praise rises. But, like the melody, what rises in the lyrics soon falls—and the singer suddenly wishes that it were night, and then, for the last time, everything goes black.

"I'm going where the Southern crosses the yellow dog," in "Nettie Moore": the conjunction of the Southern Railway and the Yazoo Delta Railroad, Moorhead, Mississippi.

Far from random, "Nettie Moore" is a song of surpassing sorrow, of every spark of hope extinguished, every certainty thwarted—"Everything I've ever known to be right has proven wrong / I'll be drifting along," Dylan sings—but there's no one left whom he can talk to, or at least no one who will understand. And gradually, a more exact possibility falls into place: the singer has stabbed his beloved but unfaithful Nettie to death with a knife; now convicted for the crime and alone in jail, with no one left to tell, he comprehends everything, declares and re-declares his love, his heart thumping loud, before his execution, when all goes black just as the springtime is cresting. Alternatively, the singer, an aging member of a cowboy band—like the Sons of the Pioneers?—is mourning the lost love of his life who may still be alive, and he lives in darkness, with no one left from the old days of "then" with whom to talk.

Or such, at least, are two reasonable readings of a song that, taking Dylan at his word, has a very exact meaning and is not arbitrary or indiscriminate. The song wafts through time and space, past and present, old songs and new, as Dylan's recent songs do. It presents itself in the fragmented, ambiguous way that has marked Dylan's music, through many phases, for decades. And it is a song that, from time to time, is as plain and obvious to me as whatever Dylan had in mind was or is to him.

To say that Dylan, by 2006, appeared to be more open and talkative with the public would be saying little, given what had long been his notorious reticence. Apart from press interviews—usually timed to coincide with the release of an album, and almost always in print, not on film—Dylan hardly ever spoke in public anymore, even through a mask, outside his lyrics and occasional liner notes. At the press conference in Park City, Utah, for the premiere of *Masked and Anonymous* he appeared briefly, wore a blond wig beneath a blue wool cap, and said nothing. One of the Web sites that tracks Dylan concert appearances and set lists even included a feature, BobTalk, that immortalized his offhand comments from the stage, on the order of "Thanks everybody! That last song was a song about trying to say goodbye to somebody. This one is about trying to say hello to somebody." True, by the 1990s, Dylan's interviewers noted that he was less cagey and combative than he had been thirty years earlier, and that, although certain topics about his private life were off-limits, he was friendly and even helpful in trying to convey how he had conceived his latest project, or how he went about writing songs. But these interviews were rare.

This began to change in *Chronicles,* where, even though the words were still printed, Dylan's candor and gratitude came through—and they were his own words, or mostly his own. It changed even more with Martin Scorsese's documentary *No Direction Home,* where selections from the total of roughly eighty hours of on-camera interviews gathered by Jeff Rosen showed Dylan telling parts of his own story, sometimes pensively, sometimes playfully, but always grasping for the right word or turn of phrase until he found it. The film begins with Dylan just talking: "I had ambitions to, ahhhhh, set out and find—like an odyssey, goin' home somewhere, set out to find, ahh, this home that I'd left awhile back and couldn't remember exactly where it was but I was, ahhh, on my way there. And, ahhh, encountering what I encountered on the, on the way was how I envisioned it all, I didn't really have any ambition at all. I was born very far from where I'm supposed to be, and so I'm on my way home." Coming so soon after *Chronicles,* the film showed Dylan opening up about himself as never before outside his songs, but also, as was said of his friend Ginsberg, composing on the tongue.*

Even more came through on *Theme Time Radio Hour with Your Host Bob Dylan,* which appeared for three seasons, and in one hundred episodes, on XM satellite radio (later Sirius-XM) beginning in May 2006. Here was a new, thoroughly digitized version of an old technology, with a national reach far greater than that of the fifty-thousand-watt stations Dylan had listened to late at night as a boy. Here was a virtual reality that was benign, indeed uplifting, the virtual community of shared tastes and desires created by any disc jockey and his listeners. The show originated from no place in particular—in fact, it was recorded and assembled for the most part in Los Angeles, edited in New York, and broadcast from the XM studio in Washington, D.C.—so Dylan, now wearing his disc jockey mask, along with the show's producers, could make real in words their own archaic fantasies about the surroundings that the listeners could never see. Appearing on a subscriber-only satellite station, the shows also had no commercials, allowing Dylan and his accomplices additional room for invention. And in his selection of themes as well as recordings, Dylan could yet again reclaim and reassemble the American musical past, providing his own patter but also, now, letting the music speak for itself—with no complicating charges of plagiarism.

One of the most interesting features of the show was Dylan the DJ, or his persona as a DJ. He never denied who it was behind the microphone,

---

* As Ginsberg also does in the film. One of the documentary's most moving moments comes when Ginsberg, who has been choosing his words carefully, momentarily chokes up when he recalls hearing Dylan on record for the first time in 1963. After listening to "Hard Rain," he recalls, he wept at the recognition that another generation had arrived to pick up "earlier bohemian or Beat illumination and self-empowerment . . . Poetry is words that are empowered that make your hair stand on end, that you recognize instantly as being some form of subjective truth that has an objective reality to it because somebody's realized it. Then you call it poetry later."

dropping, here and there, little jokes or anecdotes about his life as a musician among musicians. With his choice of themes, listeners learned, among other things, that the Bob Dylan who decades earlier wrote a song about the New York Yankees pitcher Catfish Hunter remains very much a baseball fan, enough so to offer his own a cappella singing of "Take Me Out to the Ballgame" on his show entitled "Baseball." But Dylan also took on a role, as a disc jockey from out of the past but also as instructor of music appreciation, biographer, comedian, commentator, and dispenser of recipes, household hints, and other bits of useful information.

One writer has suggestively likened the show to Samuel Johnson's *Lives of the Poets* in proclaiming the virtues of writers whose work was in danger of being misunderstood or forgotten. The comparison captures a bit of what the show conveyed, but it is incomplete and a little too high-minded. *Theme Time Radio Hour* sounded more like another conjuring—a blend of an old-time radio show, complete with little jingles, and a hometown newspaper out of the 1940s or 1950s, with its vintage ads, home entertaining features (such as instructions on how to mix an ideal mint julep on the "Drinking" show), lists of interesting things to know (on the "Weather" show, the three American cities that are windier than the Windy City, Chicago: Dodge City, Kansas; Amarillo, Texas; and Rochester, Minnesota), freely associated True History Facts (including the information, dispensed during the show called

Jaime Hernandez poster for *Theme Time Radio Hour with Your Host Bob Dylan,* XM radio, 2007.

"War," that more than three hundred soldiers under the age of thirteen served in the Civil War, most as fifers or drummers, but some as combatants, including one George S. Lamkin, who joined the Mississippi Battery when he was eleven years old and was severely wounded at Shiloh before he turned twelve), telephone call-ins and "letters" from listeners (the latter in the form of e-mails, contrived by Dylan and the producers), and plenty more besides the music.

With his co-producers, Dylan created an imaginary theater, with heavy overtones of the 1940s and 1950s. The show supposedly emanated from Studio B in something called the Abernathy Building (which in the second season became the "historic" Abernathy Building), close by to Samson's Diner and Elmo's Bar and Carl's barbershop. The actress Ellen Barkin introduced most of the shows with a noirish monologue, sound effects in the background, describing snapshots of big-city private life, somewhat in the spirit of Edward Hopper's painting *Nighthawks:* the very first of them—"It's nighttime in the Big City. Rain is falling, fog rolls in from the waterfront. A nightshift nurse smokes the last cigarette in a pack"—was typical. One imagines that the movie theaters are featuring *She Wore a Yellow Ribbon,* or maybe Victor Mature and Hedy Lamarr playing in *Samson and Delilah.* That nurse's pack of cigarettes costs fourteen cents. Everybody smokes.

From out of this past, Dylan the DJ—no latter-day Symphony Sid Torin or Alan Freed, his voice sounding as old as the hills—spun his platters (of which, of course, there were none in this digital age), playing a great deal of music that one doesn't hear on the radio anymore—except on some college stations and the odd listener-supported radio station like WWOZ in New Orleans—telling something about the performers and, often, even listing the label on which the recording appeared, as if we could run out and buy them. And Dylan's tastes turned out to be even more eclectic than most listeners could have imagined. There was, not surprisingly, plenty of blues and rhythm and blues, beginning with the very first record on the very first show, Muddy Waters performing "Blow, Wind, Blow";* and there was plenty of country (from the Carter Family onward), western swing, gospel, doo-wop, and rock and roll, by performers and groups both famous and long forgotten; and occasionally, Dylan played jazz (including, as the preface to his show "Moon," Charlie Parker playing "Ornithology," which the DJ instructor pointed out was based on the chord structure of "How High the Moon").

---

* Dylan had all sorts of fun with his selections right from the start. Describing Muddy Waters as "one of the ancients by now whom all moderns prize," he selected a number that listeners might easily associate with his own "Blowin' in the Wind," but that contained a verse which Dylan actually adapted later for "It Takes a Lot to Laugh (It Takes a Train to Cry)": "Don't the sun look lonesome / Shading down behind the trees? / Don't the sun look lonesome / Shading down behind the trees? / But don't your house look lonesome / When your baby's packed to leave?"

But Dylan also played a great deal of Glenn Miller, Frank Sinatra (the performer played most often in the first season), Patti Page, and various crooners from the 1930s through the 1950s, including Bing Crosby. He played LL Cool J and spoke knowledgeably about rap. He took time to recite repeatedly fitting lines of serious literature, from Yeats's "Drinking Song" to Lawrence Ferlinghetti's "Baseball Canto." And sometimes, instead of juxtaposing one thing and another, he threw different things into the same pot and stirred, as on the "Devil" show, when he read of Satan from *Paradise Lost,* while he played the Reverend Gary Davis in the background, performing "Devil's Dream."

By the end of the third season, close to a hundred hours existed of Dylan speaking, intermittently, in a grand act of archiving and presentation, offering a vast cabinet of curios as well as masterpieces, musical and literary—and taking glances backward over the traveled roads, from all directions, that he had followed on his long journey home. In a variation on his modern minstrel composing, Dylan had found, in radio, an imaginative medium far better suited than film for writing another song—a song that also turned out to be another kind of memoir, collecting and codifying the scriptures of a lifetime.

After five years of steady touring with new bands, built around Tony Garnier and George Recile, Dylan had hammered out a new sound in concert, louder and driven by more powerful guitar and drums, but also enhanced by his own keyboard playing—in 2003, Dylan began cutting back playing the guitar onstage—as well as the multi-instrumental talents of Donnie Herron, formerly of the updated country and western-swing band BR5-49. The concertizing was steady, usually in tandem with another act, and the venues were imaginative, like the minor-league ballparks that Dylan toured during the summers of 2005 and 2009. Of the dozen or so concerts I attended after 2002, most were uneven musically—in part because of the band's loudness, in part because of the raggedness of Dylan's voice—but all had at least a few arresting moments. None surpassed the performance at the Reverend Ike's United Church Palace in Washington Heights in Manhattan at the end of November 2008. After passing through the gilded lobby of a former Loews movie palace, covered with the reverend's "prosperity preaching" slogans—including "I Am Not Other People's Opinions"—an almost entirely white crowd filed into the theater to hear Dylan open with "Gotta Serve Somebody," a song he hardly ever performs anymore, playing a fine harmonica break and snaking through a little preacher man dance. The ensemble also played a strong arrangement of "It's Alright, Ma" (which brought out the chord structure it shares, funnily, with the Everly Brothers' "Wake Up, Little Susie") and a blues band version, with Dylan again fronting on harmonica, of "'Til I Fell in Love with You," from *Time Out of Mind*.*

By early 2009, the band, with the all-important temporary addition of the multi-instrumentalist David Hidalgo, of Los Lobos, had jelled in the studio, producing (almost out of thin air, it seemed) a new album of original songs, *Together Through Life*. But before that, Dylan released the latest in his series of so-called official bootleg albums, a three-CD set of outtakes and concert performances since 1989, called *Tell Tale Signs*.

What tales did the signs tell? The concert introduction delivered by Al Santos, the stage manager, about Dylan's progress from has-been to reborn star comes word for word from some mock afflatus in an admiring article about Dylan that appeared in the *Buffalo News* in 2002. (Dylan's appropriations extend well beyond his songs.) It jibes with *Chronicles: Volume One*, where Dylan describes the artistic crises and physical trauma that abated shortly before he recorded *Oh Mercy* in 1989. All that followed from that recovery forms one of the tales told on *Tell Tale Signs*, which starts in 1989 and ends in 2006, the year that Dylan released *Modern Times*. There are also the tales inside the signs (that is, the songs) themselves, from the formulaic, protesty "Everything Is Broken" and the heartbroken "Most of the Time" on *Oh Mercy* to "Ain't Talkin'," the final cut on *Modern Times*—a harrowing minor-key excursion through suffering, abandonment, unanswered prayers, and contemplated revenge that ends with a swelling, redemptive major chord. And although it may just be a coincidence, these tales coincide exactly with yet another story that remains in the background, unmentioned—the decline and then sudden downfall of America's age of Ronald Reagan, from the ascension of George Bush the elder in 1989 to the beginning of Bush the younger's unraveling in 2006.

The collection contains some studio gems that had not been previously released. One of Dylan's quirks as he has grown older has been to leave

---

* That said, the finest single performance of Dylan's I heard, about this time, was a heartbreaking "Nettie Moore," played during the summer of 2008 at an otherwise unremarkble concert at the Prospect Park Bandshell in Brooklyn.

some of his best work off of his albums, for no stated reason. In his liner notes, Larry Sloman remembers expressing shock in 1983 at learning that "Blind Willie McTell" would be dropped from the forthcoming *Infidels*. ("Aw Ratso, don't get so excited," he recalls Dylan saying. "It's just an album. I've made thirty of them.") Still, imagine the kind of reception *Infidels* would have received—and how the arc of Dylan's career might have bent—if "Foot of Pride" as well as "Blind Willie" had been left on. "Red River Shore," cut from *Time Out of Mind* and left unreleased, is, if not a masterpiece like "Blind Willie," better than almost all of Dylan's officially released material from the mid-1980s and the 1990s. (The legendary session keyboard player Jim Dickinson told an interviewer he thought it was the best of the songs recorded for *Time Out of Mind*.) "Marchin' to the City," also discarded, is just as good, and "Dreamin' of You"—which, after not appearing on *Time Out of Mind*, fragmented and appeared piecemeal in various other songs down the road—is not too far behind.

Then there are the concert tracks on *Tell Tale Signs*. Dylan's reworking, onstage, of his own compositions, as well as others', had been legendary since the 1970s, and even today it can frustrate those fans who adore his songs but whom he asks to think about them fresh—yet who, after all these years, still don't want to. *Tell Tale Signs* includes a remarkable performance of "Cocaine Blues" at the concert I was fortunate to attend at Wolf Trap in 1997. This version is neither the one made famous by the Reverend Gary Davis during the 1960s folk revival, nor Dave Van Ronk's adaptation of Davis's, nor Dylan's own youthful rendering of Van Ronk's. (Van Ronk, who performed the song beautifully umpteen times, sometimes turned his twilight growl into an ironic chuckle about the effects of hard drugs.) It is almost a wholly new song, with Dylan's raspy plaint more desperate than the others—the desperation soaring over the then newly added band member Larry Campbell's delicate fingerpicking. (Getting to hear several live tracks with Campbell, one of the very finest sidemen Dylan has ever hired, is one of the additional treats of *Tell Tale Signs*.) The album also shows Dylan working hard in the studio. Three versions of "Mississippi," all from the *Time Out of Mind* sessions, run from sorrowful to worn-out to courageous. They reveal how inflection and tone can make up for a constriction of vocal range, and how changes in either can completely change the mood if the song is rich enough. They also show how Dylan approaches one of his own songs, trying to figure it out as if someone else had written it, maybe an eon ago.

But the revelation on *Tell Tale Signs* is the stripped-down studio version of one of the older songs, the deceptively pretty, apocalyptic spiritual summons "Ring Them Bells" from 1989, sung and played solo on the piano. Sloman remarks that Dylan's performance of the song was so strong that for the track finally released on *Oh Mercy*, Lanois, the practiced soundscaper, added only a quiet guitar and organ backing. And it is true that Dylan's mastery of phrasing and breath is fully in evidence in the version included on *Oh Mercy*. Yet Lanois's little production touches made the song sound bright and full, almost like a glad tiding, whereas here the song sounds less certain and more urgent, as if the chimes of freedom and righteousness—tolling "for the blind and the deaf" and "for all of us who are left" and for the chosen few who will judge the many—may not flash in time. A superb, contained recording, it is one of the last gasps of the hopefulness that would seem to have vanished by the late 1990s, when things had changed and Dylan sang of being locked in tight and no longer caring.

Of course, by the time *Tell Tale Signs* appeared, there were reasons for Dylan to think that fresh signs were appearing. Without his being in any way direct about it, the smoldering but bleak and pessimistic feel of so much of Dylan's songwriting over the previous decade inescapably reflected the times. The same held for his film *Masked and Anonymous,* with its Melvillean political allegory of civil war. But just maybe, beginning in 2006, he sensed history's gears shifting again. Playing in Minneapolis on the night Barack Obama was elected president, the stubbornly reticent Dylan broke with habit and told the audience that he had been born in 1941, the year Pearl Harbor was bombed, and that he had lived in a world of darkness ever since, but that "it looks like things are gonna change now." Though I understood the symbolism and the emotive force, I was more skeptical at the time, and could imagine that Dylan was being ironic or at least ambiguous. But without betraying any kind of certainty let alone commitment, he sounded sincere and even excited, as if the markings of his music might prove not a descent into final disillusionment but the prelude to new and different kinds of tales and signs.

In any event, Dylan's surge of productivity continued with the release, at the end of April 2009, of *Together Through Life*—and while I was listening to the album's third track, something hit me. The song, "My Wife's

Willie Dixon (stand-up bass) and Muddy Waters (guitar) performing on CBC-TV's *The Blues,* a "Festival" special broadcast on February 23, 1966, in Canada.

Home Town," is basically a clever reprise of the Muddy Waters classic "I Just Want to Make Love to You," written by the Chicago blues great Willie Dixon, first recorded by Waters in 1954, and later recorded by, among others, Etta James and the (early) Rolling Stones. (The song also appears to have been part of the inspiration behind Dylan's own "All I Really Want to Do," from 1964.) The accordion part (played beautifully by David Hidalgo) drifts in and out of lines played on the original by the pianist Otis Spann and the harmonica virtuoso Little Walter. But the melody is the same, and the arrangement comes mighty close, closer than any of the borrowing on *"Love and Theft"* or *Modern Times.** And the song's credits correctly cite Dixon.

I wondered, on first hearing the track, whether Dylan was paying homage to Waters or Dixon or James or Mick Jagger, or maybe all of them. But what hit me was something else: how Dylan's voice, with age, had harshened into a blues rasp vaguely reminiscent of yet another Chicago blues great, Howlin' Wolf. And so, on an old song that Dylan had rewrit-

---

* The melody and arrangement of another song, "Beyond Here Lies Nothin'," resemble those of "All Your Love," recorded by Otis Rush in 1958. My thanks to Tony Glover on this point.

ten into a wicked number about an evil wife whose hometown is hell and who wields "stuff more potent than a gypsy's curse," strange specters appeared—shades from Chess Records sessions dating back more than half a century that suddenly materialized as Dylan, Hidalgo, and the rest of the band that Dylan assembled for *Together Through Life*. An album of songs about women and love (with most of the songs' lyrics co-credited to Robert Hunter, the Grateful Dead writer with whom Dylan had written before), it is also about music that Dylan had traveled with through his own life—and it contains some of that music.

The recording was in some ways very much of a piece with Dylan's work dating back to *"Love and Theft."* Sounds, melodies, country and pop-song lyrics—"the boulevard of broken dreams" became "the boulevard of broken cars"—snatches of classical poetry—Ovid showed up as he did on *Modern Times,* once again unnoted—got turned into something new that also sounded old. Once more, the simplest of the songs contained layers that approached allusion, but only just. In her 1974 hit "Jolene," Dolly Parton pleads with a raving beauty, "with flaming locks of auburn hair" and "eyes of emerald green," begging her not to steal her man. Dylan's "Jolene" does not even attempt to match Parton's, which is one of the great performances in country-and-western music, but it is an interesting counterpart. In Dylan's version, a toss-off steady rocker with a nice guitar hook, Jolene's eyes are brown and Dylan sings as the king to her queen, while he packs a Saturday night special—a plain enough sex song, but lurking in the lyrics and the music are also hints of Robert Johnson's "32-20 Blues," as well as Victoria Spivey's album recorded in early 1962, *Three Kings and the Queen* (on which a twenty-year-old Bob Dylan, no king, played harmonica in back of Big Joe Williams).

Even when the songs tell of loss and longing, the album has a musically warm, at times almost sunny atmosphere, as if it were being performed under the shade of a tree, weekend music for dancing couples in some lazy southwestern border town. That feeling came largely from the Tex-Mex strains of Hidalgo's squeeze box, at times paired with Dylan's current road band regular Donnie Herron playing a mariachi trumpet. And there was a good deal of throwback here too, to Dylan's own music as well as to that of others. Dylan had used Tex-Mex sounds effectively in his own work since at least 1965, when he added, at the last minute, Charlie McCoy's brilliant guitar to the studio version of "Desolation Row." At the very moment he broke with the more conventional forms of 1960s folk music, Dylan publicly acknowledged his admiration for the work of his friend the San Antonio genius Doug Sahm and Sahm's Tex-Mex rock band with a British invasion name, the Sir Douglas Quintet.

The sound of much of *Together Through Life* fit well with the mythic Old West setting that (along with the Civil War and the bluesmen's land, from Mississippi to Chicago, circa 1938 to 1955) has repeatedly sparked Dylan's imagination: matrices of American myth. Hidalgo was also the latest in a string of master keyboard players with whom Dylan had played and recorded over the decades, including Paul Griffin, Al Kooper, Garth Hudson, and Augie Meyers, not to mention his own often overlooked piano and organ playing. And while *Together Through Life* bears no obvious resemblance to *Blonde on Blonde,* the metallic glow Dylan found for that album reappears, sometimes shining softly, sometimes shimmering in a rollicking jump.

As early press reports revealed, the album grew out of a commission to write a song (which became "Life Is Hard") for a film directed by Olivier Dahan, *My Own Love Song.* There was nothing odd about that either: at Dylan's live shows, he still shows off, perched on one of the amps, the Oscar he won for "Things Have Changed" in the film *Wonder Boys* (which helped make him, along with Aaron Copland, one of the few artists ever to receive both a Pulitzer Prize and an Academy Award). One of the album's more infectious songs, "If You Ever Go to Houston" (its title taken from Leadbelly's classic "Midnight Special"), carries us back for a little while to the 1870s or so, sung in the voice of a veteran of the Mexican-American War who instructs the listener on how to walk in that city (the album has a thing about keeping your hands in your pockets), with some site check-offs for other Texas cities (like Dallas, with its Magnolia Hotel, although Houston has one of these, too)—but mainly with a lush soundscape of Tony Garnier's bass, with Mike Campbell (borrowed from Tom Petty's Heartbreakers) on a gut-stringed acoustic guitar and Hidalgo playing a repeating tune of descending note pairings.

There are no Dylan epics like "Highlands" or even "Ain't Talkin'" on the album, nor too much, really, to tax the brain, but there is plenty to dance to, shake to, even laugh to. *Together Through Life* is above all a musical album, which may have disappointed the Bob Dylan wing of English departments throughout the nation and around the world. The album's look drove that home. For the front cover, Dylan selected one of Bruce Davidson's photographs of a Brooklyn gang taken in 1959, depicting a serious make-out session in the backseat of a speeding car: love and sex. But the album's back cover is completely musical—a Josef Koudelka photograph, taken in 1968, of a band of Romanian gypsy musicians, with an accordionist and a trumpet player right in the middle.

The album included a protest song, but more humorous than accusatory, sending up the inane, omnipresent motivational-speaker cliché "It's all good!" And politically minded fans who might have expected a Dylan song entitled "I Feel a Change Comin' On" to pick up where Sam Cooke left off would be surprised by its reflective, later-in-the-day love lyric in which the singer announces his high-low taste in books and music, and which has a bridge that some would hear as a skeptical Dylan himself speaking, in the sobering early aftermath of Barack Obama's election to the White House: "Dreams never did work for me, anyway / Even when they did come true." The song also includes a lovely, poignant lifting about "the fourth part of the day"—apparently taken from Chaucer—being nearly gone.

In 1965, the year that Dylan famously played electric at the Newport Folk Festival, the fetishists of authenticity (along with fans who just loved great American music) clung to the rediscovered black blues artists who were enjoying a last taste of celebrity, singing the songs they had recorded in the 1920s and 1930s for the Vocalion and OKeh and Bluebird labels. There was Son House (who was sixty-three years old), and Mississippi John Hurt (in his early seventies), and Mance Lipscomb (exactly seventy), as well as a younger cohort that included Willie Dixon, who was fifty, and Memphis Slim, who was forty-nine. Now the untamed young musical expeditionary of 1965 was right up there with the old guys—he turned sixty-eight shortly after *Together Through Life* was released—yet he was not just reinventing and performing his old songs for college kids but also turning the old into the new and then back again, with fresh myth-laden music that made you think and feel at the same time. This time out, though, maybe more than ever, he also roused you to dance and dance, and then dance some more, and then, well . . . then we'd just see what developed.

CODA

DO YOU HEAR
WHAT I HEAR?

Christmas in the Heart, October 13, 2009

When word spread during the summer of 2009 about the contents of Bob Dylan's second album of the year, *Christmas in the Heart,* there were almost audible gasps of astonishment on the Dylan fan blogs and Web sites. It mattered little that Dylan was about the only major popular American singer or musician of modern times who had as yet failed to make a Christmas album. Bing Crosby made several, springing in part from the all-time popularity of his "White Christmas," but the list has run the gamut from Frank Sinatra to Joan Baez, to the Ventures, to the Ronettes (as part of a compilation album, *A Christmas Gift for You from Phil Spector*). Even Jewish singers, including Barbra Streisand and Neil Diamond, released Christmas albums. In 1934, Eddie Cantor (born Edward Israel Iskowitz) had a huge hit with a brand-new song that other major singers had turned down as too childish: "Santa Claus Is Coming to Town." One of the most beloved holiday standards, "The Christmas Song (Chestnuts Roasting on an Open Fire)," was cowritten by the son of Russian-Jewish immigrants whose name, before they changed it, was Torma—Mel Tormé.

One of my favorites of all the Christmas records—recorded by Elvis Presley, entitled simply *Elvis' Christmas Album,* and released in 1957—includes, on one side, old standbys such as "White Christmas" and Gene Autry's "Here Comes Santa Claus" and new rockers such as "Santa Claus

Is Back in Town" and, on the other, carols and black gospel songs. The latter include Presley and his backup singers, the Jordanaires, performing Thomas A. Dorsey's "(There'll Be) Peace in the Valley (for Me)," a performance that, for purely spiritual reasons, moves me more with each passing year. But no matter how many singers had come before, to fans who still remembered Dylan as the rebellious voice of the counterculture, or even those who had heard the older, sophisticated re-assembler of American music and literature, the thought of him recording anything as sentimental as a Christmas album seemed odd. Was Dylan up to his old tricks, changing his style dramatically just when listeners and critics thought they had him pegged? Was it all just a high-spirited spoof?

In fact, making this record was a generous act that was also oddly in keeping with Dylan's past and with his developing art. The crass reason for artists to release special albums of Christmas songs had always been to cash in on the lucrative Christmas sales market. Dylan understood as much—but in the Christian spirit of *caritas,* he donated all of his royalties ahead of time to buy holiday meals for millions of needy people through the organization Feeding America. The artistic reason for cutting special Christmas collections had always been that there are so many wonderful Christmas songs, old and new—not least those in the American songbook of the past century and a half—and ambitious musical artists have been tempted to take them on. This was Dylan's motivation as well. Some listeners heard *Christmas in the Heart,* with knowing irony, as a parody of 1950s white-bread music, but the album contains not a single ironic or parodic note. It is a sincere, croaky-voiced homage to a particular vintage of popular American Christmas music, as well as testimony to Dylan's abiding faith: hence, its title.

Like *Elvis' Christmas Album,* but in a more jumbled way, *Christmas in the Heart* mixes traditional carols (roughly one-quarter of the album) with Tin Pan Alley holiday songs, one seasonal hit that has become attached to the holiday ("Winter Wonderland"), and a novelty song or two. The album could have appeared as a large chunk of a *Theme Time Radio Hour* episode entitled "Christmas," but this time with Dylan performing all of the songs instead of acting as DJ.

But the most salient thing about the album is how much of it consists of hits written and originally recorded in the 1940s and early 1950s—the years of Dylan's boyhood, when these songs formed a perennial American December soundscape, even for a Jewish boy. "Have Yourself a Merry Little Christmas" first appeared in the film *Meet Me in St. Louis* in 1944, as sung by Judy Garland (who, as Frances Ethel Gumm, nineteen years Dylan's senior, had grown up in Grand Rapids, Minnesota, about thirty miles west of Hibbing).* Other standards on the album come from the same era: "The Christmas Song" (1944), later made famous by Nat "King" Cole; the Andrews Sisters' "Christmas Island" (1946); Autry's and, later, Presley's "Here Comes Santa Claus" (1947); and Dean Martin's "Christmas Blues" (1953).

It is just as striking that, much as Charley Patton's shade presides over "*Love and Theft,*" the benign spirit of Bing Crosby haunts *Christmas in the Heart.* This is not entirely surprising: after he recorded "White Christmas" in 1942, Crosby practically owned the franchise on making popular recordings of Christmas music. Still, it cannot be coincidental that of all the Christmas material available to him, Dylan included three of the songs most closely identified with Crosby—"I'll Be Home for Christmas" (1943), "Silver Bells" (1952), and "Do You Hear What I Hear?" (1962)—as well as others that were successful songs for Crosby, including "Here Comes Santa Claus" (written in 1947, recorded by Crosby with the Andrews Sisters in 1949), "The Christmas Song" (recorded by Crosby in 1947), and "Winter Wonderland" (written in 1934 and recorded by Crosby in 1962). In all, thirteen of the fifteen songs on *Christmas in the Heart,* including all of the carols, were also recorded by Crosby.

And so the album takes us back to the mid- to late 1940s, when Bobby Zimmerman was just a child—but it also takes us back to 1985, when Bob Dylan was touting Bing Crosby as a great master of phrasing, one of whose songs he hoped soon to record. And it also takes us back two years before that, to the Power Station recording studio in New York in late April 1983, when Dylan was recording *Infidels.* The eleventh recording session in as many days began with repeated efforts to complete "Foot of Pride," but nine takes yielded nothing usable. To unwind, the band members jumped into a reggae jam—and then Dylan led them into "The Christmas Song," followed by Louis Jordan's jump-blues hit from 1946 "Choo Choo Ch'Boogie," then "Silent Night," and then the

---

* In *Chronicles,* Dylan recalls playing Garland singing "The Man That Got Away" on the jukebox during his early days in New York: "The song always did something to me, not in any stupefying, tremendous kind of way. It didn't summon up any strange thoughts. It was just nice to hear . . . Listening to Judy was like listening to the girl next door. She was way before my time, and like the Elton John song says, 'I would have liked to have known you, but I was just a kid' " (49).

contemporary Australian Pentecostal songwriter Darlene Zschech's "Glory to the King." If a seed was planted in the era of World War II and just after, it matured in Dylan's mind for at least a quarter century before he recorded *Christmas in the Heart.*

Dylan could not, of course, keep from importing his own style and preferences and melding them with the 1940s sound. (The results are best heard on "Winter Wonderland," complete with Donnie Herron on pedal steel guitar.) His careful phrasing and arrangements could not erase the ragged effects of his badly worn and cracked vocal cords, which simply were not up to a tune as complicated as "The Christmas Song." But the season's warm and exuberant joys come alive on several tracks, not least my favorite, "Must Be Santa"—a dance-hall rendition (complete with David Hidalgo's accordion and George Recile's crash cymbal) that, although beholden to the Texas rock-polka band Brave Combo, revives the polka rave-ups of Whoopee John Wilfahrt and all the Midwestern polka band kings of Dylan's youth. And even though Dylan's voice strains and actually falters for a moment on "Hark, the Herald Angels Sing," and an interlude by a female chorale starts off sounding dippy, the chorale's line suddenly pauses, slows, and turns lovely, and Dylan joins in with "joyful, all ye nations rise / join the triumph of the skies," and the season's divinity comes to the ear, and to the heart.

For more than half a century, Bob Dylan had been absorbing, transmuting, and renewing and improving American art forms long thought to be trapped in formal conventions. He not only "put folk into bed with rock," as Al Santos still announces before each concert; he took traditional folk music, the blues, rock and roll, country and western, black gospel, Tin Pan Alley, Tex-Mex borderlands music, Irish outlaw ballads, and more and bent them to his own poetic muse. At the start of the 1960s, influenced by the songs and milieu of the Popular Front–inspired folk revival, he turned them into something else, much as the Popular Front composer Aaron Copland had turned folk songs into orchestral music. His imagination and his voice blasted open by Beat aesthetics, Dylan then pushed his own reinventions of folk music into realms that were every bit as mysterious and mythic as the old traditional music, but in a pop sensibility of his own time that shocked the folk purists. And then he turned away again, moving to Blakean and biblical parable, time-fractured songs of love and heartbreak, hellfire preaching, and onward, through his recovered and revised modern minstrelsy of the 1990s and after.

Open to artistic inspiration anywhere he found it, Dylan was not so much a sponge (although he has always absorbed prodigious amounts) as an alchemist, taking common materials and creating new art. Nothing that came within his field of vision escaped him: 1930s French films, 1850s minstrel songs, the works of Shakespeare, Dolly Parton, Saint John of Patmos, Muddy Waters—anything of beauty, no matter how terrible, became something to seize upon and make his own. And yet, as he ended his seventh decade, Dylan also in some ways spiritually resembled Blind Willie McTell, traveling endlessly, performing endlessly, sharp to the wiles of the world, taking things from everywhere but fixing them up his own way, composing new songs and performing old ones that were sometimes sacred and sometimes secular, but neither black nor white, up nor down—and that had reference to everybody.

Then, all of a sudden, late in 2009, Dylan offered a red-ribboned gift to the world, not so much slipping back and forth through time, or recombining old and new as on his previous four albums, as instead evoking and in some ways replicating his own past and America's, while providing Christmas dinner to families on relief—acting like a grander version of the Pretty Boy Floyd of his last proclaimed hero, Woody Guthrie, but as an artist, not a bank robber. Or perhaps *Christmas in the Heart* was not just a gift but another album of cover versions that, as in the past, marked an interlude before Dylan undertook yet another new phase of his career. With the masked, shape-changing American alchemist, it was impossible to know too much for sure.

ACKNOWLEDGMENTS

I am grateful above all to my editor, the incomparable Gerald Howard, and his staff at Doubleday, especially his assistant, Hannah Wood. I am also indebted to Bette Alexander, Rebecca Holland, Brandy Flora, Emily Mahon, Rachel Lapal, Jeffrey Yamaguchi, and John Pitts. Deborah Bull skillfully tracked down numerous photographs and prints.

My colleagues at Princeton, as well as Judy Hanson and the staff of the Princeton History Department, are a continuing source of inspiration and support. I owe special thanks this time to Brooke Fitzgerald for her splendid work in helping with the illustrations.

As usual, I have avoided the dance of subjectivities that goes along with extensive interviewing, but I made a couple of exceptions: Al Kooper and Charlie McCoy gave generously of their time and recollections. Thanks also to Bill Flanagan, Tony Glover, and Donn Pennebaker for recollections and clarifications.

George Hecksher very kindly permitted me to consult the collection of Dylan manuscripts he has donated to the Morgan Library and Museum in New York, and Robert Parks patiently guided me through the holdings.

Apart from the chapters revised from previously published essays, smaller fragments of this book appeared in earlier writings of mine, and I'd like to thank those responsible for giving them their first, longer trying-out, especially Tina Brown and Edward Felsenthal of the Daily Beast, and Lindsay Waters of Harvard University Press.

Writing this book would have been impossible without the munificence, expertise, and camaraderie of Robert Bower, Callie Gladman, April Hayes, Diane Lapson, Damian Rodriguez, Lynne Okin Sheridan, and Debbie Sweeney. A big tip of the cap as well to Dan Levy.

I owe more than I can say to Jeff Rosen for, among other things, countless hours of conversation, argument, and discovery—and for our continuing improvisations in music appreciation.

SELECTED READINGS, NOTES, AND DISCOGRAPHY

There is an enormous body of commentary on Bob Dylan and his work, and there are numerous valuable research tools to aid current and future writers. The following is a highly select listing of the books and resources that I found most useful, including a discography of the key recordings I have cited.

GENERAL

Historians habitually work with primary materials in libraries and archives, but no official repository has been selected (if ever one will be) to house the bulk of Dylan's manuscripts and private papers. The outstanding exception is the rich body of manuscripts of Dylan's lyrics, collected by George Hecksher, which is held by the Morgan Library and Museum in New York. I have also been privileged to enjoy access to a wide range of materials, including session tapes, overseen by Jeff Rosen and his staff at Special Rider Music.

There are several copious and helpful reference books, although they are far from flawless and must be used in close conjunction with the other basic sources: Michael Gray, *The Bob Dylan Encyclopedia* (2006; New York, 2008); Clinton Heylin, *Bob Dylan: The Complete Recording Sessions, 1960–1994* (New York, 1995); and Oliver Trager, *Keys to the Rain: The Definitive Bob Dylan Encyclopedia* (New York, 2004). Two very useful compilations of Dylan's newspaper, magazine, radio, and television interviews are Jonathan Cott, ed., *Bob Dylan: The Essential Interviews* (New York, 2006); and James Ellison, ed., *Younger Than That Now: The Collected Interviews with Bob Dylan* (New York, 2004).

Research on Dylan has been greatly facilitated by the Internet. The first place to look is Dylan's own official Web site, www.bobdylan.com. For information on past concert tours, set lists, and recording dates, as well as for leads about other useful sites, see Bill Pagel's Bob Links, www.boblinks.com; and Olof Björner's About Bob, www.bjorner.com/bob.htm. For a continuing, comprehensive aggregation of the latest information on the Internet, with an archive that dates back to 1995, see Karl Erik Andersen's indispensable site, Expecting Rain, www.expectingrain.com. Additional useful information and source material, some of it to be found nowhere else, is Giulio Molfese's Bread Crumb Sins, www.interferenza.com/bcs, although the site has not been updated in some years. Pagel's and Andersen's sites also contain links to the most important Dylan fanzines, including two (now venerable) British publications, *Isis* and *The Bridge*. See also Derek Barker's edited collections, *Isis: A Bob Dylan Anthology* (London, 2004); and *20 Years of Isis: Anthology Volume 2* (Surrey, U.K., 2005). Serious researchers will want to consult back issues of two other magazines no longer being published, *Wanted Man* and the *Telegraph,* as well as the volume edited by the late John Bauldie, *Wanted Man: In Search of Bob Dylan* (London, 1990).

Bob Dylan's *Lyrics, 1962–2001* (New York, 2004) contains the standard versions of Dylan's song lyrics through *"Love and Theft."* Readers may also consult www.bobdylan.com, which covers the lyrics of albums released since 2001 as well as all of the earlier work.

Biographies of Dylan vary widely in quality and accuracy, depending in part on their degree of celebrity worship. By far the most useful for my purposes is Clinton Heylin's *Bob Dylan: Behind the Shades: Take Two,* which has been reissued as *Bob Dylan: Behind the Shades Revisited* (New York, 2003). Other informative general biographies (although, again, of varying quality as biographies) include: Robert Shelton, *No Direction Home: The Life and Music of Bob Dylan* (New York, 1986); Anthony Scaduto, *Bob Dylan: An Intimate Biography* (New York, 1971); Howard Sounes, *Down the Highway: The Life of Bob Dylan* (New York, 2001); and Bob Spitz, *Dylan: A Biography* (1989; New York, 1991).

Among the memoirs, pride of place goes to Dylan's superb *Chronicles: Volume One* (New York, 2004); two more volumes of his memoirs are expected to appear. On Dylan's early years in New York—and, just as important, on the wider Greenwich Village scene—Suze Rotolo's charming yet tough-minded *A Freewheelin' Time: A Memoir of Greenwich Village in the Sixties* (New York, 2008) is essential. Dave Van Ronk did not, alas, live to complete the manuscript of his memoir, but Elijah Wald served his memory well in bringing to fruition *The Mayor of MacDougal Street: A Memoir* (New York, 2005). Other useful memoirs include Joan Baez, *And a Voice to Sing With* (1989; New York, 2009); Liam Clancy, *The Mountain of the Women: Memoirs of an Irish Troubadour* (New York, 2002); Levon Helm and Stephen Davis, *This Wheel's on Fire: Levon Helm and the Story of the Band* (New York, 1993); the relevant portions of Phil Lesh, *Searching for the Sound: My Life with the Grateful Dead* (New York, 2005); and, for background, Israel Goodman Young, *Autobiography: The Bronx, 1928–1938* (New York, 1969).

The number of serious studies of Dylan's work has grown large enough to constitute a small library, written in several languages and covering topics ranging from Dylan as a Zen master to his style of playing the harmonica. Some of these works are of special importance. Of the many talented writers who pioneered rock-and-roll criticism in the 1960s, Greil Marcus has established himself as the foremost cultural critic, and his abundant work on Dylan ranks among his best. Above all, readers interested in further exploring Dylan's larger cultural significance should read Marcus's *Invisible Republic: Bob Dylan's Basement Tapes* (New York, 1997), which in its paperback edition was re-titled *The Old, Weird America: The World of Bob Dylan's Basement Tapes.* Similarly stimulating, from very different perspectives, are the latest edition of Michael Gray's sprawling and endlessly fascinating *Song and Dance Man III: The Art of Bob Dylan* (London, 2000); Christopher Ricks's highly formal, playful, and brilliant close readings of Dylan's lyrics in *Dylan's Vision of Sin* (New York, 2003); and the postmodernist-influenced readings in Stephen Scobie, *Alias Bob Dylan Revisited* (Calgary, 2004). Other important and illuminating works, focused on more selective aspects of Dylan's career, include Paul Williams's multivolume study of Dylan as performer, beginning with *Performing Artist: The Music of Bob Dylan, Volume One, 1960–1973* (Novato, Calif., 1990); Aidan Day, *Jokerman: Reading the Lyrics of Bob Dylan* (Oxford, 1988); Vince Farinaccio, *Nothing to Turn Off: The Films and Video of Bob Dylan* (n.p., 2007); C. P. Lee, *Like a Bullet of Light: The Films of Bob Dylan* (London, 2000); Michael Marqusee, *Wicked Messenger: Bob Dylan and the 1960s* (2003; New York, 2005); Andy Gill and Kevin Odegard, *A Simple Twist of Fate: Bob Dylan and the Making of "Blood on the Tracks"* (New York, 2004); David Hajdu, *Positively 4th Street: The Lives and Times of Joan Baez, Bob Dylan, Mimi Baez Fariña, and Richard Fariña* (New York, 2001); Stephen W. Webb, *Dylan Redeemed: From "Highway 61" to "Saved"* (New York, 2006); and Seth Rogovoy, *Bob Dylan: Prophet, Mystic, Poet* (New York, 2009). On the comic side of Dylan's work, essential but often neglected, see Susan Wheeler's fine essay "Jokerman," in *"Do You, Mr. Jones?" Bob Dylan with the Poets and Professors,* ed. Neil Corcoran (London, 2003), 175–91. On "Visions of Johanna," see Jonny Thakar, "Visions of Infinity," *The Owl Journal* (University of Oxford, Hilary Term, 2004). The useful collections of essays and other critical writings about Dylan include Elizabeth Thomson and David Gutman, eds., *The Dylan Companion: A Collection of Essential Writings About Bob Dylan* (New York, 1990); Carl Benson, ed., *The Bob Dylan Companion: Four Decades of Commentary* (New York, 1998); Benjamin Hedin, ed., *Studio A: The Bob Dylan Reader* (New York, 2004); and Kevin J. H. Dettmar, *The Cambridge Companion to Bob Dylan* (New York, 2009).

There are also numerous films and DVDs, apart from Dylan's own films and

D. A. Pennebaker's *Dont Look Back,* that portray Dylan's life, or some portion of it. The most searching of these, even though it only covers the years through mid-1966, is Martin Scorsese's documentary *No Direction Home: Bob Dylan* (Spitfire Pictures, 2005).

CHAPTER ONE: MUSIC FOR THE COMMON MAN

The most thorough biography of Copland is Howard Pollack's discerning *Aaron Copland: The Life and Work of an Uncommon Man* (1999; Urbana, Ill., 2000). Another essential title, especially on the themes covered in this chapter, is Elizabeth B. Crist, *Music for the Common Man: Aaron Copland During the Depression and War* (New York, 2005). See also Jennifer DeLapp, *Copland in the Fifties: Music and Ideology in the McCarthy Era* (Ann Arbor, Mich., 1997). There is a fine selection of Copland's letters, Elizabeth B. Crist and Wayne Shirley, eds., *The Selected Correspondence of Aaron Copland* (New Haven, Conn., 2006), although this should be supplemented by the rich body of material in the Library of Congress's Aaron Copland Collection, some of which can be perused online at memory.loc.gov/ammem/collections/copland/index.html. Copland's own writings are best sampled in Richard Kostelanetz, ed., *Aaron Copland: A Reader: Selected Writings, 1923–1972* (New York, 2004). Useful critical interpretations of Copland's music include Neil Butterworth, *The Music of Aaron Copland* (New York, 1986); and Gail Levin and Judith Tick, *Aaron Copland's America: A Cultural Perspective* (New York, 2000). See also the essays in Peter Dickinson, ed., *Copland Connotations: Studies and Interviews* (Woodbridge, U.K., 2002), which also provides two interviews with Copland; and Carol J. Oja and Judith Tick, eds., *Aaron Copland and His World* (Princeton, N.J., 2005).

On Marc Blitzstein, see Eric A. Gordon, *Mark the Music: The Life and Work of Marc Blitzstein* (New York, 1989). Blitzstein's papers and manuscripts are kept at the Division of Archives and Manuscripts, State Historical Society of Wisconsin in Madison. There is no available recording of *Brecht on Brecht,* but Dylan listened to the recording of the 1954 Theatre de Lys production of *The Threepenny Opera,* now available on compact disc from Decca Broadway Recordings. An exceptional, if expensive, collection of Lotte Lenya's complete recorded works has been released on eleven CDs by the estimable Bear Family label, entitled *Lotte Lenya: Her Complete Recordings from 1929–1975.*

On the cultural history of the Popular Front in the United States, the most comprehensive secondary source is Michael Denning's *Cultural Front: The Laboring of American Culture in the Twentieth Century* (New York, 1997). See also, on the 1940s, the chapter about music in FDR's America in Alex Ross, *The Rest Is Noise: Listening to the Twentieth Century* (New York, 2007). On both the modernist Composers' Collective of the early to mid-1930s and the pro-Communist folk-song movement of the later 1930s and the 1940s, including Pete Seeger's People's Songs group, see Robbie Lieberman, *"My Song Is My Weapon": People's*

Songs, American Communism, and the Politics of Culture (1989; Urbana, Ill., 1995); and Richard A. Reuss with JoAnne C. Reuss, *American Folk Music and Left Wing Politics, 1927–1957* (Lanham, Md., 2000). On Charles Seeger, see Ann M. Pescatello, *Charles Seeger: A Life in American Music* (Pittsburgh, 1992).

On the folk revival and its origins, see Robert Cantwell, *When We Were Good: The Folk Revival* (Cambridge, Mass., 1996); Ronald D. Cohen, *Rainbow Quest: The Folk Music Revival and American Society, 1940–1970* (Amherst, Mass., 2002); and Dick Weissman, *Which Side Are You On? An Inside History of the Folk Music Revival in America* (New York, 2005). More particular perspectives on the revival appear in Alan Lomax, *Selected Writings, 1934–1997*, ed. Ronald D. Cohen (Oxford, 2003); and David King Dunaway, *How Can I Keep from Singing? The Ballad of Pete Seeger* (New York, 2008). On Dylan's boyhood and teenage years, in addition to the basic biographies, see Dave Engel, *Just Like Bob Zimmerman's Blues: Dylan in Minnesota* (Amherst, Wis., 1997).

19 "progress from [the] ivory tower": Carl Sands [Charles Seeger], "Copeland's [*sic*] Music Recital at Pierre Degeyter Club," *Daily Worker*, March 22, 1934.

19 "the silliest thing I did": Copland quoted in Howard Pollack, *Aaron Copland: The Life and Work of an Uncommon Man* (1999; Urbana, Ill., 2000), 276.

19 "a splendid thing": Seeger quoted in ibid., 275.

19 "Many folksongs are complacent": Seeger (as Carl Sands) quoted in Robbie Lieberman, *"My Song Is My Weapon": People's Songs, American Communism, and the Politics of Culture* (1989; Urbana, Ill., 1995), 30.

22 "It began when Victor": Copland to Israel Citkowitz, Sept. 1934, Aaron Copland Collection, Library of Congress; also in *The Selected Correspondence of Aaron Copland*, eds. Elizabeth B. Crist and Wayne Shirley (New Haven, Conn., 2006), 105–6.

22 "The summer of 1934": Pollack, *Copland*, 278.

24 "The opening night": Aaron Copland, "In Memory of Marc Blitzstein (1905–1964)," MS, Copland Collection; published in *Perspectives of New Music* 2, no. 2 (Spring–Summer, 1964), 6–7.

24 "social drama": Pollack, *Copland*, 181–82.

25 "to the mongrel commercialized interests": Diamond to Copland, June 15, 1939, Copland Collection, cited in ibid., 190.

26 "too European": Copland quoted in Pollack, *Copland*, 125.

26 "rather wary": Aaron Copland, "About Billy the Kid," n.d. [circa 1950], MS, Copland Collection.

26 "I have never been": Aaron Copland, "Notes on a Cowboy Ballet," in *Aaron Copland: A Reader: Selected Writings, 1923–1972*, ed. Richard Kostelanetz (New York, 2004), 239–40.

26 "hopelessly involved": Aaron Copland, Ibid.

27 "It's a rather delicate operation": Ibid.

28 "stammering version": Albert H. Tolman, "Some Songs Traditional in the United States," *Journal of American Folk-Lore* 29 (April–June 1916), 189.

30 "severe" music: Arthur Berger, "Copland's Piano Sonata," *Partisan Review* 10, no. 2 (March–April 1943), 187–90. Copland remained good friends with Berger despite their differences and wrote to Berger in characteristic good humor after he "came upon" Berger's *Partisan Review* essay. "I like to think," Copland remarked, "that . . . I have touched off for myself and others a kind of musical naturalness that we have badly needed—along with 'great' works." Copland to Berger, April 10, 1943, Copland Collection; also in Crist and Shirley, *Selected Correspondence*, 153–54.

30 "the speeches of Henry Wallace": Thomson quoted in Elizabeth B. Crist, *Music for the Common Man: Aaron Copland During the Depression and War* (New York, 2005), 193.

30 "mid-cult": Dwight Macdonald, "Masscult and Midcult," in *Against the American Grain: Essays on the Effects of Mass Culture* (New York, 1962), 37.

31 "The conventional concert public": Aaron Copland, "Composer from Brooklyn: An Autobiographical Sketch" (1939, 1968), in Kostelanetz, *Copland: A Reader*, xxvi.

34 "one of America's"; "straightforward without being banal": Martin Bernstein, *An Introduction to Music* (1937; New York, 1951), 430, 432.

34 "is dissolved in personal lyricism": Joseph Machlis, *The Enjoyment of Music: An Introduction to Perceptive Listening* (New York, 1955), 600.

36 "a democratic American artist": Aaron Copland, "Effect of the Cold War on the Artist in the U.S.," speech delivered to the Cultural and Scientific Conference for World Peace, New York, March 27, 1949, MS, Copland Collection.

36 "each fiat": Aaron Copland, *Music and Imagination* (1952; Cambridge, Mass., 1980), 75.

36 "a representative selection": *Life,* April 4, 1949.

38 "had never thought of myself": Copland in *Executive Sessions of the Senate Permanent Subcommittee on Investigations of the Committee on Government Operations*, 83rd Cong., 1st sess., 1953 (Washington, D.C., 2003), vol. 2, 1267–89, quotations on 1268, 1277, 1284.

38 "exactly as if": Copland quoted in Pollack, *Copland,* 516.

43 " 'Morning Anthem' ": Bob Dylan, *Chronicles: Volume One* (New York, 2004), 272.

43 "nasty song": Ibid., 275.

43 "far away from": Ibid., 276.

44 "the moral fervor": Copland, "In Memory of Marc Blitzstein."

46 "when the gifted young American": Damrosch quoted in "Nadia Boulanger, Organist, Appears," *New York Times*, Jan. 12, 1925. This quota-

tion, rendered in several different forms in subsequent biographies and critical studies, has commonly been taken as an effort by Damrosch to placate restive members of the audience who were offended by Copland's music. But the original article in the *Times* offered a very different account of what happened after Damrosch spoke: "A loud laugh went through the audience and up in his box the young American"—Copland—"laughed as loudly as the rest and applauded the sentiment."

CHAPTER TWO: PENETRATING AETHER

General appraisals of the Beat generation include Bruce Cook, *The Beat Generation* (New York, 1971); Bill Morgan, *The Beat Generation in New York* (San Francisco, 1997); John Tytell, *Naked Angels: The Life and Literature of the Beat Generation* (New York, 1976); Ann Charters, ed., *The Beats: Literary Bohemianism in Postwar America, Parts I and II,* vol. 16 of *Dictionary of Literary Biography* (Detroit, 1983); Edward Halsey Foster, *Understanding the Beats* (Columbia, S.C., 1992); Steven Watson, *The Birth of the Beat Generation: Visionaries, Rebels, and Hipsters, 1944–1960* (New York, 1995); Ann Charters, *Beat Down to Your Soul: What Was the Beat Generation?* (New York, 2001). The most useful anthology of Beat writings is Ann Charters, ed., *The Portable Beat Reader* (New York, 1992), but see also Donald M. Allen, ed., *The New American Poetry, 1945–1960* (New York, 1960); LeRoi Jones, ed., *The Moderns: An Anthology of New Writing in America* (New York, 1963); Seymour Krim, ed., *The Beats* (New York, 1960); and Elias Wilentz, ed., *The Beat Scene* (New York, 1960). Selections of critical essays can be found in Lee Bartlett, ed., *The Beats: Essays in Criticism* (New York, 1981); and Kostas Myrsiades, ed., *The Beat Generation: Critical Essays* (New York, 2002). A blend of contemporary writings about the Beats and Fred McDarrah's fine photographs appears in Fred W. McDarrah and Timothy S. McDarrah, comps., *Kerouac and Friends* (1985; New York, 2002).

The standard edition of Allen Ginsberg's poetry is Allen Ginsberg, *Collected Poems, 1947–1997* (New York, 2006). Of special importance is Bill Morgan, ed., *The Letters of Allen Ginsberg* (New York, 2008). The best biographies are Barry Miles, *Ginsberg: A Biography* (New York, 1989); and Michael Schumacher, *Dharma Lion: A Biography of Allen Ginsberg* (New York, 1992). On Ginsberg and his work, see also Jane Kramer, *Allen Ginsberg in America* (New York, 1968); and the essays in Lewis Hyde, ed., *On the Poetry of Allen Ginsberg* (Ann Arbor, Mich., 1984). On Jack Kerouac, Ann Charters's pioneering biography, *Kerouac: A Biography* (1973; New York, 1994), should be supplemented with Dennis McNally, *Desolate Angel: Jack Kerouac, the Beat Generation, and America* (New York, 1979); and Gerald Nicosia, *Memory Babe: A Critical Biography of Jack Kerouac* (New York, 1983). Of particular importance, both on Kerouac and on the Beat scene, is Joyce Johnson, *Minor Characters* (Boston, 1983). The film *Pull My*

Daisy, directed by Robert Frank and with a score by David Amram, is available on DVD in the first volume of *Robert Frank: The Complete Film Works,* released by Distributed Art Publishers.

On the literary and political worlds of the so-called New York Intellectuals, there are several places to start: Alexander Bloom, *Prodigal Sons: The New York Intellectuals and Their World* (New York, 1986); Hugh Wilford, *The New York Intellectuals: From Vanguard to Institution* (New York, 1995); and Alan M. Wald, *The New York Intellectuals: The Rise and Decline of the Anti-Stalinist Left from the 1930s to the 1980s* (Chapel Hill, N.C., 1987).

Most of Lionel Trilling's important works remain in print, but of special relevance to this chapter is *The Liberal Imagination: Essays on Literature and Society* (1950; New York, 2008). See also the excellent posthumous collection *The Moral Obligation to Be Intelligent: Selected Essays,* Leon Wieseltier, ed. (New York, 2000). A full biography has yet to be written, but for a unique perspective on Trilling's life and work, see Diana Trilling, *The Beginning of the Journey: The Marriage of Diana and Lionel Trilling* (New York, 1993). Useful studies of Trilling's criticism include William M. Chace, *Lionel Trilling: Criticism and Politics* (Stanford, Calif., 1980); Robert Boyers, *Lionel Trilling: Negative Capability and the Wisdom of Avoidance* (Columbia, Mo., 1977); Mark Krupnick, *Lionel Trilling and the Fate of Cultural Criticism* (Evanston, Ill., 1986); and the essays in John Rodden, ed., *Lionel Trilling and the Critics: Opposing Selves* (Lincoln, Neb., 1999).

On Ginsberg and Trilling's fraught relations, see Robert Genter, " 'I'm Not His Father': Lionel Trilling, Allen Ginsberg, and the Contours of Literary Modernism," *College Literature* 31, no. 2 (2004), 22–52; and Adam Kirsch, "Lionel Trilling and Allen Ginsberg: Liberal Father, Radical Son," *Virginia Quarterly Review* (Summer 2009), poems.com/special_features/prose/essay_kirsch2.php.

48 "Once I went to a movie": Jack Kerouac, "54th Chorus," in *Mexico City Blues (242 Choruses)* (1959; New York, 1994), 54.

49 "Someone handed me": Dylan as quoted in Allen Ginsberg, introduction to Jack Kerouac, *Pomes All Sizes* (San Francisco, 1992), 2.

50 "I came out of the wilderness": Dylan quoted in Cameron Crowe, liner notes to *Biograph* (1985).

50 "breathless, dynamic bop phrases": Bob Dylan, *Chronicles: Volume One* (New York, 2004), 57.

51 "the warp of wood": Jack Kerouac, *Lonesome Traveler* (1960; New York, 1994), 38.

52 "Beautiful day with Dylan": Ginsberg to Louis Ginsberg, Nov. 4, 1975, in *The Letters of Allen Ginsberg,* ed. Bill Morgan (New York, 2008), 383.

53 "He had declared": Ginsberg in Lawrence Grobel, *Endangered Species: Writers Talk About Their Craft, Their Visions, Their Lives* (New York, 2001), 169.

54 "In the early years": Ginsberg quoted in Alfred G. Aronowitz, "Portrait of a Beat," *Nugget,* Oct. 1960, in *Kerouac and Friends,* comp. Fred W. McDarrah and Timothy S. McDarrah (1985; New York, 2002), 106.

55 "a kind of intellectual calisthenic": Lionel Trilling, *The Liberal Imagination: Essays on Literature and Society* (1950; New York, 2008), 183.

56 "the value of individual existence": Lionel Trilling, "Art, Will, and Necessity," in *The Moral Obligation to Be Intelligent: Selected Essays,* ed. Leon Wieseltier (New York, 2000), 511.

56 "moral realism": Trilling, *The Liberal Imagination,* 219.

56 "unaffected by moral compunction": Ginsberg to Trilling, Sept. 4, 1945, quoted in Robert Genter, " 'I'm Not His Father': Lionel Trilling, Allen Ginsberg, and the Contours of Literary Modernism," *College Literature* 31, no. 2 (2004), 37.

56 "an absolutism": Trilling to Ginsberg, Sept. 11, 1945, quoted in ibid., 38.

56 "cheap trick": Ginsberg to John Hollander, Sept. 7, 1958, in Morgan, *Letters of Allen Ginsberg,* 215.

57 "the shadowy and heterogeneous": Ginsberg to Trilling, Dec. [?], 1948, quoted in Genter, " 'I'm Not His Father,' " 43.

59 "It's my old school": Ginsberg to Ferlinghetti, March 6, 1959, quoted in Barry Miles, *Ginsberg: A Biography* (New York, 1989), 260.

60 "goddamn anarchist": Asch quoted in Peter D. Goldsmith, *Making People's Music: Moe Asch and Folkways Records* (Washington, D.C., 1998), 4.

63 "silly milly": Ted Joans, "I Love a Big Bird," in *Bird: The Legend of Charlie Parker,* ed. Robert G. Reisner (1962; New York, 1977), 117.

63 "We all play": Monk quoted in Dylan, *Chronicles,* 95.

64 "jazz snob": Van Ronk remark in *No Direction Home: Bob Dylan,* directed by Martin Scorsese (Spitfire Pictures, 2005). See also Dave Van Ronk, *The Mayor of MacDougal Street: A Memoir* (New York, 2005).

64 "I tried to discern": Dylan, *Chronicles,* 94.

64 "listening to Ray Charles blues": Allen Ginsberg, "Kaddish," in *Collected Poems, 1947–1997* (New York, 2006), 217.

66 "There used to be": Scott Cohen, "Bob Dylan Not Like a Rolling Stone Interview," *Spin,* Dec. 1985, reprinted in *Younger Than That Now: The Collected Interviews with Bob Dylan,* ed. James Ellison (New York, 2004), 223.

66 "the French guys": Ibid.

66 "jail songs": Bob Dylan, "11 Outlined Epitaphs," liner notes to *The Times They Are A-Changin'* (1964), www.bobdylan.com/#/music/times-they-are-changin.

67 "to enlist the romantic dream": Norman Mailer, "Superman Comes to the Supermarket," *Esquire,* Nov. 1960, www.esquire.com/features/superman-supermarket-6.

67 "there's only up and down": "Transcript of Bob Dylan's Remarks at the

Bill of Rights Dinner at the Americana Hotel on 12/13/63," www.corlisslamont.org/dylan.htm.

69 "Allen was really": Aronowitz quoted in Clinton Heylin, *Bob Dylan: Behind the Shades: Take Two* (London, 2000), 139.

69 "I might become his slave": Ginsberg quoted in Miles, *Ginsberg,* 334.

69 "the colors of friday were dull": Dylan quoted in Heylin, *Behind the Shades: Take Two,* 143.

69 "Okay. Are there any poets": *Dont Look Back: A Film and Book by D. A. Pennebaker* (New York, 1968), 113.

72 "sort of a horror cowboy movie": Television interview with Les Crane, *The Les Crane Show,* Feb. 17, 1965, transcript available at Giulio Molfese's Web site, Bread Crumb Sins, www.interferenza.com/bcs/interw/65-feb17.htm.

74 "i have": Bob Dylan, liner notes to *Bringing It All Back Home* (1965), www.bobdylan.com/#/music/bringing-it-all-back-home.

74 "Do you think": Jonathan Cott, ed., *Bob Dylan: The Essential Interviews* (New York, 2006), 63.

75 "Dylan has sold out to God": Ginsberg quoted in Heylin, *Behind the Shades: Take Two,* 223.

76 "new ax for composition": Ginsberg quoted in Miles, *Ginsberg,* 381.

76 "joked that Ginsberg"; "a bit of taunt and tease": Anne Waldman, "Dylan and the Beats," in *Highway 61 Revisited: Bob Dylan's Road from Minnesota to the World,* eds. Colleen J. Sheehy and Thomas Swiss (Minneapolis, 2009), 255.

78 "ringing at dawn": Allen Ginsberg, "I Am a Victim of Telephone" (1964), in *Collected Poems, 1947–1997,* 352.

78 "which is the power": Allen Ginsberg, "Kral Majales" (1965), in ibid., 361.

78 "Angelic Dylan": Allen Ginsberg, "Wichita Vortex Sutra" (1966), in ibid., 417.

80 "There aren't any finger pointing songs": Dylan quoted in Nat Hentoff, "The Crackin', Shakin', Breakin' Sounds," *New Yorker,* Oct. 24, 1964, reprinted in Cott, *Essential Interviews,* 15–16.

80 "join[ing] images": Allen Ginsberg, *Journals: Mid-Fifties, 1954–1958,* ed., Gordon Ball (New York, 1995), 142.

80 "telescoping of images": T. S. Eliot, "The Metaphysical Poets" (1921), in *The Selected Prose of T. S. Eliot,* ed. Frank Kermode (New York, 1975), 60.

82 "a certain drear": Jack Kerouac, *Desolation Angels* (1965; New York, 1980), 222. On Dylan's modernism, special thanks to Anne Margaret Daniel.

82 "Oh, that's someplace in Mexico": Television press conference, KQED (San Francisco), Dec. 3, 1965, in Cott, *Essential Interviews,* 72.

84 "to be a rock star": Mark Shurilla quoted in Eric Hoffman, "Poetry Jukebox: How Rock and Roll Found Literature and Literature Found Rock

and Roll: The Story of Allen Ginsberg and Bob Dylan," *Isis* 145 (July–Aug. 2009), 41.

CHAPTER THREE: DARKNESS AT THE BREAK OF NOON

An earlier version of this chapter appeared as the liner notes to *The Bootleg Series, Vol. 6: Bob Dylan Live 1964: Concert at Philharmonic Hall* (Sony/Legacy Records, 2003). Unless noted below, all quotations in this chapter can be found on that album.

89 "SHUT UP": Johnny Cash, "Letter to *Broadside*," *Broadside*, March 10, 1964, in *Studio A: The Bob Dylan Reader,* ed. Benjamin Hedin (New York, 2004), 21.

89 "new songs": Irwin Silber, "An Open Letter to Bob Dylan," *Sing Out!* Nov. 1964, www.edlis.org/twice/threads/open_letter_to_bob_dylan.html.

103 "the voice of a generation": "The Rome Interview" (2001), www.expecting rain.com/dok/cd/2001/romeinterview.html.

CHAPTER FOUR: THE SOUND OF 3:00 A.M.

An earlier version of this chapter appeared as "Mystic Nights: The Making of *Blonde on Blonde* in Nashville," *The Oxford American,* no. 58 (2007), 142–49.

Unless noted below, all quotations in this chapter are from the New York and Nashville session tapes to *Blonde on Blonde,* courtesy of Special Rider Music.

105 "a minority of": Interview with Klas Burling, April 29, 1966, www .interferenza.com/bcs/interw/66-apr29.htm.

106 "that thin": Interview with Ron Rosenbaum, *Playboy,* March 1978, reprinted in *Bob Dylan: The Essential Interviews,* ed. Jonathan Cott (New York, 2006), 208.

107 "nobody has ever captured": Kooper quoted in Howard Sounes, *Down the Highway: The Life of Bob Dylan* (New York, 2001), 205.

108 "He never did anything twice": Johnston in Richard Younger, "An Exclusive Interview with Bob Johnston," n.d., www.b-dylan.com/pages/ samples/bobjohnston.html.

114 "half Gershwin": Jonathan Singer to David Hinckley, March 4, 1999, www.steelydan.com/griffin.html.

114 "We knew we had cut": Kooper, interview with author, Nov. 13, 2006.

115 "After that": McCoy, interview with Richie Unterberger, n.d., www .richieunterberger.com/mccoy.html.

116 "everybody knew": McCoy, interview with author, Nov. 20, 2006.

117 "standoffish": Robertson quoted in Sounes, *Down the Highway,* 201.

117 "Those guys welcomed us in": Kooper, interview with author.

117 "I wouldn't have *dared*": Kristofferson quoted in David Bowman, "Kris Kristofferson," *Salon,* Sept. 24, 1999, dir.salon.com/people/lunch/1999/09/24/kristofferson.

117 "It made all the difference": Buttrey quoted in Bob Spitz, *Dylan: A Biography* (New York, 1991), 339.

117 "the artist and the song": McCoy, interview with Unterberger.

117 "was just unheard of": McCoy, interview with author.

118 "Jesu, Joy of Man's Desiring": Thanks to Anne Margaret Daniel for this point.

118 "I saw Dylan sitting": Kristofferson quoted in Bowman, "Kristofferson."

118 "But he wasn't": Johnston quoted in Louis Black, "Page Two: A Personal Journey, Part 2," *Austin Chronicle,* May 25, 2007, www.austinchronicle.com/gyrobase/Issue/column?oid=oid:477920.

119 "After you've tried": McCoy, interview with Unterberger.

119 "If you notice": Buttrey quoted in Clinton Heylin, *Bob Dylan: Behind the Shades: Take Two* (London, 2000), 241.

123 "That sounds like": Johnston and Dylan quoted in Louis Black, "Momentum and the Mountainside Sound," *Austin Chronicle,* Sept. 30, 2005, www.austinchronicle.com/gyrobase/Issue/story?oid=oid:293992.

123 "It just didn't happen": McCoy, interview with author.

123 "all of us walking around"; "It's the only one time": Black, "Page Two."

125 "They couldn't have any charts": Johnston quoted in Black, "Page Two."

128 "as goofy": McCoy, interview with author.

128 "Everything was different": Ibid.

CHAPTER FIVE: CHILDREN OF PARADISE

The key sources on the Rolling Thunder Revue are Sam Shepard, *Rolling Thunder Logbook* (1977; New York, 1978); and Larry "Ratso" Sloman, *On the Road with Bob Dylan* (1978; New York, 2002). See also Sloman's liner notes to *The Bootleg Series, Vol. 5: Bob Dylan Live 1975: The Rolling Thunder Revue* (Sony/Legacy Records, 2002), a compilation of performances in Worcester, Boston, Cambridge, and Montreal. Norman Raeben and his influence on Dylan are discussed in Bert Cartwright, "The Mysterious Norman Raeben," in *Wanted Man: In Search of Bob Dylan,* ed. John Bauldie (London, 1990), 85–90, and www.geocities.com/athens/forum/2667/raeben.htm. Interesting considerations of *Renaldo and Clara* and the rest of Dylan's films appear in C. P. Lee, *Like a Bullet of Light: The Films of Bob Dylan* (London, 2000); and in Vince Farinaccio, *Nothing to Turn Off: The Films and Video of Bob Dylan* (n.p., 2007). On the background to "Tangled Up in Blue" and the rest of *Blood on the Tracks,* see Andy Gill and Kevin Odegard, *A Simple Twist of Fate: Bob Dylan and the Making of "Blood on the Tracks"* (New York, 2004). I was able to hear a compact disc made from an audience tape of the afternoon show in New Haven on November 13, 1975, which helped refresh my memories of the show; recordings of the concert also circulate as bootleg CDs under the titles *New Haven* (Morose Moose Music Company) and *New Haven, Connecticut, U.S.A., 13.11.75 Afternoon Show* (Great North Woods).

136 "It's like I had amnesia": Dylan quoted in Bert Cartwright, "The Mysterious Norman Raeben," in *Wanted Man: In Search of Bob Dylan,* ed. John Bauldie (London, 1990), 87.

136 "down, down, down": Interview with Jonathan Cott, *Rolling Stone,* Nov. 16, 1978, reprinted in *Bob Dylan: The Essential Interviews,* ed. Jonathan Cott (New York, 2006), 260.

137 "I found I could stand": Dylan quoted in Alan Jackson, "Bob Dylan: He's Got Everything He Needs, He's an Artist, He Don't Look Back," *Times* (London), June 6, 2008.

139 "rich old ladies": Dylan quoted in Cartwright, "Mysterious Norman Raeben," 86.

139 "how to see": Ibid., 87.

140 "I was just trying": Dylan quoted in Cameron Crowe, liner notes to *Biograph* (1985); also Cartwright, "Mysterious Norman Raeben," 89.

142 "something different": [Camilla McGuinn], "Roadie Report 31—the Rolling Thunder Revue," Roger McGuinn blog, rogermcguinn.blogspot.com/2007/11/roadie-report-31-rolling-thunder-revue.html.

144 "Roger!": Dylan quoted in Larry "Ratso" Sloman, *On the Road with Bob Dylan* (1978; New York, 2002), 4.

154 "That's our slogan": Dylan quoted in ibid.

156 "just like Marlon Brando": Dylan on what is familiarly known as the "Minnesota Hotel Tapes," recorded in 1960.

157 "He was having": Carolina A. Miranda, "Q&A with D. A. Pennebaker," *Time,* Feb. 26, 2007, at www.time.com/time/arts/article/0, 8599, 1593766, 00.html.

158 "Really, I'm trying to be Ibsen": Pennebaker quoted in ibid.

159 "is improvised, about a third is determined": Interview with Cott, *Rolling Stone,* Jan. 26, 1978, reprinted in Cott, *Essential Interviews,* 191.

160 "naked alienation of the inner self": Ibid., 178.

161 "a kind of *Children of Paradise*": Levy quoted in Vince Farinaccio, *Nothing to Turn Off: The Films and Video of Bob Dylan* (n.p., 2007), 93.

162 "Something like that": Sam Shepard, *Rolling Thunder Logbook* (1977; New York, 1978), 13.

167 "Bicentennial madness": Ibid., 45.

167 "a Bicentennial picture": Ginsberg to Louis Ginsberg, Nov. 4, 1975, in *The Letters of Allen Ginsberg,* ed. Bill Morgan (New York, 2008), 383.

169 "off and on": Radio interview with Cynthia Gooding, WBAI (New York), March 11, 1962, in Cott, *Essential Interviews,* 3.

169 "a route song": Dylan, concert remarks at Town Hall, New York, April 12, 1963. There have been two bootleg releases of this performance: one, on the Colosseum label, *Bob Dylan in Concert,* a "live" album that Columbia Records had intended to release but then scrapped; and a more recent release, on the Rattlesnake label, of the complete soundboard recording of the Town Hall concert, with the title *New York Town Hall 1963.*

169 "the traveling performers": "Bob Dylan Talks About the New Album with Bill Flanagan," www.bobdylan.com/#/conversation?page=5.

170 "wanna make you have two thoughts": Radio interview with Gooding, as transcribed from Bob Dylan with Cynthia Gooding, *Folksinger's Choice,* bootleg CD (Yellow Dog). Jonathan Cott's rendering, in his compilation of Dylan's essential interviews, truncates Dylan and Gooding's conversation; see the transcription at www.expectingrain.com/dok/int/gooding.html.

CHAPTER SIX: MANY MARTYRS FELL

The most exacting study of Blind Willie McTell, interwoven with the author's impressions of the American South today, is Michael Gray, *Hand Me My Travelin' Shoes: In Search of Blind Willie McTell* (2007; London, 2008). Gray includes a detailed discography of McTell's performances, but readers may also wish to consult the illustrated McTell discography at Stefan Wirz's fine Web site, American Music, www.wirz.de/music/mctelfrm.htm. The list of books, articles, and Web sites on the blues is enormous and growing rapidly. Two books deserve special mention for their pioneering and enduring contributions: Samuel Charters, *The Country Blues* (1959; New York, 1975); and Paul Oliver, *Blues Fell This Morning: The Meaning of the Blues* (New York, 1960). John Lomax's life and career are covered in *The Last Cavalier: The Life and Times of John A. Lomax, 1867–1948* (Urbana, Ill., 1996). On Alan Lomax's writings, see the selected readings for Chapter One. I was able to listen to the session tape demo of "Blind Willie McTell," as recorded in New York on May 5, 1983, which became the basis for the track released in 1991 on *The Bootleg Series, Vols. 1–3: Rare and Unreleased, 1961–1991.*

172 "I wonder": The entire dialogue between Lomax and McTell comes from the 1940 Library of Congress recording, labeled, oddly, by Lomax as "Monologue on Accidents," on disc 5 of the comprehensive six-CD selection *Blind Willie McTell: King of the Georgia Blues* (Snapper Records, 2007); as well as on a separate release of the 1940 session, *Blind Willie McTell 1940* (Document Records, 1990).

178 "I told you": Dylan, in *Saved! The Gospel Speeches,* ed. Clinton Heylin (Madras, 1990), 12–13.

182 "just made my hair stand up": Dylan quoted in "The 100 Greatest Sing-

ers of All Time: 56—Mavis Staples," *Rolling Stone,* Nov. 27, 2008, www.rollingstone.com/news/coverstory/24161972/page/56.

182 "fall into any category": Dylan quoted in Clinton Heylin, *Bob Dylan: Behind the Shades: Take Two* (London, 2000), 548.

186 "I run away and went everywhere": McTell remarks on Blind Willie McTell, *Last Session,* originally released in 1960 and rereleased on several occasions, in LP and CD form, most recently as a CD by Fantasy Records in 2007. The album is now also available for MP3 download.

188 "Baby, I was born to ramble": McTell quoted in Michael Gray, *Hand Me My Travelin' Shoes: In Search of Blind Willie McTell* (2007; London, 2008), 180.

189 "He always had him a contract": Kate McTell quoted in ibid., 235.

189 "They lived"; "He never allowed"; "a keen sense of scripture": W. Andrew Williams quoted in ibid., 240–42.

190 "brilliant but elusive": Samuel Charters, *The Country Blues* (1959; New York, 1975), 93.

190 "On Blind Willie McTell": Peter Guralnick, *Feel Like Going Home: Portraits in Blues and Rock 'n' Roll* (1971; Boston, 1999), 23.

194 "I jump 'em from other writers": McTell remarks on *Last Session.*

201 "God's in His heaven": Robert Browning, "Pippa Passes: A Drama," in *The Complete Works of Robert Browning* (New York, 1898), vol. 1, 193.

201 "But God is in Heaven": Herman Melville, "The Fall of Richmond: The Tidings Received in the Northern Metropolis (April, 1865)," in *Battle-Pieces and Aspects of the War* (New York, 1866), 136.

203 "Perhaps the most entrancing": Greil Marcus, *The Dustbin of History* (Cambridge, Mass., 1995), 84.

206 "The past is never dead": Gavin Stevens in William Faulkner, *Requiem for a Nun,* act 1, scene 3 (New York, 1951).

CHAPTER SEVEN: ALL THE FRIENDS
I EVER HAD ARE GONE

The basic secondary sources on "Delia" are John Garst, "Delia's Gone—Where Did She Come From, Where Did She Go?" paper delivered at the twentieth annual International Country Music Conference, Belmont University, Nashville, May 2003, kindly provided to the author by John Garst; and Sean Wilentz, "The Sad Song of Delia Green and Cooney Houston," in *The Rose and the Briar: Death, Love, and Liberty in the American Ballad,* eds. Sean Wilentz and Greil Marcus (New York, 2005), 147–58. This chapter draws heavily on the latter, although it has been thoroughly revised and corrected.

210 "I'd kind of reached": David Gates, "Dylan Revisited," *Newsweek,* Oct. 6, 1997, www.newsweek.com/id/97107.

210 "felt done for": Bob Dylan, *Chronicles: Volume One* (New York, 2004), 147.

213 "Sinatra, Peggy Lee, yeah": Dylan, interview with Mikal Gilmore, *Los Angeles Herald Examiner,* Oct. 13, 1985.

215 "It's never been simple": Interview with Nora Ephron and Susan Edmiston, "Positively Tie Dream," Aug. 1965, reprinted in *Bob Dylan: The Essential Interviews,* ed. Jonathan Cott (New York, 2006), 50.

215 "the songs would come": Dylan quoted in Clinton Heylin, *Bob Dylan: Behind the Shades: Take Two* (London, 2000), 671.

215 "If you can sing those": Ibid.

217 "Why, the judge": Baker quoted in Cecil Brown, "We Did Them Wrong: The Ballad of Frankie and Albert," in *The Rose and the Briar: Death, Love, and Liberty in the American Ballad,* eds. Sean Wilentz and Greil Marcus (New York, 2005), 138.

218 "I killed the President": Czolgosz quoted in *Buffalo Express,* Oct. 30, 1901.

219 "got worried about": Davis quoted in Stefan Grossman, "Reverend Gary Davis Interview," Stefan Grossman's Guitar Workshop, www.guitarvideos .com/interviews/davis.

219 "that song about Delia": Davis quoted in ibid.

220 "No, I ain't never heard of him": Davis quoted in ibid.

220 "I wouldn't want to forget": W. C. Handy, *Father of the Blues: An Autobiography* (1941; New York, 1991), 28.

223 "older and wiser": Johnny Cash with Patrick Carr, *Cash: The Autobiography* (1997; New York, 2003), 255.

230 "Now Coonie an' his little sweetheart": "Delia Holmes (Will Winn's Version)," in Chapman J. Milling, "Delia Holmes—a Neglected Negro Ballad," *Southern Folklore Quarterly* 1, no. 4 (Dec. 1937), 4–7.

235 "When Dylan sings": Bill Flanagan, "My Back Pages," *Musician,* Dec. 1993, 86.

CHAPTER EIGHT: DYLAN AND THE SACRED HARP

The pioneering scholar of shape-note music and the Sacred Harp tradition was George Pullen Jackson, whose most important studies include *White Spirituals in the Southern Uplands* (Chapel Hill, N.C., 1933); *Spiritual Folk-Songs of Early America* (Locust Valley, N.Y., 1937); *White and Negro Spirituals: Their Life Span and Kinship* (Locust Valley, N.Y., 1943); and *The Story of the Sacred Harp, 1844–1944* (Nashville, 1944). It is important to supplement Jackson's work with more recent scholarship, above all Buell E. Cobb Jr., *The Sacred Harp: A Tradition and Its Music* (1978; Athens, Ga., 1989); and Dorothy D. Horn, *Sing to Me of Heaven: A Study of Folk and Early American Materials in Three Old Harp Books* (Gainesville, Fla., 1970). On the deep historical background, see Manfred Bukofzer, "Popular Polyphony in the Middle Ages," *Musical Quarterly* 26 (Jan. 1940), 31–49.

The story of Joseph Thomas and of the composition and evolution of "The Lone Pilgrim" comes basically from the primary sources noted below. A number of them are easily accessible online at the Joseph Thomas page in the collection of Restoration Movement Texts posted by Memorial University of Newfoundland, www.mun.ca/rels/restmov/people/josthomas.html. See also Thomas Commuck, *Indian Melodies* (New York, 1845). For background on the numerous religious movements and revivals in the early American republic of which Thomas's mission was a part, the best starting place is Nathan O. Hatch, *The Democratization of American Christianity* (New Haven, Conn., 1989).

238 "Tunes, Hymns": William Walker, "Preface to the Former Edition," *The Southern Harmony and Musical Companion* (1835; Philadelphia, 1854), iii.

239 "And let this feeble body fail": Walker, "Hallelujah," in ibid., 107.

239 "great many good airs": Walker, "Preface to the Former Edition," iii.

242 "Why should we start": Walker, "Prospect," in *Southern Harmony*, 92.

243 "I have endeavoured"; "with a number"; "Those that are partial": Walker, "Preface to the Former Edition," iii.

244 "Deep on the palms": "Africa," in *The Complete Works of William Billings*, ed. Hans Nathan (Boston, 1977–90), vol. 2, 46–47.

247 "my gift in speaking": Thomas quoted in P. J. Kernodle, *Lives of Christian Ministers* (Richmond, 1909), 80.

247 "uncontrollable power": Joseph Thomas, *The Life and Gospel Labors of Joseph Thomas, Minister of the Gospel and Elder in the Christian Church* (1812), cited in Nathan O. Hatch, *The Democratization of American Christianity* (New Haven, Conn., 1989), 79.

247 "purely calculated": Joseph Thomas, *The Pilgrim's Hymn Book, Consisting of Hymns & Spiritual Songs Designed for the Public and Private Worship of God* (1816; Winchester, Va., 1817), vi.

247 "a full and faithful testimony": Joseph Thomas, *The Life, Travels, and Gospel Labors of Eld. Joseph Thomas, More Widely Known as the "White Pilgrim"* (New York, 1861), 87.

248 "the sweetest strains": The Reverend H. B. Hayes quoted in Kernodle, *Lives,* 82.

248 "bloody whips"; "the poor are rich": Joseph Thomas, "State of Ohio, Mad River, August 10th, 1817," in *The Life of the Pilgrim Joseph Thomas, Containing an Accurate Account of His Trials, Travels, and Gospel Labours, up to the Present Date* (Winchester, Va., 1817), 370–71.

253 "Let me arise": Joseph Thomas, "The Allurements of the World Forsaken," in *Life, Travels, and Gospel Labors,* 164.

253 "eerie and enticing": Robert Christgau, review of *World Gone Wrong*, www.robertchristgau.com/get_artist.php?name+bobdylan.

254 "exceptional": Clinton Heylin, *Bob Dylan: Behind the Shades: Take Two* (London, 2000), 679.

255 "It's a spooky record": David Gates, "Dylan Revisited," *Newsweek,* Oct. 6, 1997, www.newsweek.com/id/97107.

258 "I think we were": Interview with Murray Engleheart, *Guitar World* and *Uncut,* March 1999, reprinted in *Bob Dylan: The Essential Interviews,* ed. Jonathan Cott (New York, 2006), 405.

CHAPTER NINE: THE MODERN MINSTREL RETURNS

On early blackface minstrelsy, see the book whose title Dylan plainly borrowed, Eric Lott, *Love and Theft: Blackface Minstrelsy and the American Working Class* (New York, 1993); but also see Dale Cockrell, *Demons of Disorder: Early Blackface Minstrels and Their World* (New York, 1997), from which Dylan also seems to have borrowed (see the note for p. 291) and which presents a view of minstrelsy somewhat different from Lott's book. See also Lott's commentary on *"Love and Theft"* in the *Cambridge Companion* volume cited above under general reading.

A comprehensive history of George Wein's Newport Folk Festival—which celebrated its fiftieth anniversary in 2009—is long overdue. Wein devoted a chapter to the festival in his memoir, written with Nate Chinen, *Myself Among Others: A Life in Music* (2003; New York, 2004). (Most of the book concerns Wein's exploits in jazz, including his invention of the Newport Jazz Festival in 1954.) There is also a good deal of information about the festival in Eric Von Schmidt and Jim Rooney's excellent mixture of memoir and history, *Baby, Let Me Follow You Down: The Illustrated Story of the Cambridge Folk Years* (1979; Amherst, Mass., 1994).

Dylan's rock-and-roll performance in 1965—on the final evening bill immediately following the traditional country folksinger Cousin Emmy—has been the subject of endless debate and fascination. So charged was Dylan's appearance among the folk-song lovers—and especially among the festival's old guard—that contradictory stories abound, sometimes from the same person. Part of the problem is that music which appeared to some as offensive to certain folk sensibilities in 1965 went on to win acclaim as well as popularity, leading some participants to revise their stories. Pete Seeger, for one, has flatly denied that Dylan's new style upset him; and he has often claimed, as he does in Martin Scorsese's *No Direction Home,* that he objected vehemently not to the music but to the excruciating volume and distortion of the sound system. Yet a memo that Seeger wrote to himself at the time tells a different story, of a reaction to Dylan's new music in 1965 not unlike the traditional Popular Front outrage that Irwin Silber expressed the previous year in *Sing Out!* magazine, about Dylan's turn from the political to the personal. "Last week at Newport," Seeger wrote, "I ran to hide my eyes and ears because I could not bear either the screaming of the crowd nor some of the most destructive music this side of Hell." See David King Dunaway,

How Can I Keep from Singing? The Ballad of Pete Seeger (New York, 2008), 306. George Wein's memoir affirms that "at the sound of the first amplified chords, a crimson color rose in Pete's face, and he ran off. The rest of us [on the festival's official board] were just as shocked and upset . . . This was a sacrilege, as far as the folk world was concerned" (332–33).

In lieu of any thorough study of Newport, and of Dylan's performances there, see the two excellent documentary films by Murray Lerner, both available on DVD: *Festival!* containing general footage from 1963 through 1965; and *The Other Side of the Mirror: Bob Dylan at the Newport Folk Festival, 1963–1965.*

A Face in the Crowd, directed by Elia Kazan, is available on DVD from Warner Home Video.

262 "U.S. go home!": Clinton Heylin, *Bob Dylan: Behind the Shades: Take Two* (London, 2000), 258.

264 " 'Nigger' singing with them": Walt Whitman, "True American Singing," *Brooklyn Star,* Jan. 13, 1846.

269 "Faith is the key!": Bob Dylan, liner notes to *John Wesley Harding* (1968), bobdylan.com/#/music/john-wesley-harding.

269 "the brilliant, and the warm-blooded": *The Collected Works of Abraham Lincoln*, ed. Roy P. Basler (New Brunswick, 1953), vol. 1, 278.

277 "COMPLICATED"; "An I got nothin": Bob Dylan, "For Dave Glover," in the Newport Folk Festival program, 1963, posted on the site Dylan's Miscellany, homepage.mac.com/tedgoranson/BeatlesArchives/dylan writings/ Dylan_s_Miscellany/For_Dave_Glover10.html.

278 "hyper Zen": Ray quoted in liner notes to Koerner, Ray, and Glover, *Lots More Blues, Rags, and Hollers* (1964).

CHAPTER TEN: BOB DYLAN'S CIVIL WARS

288 "the emissary from a reinvented yesterday": Jon Pareles, "The Pilgrim's Progress of Bob Dylan," *New York Times,* Aug. 20, 2006.

289 "I had some vague idea": Melville to Sophia Peabody Hawthorne, Jan. 8, 1852, in Herman Melville, *Correspondence,* ed. Lynn Horth (Evanston, Ill., 1993), 219.

290 "the dark princes": "(Masked and Anonymous) Screenplay by Sergei Petrov & Rene Fontaine Revised Draft 5/21/02," 4, collection of the author.

290 "cupidity [and] corruption": Ibid., 88–89. The omitted speech, spoken to Jack Fate and the others gathered at the caudillo's deathbed, contains the following lines:

> Let me say we no longer have any cause to fear danger from abroad. Our strength and power is well known throughout the civilized

world. It is from amongst ourselves, from cupidity, corruption, disappointed ambition, and inordinate thirst for power that factions will be formed and liberty endangered. It is against such designs that we especially have to guard ourselves. Whatever disguises the actors may assume, we have the highest of human trust committed to our care.

Compare this with Jackson's Farewell Address, delivered in 1837, including the line about disguised actors (emphasis mine):

You *have no longer any cause to fear danger from abroad; your strength and power are well known throughout the civilized world,* as well as the high and gallant bearing of your sons. *It is from within, among yourselves, from cupidity, from corruption, from disappointed ambition, and inordinate thirst for power, that factions will be formed and liberty endangered. It is against such designs, whatever disguise the actors may assume, that you have especially to guard yourselves. You have the highest of human trusts committed to your care.*

In *Masked and Anonymous,* Edmund delivers a rather different version of the speech at the film's conclusion. It is unclear why the filmmakers decided to drop the Jacksonian original.

291 "masked and anonymous": Dale Cockrell, *Demons of Disorder: Early Blackface Minstrels and Their World* (New York, 1997), 122.

293 "just be another song": Television press conference, KQED (San Francisco), Dec. 3, 1965, in *Bob Dylan: The Essential Interviews,* ed. Jonathan Cott (New York, 2006), 65.

293 "like a great Bob Dylan song": Charles in Shelley Cameron, "Interview with Larry Charles," Reel Movie Critic.com, July 2003, www.reelmovie critic.com/20035q/id1996.htm.

294 "for they were employed": 1 Chronicles 9:33.

294 "Gratitude": Christopher Ricks, Inaugural Lecture as Professor of Poetry, University of Oxford, *Times Literary Supplement,* Feb. 25, 2005, 13.

295 "death, God and the universe": Bob Dylan, *Chronicles: Volume One* (New York, 2004), 81.

295 "He sang his songs": Ibid., 14.

296 "Just keep playing": Levon Helm with Stephen Davis, *This Wheel's on Fire: Levon Helm and the Story of the Band* (New York, 1993), 134.

296 "back betty": Bob Dylan, *Tarantula* (New York, 1971), 12.

298 "The world"; "if you were born": Dylan, *Chronicles,* 28–29.

298 "It was said": Ibid., 30.

299 "How much did I know": Ibid., 75–76.

299 "A political poem": Ibid., 38.

299 "cast off gloomy habits": Ibid., 56.

300 "tied to the circumstances": Ibid., 76.

301 "even in a simple, melodic"; "to change over": Ibid., 83.

301 "After a while": Ibid., 85.

301 "Back there, America": Ibid., 86.

301 "one where actions": Ibid., 235–36.

302 "printing away": Ibid., 103.

302 "If someone were to ask": Ibid.

303 "One night": Ibid., 165.

CHAPTER ELEVEN: DREAMS, SCHEMES, AND THEMES

My thinking in this chapter has been sharpened by Roy Kelly's challenging article "A Shiny Bed of Lights: Bob Dylan's Modified Versions," *The Bridge,* no. 28 (Winter 2007), 19–68.

310 "a link": Seeger quoted in David King Dunaway, *How Can I Keep from Singing? The Ballad of Pete Seeger* (New York, 2008), xii.

312 "information collage": Jon Pareles, "Plagiarism in Dylan, or a Cultural Collage?" *New York Times,* July 12, 2003.

312 "possible plagiarism": Robert Polito, "Bob Dylan: Henry Timrod Revisited," *Poetry Foundation Journal* (2006), www.poetryfoundation.org/journal/article.html?id=178703.

312 "immature poets imitate": T. S. Eliot, *The Sacred Wood and Major Early Essays* (New York, 1997), 72, originally published in 1920.

313 "The age": Bob Dylan, *Chronicles: Volume One* (New York, 2004), 86.

317 "I find the religiosity": Dylan quoted in Clinton Heylin, *Bob Dylan: Behind the Shades: Take Two* (London, 2000), 719–20.

319 "Thanks everybody!": Dylan remarks at State Theatre, Sydney, New South Wales, Australia, March 25, 1992, transcribed as BobTalk on Olof Bjorner's site, Olof's Files, www.bjorner.com/DSN12860%20-%201992%20Australian%20Tour.htm#DSN12860.

320 "I had ambitions": Dylan transcribed from *No Direction Home: Bob Dylan,* directed by Martin Scorsese (Spitfire Pictures, 2005).

325 "Aw Ratso": Dylan quoted in Sloman, liner notes to *Tell Tale Signs* (2008).

326 "it looks like things": Dylan remarks at Northrop Auditorium, University of Minnesota, Minneapolis, Nov. 4, 2008, www.youtube.com/watch?v=mVfvLEhWmbA.

330 "the fourth part of the day": Geoffrey Chaucer, *The Canterbury Tales,* trans. David Wright (New York, 2008), 113.

DISCOGRAPHY

All but one of Dylan's albums are available on compact disc and may be downloaded as MP3s on the Internet. *Dylan,* the Columbia "revenge" album released in 1973, never made it to CD in the United States, although a CD has appeared in Europe under the knowing title *Bob Dylan (A Fool Such as I).* The album may also be downloaded, if a listener is determined enough to find it. A complete list of the albums, and the lyrics to "George Jackson," which only appeared as a 45 rpm single, appear at www.bobdylan.com.

There are numerous compilations and tribute albums, the latter consisting mainly of other artists playing Dylan's songs; Dylan has also appeared on albums paying tribute to the music of others, including Jimmie Rodgers and the Stanley Brothers. My favorite of all the compilations—the one I find most illuminating as well as enjoyable—is a selection of Dylan's "Christian period" songs, *Gotta Serve Somebody: The Gospel Songs of Bob Dylan,* released by Sony/Columbia in 2003. Featuring major artists such as Shirley Caesar and Aaron Neville, as well as groups such as the Mighty Clouds of Joy, the album also includes an amusing back-and-forth between Dylan and Mavis Staples, preceding their duet performance of "Gonna Change My Way of Thinking." The album's excellent liner notes, written in part by Tom Piazza, link each song to a Bible passage, underscoring how Dylan's engagement with Christianity as well as with American sacred song did not end in the early 1980s and how it continues to this day.

However unfair to artists and their record companies, bootleg recordings, especially of concerts, are now a fact of life. Dylan and Sony/Legacy have responded by issuing an "official" bootleg series, which allows listeners to have the best-possible-quality recordings of some important outtakes and concerts without robbing the creators of compensation. Still, without access to some of the illicit variety, my own work would have been constrained. And so, without endorsing any illegality, I can recommend what I have found to be the best Web site for descriptions and reviews of Dylan bootlegs, www.bobsboots.com.

Bob Dylan in America cites numerous commercial recordings by other artists, some dating back to the 1920s. The following list includes those that loom the largest in the book. Rather than group them together by chapters or relevant themes, I have presented a simple list of titles, arranged alphabetically by the artists' last names. I have also included a few items not cited, in order to give readers additional leads on various lesser-known genres of American music. In every case, I have endeavored to include in the listings those versions of the songs that are readily available for purchase. When possible, I have also included original recording information. Many, if not most, are now available for downloading as MP3s, either through the usual Internet book and music store sites or through specific labels.

Roy Acuff, "Wait for the Light to Shine," *Old Time Barn Music,* LP, Columbia, 1951; *The Essential Roy Acuff,* CD, Sony/Legacy, 2004.

The Allman Brothers Band, "Statesboro Blues," *At Fillmore East*, LP, Capricorn, 1971; CD, 1997.

Barbecue Bob [Robert Hicks], "Barbecue Blues," 78 rpm, Columbia, 1927, and "Mississippi Heavy Water Blues," 78 rpm, Columbia, 1927; both on Barbecue Bob [Robert Hicks], *Complete Recorded Works in Chronological Order, Volume 1, 25 March 1927 to 13 April 1928*, CD, Document, 1994.

Count Basie and Sarah Vaughan, "I Cried for You," *Count Basie/Sarah Vaughan*, LP, Blue Note, 1961; CD, 1996.

Dominic Behan, "The Patriot Game," *Songs of the I.R.A. (Irish Republican Army)*, LP, Riverside, 1957; *The Rocky Road to Dublin: The Best of Irish Folk*, CD, Castle Music, 2006.

Marc Blitzstein, *The Cradle Will Rock,* original 1937 cast recording on Marc Blitzstein, *Musical Theater Premières,* 2 CDs, Pearl, 1998.

Dock Boggs, "Sugar Baby," 78 rpm, Brunswick, 1927; Dock Boggs, *Country Blues: Complete Early Recordings,* CD, Revenant, 1998.

Paul Brady, "Arthur McBride and the Sergeant," *Andy Irvine and Paul Brady,* LP, Mulligan, 1976; CD, Green Linnet, 1993.

———, "The Lakes of Pontchartrain," *Welcome Here Kind Stranger,* LP, Mulligan, 1978; CD, PeeBee, 2009.

David Bromberg, "Dehlia," *David Bromberg,* LP, Columbia, 1971; CD, Wounded Bird Records, 2007.

The Brothers Four, "I Am a Roving Gambler," *B.M.O.C. (Best Music On/Off Campus)*, LP, Columbia, 1961; The Brothers Four, *Greatest Hits,* CD, Sony, 1990.

Cab Calloway and His Orchestra, "St. James Infirmary," 78 rpm, Brunswick, 1930; Cab Calloway and His Orchestra, *The Early Years, 1930–1934,* CD, JSP Records, 2001.

Johnny Cash, "Delia's Gone," *American Recordings,* CD, American, 1994.

———, "Delia's Gone," *The Sound of Johnny Cash,* LP, Columbia, 1962.

The Clancy Brothers and Tommy Makem, "Eileen Aroon" and "The Parting Glass." Both of these songs appear on various collections, but my favorite versions appear on the 2-CD set *In Person at Carnegie Hall: The Complete 1963 Concert,* Sony/Legacy, 2009.

Sam Collins, "Yellow Dog Blues," 78 rpm, Gennett, 1927; Sam Collins, *Complete Recorded Works in Chronological Order, 1927–1931,* CD, Document, 2005.

Martha Copeland, "The Dyin' Crapshooter's Blues," recorded in 1927; Martha Copeland, *Complete Recorded Works in Chronological Order, Volume 1, September 1923 to August 1927,* CD, Document, 2000.

Aaron Copland, *The Copland Collection: Orchestral & Ballet Works, 1936–1948,* 3 CDs, Sony, 1991. Set includes *Billy the Kid, Rodeo,* selections from the score to *Of Mice and Men, Lincoln Portrait, Fanfare for the Common Man,* and *Appalachian Spring.*

————, *Piano Variations, Piano Music of Aaron Copland,* CD, Albany Records, 2008.

Bing Crosby, "Snuggled on Your Shoulder," 78 rpm, Brunswick, 1932; Bing Crosby, *A Musical Autobiography,* 4 CDs, Avid, 2005.

————, "Where the Blue of the Night (Meets the Gold of the Day)," 78 rpm, Brunswick, 1931; *Classic Crosby (1930–1934),* CD, Naxos Nostalgia, 2000.

Gary Davis, "Delia," *Delia—Late Concert Recordings, 1970–71,* CD, American Activities, 1990.

————, "Devil's Dream," *The Guitar & Banjo of Reverend Gary Davis,* LP, Fantasy/Prestige, 1964; CD, Original Blues Classics, 1990.

Reese Du Pree, "One More Rounder Gone," 78 rpm, OKeh, 1924; reissued on *Male Blues of the Twenties, Volume 1, 1922–1930,* CD, Document, 1996.

Ramblin' Jack Elliott, "Roving Gambler," *Jack Elliott,* LP, Fontana, 1964; CD, Vanguard, 2007.

Sleepy John Estes, "Someday Baby Blues," 78 rpm, Decca, 1935; Sleepy John Estes, *Complete Recorded Works in Chronological Order, Volume 1, 24 September 1929 to 2 August 1937,* CD, Document, 1994.

————, "Working Man's Blues," 78 rpm, RCA Victor/Bluebird, 1941; Sleepy John Estes, *Complete Recorded Works in Chronological Order, Volume 2, 2 August 1937 to 24 September 1941,* CD, Document, 1994.

Gil Evans, "Ella Speed," *Gil Evans and Ten,* LP, Prestige, 1957; CD, JVC Japan, 1999.

The Everly Brothers, "Roving Gambler," *Songs Our Daddy Taught Us,* LP, Cadence, 1959; CD, Rhino, 1990.

Jimmie Gordon, "Dehlia," 78 rpm, Decca, 1939; Jimmie Gordon, *Complete Recorded Works in Chronological Order, Volume 3, 1939–1946,* CD, Document, 2000.

Stefan Grossman, "All My Friends Are Gone," *Shake That Thing: Fingerpicking Country Blues,* CD, Shanachie, 1998.

Merle Haggard, "Workin' Man's Blues," *A Portrait of Merle Haggard,* LP, Capitol, 1969; CD, Beat Goes On, 2005.

Blake Alphonso Higgs (Blind Blake), "Delia Gone," *A Third Album of Bahamian Songs by Blind Blake and the Royal Victoria Hotel Calypso Orchestra,* LP, Art, 1952.

Billie Holiday and Her Orchestra, "Having Myself a Time," recorded in 1938; *The Quintessential Billie Holiday, Volume 6 (1938),* CD, Sony, 1990.

Holy Modal Rounders, "Statesboro Blues," *The Holy Modal Rounders 2,* LP, Prestige, 1964; CD, Fantasy, 1999.

Mississippi John Hurt, "Frankie [and Albert]," 78 rpm, OKeh, 1928; Mississippi John Hurt, *Avalon Blues: The Complete 1928 OKeh Recordings,* CD, Columbia/Sony, 1996.

Papa Charlie Jackson, "Bad Luck Woman Blues," 78 rpm, Paramount, 1926; "Long Gone Lost John," 78 rpm, Paramount, 1928; and "Look Out Papa

Don't Tear Your Pants," 78 rpm, Paramount, 1927, all on Papa Charlie Jackson, *Complete Recorded Works, Volume 2, February 1926 to September 1928,* CD, Document, 1991.

Lonnie Johnson, "Lonesome Road," 78 rpm, Bluebird, 1942; Lonnie Johnson, *Complete Recorded Works, 1937 to June 1947, Volume 2, 22 May 1940 to 13 February 1942,* CD, Document, 1996.

Robert Johnson, "Hell Hound on My Trail," 78 rpm, Vocalion, 1937, and "32-20 Blues," 78 rpm, Vocalion, 1937; both on Robert Johnson, *The Complete Recordings,* CD, Sony, 1996.

Colonel Jubilation B. Johnston [Bob Johnston], *Moldy Goldies: Colonel Jubilation B. Johnston and His Mystic Knights Band and Street Singers Attack the Hits,* LP, Columbia, 1966.

Nic Jones, "Canadee-i-o," *Penguin Eggs,* LP, Topic, 1980; CD, 1995.

Koerner, Ray, and Glover, *Lots More Blues, Rags, and Hollers,* LP, Elektra, 1964; CD, Red House, 1999.

Huddie Ledbetter ("Leadbelly"), "Midnight Special," recorded in 1933, and "Ella Speed," recorded in 1933; both on *Midnight Special: The Library of Congress Recordings,* 3 LPs, Elektra, 1966; CD, Rounder, 1991.

Alan Lomax, comp., "Delia Gone" (1935), *Deep River of Song: Bahamas 1935, Volume 2, Ring Games and Round Dances,* CD, Rounder, 2002.

Taj Mahal, "Statesboro Blues," *Taj Mahal,* LP, Columbia, 1968; CD, Columbia/Legacy, 2000.

Tommy McClennan, "New Highway 51," 78 rpm, RCA Victor/Bluebird, 1940; *The Rural Blues: A Study of the Vocal and Instrumental Resources,* LP, RBF Records, 1960; Tommy McClennan, *Whiskey Head Woman: The Complete Recordings, Vol. 1, 1939–1940,* CD, Document, 2002.

Kansas Joe McCoy and Memphis Minnie, "When the Levee Breaks," 78 rpm, Columbia, 1929; Memphis Minnie, *Queen of the Blues,* CD, Sony, 1997.

Blind Willie McTell, *Atlanta Twelve String,* LP, Atlantic Records, 1972.

———, *King of the Georgia Blues,* 6 CDs, Snapper, 2007. This excellent collection includes all of the important McTell recordings released before 1949, including the 1940 Library of Congress session with John and Ruby Lomax.

———, *Last Session,* LP, Bluesville, 1960; CD, Fantasy, 1992.

———, *The Regal Country Blues,* 2 CDs, Acrobat, 2005.

Blind Willie McTell and Curley Weaver, *The Post War Years, 1949–1950,* CD, Document, remastered edition, 2008.

Memphis Minnie, "Ma Rainey," 78 rpm, OKeh, 1940; Memphis Minnie, *Hoodoo Lady,* 2 CDs, Proper Pairs, 2003.

Mississippi Sheiks, "Stop and Listen Blues," 78 rpm, OKeh, 1930; Mississippi Sheiks, *Stop and Listen,* CD, Yazoo, 1992.

The Chad Mitchell Trio, "The John Birch Society," *The Chad Mitchell Trio at the Bitter End,* LP, Kapp, 1962; CD, Folk Era Records, 1997.

Geoff Muldaur, "Wild Ox Moan," *The Secret Handshake,* CD, Hightone, 1998.

Napoleon XIV [Jerry Samuels], "They're Coming to Take Me Away, Ha-Haaa!" 45 rpm, Warner Brothers, 1966; Napoleon XIV, *The Second Coming,* CD, Rhino, 1996.

The New Lost City Ramblers, "Don't Let Your Deal Go Down," *The New Lost City Ramblers,* LP, Folkways, 1958; The New Lost City Ramblers, *The Early Years, 1958–1962,* CD, Smithsonian Folkways, 1992.

Randy Newman, "Louisiana 1927," *Good Old Boys,* LP, Reprise, 1974; CD remastered, Rhino, 2003. Newman has rereleased this song in various versions, but his most moving performance of it came during a live, nationally televised joint-network telethon for the victims of Hurricane Katrina on September 9, 2005. Although Dylan did not attend, his presence was felt: the evening's entertainment was entitled "Shelter from the Storm," after the song on Dylan's album *Blood on the Tracks.* Unintentionally, the event was a poignant contrast to the unkempt, directionless telethon that had formed one of the backdrops to *Masked and Anonymous.*

Phil Ochs, "Davey Moore," recorded in 1964; *The Early Years,* CD, Vanguard, 2000.

The Pacifics, "Hopped-Up Mustang," *Hot Rods and Custom Classics,* 4 CDs, Rhino, 1999.

Dolly Parton, "Jolene," *Jolene,* RCA Victor, 1974; CD, Sony, 2007.

Charley Patton, "High Water Everywhere, Parts 1 and 2," 78 rpm, Paramount, 1930, and "Down the Dirt Road Blues," 78 rpm, Paramount, 1930; both on *"Screamin' and Hollerin' the Blues": The Worlds of Charley Patton,* 7 CDs, Revenant, 2001.

Charlie Poole and the North Carolina Ramblers, "Don't Let Your Deal Go Down Blues," 78 rpm, Columbia, 1925; *Charlie Poole and the Roots of Country Music,* 3 CDs, Sony/Legacy, 2005.

Elvis Presley, *Elvis' Christmas Album,* LP, RCA Victor, 1957; CD, RCA, 1990.

———, "Tomorrow Night," originally recorded in 1954, released with overdubs on *Elvis for Everyone,* LP, RCA Victor, 1965; CD, BMG International, 1995.

Paul Robeson, "Lonesome Road," 78 rpm, Paramount, 1929; Paul Robeson, *A Man and His Beliefs,* CD, Legacy International, 2001.

Jimmie Rodgers, "Waiting for a Train," 78 rpm, Victor, 1928; *The Essential Jimmie Rodgers,* CD, RCA, 1995.

Tom Rush, "Statesboro Blues," *Take a Little Walk with Me,* LP, Elektra, 1966; CD, Collectors' Choice, 2001.

Sacred Harp Singers, "The Lone Pilgrim," *New Year's Eve at the Iveys' 1972,* CD, Squirrel Hill, 2005.

Frank Sinatra, "Lonesome Road," *A Swingin' Affair,* LP, Capitol, 1957; CD, 1998.

Hank Snow, "I'm Movin' On," 45 rpm, RCA, 1950, and "Ninety Nine Miles an

Hour (Down a Dead End Street)," 45 rpm, RCA, 1963; both on *The Essential Hank Snow,* CD, RCA, 1997.

Sons of the Pioneers, "Gentle Nettie Moore," 33 rpm, Master, 1934; Sons of the Pioneers, *Songs of the Prairie,* 4 CDs, Bear Family, 1998.

Victoria Spivey, "Dope Head Blues," 78 rpm, OKeh, 1927; Victoria Spivey, *Complete Recorded Works, Volume 1, 11 May 1926 to 31 October 1927,* CD, Document, 2000.

Victoria Spivey with Roosevelt Sykes, Big Joe Williams, and Lonnie Johnson, *Three Kings and the Queen,* recorded in 1962; LP, Spivey Records, 1964.

The Stanley Brothers, "Highway of Regret," 45 rpm, Starday, 1959; The Stanley Brothers, *Early Starday-King Years, 1958–1961,* CD, King, 1995.

William Hamilton Stepp, "Bonaparte's Retreat," recorded in 1937; *The Music of Kentucky: Early American Rural Classics, 1927–37,* CD, Yazoo, 1995.

Sister Rosetta Tharpe, "The Lonesome Road," 78 rpm, Decca, 1938; Sister Rosetta Tharpe, *Complete Recorded Works, Volume 1, 1938 to 1941,* CD, Document, 1996.

The Three Peppers (Sally Gooding, voc.), "It Must Be Love," 78 rpm, Variety Records, 1937; *The Three Peppers, 1937–1940,* CD, Classics France/Trad Alive, 2002.

The Traveling Wilburys, *The Traveling Wilburys, Volume 1*, LP, Warner Brothers, 1988.

————, *The Traveling Wilburys, Volume 3,* LP, Warner Brothers, 1990; released together with *Volume 1* as *The Traveling Wilburys Collection,* CD, Rhino, 2007.

Dave Van Ronk, "Cocaine Blues," *Dave Van Ronk, Folksinger,* LP, Prestige, 1963; released with *Inside Dave Van Ronk* as *Inside Dave Van Ronk,* CD, Fantasy, 1991.

————, "Statesboro Blues," *No Dirty Names,* LP, Verve/Forecast, 1966; no CD is available, but a strong rendering appears on *Dave Van Ronk, Live at Sir George Williams University,* Just a Memory, 1997.

Muddy Waters, "Rollin' and Tumblin', Parts 1 and 2," 78 rpm, Parkway, 1950, "Blow, Wind, Blow," 78 rpm, Chess, 1953, and "I Just Want to Make Love to You," 78 rpm, Chess, 1954; all on *The Chess Box: Muddy Waters,* 3 LPs, 3 CDs, Chess, 1989.

Doc Watson, "The Lone Pilgrim," *The Watson Family,* LP, Folkways, 1963; CD, Smithsonian Folkways, 1993.

Kurt Weill and Bertolt Brecht, *The Threepenny Opera,* trans. Marc Blitzstein, LP, Decca, 1954; CD, Decca Broadway, 2000.

Bukka White, "Fixin' to Die Blues," 78 rpm, Vocalion, 1940; *The Country Blues,* LP, RBF Records, 1959; *The Complete Bukka White, 1937–1940,* CD, Columbia/Legacy, 1994.

Hank Williams, "Love Sick Blues," 78 rpm, MGM, 1949, and "I'll Never Get

Out of This World Alive," 78 rpm and 45 rpm, MGM, 1952; both on *The Complete Hank Williams,* 10 CDs, Mercury Nashville, 1998.

Sonny Boy Williamson, "Your Funeral and My Trial," 78 rpm and 45 rpm, Checker, 1958; Sonny Boy Williamson, *His Best,* CD, Chess, 1997, reissued on Universal Japan, 2008.

ILLUSTRATION CREDITS

75   © Jim Marshall
79   Courtesy of Department of Special Collections and University Archives, Stanford University Libraries, and Allen Ginsberg LLC.
88   © Daniel Kramer
91   © AP Images
93   © CBS Photo Archive/Getty
94   © AP Images
98   © Ed Grazda
101 © Daniel Kramer
104 © Jerry Schatzberg/Trunk Archive
106 © Michael Ochs Archives/Getty Images
107 © Michael Ochs Archives/Getty Images
109 © Jerry Schatzberg/Corbis Images
110 from "The Other Side of Nashville," directed by Etienne Mirlesse
111 © Sean Wilentz
115 From the author's collection
116 left: ©Frank Driggs Collection/Getty Images
116 center: Michael Ochs Archives/Getty Images
116 right: Courtesy of Country Music Hall of Fame® and Museum
121 © Jerry Schatzberg/Trunk Archive
127 The British Library
128 From the collection of Mitch Blank
131 Courtesy of Kevin Roche John Dinkeloo and Associates
133 top: From Marcel Carné's *Les eufants du paradis*
133 bottom: © Ken Regan/Camera 5
135 © Estate of David Gahr
138 Courtesy of John Amato
139 Courtesy of John Amato
145 © Bob Gruen/www.bobgruen.com
162 left: Courtesy Everett Collection
162 right: © Ken Regan/Camera 5
166 © Ken Regan/Camera 5
173 top: Library of Congress
173 bottom: American Folklife Center/Library of Congress
179 © Peter Noble/Redferns/Getty Images
181 © Dick Cooper
185 Georgia Department of Archives and History
187 Georgia Department of Archives and History
188 From author's personal collection
191 From the collection of Alan White—www.earlyblues.com
194 Shanachie Entertainment
203 © Jim Curnyn
214 © American Stock/Getty Images
215 © Paramount Pictures. Courtesy Photofest
220 © Joe Alper
222 New York Public Library
229 From the collection of Elijah Wald
233 © Ken Regan/Camera 5
236 © 2010 Marcus B. Johnson
239 *The Sacred Harp* digitized by the Michigan State University Libraries
241 Library of Congress, Music Division, Washington, D.C. 10540
246 P. J. Kernodle, *Lives of Christian Ministers: Over Two Hundred Memoirs* (Richmond, Va.: The Central Publishing Company, 1909)
249 both: © Sean Wilentz
252 © John Cohen/Getty Images
262 © Barry Feinstein
266 From the collection of John Tefteller and www.Bluesimages.com. Used with permission.
267 Courtesy of the North Carolina State Archives. Creative Commons license http://www

INDEX

(Italic page numbers indicate illustrations.)